Marriages of

BUTE AND WARREN COUNTIES,

NORTH CAROLINA

1764–1868

CLEARFIELD COMPANY
REPRINTS & REMAINDERS

International Standard Book Number 0-8063-1301-3

Printed in 1991 for Clearfield Company Inc.,
by Genealogical Publishing Company, Inc., Baltimore, MD

Made in the United States of America

INTRODUCTION

This volume contains abstracts of all extant marriage bonds issued in Bute and Warren counties, North Carolina from 1764-1868, when marriage bonds were discontinued. The abstracts of the bonds were made from a microfilm copy of the bonds and are arranged in alphabetical order by the name of the groom, each entry further providing the name of the bride, the date of the bond, and the names of the bondsmen, where all of these items appear on the bonds. To facilitate research, names of the brides and bondsmen are also listed in the index. Additionally, abstracts of the entries in the marriage register for Warren County, 1851-1867, are included as well, made from a microfilm copy (North Carolina Archives microfilm C.100.63002). The marriages in the register were recorded in the order in which they were turned in by the officiants. Some were recorded some time after the marriage took place. The names of the grooms and brides from the register are included in the index.

The reader should keep in mind that the name of the groom on the bond is spelled as the name was signed, or in the case of a person who could not write, the way it was signed for him. The name of the bride appears as it was spelled by the clerk or the person making out the bond. Since the bride did not sign, the spellings may vary widely from the way the name would properly be spelled.

Marriage bonds are the only public records of marriage prior to 1851. Although the marriage bond law was enacted in 1751 and remained in force until 1868, the clerk of the county court was required only from 1851 to keep a register of all marriages performed by license (issued with the bond).

The researcher should bear in mind that bonds alone are not proof that a marriage took place, only that a marriage was intended. The entries in the register are proof that the couple was married. Also, not everyone who married in Bute and Warren counties between 1764 and 1868 is identified in this work, for some marriages were performed after publication of banns and no bond, license, or other public record of marriage was required.

BRENT HOWARD HOLCOMB, C. G.
Columbia, South Carolina

BUTE COUNTY MARRIAGES

BUTE COUNTY MARRIAGES

Acock, Abner & Sarah Harper, 7 July 1778; John Acock, bm; Thos Machen ,wit.

Alford, Warren & Betty Ward, 25 Nov 1778; Benjamin Ward, bm.

Baley, William Flemming & Molley Sprunt, 9 July 1778; Baley Fleming, bm; Thos Machen, wit.

Bell, Jno & Sarah Green (dau Peter Green), 28 Nov 1764, William House, bm; Jno Bowie, wit.

Blalock, David & Anne Beal, 8 March 1773; John Scott, bm.

Brown, Mitchell & Tabitha Beckham, 4 Aug 1778; John Watson, bm; Thos Machen, wit.

Burt, William & Ann Turner (dau Thos Turner), 30 Mar 1779.

Carlile, James & Rebecca Johnson, 19 Dec 1778; James Collens, bm.

Cheek, John & Sarah Tharp, 21 Dec 1773; James Thompson, bm; Thos Machen, wit.

Collins, Michael & Elizabeth Drake, 10 June 1773; William Bridges, bm; Alexr Muirhead, wit.

Cooper, Henry & Molley Blackman, 5 Oct 1778; Vencint Bodine, bm; Thos Machen, wit.

Darnel, Moses & Susannah Massie, 7 Jan 1779; John Prim, bm; Jesse Mabry, Chas Cupples, wit.

Davis, Dioclesian & Nancy Fluker, 7 Dec 1778; William Burrow, bm.

Dunstan, William & Fannie Bibbie, 11 July 1778; John Myrick, bm; Reps Brewer, bm.

Edwards, Charles & Jenny Lowe, 12 Nov 1774; James Martin, bm; Thos Machen, wit.

Ellkins, John & Sarah Stringfellow, 27 June 1778; Charles Cupples, bm; Thos Machen, wit.

Emmerson, James & Judy Oliver, 8 Sept 1773; Robert Caller, bm; Thos Machen, wit.

Faulcon, John & Lucretia Person, 27 May 1773; William Park, bm; Thomas Machen, wit.

Felts, Randolph & Rebecca Bobbett, 1 Apr 1778; Nathaniel Harris, bm.

Frazier, Alexander & Sarah Terrill, 19 June 1778; James Meroney, bm; Thos Machen, wit.

Freeman, Joseph & Aggy Freeman, 11 Nov 1778; John Ross, bm.

Freeman, William & Priscilla Hunt, 5 Sept 1778; John Withers, bm.

3

Gardner, Thomas & Betty Waller, 9 Feb 1778; Robert Waller, bm.

Green, Isham & Mary Green, 23 Apr 1777; Obed Green, bm.

Green, Josiah & Mary Williford, 10 May 1773; John Duke, bm; Thos Machen, wit.

Hammond, Job & Lucy Howard, 22 Dec 1775; Julius Howard, bm.

Harris, Roe & Betsy Brinkley, 9 Jan 1778; W. Wortham, bm; Thos Machen, wit.

Harris, Solomon & Milley Watkins, 11 March 1778; Richard Hill, bm; Thos Machen, wit.

Harrison, Richard & Ann Pattillo, bm; 16 Dec 1774; Philemon Hawkins, Jr., bm; Thos Machen, wit.

Hawkins, John & Salley Macon, 27 Feb 1765; James Ransom, bm; John Bowie, wit.

Hicks, Lewis & Sarah Hill, 6 Apr 1773; Joseph Seawell, bm; Thos Machen, wit.

Hightower, Robert & Anne Ward, 30 June 1773; Philip Hawkins, Jur., bm; Thos Machen, wit.

Hill, Richard & Lidia Watkins, 11 March 1778; Solomon Harris, bm; Thos Machen, wit.

Hunt, John (of Granville Co.) & Mary Jeffreys (of Bute Co), 13 Sept 1778; John William, Jr., of Granville Co., bm.

Ingram, Joseph & Winney Nelms, 10 Sept 1774; John Myrick, bm; Thos Machen, wit.

James, Isaac & Patty Burrow, 7 Dec 1778; Dioclesian Davis, bm.

Jones, Drury & Amey Kimball, 6 Nov 1775; Benjamin Kimball, bm.

Jones, John & Elizabeth Brown, 12 Apr 1774; John Brown, Jr., bm.

Kitchen, Joseph & Patience Bridges, 17 Sept 1778; James Bryant, bm.

Lancaster, John & Apsley Osheal, 18 Aug 1778; Lawrence Lancaster, Sr., bm.

Lancaster, John & Martha Lancaster, 7 Sept 1778; Jordan Harris, bm; Thos Machen, wit.

Lanier, Robert & Jane Pattillo, 12 June 1775; Philemon Hawkins, Jr., bm.

Linch, Bryant & McKay Butler, 19 Aug 1778; John Rice, bm.

Long, Drury & Sally Green, 19 July 1773; John Duke, bm; Thos Machen, wit.

McKissock, Thomas & Lucy Edwards, 8 Feb 1779; William Hudson, bm; Thos Machen, wit.

Mabry, David & Jean Bledsoe, 4 Aug 1778; Andrew Railey, bm; Thos Machen, wit.

Martin, James & Salley Lyles, 12 May 1773; Jethro Sumner, bm; Thos Machen, wit.

Martin, Joseph & Sarah Smith, 7 Feb 1778; John Emerson, bm.

Mayfield, John & Mary Syms (dau Edword Syms), 23 Feb 1773; Drury Jackson, bm; Thos Machen, wit.

Mitchel, James & Nancy Colclough, 20 Nov 1778; William Durham, Jr., bm.

Morgan, Hardy & Sarah Alston, 24 May 1777; James Alston, bm; Thos Machen, wit.

Murry, James, Jr., & Nanney Stone, 21 July 1778; John Hopkins, bm; Thos Machen, wit.

Oglby, John & Ann Thornton, ___ 177–; William Park, bm.

Perry, James & Mary Cooper, 14 Aug 1778; Thomas Sherrod, bm.

Perry, Jeremiah & Frances Massey, 26 May 1778; Willis Perry, bm.

Pope, Isaac Ricks & Elizabeth Kearny, 23 Oct 1773; Isaac Winston, bm; Thos Machen, wit.

Powell, Honorius & Anne Brown, 23 Feb 1773; Thomas Machen, bm.

Powell, John & Mary Whithurst, 29 Dec 1775; John Turner, bm; M. D. Johnson, wit.

Power, John & Henritta Christmass, 28 July 1775; James Ransom, Jr., bm; Thos Machen, wit.

Pride, Edward & Elizabeth Kearne (dau Shel. Kearne) ,16 Apr 1778; Edward Pegram, bm;

Railey, John & Judith House, 5 July 1775; Andrew Railey, bm; Thos Machen, wit.

Ransom, Reuben & Salley Leaman, 1 Feb 1779; Isaac Collier, bm;

Riggin, Charles & Zillah Lindsey, 10 Jan 1774; Joseph Lindsey, bm; Thos Machen, wit.

Rush, Benjamin & Sarah White, 26 May 1773; Robert Peyton, bm; Thos Machen, wit.

Rush, William & Abigail Terrill, 6 Feb 1775; James Martin, bm; Thos Machen, wit.

Sledge, James & Rebecca Person, 22 Nov 1777; Daniel Sledge, bm.

Smith, Robert & Sarah Page, 29 Aug 1778; Nimrod Williams, bm.

Snow, Spencer & Frances Self, 1 Jan 1778; Charles Blackard, bm; Thos Machen, wit.

Strickland, Mathew & Mary Perry, 5 Jan 1774; John Richards, bm; Thos Machen, wit.

Tanner, John & Darcus Pickerill, 19 Oct 1775; Nimrod Williams, bm.

Tassie, George & Mary Armistead, 27 Sept 1774; Thomas Machen, bm; Letty Machen, wit.

Thomas, Micajah & Anne Hawkins, 7 Jan 1778; Benjamin Hawkins, bm; Thos Machen, bm.

Turner, William & Rebecca Nicholson, 31 Aug 1775; Benjamin Kimball, bm; Thomas Machen, wit.

Turpin, Hugh & Jane Murry, 5 Jan 1774; William Elliott, bm.

Twitty, John & Mildred Burford (dau Phil. Burford), 24 Feb 1773; Philemon Hawkins, Jr., bm.

Vaughan, Thomas & Susannah Hunt (of Northampton Co.), 30 Jan 1775; Mary Butler, William Jones, wit.

Vaughan, William & Sarah Person (consent of William Person), 11 Dec 1777; William Park, bm; Thos Machen, wit.

Watson, William & Salley Caller, 26 July 1775; Robert Caller, Junr, bm; Thos Machen, wit.

Weldon, William & Betty Plummer, 21 May 1776; John Willis, bm; Thos Machen, wit.

Wilson, Jno & Mary Lide, 4 Apr 1777; Nathl. Kimbrough, bm.

Wortham, John & Mary Marshall, 9 Aug 1775; Wm Wortham, bm; Thos Machen, wit.

Wren, Joel & Bettsy Allen, 5 July 1777; Thos Machen, C. C., wit.

WARREN COUNTY MARRIAGES

Abbet, Mackon & Meranda Askew, 19 Mar 1856; M. R. Pennell, bm; Jno W. White, wit; m 20 Mar 1856 by P. H. Smith, M. G.

Abbit, John & Delia Perdue, 25 Dec 1811; Anthoney Dowtin, bm; Jno. H. Green, wit.

Abernathy, Sidney S. (son of Clayton & Matilda Abernathy) & Bettie C. Allen (dau of Turner & Betsey Allen, 7 Dec 1867; William W. White, wit; m 17 Dec 1867 by N. A. Purefoy, M. G.

Acock, Ransome & Elizabeth Dowlen, 30 Jul 1802; Peterson Person, bm; Sugar Johnson, wit.

Acock, Robert & Mary Blanchett, 25 Jul 1780; Abner Acock, bm; Thos Machen, wit.

Acre, James & Scinthia Meadows, 6 Sept 1842; Wm. H. Shearin, bm; M. J. Montgomery, wit.

Acre, Willie & Minerva Moody, 23 Dec 1826; Thomas Bell, bm; M. M. Drake, wit.

Acree, Joshua & Lydianna Mitchell, 14 Nov 1809; Benjamin Colclough, bm; Jno C. Johnson, D. C., wit.

Acree, Shearin & Susanah Russell, 15 Apr 1793; Isaac Acree, Jr., bm; M. D. Johnson, C. C. C., wit.

Acrey, Abreham & Fanney Colcolough, 12 Nov 1798; Isaac Acree, bm; S. Green, wit.

Adams, David & Rebecca Coleman, 18 Aug 1796; Thomas Brodnax, bm; M. Duke Johnson, C. C., wit.

Adams, David & Patsey Kimbell, 24 Apr 1821; John Kimbell, bm; C. Drake, C. W. C. C., wit.

Adams, Jno A. & Silvey Stokes, 7 Oct 1852; A. J. Johnston, bm; Jno W. White, wit; m. 10 Oct 1852 by J. B. Solomon.

Adams, Thomas & Abigal Ellis, 15 Sept 1781; William Ellis, bm; Thos Machen, wit.

Adams, William Avery & Fanny Senter, 19 Dec 1813; John Burgess, bm; Wm. Green, C. C., wit.

Adkins, James & Susan Short, 1 Nov 1860; Isaac Loyd, bm; Wm. A. White, wit; m 1 Nov 1860 by A. L. Steed, J. P.

Aikin, Thomas & Susan Brown, 27 Aug 1833; Dudley Mingey, bm; M. M. Drake, wit.

Alexander, Ellick (col) & Clora Somerville, 8 Sept 1865; Roderick Somerville, bm; William A. White, clk., wit; m 13 Sept 1865 by W. Hodges, M. G.

Alexander, Ferry (col) & Ginney Jefferson, 21 Dec 1866; William A. White, clk , wit; m 22 Dec 1866 by Jas T. Russell, J. P.

Alexander, John & Lucy Robertson, 8 Sept 1812; Benjamin Riggan, bm; Wm. Green, C. C., wit.

Alexander, Mark & Sally P. Turner, 20 May 1831; Peter Mitchell, bm; C. Drake, C. C. wit.

Alexander, Robert & Elizabeth Smith, 19 Apr 1788; James Williams, bm; M. Duke Johnson, C. C., wit.

Algard, David & Mary Roberds, 1 Mar 1833; M. A. Burnett, bm; Burl Pitchford, J. P., wit.

Algier, Robert & Elizabeth Gordon, 8 Jan 1831; James Stegall, bm; M. M. Drake, wit.

Algood, Samuel (col) & _____, 9 Apr 1866; Hartwell Hill, bm; William W. White, wit.

Allen, Charles, Jr. & Patty Jenkins, 19 Sept 1781; John Jenkins, bm.

Allen, Charles, Sr. & Mary C. Tunstall, 10 Dec 1813; John H. Hawkins, bm; Wm. Green, C. C., wit.

Allen, Chasten & Jincy W. Turner, 23 Nov 1822; Stephen Turner, bm.

Allen, Edmd & Sally P. Watson, 28 Dec 1830; Lewis Turner, bm; C. Drake, C. C., wit.

Allen, Francis D. & Nancy E. Coleman, 30 Aug 1819; Richd Allen, bm; C. Drake, C. W. C. C., wit.

Allen, George & Salley Ray, 4 Feb 1790; Richard Marshall, bm; M. Duke Johnson, C. C., wit.

Allen, George (col) & Ellen Carroll, 4 Aug 1866; Geo R. Sledge, bm; William A. White, clk, wit; m 4 Aug 1866 by R. D. Paschall, J. P.

Allen, George M. & Harriet J. Yancey, 13 Jan 1829; John V. Cawthorn, bm; E. D. Drake, wit.

Allen, Henry & Nancey Walker, 19 Dec 1809; Henley Turner, bm; Jno C. Johnson, D. C., wit.

Allen, Henry T. & Mary Ann Stiner, 21 Nov 1836; John G. Yancey, bm; E. D. Drake, clk, wit.

Allen, Ira & Mary Powell, 22 Dec 1813; Thomas H. Person, bm; Wm. Green, C. C. C., wit.

Allen, James & Mary H. Macon, 8 Jul 1813; Peter R. Davis, bm; Jno H. Green, wit.

Allen, John & Polley Davis, 13 Feb 1800; Wyatt Williams, bm; Shd Green, wit.

Allen, John & Winnefred Vanlandingham, 2 Mar 1805; Philemon Hawkins, bm; M. D. Johnson, C. C., wit.

Allen, John (son of Washington & Marlin) & Mollie Plummer (dau of Eliza), 22 Sept 1867; William A. White, clk; m 22 Sept 1867 by Wm Wallace White, J. P.

Allen, Lewis (col) (son of Thomas & Emily), & Luvenia Champion (dau of Wright & Sarah), 6 June 1867; William W. White, clk, wit; m 6 June 1867 by P. H. Joyner.

Allen, Michael & Nanney Cawdle, 19 Sept 1783; Benjamin Stiles, bm; M. Duke Johnson, C. C., wit.

Allen, Miles C. & Ronia Tomlinson, 27 Sept 1862; R. W. Lowry & Jno M. Wilson, bm; Wm. A. White, wit.

Allen, Nathaniel & Mary E. Powell, 14 Mar 1859; Jno C. McCraw, bm; John W. White, Clk, wit; m 15 Mar 1859 by N. A. Purefoy, M. G.

Allen, Richard & Nancy Pride, 6 Jan 1808; James Allen, bm; J. C. Johnson, wit.

Allen, Sandford G. & Nancy Allen, 29 May 1829; Gordon Cawthorn, bm.

Allen, Thomas & Elizabeth Baxter, 30 Dec 1800; Thadeous Murray, bm; M. Duke Johnson, C. C., wit.

Allen, Turner & Martha Montgomery, 18 Jan 1828; Zachariah Wright, bm; M. M. Drake, wit.

Allen, Turner & Elizabeth Watson, 6 Nov 1832; John Stainback, bm; C. Drake, C. C., wit.

Allen, William & Sarah Williams, 5 Apr 1788; Jno Dawton, bm.

Alley, James & Ann P. Connell, 22 Dec 1813; Benjamin King, bm; Wm. Green, C. C., wit.

Allin, Grant (of Granville Co) & Tabitha Marshall, 29 Jan 1783; John Wortham, bm; M. Duke Johnson, wit.

Alsobrook, Lunsford L. & Temperance B. Eaton, 7 June 1826; Robert Ransom, bm; M. M. Drake, wit.

Alston, Adam (col) & Pattie Alston, 2 Jan 1867; William A. White, clk, wit; m 18 Jan 1867 by J. Buxton Williams, J. P.

Alston, Alfred & Mary A. Plummer, 23 Sept 1813; John M. Johnson, bm; Jno H. Green, wit.

Alston, Alfred & Polly D. Kearney, 20 Apr 1853; Wm. T. Alston, bm; Jno W. White, Clk, wit; m 20 Apr 1853 by Robt O. Burton, M. G.

Alston, Anderson (col) & Miranda Alston, 26 Dec 1865; Wm. T. Alston, bm; William A. White, wit.

Alston, Auguston & Martha Macon, 27 July 1813; Thomas Allen, bm; Wm. Green, C. C. C. wit.

Alston, Augustus & Mary A. Hawkins, 18 Nov 1829; John B. Somervill, bm; E. D. Drake, wit.

Alston, Brister (col) & Susan Alston, 9 Mar 1867; Wm. T. Alston, bm; William W. White, clk, wit; m 9 Mar 1867 by William Hodges, M. G.

Alston, Buckner (col) & Lucy Clements, 14 Nov 1866; James T. Rice, bm; William A. White, clk, wit; m 18 Oct 1867 by John S. Cheek, J. P.

Alston, Eaton (col) & Sally Ann Williams, 26 Feb 1867; N. F. Alston, bm; William A. White, clk., wit; m 12 Mar 1867 by J. Buxton Williams.

Alston, Frank (col) & Mary A. E. Alston, 23 July 1866; P. J. Turnbull, bm; William A. White, clk, wit; m 25 July 1866 by J. Buxton Williams, J. P.

Alston, George W. & Marina P. Williams 14 Feb 1829; James J. Alston, bm; E. D. Drake, bm.

Alston, George W. (son of Geo W. & Merina P. Alston) & Hattie Faulcon Alston (dau of Samuel T. & Ruina T. Alston), 16 Oct 1867; William W. White, Clk, wit; m 23 Oct 1856 by J. P. Moore, M. G.

Alston, Gideon & Evelina Alston, 7 Feb 1832; William H. Williams, bm.

Alston, Isham (col) (son of Washington & Ailsey) & Margaret Williams (dau of Wm & Caroline), 26 Aug 1867; William A. White, clk, wit; m 31 Aug 1867 by J. Buxton Williams.

Alston, James & Salley Kearny (dau of Edward), 23 Jan 1780; Isaac Acree; bm.

Alston, James (col) & Louisa Burgess, 30 Mar 1867; Robt W. Alston, bm; William A. White, clk., wit; m 7 Apr 1867 by M. P. Perry, J. P.

Alston, James J. & Mariah A. Somerville, 17 Oct 1866; James B. Somerville, bm; William W. White, C. C. C., wit; m 18 Oct 1866 by William Hodges, M. G.

Alston, James W. & Laura C. Terrell, 27 Apr 1865; William T. Alston, bm; William A. White, clk, wit; m 11 Mar 1866 by N. A. Purefoy, M. G.

Alston, Jesse A. & Mary A. T. Newell, 11 Feb 1841; F. A. A. Bobbitt, bm; Edwd W. Best, Clk, wit.

Alston, Joseph (col) & Pleasant Williams, 13 Feb 1867; William A. White, clk, wit; m 15 Feb 1867 by J. Buxton Williams.

Alston, June (col) & Julia Burgess, 26 Feb 1867; Dr. M. P. Perry, bm; William A. White, Clk, wit; m 7 Apr 1867 by M. P. Perry, J. P.

Alston, Nathaniel M. & Martha Williams, 22 Dec 1829; Whitmell H. Kearny, bm; C. Drake, C. C., wit.

Alston, Nelson (col) & Lucinda Alston, 28 Dec 1866; William A. White, clk, wit; m 4 Jan 1867 by J. Buxton Williams.

Alston, Rhoden (col) & Judy Williams, 22 Jan 1867; William A. White, clk, wit; m 2 Feb 1867 by J. Buxton Williams.

Alston, Robert & Ann Maria Alston, 18 Oct 1836; Solomon Williams, bm; E. D. Drake, clk, wit.

Alston, Thomas N. F. & Mary R. Brodie, 25 Oct 1834; Jno B. Williams, bm.

Alston, Thomas P. & Sarah A. M. Newell, 21 Jul 1856; Thos H. Christmas, bm; Jno W. White, wit; m 30 Jul 1856 by N. Z. Graves.

Alston, Wake (col) (son of Warren & Grace) & Matilda Williams (dau of Solomon & Jane), 26 Oct 1867; William A. White, clk, wit; m 26 Oct 1867 by Edward Eagles, M. G.

Alston, William (col) & Nancy Williams, 15 Mar 1867; W. Henry Harrison, bm; William A. White, wit.

Alston, William T. & Laura Eaton, 14 Oct 1851; Benj Wilson, bm; Jno W. White, clk, wit; m 15 Oct 1851 by Cameron S. McRae, M. G.

Amis, James & Celistia Hawkins, 29 Oct 1831; Nathal T. Green, bm.

Amis, Junius & Henretta Hawkins, 19 Aug 1837; R. H. Long, bm.

Amis, Thomas & Sarah Davis, 22 Dec 1834; Joseph J. Bell, bm; E. D. Drake, clk, wit.

Anderson, Martin & Barbary Kersey, 30 Dec 1828; William Evans, bm; E. D. Drake, wit.

Anderson, Robert F. & Kinnis Anderson, 18 May 1856; Henry Nuckles, bm; Thomas P. Paschall, wit; m 18 May 1856 by Thomas P. Paschall, J. P.

Andrews, Abram & Nancy Sims (no date); Allan Sims, bm; M. D. Johnson, C. C. C., wit.

Andrews, Benjamin W. & Narcissa Mundford, 28 Mar 1836; Edwin Ashley, bm.

Andrews, Burwell G. & Mary Ann Ogburn, 24 Nov 1817; Armstead Blankinship, bm; W. A. K. Falkener, bm.

Andrews, Drury & Henrietta Power, 23 Dec 1801; James Caller, bm; M. Duke Johnson, C. C., wit.

Andrews, Green & Mercilla Ransom, 21 Mar 1780; Joseph Ward, bm; Thos Machen, wit.

Andrews, Green & Polley Ward, 17 Jan 1804; Jas Harrison, bm; M. D. Johnson, C. C., wit.

Andrews, Henry & Martha E. Moore, 4 Nov 1841; Matthew W. Williams, bm; M. J. Montgomery, wit.

Andrews, John & Elizabeth Fleming, 21 Jan 1800; Jno F. Andrews, bm; Thomas F. Paschall, wit.

Andrews, John & Ellen A. Paschall, 22 Jan 1829; William E. Mayfield, bm; E. D. Drake, wit.

Andrews, John W. & Susan A. Fleming, 20 Dec 1858; John W. H. Paschall, bm; Thomas F.Paschall, wit; m 22 Dec 1858 by Thos P. Paschall, J. P.

Andrews, Lankston C. & Sarah A. Hudson 6 Feb 1846; Drury Gill, bm; M. J. Montgomery, bm.

Andrews, Lowry & Mrs. Nancy Andrews (both of Lunenburg Co., VA), 15 Mar 1821; Elisha Andrews, bm; Cas. Drake, C. W. C. C., wit.

Anstead, Henry & Elizabeth Mann, 2 Mar 1807; Joseph Anstead, bm; Jo Terrell, D. C., wit.

Archer, William T. & Sally James, 28 Mar 1836; Jesse Pittard, bm.

Arnold, John & Elisabeth Brogdon, 21 Jul 1786; Chas Asque, bm; M. Duke Johnson, wit.

Arrington, Gideon & Rhody Carter, 20 Dec 1826; Lewis Morris, bm; M. M. Drake, wit.

Arrington, Henry & Caroline Powell, 27 Nov 1837; Edwin D. Drake, bm.

Arrington, John & Mary A. Boyd, 2 Apr 1850; Thos S. Campbell, bm; Jno W. White, wit.

Arrington, Peter W. & Alice A. Watson, 3 Nov 1866; R. T. Arrington, bm; William A. White, clk, wit; m 8 Nov 1866 by William Hodges, M. G.

Arrington, Richard & Maria D. Johnson, 9 Feb 1810; Sugan Johnson, bm; M. Duke Johnson, C. C., wit.

Arrington, Richard T. & Bettie J. Plummer, 31 Oct 1853; David C. Hall, bm; Jno W. White, wit; m 2 Nov 1853 by L. L. Smith, Clergyman.

Arrington, Samuel P. & Sue Eaton, 6 May 1858; Thos D. Williams. bm; Jno W. White, clk, wit; m 6 May 1858 by William Hodges, M. G.

Arrington, Saml P. & Hannah B. White, 11 Dec 1860; M. M. Ward, bm; m 12 Dec 1860 by William Hodges, M. G.

Arrington, William W. & Nancy Southall, 13 Oct 1828; Joel Rosser, bm; M. M. Drake, wit.

Artis, Amos & Nancy Green, 9 Jan 1854; James Dunston, bm; Jno W. White, C. C. C., wit, m; 17 Jan 1854 by John S. Cheek, J. P.

Artis, Jack & Roberta Mills, 27 Nov 1860; Alford Artiss, bm; m 29 Nov 1860 by R. Brown, J. P.

Artist, Robertson (col) & Louisa Williams, 26 Feb 1867; Thomas J. Harriss, bm; William A. White, clk, wit; m 27 Feb 1867 by John W. Riggan, J. P.

Ascue, John & Martha Nicholson, 7 Oct 1830; Jno Bellamy, bm.

Ascue, Joseph & Milly Marcus, 6 Dec 1806; Atkins McLemore, bm; Jo Terrell, D. C., wit.

Ascue, Thomas & Rackey Jones, 21 Jan 1813; Philemon Hawkins, bm; Wm. Green, C. C. C., wit.

Ash, Edward & Martha Roney, 15 July 1830; Green D. Jenkins, bm; C. Drake, C. C., wit.

Ash, Lewis & Elizabeth Carter, 2 Mar 1859; Ridley Browne, bm; William A. White, wit; m 4 Mar 1859 by Ridley Browne, J. P.

Ashe, Noah (col) & Rosa Cheek, 2 Dec 1867; Wm. C. Williams, bm; William A. White clk, wit; m 2 Dec 1865 by W. Hodges, M. G.

Askew, George & Christian Lemon, 17 Dec 1818; Jno L. Ward, bm.

Askew, John & Nancy Vanlandingham, 20 Oct 1846; James Cottrell, bm; Jno W. White, wit.

Askew, Osborne L. (son of Tanner Askew) & Louisa Collier (dau of Artilious & Elizabeth Collier), 25 Nov 1867; William A. White, clk, wit; m 26 Nov 1867 by M. P. Perry, J. P.

Askew, Wilis (col) & Miranda Falkener, 27 Dec 1866; John Askew, bm; William A. White, clk, wit; m 30 Dec 1865 by Jas A. Egerton, J. P.

Askue, John & Fereby Dickerson, 7 May 1831; Capt John Williams, bm. C. Drake, C. C. wit.

Askue, John & Betsey Askue, 28 Jun 1831; Plummer Peebles, bm; C. Drake, C. C., wit.

Asslien, David & Martha Shearin, 10 Nov 1801; Charles Bell, bm; Sugan Johnson, wit.

Austin, Octavus & Pattie A. Burges, 29 Sept 1855; W. T. Alston, bm; Jno W. White, clk, wit; m 5 Oct 1855 by L. S. Burkhead, M. G.

Avent, Thomas W. & Mary E. Williams, 15 Dec 1838; William T. Williams, bm;

Avrett, James M. & Nancy Rice, 6 Sept 1825; James N. Towler, bm; Burl Pitchford, wit.

Aycock, Abner & Nancy White, 16 Nov 1829; Luces Lancaster, bm; E. D. Drake, wit.

Aycock, Abner & Sarah Bartlette, 1 Nov 1854; Wm H. White, bm; Jno W. White, C. C. C., wit; m 2 Oct 1854 by John H. Hawkins, J. P.

Aycock, Augustus S. & Mary M. Aycock, 2 Jan 1854; Isham H. Bennett, bm; Jno W. White, C. C. C., wit; m 5 Jan 1854 by H. J. Macon, J. P.

Aycock, Clabour & Nancy Arrington, 9 Mar 1825; Abner Aycock, bm; E. D. Drake, wit.

Aycock, Doctor L. & Lucetta W. Bennett, 22 Dec 1851; Ambrose Aycock, bm; Jno W. White, clk, wit; m 23 Dec 1851 by H. J. Macon, J. P.

Aycock, Henry & Elizabeth Blackburn, 5 Dec 1828; Abner Acock, bm; M. M. Drake, wit.

Aycock, Henry & Maria Bennett, 18 Apr 1836; Abner Aycock, bm; E. D. Drake, clk, wit.

Aycock, Henry H. & Nancy Balthrop, 2 Jan 1805; Mark W. Harwell, bm; M. Duke Johnson, C. C., wit.

Aycock, John T. & Martha B. Shearin, 13 Feb 1844; George S. Smith, bm; W. W. Vaughan, wit.

Aycock, Joseph H. & Amy King, 1 Mar 1828; William B. Reed, bm; M. M. Drake wit.

Aycock, Ransome & Tab(?) Patrick, 18 May 1818; John Allen, bm; Wm. Green, wit.

Aycock, Robert L. & Emily Christial, 18 Jan 1853. Joseph Read, bm; Jno W. White, wit.

Aycock, Samuel & Lucy Sledge, 2 Feb 1820; Arthur Davis, bm; Cas Drake, C. W. C. W., wit.

Aycock, Samuel & Sally Ann Conn, 27 Nov 1860; R. T. Aycock, bm; William W. White, wit; m 27 Nov 1860 by W. A. Dowtin, J. P.

Ayscue, W. E. & Amanda Lancaster, 17 Oct 1859; Samuel Duke, bm; Jno W. White, Clk, wit; m 19 Oct 1859 by C. F. Harris.

Azlien, Samuel & Amey Shearin, 20 Dec 1803; Reubin Baxter, bm; M. Duke Johnson, C. C., wit.

Bacon, Gillie M. & Marian M. Bacon, 9 Jan 1840; Malachi Dupriest, bm.

Badger, Geo E. & Rebecca Turner, 23 Dec 1818; Geo Anderson, bm.

Bagnal, James & Mary George, 26 Oct 1825; Benjamin Johnson, bm.

Baird, William & Lucy Holden, 20 Sept 1810; Samuel Holding, bm; Jno C. Johnson, D. C., wit.

Baker, Blake B. & Arilla Johnston, 11 Apr 1857; R. J. Harriss, bm; C. M. Cook, wit; m 15 Apr 1857 by C. M. Cook, J. P.

Baker, Claborn & Frances Baker, 11 Aug 1803; J. Hawkins, bm; M. Duke Johnson, C. C. C., wit.

Baker, Lundsford & Nancy Good, 26 Nov 1833; Edwd Williams, bm; E. D. Drake, clk, wit.

Baker, Simons J. & Elizabeth M. Hawkins, 23 Nov 1837; James L. G. Baker, bm.

Baker, Thomas D. & Lucy Robinson, 16 Nov 1813; Francis Carter, bm; Wm. Green, C. C. C., wit.

Baker, William & Cintha Robertson, 16 Feb 1838; Kinchen D. Taylor, bm; Henry T. Allen, wit.

Baker, William T. & Catharine Baker, 29 Nov 1856; B. H. Priddie, bm; Jno W. White, clk., wit; m 30 Nov 1856 by Thos S. Campbell.

Ball, Feils (Fields) R. & Mary Parish, 4 Mar 1840; L. Swepson Sims, bm.

Ball, Henry (col) (son of Daniel Hayes & Mariah Ball) & Missoura Carroll (dau of Elias & Huldah Boykin), 13 July 1867; William A. White, clk, wit; m 13 July 1867 by P. H. Joyner.

Ball, James & Temperance Faulkner, 24 June 1779; Daniel Ball, bm; Thos Machen, wit.

Ball, James & Nancy G. Rudd, 24 Sept 1823, Richard Duke, bm.

Ball, James & Mary Weldon, 15 June 1833; William R. Wright, bm; Benj E. Cook, wit.

Ball, James & Mary Ball, 14 Sept 1838; Jordan H. Foster, bm; Jno W. White, wit.

Ball, Robert & Caroline Ayscew (Askew), 13 Apr 1860; Daniel Burchitt, bm; m 13 Apr 1860 by Thomas P. Paschall, J. P.

Ball, Warren & Rhoda Askew, 4 Jan 1832; John Askew, bm; C. Drake, C. C., wit.

Ballard, Benjamin & Eliza Ann James Williams Thorn, 18 Jan 1813; Wm Green, bm; Wm. Green, C. C. C., wit.

Ballard, Dudley & Salley Duke, 21 Sept 1782; John Thomas, bm; M. Duke Johnson, wit.

Ballard, Edmund & Jemima Willson, 2 July 1803; Samuel Bartlet, bm; James Moss, wit.

Ballard, Jesse & Mary Smith, 22 Sept 1785; Adam Milam; bm; M. Duke Johnson, wit.

Ballard, Owen & Mary Brinkle, 6 Sept 1783; Richard Thomas, bm; M. Duke Johnson, wit.

Ballard, Rufus & Lucy Ballard, 29 Oct 1814; W. Green, C. C., wit.

Ballard, Wyatt & Disey Ballard, 28 Oct 1783; Owen Ballard, bm; M. D. Johnson, wit.

Balthrop, Augustine & Holly Burrow, 7 Apr 1813; Edward Pattillo, bm; W. Green, C. C. C., wit.

Balthrop, Francis & Polley Gardner (no date); Jno Balthrop, bm; M. Duke Johnson, C. C., wit.

Balthrop, Francis & Sally Rodwell, 23 Nov 1813; Wilis Balthorp, bm; Wm. Green, C. C. C., wit.

Balthrop, James M. & Matilda A. Johnson, 13 May 1835; William H. Foote, bm; E. D. Drake, Clk, wit.

Balthrop, John & Anna Rodwell, 4 Jan 1806; John Rodwell, bm; Jo Terrell, D. C. C., wit.

Balthrop, John W. & Harret W. Daniel, 28 Aug 1838; Daniel Shearin, bm; Edwd W. Best, clk, wit.

Baltrop, Augustin & Mary Todd, 22 Apr 1784; John Balthrop, bm; M. D. Johnson, wit.

Barham, William & Elizabeth Smith, 27 Jan 1836; Daniel Bowdon, bm; E. D. Drake, clk, wit.

Barker, Richard & Ann Jones, 7 Jan 1851; Richard Konner, bm; R. B. Robinson, wit.

Barner, John F. & Nancy Matthews, 18 July 1856; E. H. Riggan, bm; Philip Love, wit; m 18 Jul 1856 by Richd B. Robinson, J. P.

Barner, William & Catharine Steed, 10 Feb 1817; John H. Mulholland, bm; Wm Green, C. C. C., wit.

Barnes, Benjamin & Anne F. Ward, 19 Aug 1805; William Williamson, bm; Jo Terrell, D. C., wit.

Barnes, James & Elizabeth Tucker, 13 Jan 1821; Richard Wadkins, bm;

Barnes, William & Milly Williams, 8 Apr 1810; John Ellington, bm; Jno C. Johnson, D. C. C., wit.

Barnett, Germon B. & Apha Rottenberry, 26 Dec 1832; Thomas Purly, bm; Burl Pitchford, J. P., wit.

Barrow, Charles & Nancey Sherrin, 12 Nov 1807; Jacob Bell, bm; Robt R. Johnson, wit.

Barrow, Danl & B. Milles, 7 June 1786.

Barry, Col. John D. & Fanny L. Jones, 1 Dec 1864; John Worster, bm; William A. White, clk, wit; m 1 Dec 1864 by William Hodges, M. G.

Bartholomew, Lewis & Lucy Bennit, 29 Dec 1791; Moses Bennitt, bm; M. D. Johnson, C. C., wit.

Bartholomew, Samuel & Sarah E. Johnson, 15 Sept 1856; W. B. Joyner, bm; William A. White, wit.

Bartlet, Churchwel & Rebecca Hawks, 19 Dec 1822; Thos Hawks, bm;

Bartlet, Spious & Rebecca King, 15 Oct 1807; Obediah Ellis, bm; Jo Terrell, D. C. C., wit.

Bartlet, William & Elisabeth Wood, 15 June 1798; Charles Mabry, bm; J. Moss, wit.

Bartlet, William & Elizabeth Paschall, 15 Mar 1808; Sterling Pitchford, bm; M. Duke Johnson, wit.

Bartlett, Lunceford L. & Sarah Elizabeth Rideout, 17 Dec 1853; J. J. M. Collins, bm; Jno W. White, C. C. C., wit; m 18 Dec 1853 by H. J. Macon, J. P.

Bartlett, William H. & Elizabeth R. Bennett, 30 Oct 1852; Alex Bennett, bm; Will A. White, wit.

Bartlett, William H. & Nancy H. Robertson, 23 July 1856; N. D. Brickell, bm; Jno W. White, wit; m 24 July 1856 by N. A. Purefoy, M. G.

Barton, Richard W. & Caroline Marx, 29 Apr 1833; Charles Marx, bm; Henry Fitts, wit.

Basford, Benson & Tempy Wood, 11 May 1798; Jesse Carter, bm; James Moss, wit.

Baskerville, Benjamin (col) & Harriett Mayho, 21 Aug 1865; Frederick King, bm; William A. White, clk, wit; m 23 Aug 1865 by Jno W. Pattillo, J. P.

Baskerville, Ferry & Roan Stewart, 22 Apr 1848; Gabriel Garner, bm; Jno W. White, wit.

Baskerville, Thomas & Jane Macklen, 13 Dec 1859; George Stewart, bm; Jno. W. White, wit.

Basket, Alexander M. & Dynitia T. Burroughs, 30 Sept 1850; Willis P. White, bm; Jno W. White, wit.

Basket, Joseph & Mary Burroughs, 4 Dec 1832; Richard Jordan, bm.

Basket, Pleasant & Nancy Bowdown, (no date); Vincent Allen, bm; M. Duke Johnson, C. C., wit.

Basket, Pleasant & Rebeccah Given, 12 Mar 1830; Peter R. Davis, bm.

Baskett, Green & Elizabeth Stewart, 8 Sept 1866; William A. White, clk, wit; m 8 Sept 1866 by R. D. Paschall, J. P.

Baskett, Pleasant & Hicksey Brown, 11 Jan 1810; Nathaniel Brown, bm; M. Duke Johnson, C. C., wit.

Baskett, Robert & Mary Bowdon, 6 Aug 1835; William C. Butler, bm; E. D. Drake, clk, wit.

Batchelor, Joseph B. & Mary Cary Plummer, 26 June 1850; Matt W. Ransom, bm.

Bates, William & Rebecca Laughter, 18 Aug 1816; John Mulholland, bm; Wm. Green, C. C. C., wit.

Batson, D. F. & Mrs. Sarah W. Weaver, 16 Jan 1864; W. W. Butts, bm; William A. White, clk, wit; m 19 Jan 1864 by Thos W. Rooker, J. P.

Battle, Hillard (col) & Bettie Jones, 26 Dec 1865; Haywood Durham, bm; William A. White, wit.

Battle, William H. & Lucy M. Plummer, 18 May 1825; James H. Otey, bm.

Baxter, James & Polley Brown, 24 Feb 1790; Repps Duke, bm.

Baxter, James & Amey Thompson, 5 Feb 1799; Nathl Baxter, bm; Shd Green, wit.

Baxter, Jeremiah & Caty Hardridge, 18 Oct 1797; Jesse Bell, Jr., bm; Shd Green, wit.

Baxter, John & Martha Acrey, 26 Oct 1799; James Baxter, bm; Shd Green, wit.

Baxter, John & Nancy Norsworthy, 31 Dec 1803; Nathaniel Baxter, bm; M. D. Johnson, C. C., wit.

Baxter, Plummer & Nancy Hawks, 21 Aug 1829; William C. King, bm; C. Drake, C. C., wit.

Baxter, Reuben & Phebey Laughter, 17 Dec 1792; Wm Laughter, bm; B. Davis, wit.

Baxter, Richard & Nancy Kimbell, 9 July 1810; James Williams, bm; Jno C. Johnson, D. C., wit.

Beard, Benjaman & Nancy Long, 17 Dec 1803; William Robens, bm; Gideon Johnson, wit.

Beard, Littleton & Elizabeth Newton, 5 Dec 1823; Phil Hawkins, bm.

Beard, Littleton & Elizabeth Holden, 10 Apr 1834; James Taylor, bm; Burl Pitchford, J. P., wit.

Beasley, John W. & Margaret Pearsey, 8 Oct 1858; Lewis B. Collins, bm; Jno W. White, wit.

Beasley, William & Delilah Jones, 16 Aug 1788; Dinatious Dinkins, bm; M. Duke, Johnson, C. C., wit.

Beasly, John & Lucy Ellis, 26 Nov 1800; Thomas Beasly, bm.

Beazley, Pitts & Martha Acree, 11 Nov 1807; James Kidd, bm.

Beckham, Benjamin & Amelia Ballard, 19 Oct 1783; Phillemon Beckham, bm; M. Duke Johnson, wit.

Beckham, Green & Elizabeth Towns, 10 Feb 1808; Ambrose Minga, John Butler, bm; J. C. Johnson, wit.

Beckham, Green & Martha Proctor, 10 Feb 1808; Ambrose Murry, bm; M. Duke Johnston, C. C., wit.

Beckham, John & Sally Wren, 4 Dec 1818; Daniel A. Pardue, bm; Wm. Green, wit.

Beckham, Moses & Martha B. Hilliard, 22 Oct 1829; John V. Cawthorn, bm; E. D. Drake, wit.

Beckham, Solomon & Nancy Watson, (no date); Stephen Bekhm, bm.

Beckham, Solomon & Elizabeth Grime(?), 6 Aug 1796; George Allen, bm; Shd Green, wit.

Beckham, Stephen & Catherine Merrit, 23 May 1787; Archibald Brown, b; M. Duke Johnson, C. C., wit.

Beckham, Stephen & Sarah Gray, 22 Nov 1804; Solomon Beckham, bm; M. D. Johnson, C. C., wit.

Beckham, William & _____ Laughter, (no date); Archd Brown, bm.

Beckham, William & Rebekey Swinney, 13 Oct 1797; Arch Brown, bm; Shd Green,w it.

Beckham, Zachakry & Martha Knight, 13 Mar 1804; James Allen, bm; John Bowdon, wit.

Beddingfield, Charles & Elizabeth Williams, 30 Sept 1863; John W. Williams, bm; William A. White, clk, wit; m 30 Sept 1863 by Henry Petty, M. G.

Bell, Benjamin & Healhey Foote, 20 Dec 1792; William Russell, bm; M. D. Johnson, clk, wit.

Bell, Charles & _____, (no date); Jacob Bell, bm; M. Duke Johnson, C. C., wit.

Bell, Jacob & Nancy Pegram, 24 Dec 1800; Charles Bell, bm; M. D. Johnson, C. C., wit.

Bell, Jesse & Polley Lawter, 4 Dec 1798; Jacob Bell, bm; Sherwood Green, wit.

Bell, John G. & Margaret Shearin, 15 Aug 1823; Thomas Paine, bm.

Bell, Joseph H. & Amey Duke, 17 Dec 1810; Luis Rose, bm; M. Duke Johnson, C. C., wit.

Bell, Thomas & Pattey Pegram, 12 Nov 1782; Daniel Pegram, bm; M. D. Johnson, wit.

Bell, Thomas & Betsey Ellis, 4 Mar 1801; Zachariah Lewis, bm; M. D. Johnson, C. C., wit.

Bell, Thomas & Judah Shearin, 20 Dec 1809; William Little, bm; J. C. Johnson, D. C. C., wit.

Bell, William & Elizabeth Acre, 27 Aug 1832; Wilie Acre, bm; C. Drake, C. C., wit.

Bell, William & Lucy Wright, 21 Sept 1865; Thomas D. Rodwell, b;m William A. White, clk, wit; m 26 Sept 1865 by B. F. Long, M. G.

Bell, William S. & Martha J. Felts, 21 Dec 1857; William Edmonds, bm; Jno W. White, clk, wit; m 24 Dec 1857 by M. M. Drake, J. P.

Bell, Zachariah & Nancy Walker, 8 May 1812; Micajah Walker, bm; Wm. Green, C. C. C., wit.

Bellamy, John & Ann Pattillo, 10 Aug 1826; Marble W. Dunnavant, bm; M. M. Drake, wit.

Bennet, Duke & Martha Fleming, 24 Mar 1797; Edward Moore, bm; Thos Malone, wit.

Bennet, John & Salley Allan, ___ 1797; W. Fann, bm.

Bennett, Alexander & Martha A. White, 6 Oct 1852; Wm. H. Bartlett, bm; William A. White, wit.

Bennett, Charles & Mary Clark, 17 Apr 1857; Saml N. Mills, bm; Jno W. White, clk, wit; m 22 Apr 1857 by A. Steed, J. P.

Bennett, Charles C. & Eveline Bennett, 28 July 1828; George W. Barnes, bm.

Bennett, Chas H. & E. B. White, 9 Aug 1858; A. R. Bennett, bm; Jno W. White, clk, wit; m 10 Aug 1858 by Wm. Hodges, M. G.

Bennett, Isham & Elizabeth White, 6 Dec 1821; James Marton, bm; Gordon Cawthorn, wit.

Bennett, Isham H. & Sarah Jane Yarbrough, 15 Aug 1846; Isham Bennett, bm; Jno W. White, wit.

Bennett, James & Lucretia Read, 20 Oct 1857; George D. Harris, bm; Jno W. White, clk, wit; m 24 Oct 1857 by Wm. A. Dowtin, J. P.

Bennett, James C. & Charity Bennett, 29 July 1819; James C. Powel bm; ___ Drake, wit.

Bennett, John & Lucy King, 23 Feb 1858; Allen M. King; bm; m 23 Feb 1858 by W. A. Dowtin, J. P.

Bennett, Joseph & Polly Stephenson, 25 Jan 1797; Sol Beckham, bm; Shd. Green, wit.

Bennett, Lemul & Elizabeth Sledge, 11 Dec 1826; James A. Lancaster, bm; M. M. Drake, wit.

Bennett, Thomas & Rebecah Capps, 31 Jan 1811; Randolph Gordan, bm; Jno C. Johnson, C. C., wit.

Bennett, William & Kizany P. Capps, 5 June 1822; James Martin, bm.

Bennitt, Charles & Rebecca Bennett, 3 Sept 1796; Samuel Smith, bm; Shd. Green, wit.

Bennitt, Reubin & Betsey Beckham, 26 May 1786; Ben Beckham, bm; M. Duke Johnson, wit.

Benter, Hennery & Susanna Matthews, 12 June 1830; Jno C. Johnson, Burl Pitchford, J. P., wit.

Berry, Andrew J. & L. W. Walton, 14 Apr 1849; D. P——— Taylor, bm; Jno W. White, wit.

Berry, William & Jerusha Paschael, 9 Feb 1785; Thos Hilliard, bm; M. D. Johnson, wit.

Bertain, David & Rebecca Tucker, 15 Oct 1808; Willie Duncan, bm; J. C. Johnson, D. C., wit.

Best, Benjamin & Susan Clark, 23 Sept 1841; Samuel Edwards, bm.

Betty, Henry & Sally Davis, _____ 180-; William Powell, bm; Sugan Johnson, wit.

Betty, Rowland & Elizabeth Walker, 23 Oct 1805; Richard Tunstall, bm; Jo Terrell, D. C. C., wit.

Bierd, Jones & Elizabeth Rottenberry, 8 May 1822; Warren Holden, bm; Cas. Drake, Clk, wit.

Bigelow, Roderick & Elizabeth Pattilloe, 20 Nov 1811; Joe Terrell, Jr., bm.

Bilbo, John P. & Lucy Paine, 18 Nov 1818; Thomas Paine, bm; W. A. K. Falkener, wit.

Bilbro, Jno & Mary Clemmons, 4 Nov 1788.

Birchett, Edward & Betsy Smith, 3 Dec 1816; Daniel Burchett, bm; Wm. Green, C. W. C. C., wit.

Birchett, Isaac & Mary Tucker, 11 Nov 1787; James Ellington, bm; M. D. Johnson, C. C., wit.

Bishop, Alfred & Mary Hicks, 20 Nov 1860; William P. Rose, bm; Jno W. White, clk., wit; m 21 Nov 1860 by Jno. W. Pattillo, J. P.

Bishop, James & Lucy Brown, 15 Jan 1810; Matthew Marshall, bm; M. Duke Johnson, D. C., wit.

Bishop, James & Caroline Mills, 10 June 1861; Redman J. Booth, bm; Jno W. White, wit.

Bishop, Weldon E. & Ann W. Lancaster, 15 Dec 1854; B. F. Powell, bm; Jno W. White, C. C. C., wit.

Blacknell, John & Ann Plummer, 22 Dec 1780; John Willis, bm.

Blackwell, Thomas F. & Sally Wortham, 2 June 1834; Jno. P. Blackwell, bm.

Blackwell, William M. & Winefred W. Cook, 16 Jan 1839; Lewis D. Burwell, bm.

Blair, H. M. & Harriet Talley, 8 Apr 1865; L. C. Perkinson, bm; William A. White, clk, wit; m 8 Apr 1865 by L. C. Perkinson, M. G.

Blanch, Ezekial A. & Emily Fitts, 15 June 1840; Jos Speed Jones, bm.

Blanch, Ezekiel & Salley Mitchell, 25 Apr 1785; Jno White, bm; M. D. Johnson, C. C,. wit.

Blanch, Henry (col) & Della Milam, 19 Apr 1867; Nathan Milam, Jno McCraw, bm; m 24 Nov 1866 by Saml Bobbitt, J. P.

Blanchett, Hudson & Edith Floyd, 7 Apr 1783; Thomas Blanchet, bm; M. Duke Johnson, wit.

Blankenship, Allen & Mary Webb, 18 Aug 1808; Amasay Webb, bm; J. C. Johnson, D. C. C., wit.

Blankinship, Benjamin & Sarah B. Web, 16 July 1808; John Webb, bm; J. C. Johnson, D. C., wit.

Blanton, Christopher & Patty Thompson, 4 Oct 1780; John Williams, bm; Thos Machen, wit.

Blanton, Green & Elizabeth Lambert, 28 Dec 1852; William Mallett, bm; Jno W. White, wit.

Blanton, James & Elizabeth McDaniel, 23 Jan 1799; Saml Lambert, bm; Shd Green, wit.

Blanton, William & Millison Worsham, _____; Jechoriah Toler, bm; M. Duke Johnson, wit.

Blanton, William & Priscilla Ellis, 16 Nov 1834; Wm. U. Meacham, bm;

Blanton, William A. & Rebecca Burton, 3 Apr 1831; Marcy Jones, bm; Burl Pitchford, J. P., wit.

Blunt, Joseph & Martha Arington, 26 Nov 1803; Willis Arrington, bm; M. Duke Johnson, C. C., wit.

Bobbit, Harvey M. & Ann Eliza Pegram, 9 Mar 1842; Henry J. Macon, bm; M. J. Montgomery, Wit.

Bobbit, John & Elizabeth Dowden, 19 Mar 1796; Sherwood Green, bm; M. Duke Johnson, clk, wit.

Bobbitt, Charles H. & Mary A. Alston, 14 Mar 1821; Anthony Dowtin, bm; Cas Drake, C. C. C., wit.

Bobbitt, Drury & Rebecca Burrow, 26 Dec 1804; John Gardner, bm; M. D. Johnson ,C. C., wit.

Bobbitt, Drury & Sally Braddley, 4 Aug 1818; Stephen Bobbitt, bm; W. A. K. Falkener, wit.

Bobbitt, Edward F. & Indianah F. Brame, 7 Nov 1853; Sol Stallings, bm; Jno W. White, wit; m 23 Nov 1853 by Robt O. Burton, M. G.

Bobbitt, Harriss & Partheny Harris, 11 Mar 1801; Joel Harris, bm.

Bobbitt, James & Polley Gunn, 10 Feb 1809; Abraham Clanton, bm; M. Duke Johnson, C. C., wit.

Bobbitt, John & Patience Harris, 16 Jan 1789; Lend Kimbel, bm.

Bobbitt, John R. & Mary A. Shearin, 12 Feb 1848; William H. Bobbitt, bm; Jno W. White, wit.

Bobbitt, Joseph H. (son of Samuel & Martha A. Bobbitt) & M. S. Mills (dau of Samuel N. & Mildred Mills), 28 Sept 1867; William A. White, clk, wit; m 2 Oct 1867 by T. B. Kingsbury at Samuel N. Mills' house.

Bobbitt, Joshua & Patsy Haithcock, 19 Feb 1813; William Bobbitt, bm; Wm. Green, C. C., wit.

Bobbitt, Kinchen & Sally Dobbin, 12 Jan 1833; John P. Shearin, bm; C. Drake, C. C., wit.

Bobbitt, Lewis & Nancy Lancaster, 29 Dec 1814; John Lancaster, bm; W. Green, C. C., wit.

Bobbitt, Lewis & Mary F. Minor, 17 Oct 1855; William M. Wilson, bm; Jno W. White, clk, wit; m 24 Oct 1855 by Thos S. Campbell, M. G.

Bobbitt, Miles & Susan Gunn, 19 Oct 1814; Turner Jinkins, bm; W. Green, C. C., wit.

Bobbitt, Miles & Martha Davis, 1 Jan 1827; James Martin, bm; M. M. Drake, wit.

Bobbitt, Samuel & Martha Ann Dawtin, 25 Dec 1838; Francis McHenry, bm.

Bobbitt, Stephen & Elizabeth A. Bradley, 22 Jan 1814; Robert Robertson, bm; Jno H. Green, wit.

Bobbitt, Stephen E. & Mary E. Kearney, 19 Mar 1855; Robert A. Shearin, bm; Jno W. White, bm.

Bobbitt, Washington (col) & Nancy Brown, 19 Nov 1866; Saml Bobbitt, bm; m 24 Nov 1866 by Saml Bobbitt, J. P.

Bobbitt, William & Sukie James, 15 May 1784; George James, bm; M. D. Johnson, wit.

Bobbitt, William & Winny Bennett, 19 Jan 1810; Robert Moore, bm; Jno C. Johnson, D. C., wit.

Bobbitt, William H. & Lutitia A. Burrows, 2 Sept 1839; Thos J. Judkins, bm.

Bobbitt, Wm. Henry & Winnie C. Fleming, 12 Jan 1864; Alpheus Bobbitt, bm; m 13 Jan 1864 by Henry Petty, M. G.

Bobbitte, Arthur & Mary Smelly, 4 Jan 1802; Joel Harris, bm; J. C. Johnson, D. C., wit.

Bolton, Bolling & Polley Dunnavand, 22 Mar 1782; Wm Johnson, bm; M. Duke Johnson, C. C., wit.

Bolton, Henry & Martha Parrish, 5 Apr 1847; Armistead King, bm; Jno W. White, wit.

Bolton, Henry & Margaret Bishop, 20 Oct 1851; John Smith, bm; Jno W. White, wit; m 22 Oct 1851 by Jas T. Russell, J. P.

Bolton, James & Lethea Talley, 24 Feb 1830; Ebenezer Coleman, bm; Burl Pitchford, J. P., wit.

Bolton, John & Judiath Newman, 6 Mar 1831; Mathew Bolton, bm; Burl Pitchford, J. P., wit.

Bolton, M. T. & Elizabeth P. Hawks, 26 July 1866; Wm. R. Coleman; bm; William A. White, wit; m 27 July 1866 by Jno W. Pattillo, J. P.

Bolton, Matthew & Sarah Darnel, 30 June 1806; John Darnol, bm; M. Duke Johnson, C. C., wit.

Bolton, Matthew & Frances Whitler, 29 Apr 1831; Ebenezer Coleman bm; C. Drake, C. C., wit.

Bolton, Wm. H. & Sally Smith, 1 Aug 1844; Wm. W. Davis, bm; M. J. Montgomery, wit.

Boorey(?), John & Betsey Partrick, 26 Dec 1799; David Thomas, bm; Shd Green, wit.

Booth, Eppa & Eluena Pascal, 1 Nov 1791; John Paschal, bm.

Booth, Luis & Hannah M. Carter, 12 June 1820; John C. Riggan, bm; Cas. Drake, C. C., wit.

Booth, Redmond J. & Nancy E. Carter, 7 Dec 1861; Peter J. Turnbull, bm; Jno W. White, wit.

Boss, Samuel & Emily Macklin, 21 May 1847; James Macklin, bm; Jno W. White, wit.

Bottom, J. M. & Bettie E. Paschall, 5 June 1861; John W. Bellamy, bm; Jno W. White, clk, wit; m 6 June 1861 by Henry A. Foote, J. P.

Bottom, John H. & Dorotha F. Overbey, 18 June 1830; George W. Barnes, bm; H. Pope, wit.

Bottom, William M. & Cinderrilla Pitchford, 11 Apr 1842; Seth W. Mabry, bm; Burl Pitchford, J. P., wit.

Bowdon, Andrew J. & Arabella G. Duke, 28 Jan 1854; John Bowdon, Jr., bm; Jno. W. White, wit.

Bowdon, Daniel & Parthena S. Basket, 11 Dec 1839; Lewis Turner, bm.

Bowdon, John Jr., & Mary A. Newton, 28 Aug 1848; Jno White, bm.

Bowdon, Robert & India F. Perkinson, 5 Feb 1866; John R. Bynum, bm; William A. White, clk, wit; m 15 Feb 1866 by S. P. J. Harris, M. G.

Bowers, Giles & Nancy Felts, 7 Feb 1854; Blake Baker, bm; W. B. Thornton, wit; m 14 Feb 1854 by Henry Harris, J. P.

Bowers, James & Henriter Duke, 30 Aug 1797; James Glen, bm; Shd Green, wit.

Bowin, Jonathan & Tempe Tarbrough, 16 Mar 1780; John Laughter, bm.

Boyce, William & Elizabeth Person, 17 Aug 1802; Jesse Person, bm; S. Johnson, wit.

Boyd, Conrad S. & Alice E. Stewart; R. D. Fleming, bm; Jno W. White, wit; m 6 July 1859 by J. B. Solomon, M. G.

Boyd, Conrard S. & Mary A. Kearney, 14 Aug 1828; Jno W. Lewis, bm; M. M. Drake, wit.

Boyd, James & Lucy Ann Lyne, 15 July 1808; Richard Boyd, bm; John C. Johnson, wit.

Boyd, Jno E. & Ann B. Jones, 27 Feb 1834; Henry G. Fitts, bm.

Boyd, Richard S. & Mary E. Coleman, 23 Apr 1828; Edwin D. Drake, bm; M. M. Drake, wit.

Boyd, Wm Henry (col) & Betsey Ann Collins, 22 Sept 1866; William A. White, clk, wit; m 7 Oct 1866 by W. W. White, J. P.

Brack, Baker B. & Mary F. Thompson, 19 Jan 1858; Henry Y. Harriss, bm; Wm. A. White, wit; m 30 Jan 1858 by Saml Bobbitt, J. P.

Brack, George W. & Elizabeth Pegram, 25 Mar 1856; William A. J. Nicholson, bm; Jno W. White, wit.

Brack, Samuel & Sally Brewer, 11 Feb 1813; Randolph Gordan, bm; Jno H. Green, wit.

Bradley, John & Priscilla Mabry, 6 July 1830; William Little, bm; C. Drake, C. C., wit.

Bradly, Stephen & Martha Whitaker, 15 May 1839; Geo E. Spruill, bm.

Bradly, William & Elisabeth Atkins, 1 Oct 1788; Philip Harris, bm; M. Duke Johnson, C. C., wit.

Bradshaw, Mordecai & Amy J. Byrum, 3 Feb 1838; Griffin Williams, bm.

Bragg, Thomas & Margaret Crosland, 20 Dec 1803; Thomas Griffin, bm; M. Duke Johnson, C. C., wit.

Bragg, William & Drucilla Harton, 24 Dec 1838; William Dickerson, bm; Richd Jordan, wit.

Brame, Anderson F. & Alice Milam, 3 Feb 1823; Alexander Crossland, bm; C. Drake, C. C., wit.

Brame, Armistead (col) & Fanny Cheek, 25 Mar 1867; William A. White, clk, wit; m 30 Mar 1867 by P. H. Joyner,

Brame, Elbert & Indianah King, 4 Dec 1851; W. W. King, bm; Jno W. White, clk, wit; m 10 Dec 1851 by O. D. Fitts, J. P.

Brame, Henry & Martha Milam, 16 Dec 1825; Jesse B. White, bm; M. M. Drake, wit.

Brame, John & Sarah C. Butler, 10 Nov 1823; John O. Butler, bm.

Brame, Marcus & Ann Foote, 15 Dec 1831; Matthew M. Drake, bm; C. Drake, C. C., wit.

Brame, Nelson & Elizabeth Wortham, 27 Nov 1855; William Bragg, bm.

Brame, Oliver & Elizabeth Archer, 30 Dec 1832; Asa George, bm.

Brame, Thomas R. & Almeda J. W. Kearney, 29 Nov 1836; William C. Clanton, bm.

Brame, William & Nancey Fitts, 27 Dec 1793; Thomas Reavis, bm; Richd Russell, wit.

Brame, William (col) & Chany Ellis, 24 Dec 1866; William A. White, clk, wit; m 25 Dec 1866 by J. M. Brame, J. P.

Brame, William A. & Orcia E. Joyner, 12 Dec 1856; E. E. Parham, bm; Jno W. White, clk, wit; m 17 Dec 1856 by James Reid, M, G.

Branch, G. A. & Rebecca Womble, 25 Feb 1867; Robt J. Day, bm; William A. White, wit.

Branch, John (col) & Harriet Williams, 15 Nov 1866; Wm J. Norwood, bm; William A. White, clk, wit; m 15 Nov 1866 by William H. Bishop, M. G.

Brandom, Jesse & Parthena Drew, 2 July 1822; William Carsey, bm.

Brandom, Samuel W. & Mary G. Evans, 21 Dec 1837; James Thomas, bm; Burl Pitchford, J. P., wit.

Brandom, Wiet & Salley Moon, 19 Dec 1832; Thomas Brandom, bm; Burl Pitchford, J. P.

Brandt, John T. & Czorilda A. Stansfield, 1 May 1852; F. S. Norwood, bm; Jno W. White, wit.

Branowski, Joseph & Sally Drake, 24 Aug 1852; Thomas W. Rooker, bm; Jno W. White, clk, wit; m 27 Aug 1852 by B. Eaton, J. P.

Brasell, William & Mary Daniel, 31 Oct 1829; James Daniel, bm; E. D. Drake, wit.

Braswell, Jacob & Parthenia H. Cotton, 18 Jan 1819; Jno. C. Johnson, bm; Wm. A. K. Falkener, bm.

Breedlove, Nathan & Holly Weaver, 6 Dec 1805; Sherod Wilson, bm; Jo Terrell, C. C. C., wit.

Breedlove, Shelton & Eveline H. Stewart, 22 Dec 1832; John Edwards, bm; C. Drake, C. C., wit.

Brehon, Samuel (son of George & Mariah) (col) & Lila Sykes (dau of Luke & Mahala), 8 Nov 1867; William A. White, clk, wit; m 8 Nov 1867 by N. A. Purefoy, M. G.

Brewer, Harday & Salley Lamkin, 19 Sept 1788(?); Martin Dye, bm; Thos Mackin, wit.

Brewer, Hardy & Mary Freeman, 19 Oct 1820; Wm. F. Lamkin, bm.

Brewer, John & Sarah Hamilton, 27 Feb 1814; William Miller, bm; Wm. Green, C. C., wit.

Brewer, John & Betsey Carroll, 4 Oct 1819; Jonas Jeffres, bm; Cas Drake, C. C. C., wit.

Brickell, Nathl D. & Matilda Yarbrough, 20 Mar 1852; William H. Bartlett, bm; Jno W. White, wit.

Brickell, Nathl D. & Julia A. Bartlett, 21 July 1856; John C. McCraw, bm; Jno W. White, wit; m 22 July 1856 by J. B. Solomon, M. G.

Brickell, Thomas & Salley Hill Jones, 4 Dec 1783; John Macon, bm; M. Duke, Johnson, wit.

Brickell, Thomas & Sally Gloster, 25 June 1807; Joshua Archer, bm; Jo Terrell, D. C. C., wit.

Brickle, Nathaniel D. & Emeline M. Duke, 28 Mar 1836; James S. Walker, bm; E. D. Drake, clk, wit.

Bridgers, Frank (col) & Priscilla Allen, 2 Mar 1867; Revd. J. B. Solomon, bm; William A. White, clk, wit; m 2 Mar 1867 by P. H. Joyner.

Bridges, Benja B. & Rebecca P. Southerland, 3 Jan 1834; John V. Crossland, bm; E. D. Drake, clk, wit.

Brintle, Jesse & Rebecca Bell (no date); John Tansil, bm; M. D. Johnson, C. C., wit.

Brocket, James (col) & Martha A. Burnett, 1 Dec 1866; J. H. Bennett, D. C., wit; m 2 Dec 1866 by C. M. Cook, J. P.

Brodie, John & Martha E. Williams, 15 Dec 1809; John M. Johnson, bm; M. Duke, Johnson, C. C., wit.

Brodie, William L. & Drucilla Green, 9 May 1853; Jno White, bm; Jno W. White, clk, wit; m 11 May 1853 by Numa F. Reid, M. G.

Brodnax, Thomas & Mary Call, 6 Mar 1792; John Power, bm; M. D. Johnson, C. C. C., wit.

Brogdon, John & Salley Gurley (no date); Sugan Kimbell, bm; M. Duke Johnson, C. C., wit.

Brooks, Robert & Ann Salmon, 15 Nov 1850; Nathan Milam, bm.

Brooks, Wade & Sarah Beazley, 13 Aug 1782; John Pitts Beasley, bm; M. Duke Johnson, Joseph Taylor, wit.

Brooks, Wade & Elizabeth Carol, 14 Apr 1802; James Beazly, bm; Gideon Johnson, wit.

Brosius, Wm. K. & Maggie J. Norfleet, 15 Sept 1865; K. W. Coghill, bm; William A. White, clk, wit; m 21 Sept 1865 by P. H. Joyner.

Brown, Archibald, Jr., & Martha Smith, 15 Dec 1830; Joseph Clark, bm; C. Drake, D. C. C., wit.

Brown, Charles & Salley Foote, 24 Dec 1834; Jno E. Twitty, bm.

Brown, Charles Z. & Mary A. Wells, 4 Apr 1865; Richard W. Kearney, Jr., bm; William A. White, wit; m 5 Apr 1865 by T. Page Ricaud, M. G.

Brown, Harry (col) & Hannah Browne, 6 Nov 1866; William E. Brown, bm; William A. White, clk, wit; m 10 Nov 1866 by Saml Bobbitt, J. P.

Brown, Jacob & Emily B. Mudd, 12 Nov 1863; W. S. Wanwright, bm; John C. McCraw, D. C., wit; m 12 Nov 1863 by Henry Petty, M. G.

Brown, James & Angilica Warton (no date); Chas Elloms, bm; M. Duke Johnson, wit.

Brown, James & Elizabeth Renn, 20 Mar 1801; Charles Bell, bm; M. D. Johnson, C. C., wit.

Brown, James T. & Mary C. Harris, 14 Dec 1830; James Y. Harriss, bm; C. Drake, C. C., wit.

Brown, James T. & Susan Clanton, 19 Dec 1833; John Egerton, bm; E. D. Drake, clk, wit.

Brown, Jerry (col) & Julia Sutton, 19 Nov 1866; Turner Allen, bm; J. H. Bennett, wit; m 20 Nov 1866 by N. A. Purefoy, M. G.

Brown, John (col) & Mary Hawkins, 19 May 1866; Reubin Hawkins, bm; William A. White, clk, wit; m 19 May 1866 by R. D. Paschall, J. P.

Brown, John E. & Martha G. Hase, 12 June 1833; Allen B. Pitchford, bm; Burl Pitchford, J. P.

Brown, John E. & Elizabeth D. Dobbins, 24 Feb 1852; C. N. Riggan, bm; Jno W. White, wit; m 25 Feb 1852 by B. Eaton, J. P.

Brown, John H. & Nancy Beckham, 23 Jan 1849; Benjamin H. Johnson, bm; Jno W. White, wit.

Brown, Julius S. & Sarah A. Walker, 3 Feb 1862; P. R. Uzzle, bm; Jno W. White, clk, wit; m 4 Feb 1862 by Chas Skinner, J. P.

Brown, Lafayette & Mary A. Faulcon, 26 Apr 1827; Henry Fitts, bm.

Brown, Nathaniel & Sarah Riggan, 9 Nov 1808; Elias Gwin, bm; J. C. Johnson, D. C., wit.

Brown, Peyton & Sally Turner, 20 Apr 1856; William Watson, bm; E. D. Drake, clk, wit.

Brown, R. F. (Dr.) & Elizabeth H. Mitchell, 2 Aug 1856; Will A. Jenkins, bm; Jno W. White, clk, wit; m 5 Aug 1856 by L. L. Smith.

Brown, Sterling & Polly Bobbett, 12 Jan 1822; Robert Riggan, bm; Cas. Drake, wit.

Brown, Thomas & Mary R. Foot, 22 Aug 1828; Nathaniel Brown, bm; M. M. Drake, wit.

Brown, William & Polly Smith, 30 June 1800; Archd Brown, bm; S. Johnson, wit.

Brown, William & Mary Myrick, 19 Dec 1809; Joshua Archer, bm; Jno C. Johnson, D. C. C. C., wit.

Brown, William H. & Martha Egerton, 2 Sept 1804; Gilbert G. Egerton, bm; M. Duke Johnson, C. C., wit.

Browne, Howard (col) & Letitia Thornton, 28 Dec 1866; William A. White, clk, wit; m 29 Dec 1866 by R. S. F. Peete, J. P.

Browning, Benjamin & Nancy Bobbitt, 11 Sept 1849; R. Browning. bm; Jno. W. White, clk, wit.

Browning, James W. & Mary Ann Shearin, 11 Jan 1853; L. D. Browning, bm; Jno W. White, clk, wit; m 12 Jan 1853 by B. Eaton, J. P.

Browning, Louis D. & S. Robertson, 3 Feb 1857; W. H. Browning, bm; Jno W. White, wit.

Browning, William & Winifred M. Bobbitt, 28 May 1827; Jesse Myrick, bm; M. M. Drake, wit.

Bryan, H. B. & Mary P. Jenkins, 4 Sept 1848; Jno W. Bellamy, bm; Jno W. White, wit.

Buchanan, Alexander S. & Mary M. Tunstall, 17 Feb 1853; M. G. Newman, bm; Jno W. White, wit.

Buchanan, James C. & Martha Mabrey, 15 Dec 1829; John Ellington, bm; E. D. Drake, wit.

Buchanan, M. S. & Mrs. Eliz M. Loyd, 7 Dec 1866; William A. White, C. C., C., wit; m 8 Dec 1866 by N. A. Purefoy, M. G.

Buchanan, Samuel & Mary H. Sandiford, 12 Oct 1802; Henry Williams, bm; M. Duke Johnson, C. C., wit.

Buchanan, William C. A. & Permealea Ellington, 24 Dec 1834; William F. Hilliard, bm; Burl Pitchford, J. P., wit.

Buckhanan, David D. & Nancy B. Turner, 31 Dec 1846; James R. Watkins, bm; Jno W. White, wit.

Bugg, Samuel F. & Saluda A. Pattillo, 30 Nov 1833; Zachariah Herndon, bm; C. Drake, C. C., w.it.

Bugg, Samuel R. & Frances D. Hatchel, 20 Nov 1833; George W. Norvell, bm; Burl Pitchford, J. P.

Bugg, William & Martha Hutson, 15 Feb 1834; John Hutson, bm; Burl Pitchford, J. P., wit.

Bull, Eli W. & Sarah A. Renno, 22 Dec 1860; John G. Hubbard, bm; William A. White, clk, wit; m 28 Dec 1860 by R. D. Paschall, J. P.

Bullock, Ancil (col) & Mary Williams, 30 Aug 1866; William A. White, clk, wit; m 1 Sept 1866 by R. D. Paschall, J. P.

Bullock, Parker & Charlotte Hargrove, m 30 Dec 1866 by L. Henderson, J. P.

Bullock, Richard, Jr., & Cornelia A. Boyd, 29 Dec 1849; Wm R. Thornton, bm; Jno W. White, wit.

Bullock, Richard A. & Isabella B. Bullock, 18 May 1867; William A. White, clk, wit; m 29 May 1867 by F. N. Whaley, M. G.

Burchet, Jack & Sarah Drue, 6 Apr 1837; Christopher Roberson, bm; Burl Pitchford, J. P., wit.

Burchet, John & Eliza Mewshaw, 8 Jan 1838; Christopher Robertson, bm; Burl Pitchford, J. P., wit.

Burchett, Daniel & Leathea E. Smith, 28 May 1825; Howel Hagood, bm; Burl Pitchford, wit.

Burchett, Ezekial & Mariah Taylor, 11 June 1825; Daniel Burchett, bm; Burl Pitchford, wit.

Burchett, John L. & Martha A. Tucker, 9 Dec 1856; R. J. Robinson, bm; Jno. W. White, clk, wit; m 11 Dec 1856 by Wm. A. Burwell, J. P.

Burchett, Robert & Ann Eliza Fletcher, 10 Jan 1842; Thomas J. Rainey, bm; M. J. Montgomery, wit.

Burchette, John L. & Martha A. Vaughan, 30 July 1862; William H. Richardson, bm; m 30 July 1862 by Thomas P. Paschall, J. P.

Burchitt, Joseph & Martha Wilson, 18 Sept 1782; Wyatt Hawkins, bm.

Burford, Philip & Rebecah Clark, 8 Jan 1782; Euel Engliss Wright, bm.

Burge, William & Eliza A. W. Alston, 23 Jan 1837; Green D. Jenkins, bm; Benj E. Cook, wit.

Burges, John & Martha J. Alston, 24 July 1824; William Williams, bm; C. Drake, C. C., wit.

Burgess, Cyrus (col) & Nancy Williams, 6 Dec 1866; William A. White, clk, wit; m 28 Dec 1866 by M. P. Perry, J. P.

Burgess, James & Maria Burrows, 26 Dec 1822; Freemond Lewis, bm; Cas. Drake, C. C., wit.

Burgess, James & Julia Freer, 25 June 1832; George W. Barnes, bm; C. Drake, C. C., wit.

Burgess, John & Polley Wuggins, 16 July 1796; Benja Crenshaw, bm; Shd Green, wit.

Burgess, Lovitte & Frances Cocke, 16 Sept 1828; Samuel T. Alston, bm; M. M. Drake, wit.

Burgess, Thomas L. & Harriet C. Burt, 6 June 1853; A. H. Davis, bm; Jno. W. White, wit; m 8 June 1853 by Robt O. Burton, M. G.

Burks, Luke & Jane Guise, 24 Nov 1824; Willis Guise, bm; Burl Pitchford, wit.

Burnam, Alexander & Phebe Pardue, 5 July 1782; Morriss Pardue, bm; M. Duke Johnson, wit.

Burnet, Micajah & Martha A. Mills, 28 Dec 1859; Thos H. Read, bm; Jno. W. White, clk, wit; m 29 Dec 1859 by N. A. Purefoy.

Burney, John R. & Winnie A. Milam, 8 May 1858; Paul Palmer, bm; Jno W. White, wit; m 12 May 1858 by T. G. Lowe, M. G.

Burroughs, Bazzal & Rebecca M. Turner, 1 Feb 1828; Sandey L. Thurmon, bm.

Burroughs, Clement & Nancy Summerhill (no date); Thos Smith, bm; M. Duke, Johnson, C. C., wit.

Burroughs, James (of Caswell Co) & Salley Watson, 31 Dec 1803; John Watson, bm.

Burroughs, James & Lucy Jordan, 4 Jan 1837; Gideon M. Green, bm; E. D. Drake, clk, wit.

Burroughs, John & Mrs. Lucy W. Pinnell, 10 Oct 1866; Isaac Loyd, bm; William A. White, C. C. C., wit; m 14 Oct 1866 by S. P. J. Harris, M. G.

Burroughs, William & Agnes Vanlandingham, 6 Dec 1797; Henry Cauthan, bm; Sherwood Green, wit.

Burroughs, William W. & Harriet H. Turner, 19 Dec 1843; William Vanlandingham, bm; M. J. Montgomery, wit.

Burrow, Francis & Elizabeth Jones, 24 June 1806; Joseph Kimbell, bm; M. Duke Johnson, C. C., wit.

Burrow, James & Rebecca Cheek, 31 May 1788; John Bobbitt, Jr., bm; M. Duke Johnson, C. C., wit.

Burrow, James & Mary Shearin, 2 Jan 1817; Joshua Haywood, bm; Wm. Green, C. C. C., wit.

Burrow, Thomas & Patsey Green, 14 Dec 1788; George Dorden, bm; M. Duke, Johnson, C. C., wit.

Burrow, William & Holley Bobbitt, 15 Dec 1798; David W. Newell, bm; Shd Green, wit.

Burrows, Archibald D. & Polly Fowler, 18 July 1820; Gordon Cawthorn, bm; Cas Drake, C. C. C., wit.

Burrows, James & Nancy Shearin, 6 Mar 1824; Littleberry L. Robertson, bm.

Burrows, Robert D. & Senoria Harris, 22 Apr 1851; Danl Hardy, bm; Jno W. White, clk, wit; m 24 Apr 1851 by M. M. Drake, J. P.

Burrows, William P. & Ann Riggan, 22 Dec 1841; John W. Balthrop, bm;

Burt, John A. & Emily M. Cheek, 9 Oct 1830; Edwin D. Drake, bm.

Burton, Allen & Elizabeth Brooks, 12 Mar 1800; James Kidd, bm; S. Johnson, wit.

Burton, Frederick J. & Elizabeth Cole, 2 Jan 1850; M. R. Seymour, bm; Phillip Love, wit.

Burton, Horace N. & Margaret D. Williams, 24 May 1825; Daniel Turner, bm; M. M. Drake, wit.

Burton, John & Tempy Jones, 22 Jan 1817; Willson Harris, bm; Wm. Green, C. C. C., wit.

Burwell, Jno S. & Sarah E. Hayes, 23 Oct 1834; William Davis, bm; E. D. Drake, clk, wit.

Burwell, John S. S. R. & Panthea E. Boyd, 21 Aug 1840; Joshua Davis, bm.

Burwell, William A. & Mary G. Williams, 13 Dec 1834; William Davis, bm; E. D. Drake, clk, wit.

Bush, Jeremiah & Mary Duke, 2 July 1789; Dwelley Darnald, bm; M. Duke Johnson, C. C., wit.

Bush, John & Mary Dickens, 21 Jan 1793; John Dickins, bm; M. Duke Johnson, C. C., wit.

Butler, John & Polly Turner, 24 May 1822; John Egerton, bm; Cas. Drake, wit.

Buttrill, Thomas & Peggey Malone, 23 Dec 1785; Fredk Malone, bm; M. Duke Johnson, wit.

Byrd, James & Lucy Lanier, 17 Dec 1798; James Caller, bm; M. Duke Johnson, C. C., wit.

Cabanne, L. D. & Susan Plummer, 17 Jan 1838; Jno T. Williams, bm.

Cain, John & Polley Thomas, 27 Dec 1827; Steven Thomas, bm; Burl Pitchford, wit.

Calafer, William & Emily R. Bennett, 12 July 1837; Simon B. Everitt, bm.

Callahan, James & Martha Cooper, 3 Sept 1862; William Wynn, bm; Wm. A. White, clk, wit; m 3 Aug 1852 by Jas C. Robinson, J. P.

Caller, John & Sarah Wood, 15 Jan 1781; Euel Wright, bm; M. D. Johnson, wit.

Caller, Thomas & Nancy Mayfield, 17 June 1793; Jas Caller, bm; Richd Russell, wit.

Callier, Charles & Susan Leonard, 5 Nov 1805; Thomas Stackhouse, bm; Jo Terrell, D. C., wit.

Camp, Amiel & Martha R. Myrick, 11 June 1832; George W. Barnes, bm; C. Drake, C. C., wit.

Campbell, _____ & _____ Davis (no date).

Campbell, Thomas S. & Elizabeth D. Collins, 16 Nov 1846; Oliver D. Fitts, bm.

Cannon, James & Peggy Finley, 14 Jan 1812; Jesse Stegall, bm; Wm. Green, C. C. C., wit.

Cannon, John & Sally Wright, 22 June 1820; Archd D. Burrows, bm; Cas. Drake, C. C., wit.

Cannon, Robert & Louisa Victoria Blanton, 5 Dec 1860; David W. Harris, bm; William A. White, wit; m 5 Dec 1860 by Thos A. Montgomery, J. P.

Cannon, Thomas & Mary Brooks, 23 Jan 1809; Thomas Beasley, bm; J. C. Johnson, C. C., wit.

Cannon, Willis & Elizabeth Griffis, 20 Apr 1849; James A. Taylor, bm; Jno W. White, wit.

Capps, Cylus & Jane Marshall, 11 Aug 1809; William Capps, bm; Jno C. Johnson, D. C., wit.

Capps, Francis & Fanney Capps, 9 Oct 1797; Phil Bennett, bm; Shd Green, wit.

Capps, Henry & Nancy Lyles, 15 Sept 1800; Joshua Capps, bm; M. D. Johnson, C. C., wit.

Capps, Hillary & Rebecca Bobbitt, 1 Oct 1811; James K. Clark, bm; Jno. H. Green, wit.

Capps, Hillery & Nancy Walker, (no date); Joshua Capps, bm.

Capps, John & Salley Kimbell, 13 Jan 1801; Edwd Tanner, bm; M. Duke Johnson, C. C., wit

Capps, John & Mary House, 30 Mar 1807; Jeremiah Lancister, bm; Robt Jones, wit.

Capps, Jordan & Harriot Bennett, 21 Jan 1831; James Martin, bm; C. Drake, C. C., wit.

Capps, McKinny & Mary Heathcock, 25 Nov 1841; Miles Bobbitt, bm; M. J. Montgomery, wit.

Capps, Macon & Mary Moore, 4 Dec 1844; Alfred A. Sledge, bm; M. J. Montgomery, wit.

Capps, Makenny & Mary Conn, 28 May 1858; Littleton Thompson ,bm; Jno W. White, clk, wit; m 29 May 1858 by William A. Dowtin, J. P.

Capps, Moses & Polley Asslin, 4 Dec 1798; John Capps, bm; Sherwood Green, wit.

Capps, Oratioe & Sarah Bartholomew, 8 Dec 1801; Honorious Powell, bm; S. Johnson, wit.

Capps, Robert Y. (son of Henry B. & Darcus Capps) & Martha E. Paschall (dau of Wm. E. & Susan Paschal), 4 Sept 1867; William A. White, clk, wit; m 4 Sept 1867 by Thomas P. Paschall, J. P.

Capps, Thomas & Mildred P. Regans, 21 Sept 1864; Michael W. Paschall, bm; Thos P. Paschall, wit; m 22 Sept 1864 by L. Henderson, J. P.

Capps, Warren H. & Mary L. Regans, 16 Dec 1858; Solomon Fleming, bm; Thomas P. Paschall, wit; m 22 Dec 1858 by Wm. A. Burwell, J. P.

Capps, Whitmell & Sarah Willey, 9 Sept 1852; Geo R. Sledge, bm; Jno W. White, wit.

Capps, William & Anne Martin, 27 Nov 1792; Henry Capps, bm; M. D. Johnson, C. C., wit.

Capps, William & Jinsey Marshall, 25 May 1797; James Emmerson, bm.

Capps, Zachariah & Pattey Brewer, 23 Feb 1790; Ransom Hagood, bm; M. D. Johnson, C. C., wit.

Caps, Henry B. & Darkes Dowland, 11 Dec 1837; Daniel Burchett, bm; Burl Pitchford, J. P.

Caps, Thomas & Rebecca Langford, 8 Sept 1827; John Andrews, bm; Burl Pitchford, bm.

Carlew, Belford & Milley Williford, 26 Dec 1794; Samuel Willeford, bm; M. D. Johnson, C. C., wit.

Carr, Albert & Nancy Breen, 6 Aug 1841; Jos Speed Jones, bm.

Carr, Elias & W. Eleanor Kearney, 19 May 1859; Tho J. Hasking, bm; William A. White, wit, m 24 May 1859 by Thos G. Lowe, M. G.

Carr, Richard (son of David & Mourning) (col) & Sabina Davis (dau of Charles & Hanreitta); 8 Aug 1867; William A. White, clk, wit; m 10 Aug 1867 by A. L. Steed, J. P.

Carral, William & Sarah Cleton, 10 Jan 1841; John R. Roberts, bm; Burl Pitchford, J. P., wit.

Carrall, James H. & Diomysia F. Bartlet, 21 Jan 1858; William A. Walch, bm; William A. White, wit; m 2 Jan 1858 by J. B. Solomon.

Carrel, William & Nancy Capps, 24 May 1820; Moses Bennett, bm.

Carrell, James & Patsey Shell, 27 Feb 1805; Stephen Ellis, bm; M. D. Johnson, C. C., wit.

Carrell, Thomas & Sarah A. Robinson, 10 Dec 1827.

Carrol, Grief & Polly Nanney, 29 Aug 1818; Allen Rainey, bm; Wm. Green, C. C., wit.

Carrol, Grief & Elizabeth Taylor, 2 Dec 1824; Edward Lambert, bm; C. Drake, C. C., wit.

Carrol, Joel & Catharine Rottenberry, 5 Feb 1828; Ruben Newman, bm; Burl Pitchford, wit.

Carrol, Mecham & Susan Williams, 8 Aug 1813; James Edwards, bm; Wm. Green, C. C., wit.

Carrol, William & Elizabeth Cunningham, 3 July 1818; Willis Cunningham, bm; Wm. Green, clk, wit.

Carroll, Benjamin & Frances Rottenberry, 19 Apr 1810; Matthew Bolton, bm; M. Duke Johnson, C. C., wit.

Carroll, Edmond & Rebekah Burton, 7 July 1825; Reuben Newman, bm; Burl Pitchford, wit.

Carroll, Ezekiel & Tabitha Moore, 7 July 1824; Joseph Carter, bm; C. Drake, C. C., wit.

Carroll, George & Eliza Tucker, 10 Nov 1818; Edward Birchett, bm; Will Green, C. C. C., wit.

Carroll, Jas. A. T. (col) & Mariah Jefferson, 29 Dec 1866; William W. White, clk, wit; m 13 Jan 1867 by R. D. Paschall, J. P.

Carroll, John & Sally Wright, 13 June 1818; Robert Tally, bm; W. A. K. Falkener, wit.

Carroll, Joseph W. & Sarah E. Carroll, 24 July 1853; Geo W. Holloman, bm; Jno W. White, wit.

Carroll, Reubin (col) & Minerva Wheeless, 14 May 1867; Revd. P. H. Joyner, bm; Wm. A. White, wit.

Carroll, Robert & Sarah Mustian, 25 Sept 1865; Thomas J. Judkins, bm; William A. White, clk, wit; m 1 Oct 1865 by T. Page Ricaud.

Carroll, Samuel (col) & Chany Paschall, 15 Dec 1866; William W. White, clk, wit; m 28 Dec 1866 by Thomas T. Paschall, J. P.

Carroll, Sterling & Elizabeth R. Moore, 19 Dec 1832; Amos White, bm; M. M. Drake, wit.

Carroll, William & Mary Barner, 25 Feb 1828; John Robinson, bm.

Carroll, William & Rebecca A. Edwards, 24 Apr 1833; Augustin C. Pattillo, bm; C. Drake, C. C., wit.

Carroll, Wm. H. & Pattie Capps, 24 Dec 1866; William A. White, C. Clk, wit; m 26 Dec 1866 by J. M. Brame, J. P.

Cartain, Thomas & Elizabeth Paschael, 15 Jan 1782; Rawleigh Hammon, bm; M. D. Johnson, wit.

Carter, Eaton & Patsey Toney, 25 Dec 1832; William Carter, bm; C. Drake, C. C., wit.

Carter, Francis M. & Sally Newell, 2 May 1800; David M. Newell, bm; S. Johnson, wit.

Carter, Giles & Jenney Kelley, 29 Oct 1783; "old" Thomas Twitty, bm; M. Duke Johnson, wit.

Carter, Hawkins & Elizabeth Wiggins, 10 Jan 1845; E. H. Riggan, bm; M. J. Montgomery, wit.

Carter, Hawkins (col) & Thomas Elizabeth Toney, 21 May 1866; Samuel Green, bm; William A. White, clk, wit; m 23 May 1866 by Ridley Browne, J. P.

Carter, Henry (col) & Priscilla Toney, 6 Aug 1866; Samuel Green, bm; William A. White, clk, wit; m 8 Aug 1866 by Ridley Browne, J. P.

Carter, Jesse & Rebecca Myrick, 18 Feb 1797; Drury Bobbitt, bm; M. Duke Johnson, C. C., wit.

Carter, Jesse & Sally Ann Whitaker, 11 Dec 1843; Benjamin Jenkins, bm; M. J. Montgomery, wit.

Carter, John (son of Hawkins & Elizabeth) (col) & Emma Perry (dau Watt Samper & Eliza Perry), 26 Nov 1867; William A. White, clk, wit; m 29 Nov 1867 by M. P. Perry, J. P.

Carter, John T. & Rebecca F. Thomas, 30 Sept 1858; Saml Bobbitt, bm; J. C. McCraw, wit; m 30 Sept 1858 by Saml Bobbitt, J. P.

Carter, Matthew (son of Plummer & Amy Carter) & Bettie Wilkins (dau of Wilson & Mary Wilkins), 26 Dec 1867; William A. White, clk, wit; m 26 Dec 1867 by Thos A. Montgomery, J. P.

Carter, Newell & Temperance King, 24 Nov 1841; Allen M. King, bm; M. J. Montgomery, wit.

Carter, Perry & Betsey Williams, 4 May 1799; Barnet Beasley, bm; Shd Green, wit.

Carter, Peter F. & Martha Wood, 1 Aug 1829; Gideon Arrington, bm; E. D. Drake, wit.

Carter, Plummer & Amy Hawkins, 11 Jan 1838; Washington Carter, bm; John W. White, wit.

Carter, Plummer & Hester Mills, 19 Oct 1852; Richard Shearin, bm; Jno W. White, wit.

Carter, Thomas & Jane Brack, 11 Jan 1862; William T. Pegram; bm; Jno. W. White, clk, wit; m ___ Jan 1862 by Nathl Nicholson, J. P.

Carter, Washington & Elizabeth Mills, 7 May 1850; William L. Harris, bm; Jno W. White, wit.

Carter, Weldon & Dorothy Shearin, 26 Dec 1839; Edmund H. Riggan, bm.

Carter, William & Eliza Pike, 16 May 1818; Michael Nicholson, bm; Wm. Green, wit.

Carter, William & Martha King, 14 Feb 1848; William Ellington, bm; Jno. W. White, wit.

Carter, William & Nancy Cleaton, 24 Oct 1856; H. Kenedy, bm; Jno W. White, wit; m 26 Oct 1856 by Saml Bobbitt, J. P.

Carter, Wm. J. & Martha J. King, 24 May 1864; M. E. Beckham, bm; William A. White, clk, wit; m 25 May 1864 by L. C. Perkinson, M. G.

Carter, Wilson C. & Mary Brickell, 29 June 1807; Edward J. Jones, bm; M. Duke Johnson, clk, wit.

Casy, Benjamin & Sally Harris, 16 Dec 1813; Jordan Harris, bm; Wm. Green, C. C. C., wit.

Cates, S. M. & Amanda Rooker, 30 June 1853; P. T. Norwood, bm; Jno W. White, clk, wit; m 30 June 1853 by Will Plummer, J. P.

Cauthan, Vincent & Nancy Beckham, 1 Jan 1808; William Brown, bm; Jo Terrell, C. C., wit.

Cauthen, Henry & _____, 10 Nov 1796; William Short, bm; Shd Green, wit.

Cauthon, Benjamin & Salley Smith, 25 Dec 1792; William Smith, bm; M. D. Johnson, C. C., wit.

Cauthon, Reubin & Sarah Stallions, 25 Dec 1801; Vincent Cauthon, bm; M. D. Johnson, C. C., wit.

Cawthorn, John V. & Mary H. Pope, 8 Mar 1844; Joseph Speed Jones, bm; M. J. Montgomery, wit.

Cawthorn, John V. & Sarah E. Blount, 21 Dec 1847; E. W. Best, bm.

Cawthorn, Stephen G. & Delia Jolley, 19 Apr 1859; Wm. H. Suit, bm; Jno. W. White, clk, wit; m 27 Apr 1859 by R. D. Paschall, J. P.

Cawthorne, Alfred (col) & Mariah Williams, 18 Mar 1867; Caesar Johnson, bm; William W. White, clk, wit; m 19 Mar 1867 by William Hodges, M. G.

Cemp (Kemp), Stripplehill & Rebecca Johnston (no date); Francis Smith, bm.

Certain, Job & Nancy Kelley, 29 Oct 1788; John Certain, bm; M. Duke Johnson, C. C., wit.

Chambers, Edward & Polly Towns, 2 June 1812; Alanson Williams, bm; Wm. Green, C. C. C., wit.

Chambles, James & Rebecca Solomons, 1 July 1793; Ransom Duke, bm; B. Davis, wit.

Chambliss, Jackson (Dr) & Catharine V. Williams, 24 Aug 1858; Thomas J. Foote, bm; William A. White, wit; m 25 Aug 1858 by William Hodges, M. G.

Champion, C. W. & M. E. Thompson, 15 Oct 1860; Thos A. Langford, bm; A. L. Steed, wit; m 17 Oct 1860 by L. K. Willis, M. G.

Champion, Claiborn & Margaret Fortner, 19 Dec 1836; Edwin D. Drake, bm; E. D. Drake, clk, wit.

Chandler, Adolphus & Jane Vanlandingham, 29 Dec 1841; Jno C. Johnson, bm; M. J. Montgomery, wit.

Chanler, William & Nelepsy Macklen, 12 Feb 1834; John Walden, bm; Burl Pitchford, J. P., wit.

Chavers, Jacob & Eady Bassfield, 1 Jan 1850; James Valentine, bm; Jno W. White, wit.

Chavers, William & Jane Stewart, 20 Oct 1825; Chesley Stewart, bm; M. M. Drake, wit.

Chavis, James W. R. & Sarah C. Kearsey, 9 Oct 1862; John H. Chavis, bm; William A. White, clk; m 15 Oct 1862 by S. V. Hoyle, M. G.

Chavis, John H. & Mary J. Kersey, 17 Nov 1857; Jno W. R. Evans, bm; Jno W. White, clk, wit; m 19 Nov 1857 by W. N. Bragg, M. G.

Chavis, Tony & Mary A. Vaughan, 25 Apr 1855; Edward Harris, bm; Thos P. Paschall, wit; m 26 Apr 1855 by Thomas P. Paschall, J. P.

Chavous, Boling & Nancy Thomerson, 14 June 1793; Eaton Walden, bm; R. Russell, wit.

Chavous, John & Betsey Carsey, 6 July 1803; Hutchings Mayo, bm; James Moos, wit.

Chavus, Nathan & Frances Mooshaw, 26 Oct 1847; Washington Pennell, bm; Jno W. White, wit.

Cheatham, James A. & Lucy A. White, 9 Feb 1855; Jas R. Carroll, bm; Jno W. White, wit; m at Ridgeway 13 Feb 1855 by A. C. Harris, M. G.

Cheek, Augustus A. & E. J. Newell, 17 Sept 1858; G. H. Macon, bm; Jno W. White, clk, wit; m 21 Sept 1858 by R. C. Barrett.

Cheek, Benjamin A. (Dr.) & Laura W. Bobbitt, 26 Apr 1865; W. A. J. Nicholson, bm; m 30 Apr 1865 by T. B. Kingsbury, M. G.

Cheek, Elbert A. & Susan S. Hayes, 30 May 1825; B. N. Pugh, bm; M. M. Drake, wit.

Cheek, John (col) & Cherry Alston, 18 Jan 1867; William A. White, clk, wit; m 2 Feb 1867 by John S. Cheek, J. P.

Cheek, Randolph & _____ Green (no date); Henry Alston, bm.

Cheek, Robert T. & Mary H. Alston, 14 Apr 1802; James Kearny, bm; Sugan Johnson, wit.

Cheek, Stephen (son of Chavis Clanton & Aggy Hazell) (col) & Susan Kearney (dau of Lewis & Nancy), 2 Dec 1867; William W. White, clk., wit; m 6 Dec 1867 by Thos A. Montgomery, J. P.

Cheek, Thomas (col) & Nicey Jonston, 21 May 1866; Dr. Benjamin Cheek, bm; William A. White, clk, wit; m 26 May 1866 by Ridley Browne, J. P.

Cheek, William (col) & Sarah Davis 3 May 1867; W. W. Williams, bm; William A. White, Clk, wit; m 14 May 18867 by Thos J. Pitchford, . P.

Cheek, William A. & Angelina A. Clanton, 19 May 1846; Thomas A. Montgomery, bm; M. J. Montgomery, wit.

Cheek, Col. William H. & Alice M. Jones, 7 June 1864; Thomas Littlejohn Jones, bm; William A. White, clk, wit; m 9 June 1854 by W. Hodges, M. G.

Childres, Robert & Liddia Wilkerson (no date); Seth Williams, bm; M. Duke Johnson, wit.

Childress, John & Salley Howard, 21 Dec 1782; William Ransom, bm; M. D. Johnson, wit.

Childress, William & Dilley Ballard, 12 Oct 1782; James Ballard, bm; M. Duke Johnson, wit.

Childris, Pleasant & Sarah Bush, 4 May 1793; Russel Sullivant, bm; Richd Russell, wit.

Choley, Macon & Ginsey Renn, 5 Dec 1848; Henry Cawthorn, bm; Jno W. White, wit.

Christian, Drury & Betsey Brewer (no date); Allen Brewer, bm.

Christian, William & Tabitha House, 8 July 1794; Ransom Kimbel, bm.

Christmas, Henry (son of Richard Christmas & Ellen Watson) (col) & Lizzie Carroll (dau of Nathan & Easther), 7 Nov 1867; William A. White, clk, wit; m 10 Nov 1867 by Kemp Plummer, J. P.

Christmas, James Y. & Mrs. Rhoda G. Whitney, 9 Oct 1863; Joseph H. Cook, bm; William A. White, clk, wit; m 9 Oct 1863 by John B. Williams, M. G.

Christmas, John (col) & Nelly Green, 1 Aug 1866; Frank T. Green, bm; William A. White, clk, wit; m 1 Aug 1866 by William Hodges.

Christmas, Thomas & Sarah Duke, 26 Nov 1764 (Bute Co); Green Duke, bm; Jno Davis, wit.

Christmas, Thomas H. & Margaret L. J. Williams, 23 May 1815; William Green, bm.

Christmas, Thomas H. & Elizabeth C. Davis, 8 Feb 1817; Robert R. Johnson bm; Wm. Green, C. C., wit.

Christmas, Washington (col) & Emily Drake, 17 Dec 1866; William A. White, clk, wit; m 29 Dec 1866 by Thomas Reynolds, J. P.

Christmas, William & Abigail McLamore, 28 Aug 1780; John Scott, bm; Thos Machen, wit.

Christmas, William & Betsey Ford Jinkins, 23 May 1790; Jesse Jenkins, bm; M. Duke Johnson, C. C., wit.

Cifers, Samuel & Thursday Marks, 21 June 1838; John Stewart, bm; Burl Pitchford, J. P.

Clack, Sterling & Mary Wood, 15 Aug 1780; Philemon Hawkins, bm.

Clack, Sterling & Nancy Wesson, 17 Dec 1865; Cornelius Blackwell, wit; m 17 Dec 1865 by E. W. Wilkins, J. P.

Claiborne, Devoreux & Martha S. Jones, 8 Apr 1825; John Robinson, bm; C. Drake, C. C., wit.

Claiborne, George & Ann Robertson, 18 July 1803; Clark Robertson, bm; M. Duke Johnson, C. C.

Clanton, Abraham & Lucretia Sledge (no date), Sherwood Sledge, bm.

Clanton, George & Frances Wells, 3 Jan 1798; Benj Wells, bm; Shd Green, wit.

Clanton, Landon & Hariot R. Williams, 3 Jan 1825; Genl William Williams, bm.

Clanton, Mark & Parthenia Wilson, 4 Feb 1823; Thomas Wilson, bm; Edwin D. Drake, wit.

Clanton, Robert & Mary A. Williams, 17 Nov 1851; Wm. G. Clanton, bm; Jno W. White, clk, wit; m 20 Nov 1851 by Tho S. Campbell, M. G.

Clanton, William C. & Martha Kearney, 11 Feb 1817; J. H. Person, bm; Wm. Green, C. C. C., wit.

Clardy, John (of Mecklenburg Co, VA) & Elizabeth Hogwood, 24 June 1811; Stephen Hendrick, bm; Wm. Green, C. C. wit.

Clardy, John H. & Ann E. Watkins, 28 Nov 1842; Edward W. Watkins, bm.

Clarey, Robert & Mary A. E. Carroll, 16 Jan 1851; William Clary, bm; Richard B. Robinson, wit; m 16 Jan 1851 by Richd B. Robinson, J. P.

Clark, Benjamin & Sally Loyd, 1 Jan 1817; James Clark, bm; W. Green, C. C. C., wit.

Clark, George & Martha E. Hoyle, 9 May 1865; N. H. Breedlove, bm; William A. White, wit.

Clark, James & Sally Murray, 6 Aug 1812; James K. Clark, bm; Jno. H. Green, wit.

Clark, James & Lucy Marshall, 18 Nov 1817; William Turner, bm; W. A. K. Falkener, wit.

Clark, John & Martha Bird, 17 May 1780; Samuel Willeford, bm; Thos Machen, wit.

Clark, John & Polly Loyd, 19 Dec 1825; James Pardue, bm; C. Drake, C. C., wit.

Clark, John & Winnifred Clark, 3 Dec 1842; Neverson Faulkner, James R. Renn, bm; M. J. Montgomery, wit.

Clark, Joseph & Betsey Smith, 15 Dec 1830; Archibald Brown, bm; C. Drake, C. C. C., wit.

Clark, Marshall & Sarah Jane Edmundson, 27 Jan 1848; Jeremiah M. Fleming, bm; Jno. W. White, wit.

Clark, Reubin & Mary Folkner, 15 Mar 1800; Charles Drury, bm; M. D. Johnson, C. C., wit.

Clark, Thomas & Nancy Alexander, 16 Dec 1800; Samuel Bartlett, bm; S. Johnson, wit.

Clark, Thomas & Dicie Loyd, 25 Jan 1831; Lewis Turner, bm; C. Drake, C. C., wit.

Clark, Timothy & Elizabeth Mangum, 15 June 1805; William Mangum, bm; Jo Terrell, D. C., wit.

Clark, William & Nancy Mangum, 28 Aug 1810; Tolomy Forkner, bm; Jno C. Johnson, wit.

Clark, William N. & Elizabeth Perdue, 10 Nov 1849; Thomas Stanback, bm; Jno W. White, wit.

Clarke, George C. & Emeline W. Fortner, 18 Dec 1865; Scilus Powell, bm; William A. White, C. C., wit; m 19 Dec 1865 by P. H. Joyner.

Clary, Benjamin & Martha George, 31 Oct 1821; Charles Thomas; bm; Frs. Jones, wit.

Cleaves, John & Nancy Jones, 29 Feb 1804; Benjamin Bradley, bm; M. Duke Johnson, C. C., wit.

Clegg, Baxter & Temperance L. Collins, 8 June 1839; Edwin D. Drake, bm.

Clegg, William & Mary E. Collins, 20 Feb 1867; William A. White, clk, wit; m 9 March 1867 by William Hodges, M. G.

Clements, Oscar (col) & Cornelia Alston, 11 Sept 1866; William A. White, clk, wit; m 15 Sept 1866 by J. Buxton Williams, J. P.

Clements, Robert (of Martin Co.) & Delia Kearney, 18 Apr 1853; John S. Cheek, bm; Jno W. White, wit; m 20 Apr 1855 by Robt O. Burton, M. G.

Clements, William E. & Julia R. Taylor, 18 Sept 1850; John C. McCraw, bm; Jno W. White, wit.

Cleny, John & Elizabeth George, 28 Feb 1826; Thomas Paine, bm.

Clerk, William & Media Marshall, 14 Aug 1784; Charles Drury, bm; M. Duke Johnson, wit.

Cliborn, John & Sarah Shearin, 17 Oct 1854; John W. Riggan, bm; Jno W. White, C. C., wit; m 18 Oct 1854 by Nathl Nicholson, J. P.

Cliborne, William H. & Lucy A. Nicholson, 24 Nov 1852; R. W. Cliborne, bm.

Clibourne, John & Canady Harvey, 3 Sept 1853; John Hardy, bm; m 6 Sept 1853 by Nathl Nicholson, J. P.

Cocke, Joseph (of Halifax Co.) & Winnifret Hill, 20 Nov 1782; M. Duke Johnson, wit.

Coclough, James & Polly Dinckins, 25 Nov 1817; Wm. Hicks, bm.

Cofer, Marit & Cynthia Bennitt, 8 Feb 1832; William M. Powell, Jr., bm; C. Drake, C. C., wit.

Coghill, Isram & Elizabeth Finch, 4 Jan 1816; Edward Pattillo, bm; Will Green, C. C. C., wit.

Coghill, Marion T. & Sarah Ann Wright, 9 Apr 1856; H. H. Renn, bm; m 16 Apr 1856 by A. C. Harris, M. G.

Coghill, Reubin & Mary Coghill, 20 Dec 1791; James Coghill, bm;

Cogwell, Fredrick & Fanny Ascue, 17 Mar 1807; P. Hawkins, bm; John C. Johnson, wit.

Cogwell, Zachariah & Mary Bobbitt, 14 Dec 1822; Reuben Coghill, bm.

Cogwell, Zachariah & Willie Jarrott, 1 Sept 1804; Reuben Coghill, bm; J. Malone, wit.

Colclough, Benja & Mary Rodwell, 17 Mar 1821; Clack Robinson, bm.

Cole, Daniel & Catharine Newman, 21 Oct 1823; Burrell Pitchford, bm.

Cole, Edmund W. & Mary Joyce, 15 Apr 1850; Z. M. P. Cole, bm; Jno W. White, wit.

Cole, Edward J. & Athaiah D. Andrews, 31 Dec 1861; Jno F. Rainey, bm; Jno W. White, wit.

Cole, Henry & Eliza Baskervill, 20 June 1843; Oscar F. Alston, bm; M. J. Montgomery, wit.

Cole, Isaac & Alice H. White, 21 Dec 1812; Wm Wilson, bm; Wm Green, C. C. C., wit.

Cole, John D. & Ellen J. Newman, 6 May 1841; William A. White, bm; Jno W. White, clk, wit; m 8 May 1861 by Lemmon Shell, M. G.

Cole, Zebulon M. P. & Lucy Ann Davis, 8 Nov 1845; F. A. Thornton, bm; M. J. Montgomery, wit.

Coleman, Carter & Martha Talley, 8 Oct 1791; David Thomas, bm; M. Duke Johnson, C. C. C., wit.

Coleman, Carter & Nancy Darnell, 14 Oct 1824; Thomas Tally, bm; C. Drake, C. C., wit.

Coleman, Ebeneza & Sally Perkinson, 20 Sept 1823; Guilford Talley, bm.

Coleman, Edward & Lucy Nicholson, 18 May 1785; Urbane Nicholson, bm.

Coleman, Hagwell & Rebecca King, 2 Oct 1828; Matthew Bolton, bm; M. M. Drake, wit.

Coleman, Henry E. & Ann Turner, 3 Apr 1832; George D. Baskervill, bm; C. Drake, C. C., wit.

Coleman, Henry V. & Virginia B. Foster, 1 Dec 1836; Thomas Johnson, bm; Burl Pitchford, J. P., wit.

Coleman, Jacob & D. Polly Cheek, 12 Dec 1796; David H. Newell, bm; Shd Green, wit.

Coleman, John & Frances Harris, 29 Apr 1785; William Holliman, bm; M. D. Johnson, C. C., wit.

Coleman, John & Amanda Carter, 23 Jan 1836; B. R. Browning, bm; Jno. W. White, wit.

Coleman, Levi P. & Virginia Ann White, 20 Oct 1848; Robt J. Perkinson, bm; Jno W. White, wit.

Coleman, Peter & Salley Jones (no date); Jesse Bell, bm; M. Duke Johnson, C. C., wit.

Coleman, Peter & Precella Young, 13 Feb 1809; Jonathan King, bm; J. C. Johnson, D. C. C., wit.

Coleman, Peter & Mary A. Rainey, 11 May 1835; William Palmer, bm; E. D. Drake, clk, wit.

Coleman, Samuel & Patsey Holiman, 30 Dec 1784; Isham Felts, bm; M. Duke Johnson, wit.

Coleman, Wiley G. & J. A. Shearin, 13 Mar 1864; Lafayette B. Myrick, bm; William A. White, clk, wit; m 30 Mar 1864 by N. A. Purefoy.

Colemon, Wm. R. & Lucy A. Hicks, 14 Apr 1859; Thomas H. White, bm; Jno W. White, wit.

Coley, John & Elizabeth Turner, 21 Jan 1859; Jerry Turner, bm; Cas. Drake, wit.

Coley, Joseph & Nancy Nuckles, 13 May 1837; Littleton Ferrell, bm; E. W. Best, wit.

Coley, Lewis & Delia Askew, 1 Mar 1859; James R. Smithwick, bm; William A. White, wit; m 5 Mar 1859 by Abner Steed, J. P.

Coley, Lewis & Mrs. Malissa Ann Breedlove, 10 Dec 1866; William A. White, C. C. C., wit; m 11 Dec by A. L. Steed, J. P.

Coley, Macon & Julia Ann Shearin, 1 July 1845; John Mulholland, bm; M. J. Montgomery, J. P.

Coley, Richard & Creasy Tucker, 14 Aug 1807; Joseph Anstead, David Marshall, bm; Jo Terrell, D. C. C., wit.

Collen, Robt & Mourning Evins, 27 Aug 1798; John Winkler, bm; S. Green, wit.

Collier, Benjamin & Mary Power, 16 Oct 1837; William Murray, bm; John W. White, wit.

Collins, Amos (col) & Rhoda Newell, 16 May 1866; William P. Rose, bm; William A. White, clk, wit; m 1 June 1866 by T. Page Ricaud, M. G.

Collins, Anthony & Eliza Thompson, 14 June 1832; Richard Davis, bm; C. Drake, C. C., wit.

Collins, John & Louiza V. Myrick, 28 Nov 1865; W. S. Wainwright, bm; William A. White, clk, wit; m 29 Nov 1865 by B. F. Long, M. G.

Colman, William & Martha E. Pegram, 2 Dec 1855; J. J. Rodwell, bm; Jno W. White, wit.

Colvert, John & Nancy Edwards, 30 Jan 1830; James Carrell, bm; C. Drake, C. C., wit.

Congleton, John R. & Rebecca V. Riggan, 30 Jan 1858; John W. Williams. bm; William A. White, wit; m 31 Jan 1858 by J. B. Solomon.

Conn, Dickson & Elizabeth Southall, 18 Dec 1821; John Southall, bm.

Conn, Edward & Lucy Stokes, 26 Jan 1847; Burrell King, bm; Jno W. White, wit.

Conn, Hugh & Rebecca Tucker, 15 Nov 1847; Kemp P. Alston, bm.

Connell, John G. & Elizabeth Thompson, 9 May 1818; William Nash, bm; Wm. Green, wit.

Conner, Avery & Martha Pettillo, 15 Dec 1789; Wm. Knoles, bm; M. Duke Johnson, C. C., wit.

Conner, George & Mrs. Catie Nancy, 31 Dec 1866; William A. White, C. C. C., wit; m 1 Jan 1867 by Thos B. Ricks, M. G.

Conner, Richard & Emily Mosely, 29 Dec 1853; William Barber, bm; Jno W. White, clk, wit; m 29 Dec 1855 by Richd B. Robinson, J. P.

Cook, Benjamin E. & Sally H. Marshall, 25 Oct 1817; Frs. D. Allen, bm; Wm. Green, C. C., wit.

Cook, Benjamin E., Jr., & Ann Hall, 13 Dec 1853; W. K. Plummer, bm; Thos A. Montgomery, wit; m 15 Dec 1853 by T. B. Ricks, M. G.

Cook, Charles M. & Hanna L. Alston, 16 Sept 1847; Thomas E. Green, Jr., bm; Jno W. White, wit.

Cook, James M. & Fannie T. Fotty, 8 Sept 1857; C. M. Farris, bm; Jno W. White, clk, wit; m 10 Sept 1857 by H. J. Macon, J. P.

Cook, John & Catharine Harwell, 3 Sept 1807; Wilson Ward, bm; Jo Terrell, D. C. C., wit.

Cook, Robert & Nancy S. Clanton, 15 Feb 1823; Asa G. Sledge, bm.

Cooper, Davis & Becky Bowdown, 24 Mar 1802; George Allen, bm; Sugan Johnson, wit.

Cooper, Edward & Jane Singleton, 30 July 1836; John Hundley, bm; E. D. Drake, clk, wit.

Cooper, Howell & Holanberry Cooper, 12 Dec 1784; Stephen Beckham, bm; M. Duke Johnson, wit.

Cooper, Jacob & James Ransom, 18 Oct 1779; James Ransom, bm; William Park, wit.

Cooper, John & Martha Cooper, 3 Sept 1862; William Wynn, bm; Wm. A. White, clk, wit; m 3 Aug [sic] 1862 by Jas C. Robinson, J. P.

Cooper, William & Mary Taylor, 12 Sept 1838; John Hundly, bm; D. Parrish, J. M. Price, L. M. Long, wit.

Copeland, Hesekiah & Nancy Red, 17 Oct 1849; Sidney Weller, bm; Jno W. White, wit.

Cordle, Charles & Rebecca Lashley, 18 June 1806; Jno F. Moore, bm; M. Duke Johnson, clk, wit.

Cordle, Haywood & Mary Evans, 21 Jan 1845; Allen Wright, bm; M. J. Montgomery, wit.

Corthon, James & Milley Paschael, 4 Sept 1783; Wm. Paschael, bm; M. Duke Johnson, wit.

Cousins, Wm & Elizabeth Baskerville, 25 Feb 1862; Jno Read, bm; Jno W. White, wit.

Cowley, Drewrey & Margaret Conner, 10 Jan 1851; Landon Cowley, bm; R. A. Ezell, wit.

Cowley, John & Elizabeth Turner, 10 May 1824; Thomas V. Duke, bm; M. M. Drake, wit.

Crabb, John & Winifred William, 23 Aug 1790; William Williams, bm; Ja. Turner, wit.

Crawley, David & Mary Coleman, 2 Sept 1780; John Coleman, bm; Thomas Machen, wit.

Crawley, David (of Halifax Co) & Polly Green, 28 Feb 1782; William Green, bm; M. Duke Johnson, wit.

Crenshaw, John R. & Sarah E. Neal, 6 Oct 1840; Edward M. Pettillo, Joel P. Bragg, bm; Edwd W. Best, clk, wit.

Crichton, Winfield & Harriet R. Hicks, 20 Nov 1844; Peter J. Turnbull, bm; M. J. Montgomery, wit.

Criswick, William & Ursley Cole, 26 Apr 1785; Jenkins Divaney, bm; M. D. Johnson, C. C., wit.

Crittington, John & Anna Granger, 2 Nov 1801; John Cunningham, bm; M. Duke Johnson, C. C., wit.

Crocker, L. R. & Pattie G. Turner, 28 Sept 1862; T. A. Langford, bm; William A. White, wit; m 29 Sept 1863 by W. W. Spain.

Croker, Robert & Susanah Lancaster, 7 Sept 1785; Jno Lancaster, bm; M. Duke Johnson, wit.

Cross, James & Polly Topp, 9 Jan 1838; Philemon Hawkins, bm.

Crossan, Dexter (son of Henry and Rena Crossan) (col) & Zilphay Ann Crossan (dau of Saml and Hannah Crossan), m 8 June 1867 by J. B. Solomon, M. G.

Crossan, Douglas (col) & Priscilla Crossan, 25 Dec 1865; P. J. Turnbull, bm; William A. White, wit.

Crossan, Thos M. & Rebecca Brehon, 10 July 1854; W. T. Alston, bm; Jno W. White, clk, wit; m 10 July 1854 by L. L. Smith, M. G.

Crossland, Alexander & Lucy Blacknell, 18 Jan 1815; Thos Bragg, bm; W. Green, clk, wit.

Crowder, Bartlet & Rebecca Ann McDaniel, 21 Jan 1813; Stephen Davis, bm; Wm. Green, C. C. C., wit.

Crowder, Bartlette & Mary Taylor, 23 Apr 1853; Henderson Crowder, bm; Jno W. White, clk, wit; m 28 Apr 1853 by R. B. Robinson, J. P.

Crowder, Edward & Mary Hendrick, 27 Apr 1844; Richard Omary, bm; M. J. Montgomery, wit.

Crowder, John & Fanny Hatchell, 24 June 1844; Hartwell Wilson, bm; M. J. Montgomery, wit.

Crowder, Richard & L. Rivers, 17 Mar 1864; Odelphus Omary, bm; William A. White, clk, wit; m 18 Mar 1864 by L. C. Perkinson, M. G.

Crowder, William & Nancy Fann, 12 July 1787; Alexandr. Nicholson, bm.

Crowder, Willie, Jr., & Winifred King, 20 Oct 1855; Bartlet Crowder, bm; Jno. W. White, wit.

Crowder, Wily & Sarah Ellis, 16 Dec 1833; Churchwell C. Bailey, bm.

Crowder, Zearell & Surphrone Renn, 29 Dec 1857; George J. Hendrick, bm; Jno W. White, clk ,wit; m 31 Dec 1857 by A. L. Steed, J. P.

Crump, Leroy R. & Mary A. Matthews, 8 Nov 1849; Wm. H. White, bm; Jno W. White, wit.

Crutchfield, Charles & Salley Neal, 25 Dec 1802; Dicky Neal, bm; M. Duke Johnson, C. C., wit.

Culpepper, Erasmus & Ann Arrington, 15 Sept 1804; Willis Arrington, bm; J. Malone, wit.

Cuningham, George & Susan Rieves, 27 Feb 1839; Jno C. Johnson, bm.

Cuningham, Jesse & Patsey Elleton, 12 Apr 1791; Richard Sutton, bm; M. Duke Johnson, C. C., wit.

Cuningham, Jno. W. & Martha Helen Somerville, 3 July 1860; David A. Barnes, Philemon B. Hawkins, bm; Jno W. White, clk, wit; m 4 July 1860 by Wm. Hodges, M. G.

Cuningham, Wm. & Jeaney Darnol (no date), Daniel Smith, bm; M. D. Johnson, wit.

Cuningham, William & Mary Riggan, 25 Nov 1801; Benjamin Thurman, bm; M. D. Johnson, C. C., wit.

Cunningame, William (of Mecklenburg Co., VA) & Ellida Hammock, 11 Mar 1782; James Birchett, bm; M. Duke Johnson, wit.

Cunningham, John & Sally Earles, 8 Oct 1818; Jno Paschall, bm; W. A. K. Falkener, wit.

Cunningham, William & Nancy Bell, 6 Jan 1782; John Mayfield, bm; M. D. Johnson, wit.

Curtis, Churchwell & Harriet Wortham, 26 Nov 1847; Robert A. White, bm; Jno. W. White, wit.

Cury, Alexr & Jane Carter, 31 May 1866; T. J. James, bm; William A. White, clk, wit; m 8 June 1866 by Samuel W. Dowtin, J. P.

Cyphrus, John & Martha Mills, 13 Nov 1848; James Macklin, bm; Jno. W. White, wit.

Cyprus, William & Mary George, 13 July 1850; Richard Stegall, bm; Jno W. White, wit.

Czurda, V. & Amelia Limmer, 20 Nov 1854; P. S. Norwood, bm.

Daily, Jno & Ann S. Thrower, 26 Mar 1834; James Twitty, bm; E. D. Drake, wit.

Dancy, David & Fanny Wood, 15 May 1806; Sugan Johnson, bm.

Daniel, Harroll & Louisa Harriss, 18 Dec 1855; James Loyd, bm; Thos P. Paschall, wit; m 18 Dec 1855 by Thomas P. Paschall, J. P.

Daniel, John & Elizabeth M. Earls, 24 Aug 1808; William Burroughs, bm;

Daniel, John M. & Cornelia G. Paschall, 10 Mar 1851; James M. Daniel, bm; Thos P. Paschall, wit.

Daniel, Nathaniel C. & Ann H. Bullock, 21 Jan 1828; John C. Green, bm; M. M. Drake, wit.

Daniel, Peter & Jeane Mayfield, 15 Aug 1788; Reubin Smith, bm; M. Duke Johnson, clk, wit.

Daniel, Robert B. & Sally Brinkley, 14 Apr 1814; Xanthus Snow, bm; W. Green, C. C., wit.

Daniel, Tilman R. & Nancy Lucy, 29 June 1812; Jeremiah Allen, bm; Jno. H. Green, wit.

Daniel, William A. & Mary C. Joyner, 5 Sept 1850; Henry J. Macon, bm; Jno W. White, wit.

Darnald, Dwelly & Susan Rivers, 12 May 1842; William Tanner, bm; Jno W. White, wit.

Darnald, Benjamin W. & Mary J. Paschall, 9 Apr 1861; William H. Felts, bm; Jno W. White, C. C. C., wit; m 10 Apr 1861 by Jno W. Pattillo, J. P.

Darnell, Dwelly & Matilda Paschall, 14 Aug 1855; H. P. White, bm; Jno W. White, clk, wit; m 16 Aug 1855 by Robt D. Paschall, J. P.

Darnell, Eaton & Rebecca Felts, 18 Mar 1834; John P. Beasley, bm; E. D. Drake, clk, wit.

Darnell, Henry J. & Mary D. Floyd, 24 Dec 1866; William A. White, C. C., wit; m 27 Dec 1866 by Jno W. Pattillo, J. P.

Darnell, James R. & Winnifred P. Mustain, 20 Nov 1866; Nathaniel S. Hawks, bm; William A. White, wit; m 22 Nov 1866 by Jno W. Pattillo, J. P.

Darnold, James & Miss ___ Paschall, 14 July 1811; William Darnold, bm; Wm. R. Johnson, wit.

Darnold, James Wesley & Sarah Salmon, 16 Feb 1864; Rodolphus Omary, bm; William A. White, clk, wit; m 20 Feb 1864 by L. C. Perkinson, M. G.

Darnold, John & Sally Wilson, 15 Aug 1800; Isaac Wood, bm; S. Johnson, wit.

Darnold, Wm & Nancy Capps, 15 Aug 1811; Tilmon Felts, bm; Wm. Green, wit.

Davis, Allen (col) & Eliza Ann Shearin, 9 Feb 1867; William A. White, clk, wit; m 10 Feb 1867 by J. M. Brame, J. P.

Davis, Allen Y. & Sarah J. Bennett, 13 June 1827; Carter Nunnery, bm.

Davis, Archabald & Caroline C. Kearney, 16 Oct 1837; Wm. K. Kearny, bm.

Davis, Archibald & Catharine Hindsman, 20 Oct 1819; Moses Bennett, bm; Cas Drake, wit.

Davis, Archibald H. & Charlotte E. Harris, 14 Sept 1857; N. F. Alston, bm; William A. White, wit; m 15 Sept 1857 by N. Z. Graves.

Davis, Archibald H. & Fannie T. Southerland, 2 Nov 1865; Rev. T. B. Kingsbury, bm; William A. White, wit; m 2 Nov 1865 by T. B. Kingsbury, M. G.

David, Archibald Hamilton, Jr., & Lucy E. A. Stallings, 14 Aug 1848; Matt W. Ransom, bm; Jno W. White, wit.

Davis, Arthur & Nancy Verser, 25 Nov 1823; Joshua Harper, bm; C. Drake, C. W. C. C., wit.

Davis, Baxter & Unity C. Power, 18 Jan 1808; Ephraim Ellis, bm; M. Duke Johnson, C. C. Wit.

Davis, Benjamin & Mary Andrews, 8 Feb 1813; Richard Power, bm; Jno. H. Green, wit.

Davis, Benjamin P. & Martha A. Fleming, 5 Sept 1857; John D. Shearin, bm; William A. White, wit; m 16 Sept 1857 by Wm. C. Clanton, J. P.

Davis, Burwell P. & Caroline N. Allen, 18 Oct 1866; Will A. Jenkins, bm; William A. White, clk, wit; m 24 Oct 1866 by N. A. Purefoy, M. G.

Davis, Eaton (col) & Frances Davis, 12 May 1866; Weldon E. Davis, bm; William A. White, clk, wit; m 19 May 1866 by Jno W. Pattillo, J. P.

Davis, Edward & Mary Wall, 23 Dec 1805; Charles Davis, bm; Jo Terrell, D. C. C., wit.

Davis, Edward & Rebecca O. Pitchford, 22 Dec 1829; Isham H. Davis, bm.

Davis, Ellick (col) & Susanna Bullock, 13 Dec 1865; David Parrish, bm; William A. White, clk, wit; m 23 Dec 1865 by Wm. Wallace White, Jr.

Davis, Giles & Bettsey Powell, 13 Apr 1784; Francis Smart, bm; M. D. Johnson, wit.

Davis, Harry (col) & Mariah Mayho, 23 Sept 1865; Edward H. Plummer, bm; W. A. K. Falkener, wit; m 25 Sept 1865 by L. C. Perkinson, M. G.

Davis, Isham (formerly slave of A. H. Davis) & Rebecca Hooper (formerly slave of Dr. W. Hooper, 13 Oct 1866; Willis Alston, bm; Z. Perkinson, wit; m 14 Oct 1866 by G. M. Cook, J. P.

Davis, Isham H. & Mollie A. Pitchford, 21 Jan 1860; George W. Davis, bm; Jno W. White, clk, wit; m 7 Feb 1860 by John S. Cheek, J. P.

Davis, Jacob & Rhoda Turner, 19 Oct 1808; Mark C. Duke, bm; J. C. Johnson, D. C., wit.

Davis, James & Martha Morgan, 17 Sept 1782; Jeremiah Brown, bm; M. Duke Johnson, wit.

Davis, James A. & Mary C. Cheek, 14 July 1857; Thos B. Fleming, bm; Jno W. White, clk, wit; m 26 Jan 1858 by Mark C. Duke, J. P.

Davis, James W. & Martha A. E. Tucker, 9 Sept 1835; Joel G. Shackleford, bm; Burl Pitchford, J. P., wit.

Davis, Joe (son of Dempcey Alston & Cherry Davis) (col) & Sally Dowtin (dau of Henryetta Maxwell), 30 Sept 1867; William A. White, clk, wit; m 30 Sept 1867 by Thos J. Pitchford, J. P.

Davis, John & Quinncy Blunt, 1 Oct 1808; Benjamin Powell, bm; Jno C. Johnson, D. C. C., wit.

Davis, John & Mary Christmas, 13 Apr 1815; William Hunter, bm; W. Green, C. C. C., wit.

Davis, John C. & Lucy F. Alston, 10 Mar 1831; Samuel T. Alston, bm; C. Drake, C. C., wit.

Davis, John S. & Martha B. Powell, 5 Oct 1830; James Maxwell, bm.

Davis, Joseph & Harriet Fisher, 30 July 1826; Thomas D. Algood, bm; Burl Pitchford, wit.

Davis, Joshua & Matilda S. Boyd, 4 Aug 1830; Elbert A. Cheek, bm; E. D. Drake, wit.

Davis, Joshua E. & Sarah F. Hicks, 11 Dec 1837; James Maxwell, bm.

Davis, Nelson (col) & Lucy Davis, 4 June 1866; Col Wm. S. Davis, bm; William W. White, clk, wit; m 7 July 1866 by Jno W. Pattillo, J. P.

Davis, Oron D. & Nancy Rivers, 23 Mar 1816; Ransom Felse, bm; Will Green, C. W. C. C., wit.

Davis, Peter R., Jr., & Catharine M. White, 5 Nov 1839; William G. Noble, bm.

Davis, Richard & Winnifred Powell, 22 Mar 1815; Anguston Alston, bm; W. Green, C. C., wit.

Davis, Robert & Nelley Gosee, 31 Mar 1795; John Gosee, bm; M. D. Johnson, C. C., wit.

Davis, Rufus (col) & Ella Mayfield, 13 Sept 1866; William A. White, wit; m 16 Sept 1866 by L. C. Perkinson, M. G.

Davis, Samuel & Amanda Kearney, 11 Mar 1847; B. J. Egerton, bm; Jno. W. White, wit.

Davis, Stephen & Sally E. Johnston, 23 Feb 1815; W. Green, bm.

Davis, Thos & Betsey Hazard, 10 Nov 1796; Sher'd Green, bm; Sher'd Green, wit.

Davis, Thomas & Elizabeth Jinkins, 9 Apr 1809; David Slater, bm; M. Duke Johnson, C. C., wit.

Davis, Thomas & Mary Ann Slade, 28 Aug 1832; Matthew M. Drake, bm; C. Drake, C. W. C. C. wit.

Davis, Thomas H. & Ann Green, 4 Nov 1806; Lot Hazard, bm; M. Duke Johnson, C. C., wit.

Davis, Thomas H. & Ann E. Aycock, 23 June 1825; George W. Fuller, bm; M. M. Drake, wit.

Davis, Thomas T. & Mary A. Harris, 10 June 1843; William P. Sledge, bm; M. J. Montgomery, wit.

Davis, Wesley (son of Nannie Davis) (col) & Hagar Burgess (dau of Albert & Jane), 17 Aug 1867; William W. White, clk, wit; m 16 May 1868.

Davis, William D. & Elizabeth Ann O'Bryan, 4 Oct 1842; F. McHenry, bm; M. J. Montgomery, wit.

Davis, William S. & Bettie Jones, 25 Dec 1863; John E. Boyd, bm; William A. White, clk, wit, m 28 Dec 1863 by Lemmon Shell, M. G.

Davis, Willie J. & Betsey Nelms, 17 July 1799; George Myrick, bm; S. Green, wit.

Dawson, Henry & Sarah Alston, 3 Mar 1808; Rob R. Johnson, bm; M. Duke Johnson, clk, wit.

Dawson, Jno & _____, ___ 1798; Matthew Myrick, bm; James Moss, wit.

Dawson, John & Olive Randolph, 10 Jan 1801; Henry Robertson, bm; S. Johnson, wit.

Dawson, John & Patsey G. Hunter, 18 Oct 1814; William Hunter, bm; W. Green, C. C. C., wit.

Dawson, Larkin & Winifred Sledge, 31 Jan 1786; Daniel Sledge, bm.

Deaderick, Dr. E. L. (son of J. F. & Rebecca L. Deaderick) & Rebecca R. Williams (dau of Joseph & Lucinda W. Williams), 10 Dec 1867; m 11 Dec 1867 by Mat M Marshall, M. G.

deCiCaty, Beraud & Holly Carroll, 6 Dec 1780.

Delbridge, John C. & Martha L. Pierson, 20 Feb 1856; Peter E. R. Phillips, bm; Francis J. Ellis, wit; m 20 Feb 1856 by Richd B. Robinson, J. P.

Deloney, William H. & Susan Sledge, 30 Oct 1826; Thomas J. Judkins, bm; M. M. Drake, wit.

Denson, William & Mary Kerney (no date); Wm Paschal, bm; M. D. Johnson, C. C., wit.

Denton, James & Martha Bennit, 2 July 1788; John Williams, bm; M. D. Johnson, C. C., wit.

Derden, Jesse & Martha Vinson, 31 Jan 1827; Alexander Lunsford, bm; M. M. Drake, wit.

Derin, James & Alletha J. Floyd, 6 July 1852; James House, bm; Jno W. White, clk, wit; m by Amber Steed, J. P.

Dering, Emelius & Sarah Hazelwood, 11 Apr 1782; Joshua Capps, bm; M. Duke Johnson, wit.

Devine, Hugh & Eliza J. Vaughan, 21 May 1838; William L. Harriss, bm; Edwd W. Best, clk, wit.

Dewty, Thomas & Elizabeth Clark, 3 Oct 1797; Charles Drewery, bm; Shd Green, wit.

Dickens, Benjamin A. & Ella R. Eaton, 28 Oct 1847; K. H. Lewis, bm; Jno W. White, wit.

Dickerson, Chasteen & Mary Hayes, 19 Dec 1854; Isham Dickerson, bm; Jno W. White, wit; m 20 Dec 1854; by A. C. Harris, M. G.

Dickerson, Isham M. & Celestia Coley, 18 Apr 1859; James S. Bridgers, bm; William A. White, wit; m 20 Apr 1859 by G. J. Jones, J. P.

Dickerson, James & Catherine Roberson, 5 Sept 1853; Wm Matthews, bm; Jno W. White, wit.

Dickerson, John & Martha Fowler, 20 Dec 1783; William Cooper, bm; M. Duke Johnson, wit.

Dickerson, Nathl & Margret Mirrik (no date); Hardy Faulkener, bm.

Dickerson, William & Catharine Bragg, 27 Apr 1837; Spell Mounger, bm; E. W. Best, D. C., wit.

Dickerson, William & Mary E. Lancaster, 2 Apr 1844; Samuel B. Lancaster, bm; M. J. Montgomery, wit.

Dickerson, Wm. A. & Mary J. Parrish, 22 June 1866; J. B. Solomon, bm; W. T. Solomon, wit; m 23 June 1866 by J. B. Solomon.

Dickeson, William & Nancy Hogwood, 13 Dec 1797; Isaac Jackson, bm; Shd Green, wit.

Dickins, Demps (formerly slave of Kelly Dickins) & Ann Mariah Johnston (formerly slave of A. M. Johnston), 5 Feb 1866; Anthony M. Johnston, bm; C. M. Cook, wit; m 5 Feb 1866 by C. M. Cook, J. P.

Dinkins, James & Lucy Kendrick, 5 Jan 1796; John Stephens, bm; M. Duke Johnson, wit.

Dinkins, John & Sarah Wright, 4 Oct 1804; John Wright, bm; M. Duke Johnson, C. C., wit.

Disbon, Charles (col) & Lettuce (or Letitia) Kearney, 24 Sept 1866; John Hyman, bm; William A. White, clk, wit; m 24 Sept 1866 by John S. Cheek, J. P.

Dixon, Americus V. & Lucy P. Jeffreys, 3 July 1813; Alexander Butler, bm; Wm. Green, C. C. C., wit.

Dixon, John (col) & Inez Browne, 24 Dec 1866; William A. White, clk, wit; m 25 Dec 1866 by Ridley Browne, J. P.

Dodson, William & Caty Williams, 9 Jan 1792; Peter Twitty, bm.

Dodson, William & Charlotte Howard, 5 Oct 1793; L. Sanders Sims, bm.

Dortch, Noah & Rebeccah James Harwell, 12 Nov 1810; James Watson, bm; Jno C. Johnson, D. C. C., wit.

Dortch, William A. & Sarah G. Poythress, 31 Jan 1837; John L. Smith, bm; Burl Pitchford, J. P., wit.

Dortch, William A. & Elizabeth A. Mise, 9 May 1854; George W. King, bm; R. B. Robinson, wit; m 9 May 1854 by Richd B. Robinson, J. P.

Douglas, Alfred & Francis Maclin, 28 Nov 1839; Ephraim Maclin, bm; Wm. A. White, wit.

Dowlen, Amos & Ann Marshall, 30 Oct 1787; Saml Marshall, bm; Shd Green, wit.

Dowlen, James & Lucy Blanchett, 6 June 1781; Thomas Blansit, bm; Thos Machen, wit.

Dowlend, John & Rebeccah Watkins, 31 Jan 1809; Joseph Lees, bm; J. C. Johnson ,D. C. C., wit.

Dowling, William & Mary Taylor, 25 Feb 1845; John D. Tucker, Jr., bm; M. J. Montgomery, wit.

Dowtin, Anthony & Tempy Bobbitt, 30 Sept 1798; Matthew Duke, bm; S. Green, wit.

Dowtin, Haywood (col) & Mary Browne, 5 Oct 1866; William A. White, clk, wit; m 6 Oct 1866 by Saml Bobbitt, J. P.

Dowtin, John & Milly Williams, 5 Nov 1782; William Wilson, bm; M. Duke Johnson, wit.

Dowtin, Richard (col) & Hannah Dowtin, 24 Dec 1865; Ebenezze Respass, bm; m 24 Dec 1865 by T. P. Alston, J. P.

Dowtin, Samuel B. & Nancy Morris, 18 Dec 1810; John M. Johnson, bm; Jno C. Johnson, D. C. C., wit.

Dowtin, Samuel W. & Bettie M. Price, 19 Sept 1863; Isham H. Bennett, bm; William A. White, clk, wit; m 23 Sept 1863 by John Bryan Williams, M. G.

Dowtin, Wm. A. & Sarah Rodwell, 8 Nov 1852; Jno M. Wilson, bm; Jno W. White, clk, wit; m 11 Nov 1852 by N. Z. Graves, M. G.

Dowtin, William A. & Mary C. Watson, 29 Nov 1854; S. A. Newell, bm; Wm. A. White, clk, wit; m 5 Dec 1854 by N. A. Purefoy, M. G.

Doyel, Warwick & Polley Jones, 25 Dec 1799; Sugan Johnson, bm; R. B. Johnson, wit.

Doyell, Edmound & Susanah Hilton, 19 Dec 1801; Zenus Fore, bm; Sugan Johnson, wit.

Doyle, Joshua & Charlot Tucker, 10 Nov 1794; Michal Harris, bm; M. D. Johnson, C. C., wit.

Drake, Guilford (col) & Hannah Rodwell, 13 Sept 1865; Jno O. Drake, bm; William A. White, clk, wit; m 23 Sept 1865 by T. B. Ricks, M. G.

Drake, Hartwell & Jane Norwood, 9 June 1835; George W. Barnes, bm.

Drake, Henry B. & Sarah Robertson, 27 June 1844; George S. Smith, bm; W. W. Vaughan, wit.

Drake, Matthew M. & Winnifred Fitts, 3 Nov 1825; Michael Collins, bm.

Drake, William C. & Sallie F. Twitty, 10 Oct 1854; Jos E. Drake, bm; Jno W. White, C. C. C., wit; m 18 Oct 1854 by Thos G. Lowe, M. G.

Draughan, James & Nancy Braddly, 20 Dec 1818; Benjamin Hill, bm.

Drew, Allexander & Eliza Durham, 29 Jan 1858; Willis Kersey, bm; Thomas P. Paschall, wit.

Drew, John & Ann Sewell, 20 Feb 1851; Willis Kersey, bm; Jno W. White, wit.

Drew, John & Julia Durham, 29 Dec 1864; Willis Kersey, bm; Thomas P. Paschall, wit; m 31 Dec 1864 by John H. Bullock, J. P.

Drewry, Charles & Charity Marshall, 8 Feb 1797; John Clark, bm; Shd Green, wit.

Drewry, Marshall & Sally Edwards, 24 Apr 1834; William Southall, bm; E. D. Drake, clk, wit.

Drewry, Robert W. & Annie Hudgins, 16 Nov 1861; James W. Downey, bm; Jno W. White, wit; m 28 Nov 1861 by Wm. Hodges, M. G.

Drury, John & Hollay Stephens, 20 May 1791; Charles Drury, bm; M. D. Johnson, C. C., wit.

Dugger, Daniel & Mary E. Green, 20 Mar 1834; Stephen Davis, bm.

Dugger, George & Sarah Ann Bost(?), 9 Nov 1829; Ezra Dugger, bm; E. D. Drake, wit.

Dugger, James B. & Mary Harris, 30 May 1833; Hilliard J. Mannings, bm; C. Drake, C. W. C. C., wit.

Dugger, Richmond & Martha A. Foster, 29 May 1844; Thomas P. Walker, bm; M. J. Montgomery, wit.

Dugless, David W. & Minervey Rottenberry, 25 May 1837; Richardson Douglass, bm; Burl Pitchford, J. P., wit.

Dugless, William P. & Middey Bard, 6 Jan 1829; Littleton Bard, bm; Burl Pitchford, J. P., wit.

Duke, A. P. & Hester C. Duke, 14 Dec 1866; William A. White, C. C. C., wit; m 20 Dec 1866 by Ira T. Wyche, M. G.

Duke, Abner (col) & Margaret Jackson, 18 May 1867; William A. White, clk, wit; m 19 May 1867 by L. C. Perkinson, M. G.

Duke, Albert E. & Mary Ann Talley, 10 Sept 1850; Nathl D. Brickell, bm; Jno W. White, wit.

Duke, Buckner & Susanna Hogwood, 4 July 1805; Willie Dunkin, bm; Jo Terrell, D. C., wit.

Duke, Doctor M. & Kitty Warrell, 12 May 1840; William P. Rose, bm.

Duke, George A. & Martha R. Sledge, 12 June 1848; Mark C. Duke, bm; Jno W. White, wit.

Duke, Green B. & Rebecca Robertson, 22 Oct 1806; David Terry, bm; M. Duke Johnson, C. C., wit.

Duke, Hardaway & Elisa Harris, 23 Oct 1787; Robert Harris, Jr., bm.

Duke, Harrell & Huldy McGee, 16 June 1781; John Duke, bm; Thos Machen, wit.

Duke, Henly T. & Jane Rodwell, 9 Dec 1853; Matthew Duke, bm; Jno W. White, wit.

Duke, Henry T. & Frances X. Kearney, 14 Nov 1855; Lewis B. Collins, bm; Jno W. White, wit; m 15 Nov 1855 by Wm. C. Clanton, J. P.

Duke, James L. & Betsy P. Baskerville, 15 July 1844; K. P. Alston, bm; M. J. Montgomery, wit.

Duke John & Molley Archer (no date); John Wadkins, bm.

Duke, Lewis P. & Mary Ransom, 11 Mar 1813; John Snow, bm; Jno H. Green, wit.

Duke, Lewis S. & Phoebe G. Mabry, 7 Dec 1850; Simon G. Duke, bm; Jno. W. White, wit.

Duke, Mark C. & Temperance Davis, 26 Apr 1809; John B. Powell, bm; Jno C. Johnson, D. C., wit.

Duke, Mark C. & Martha Ann Pitchford, 20 Nov 1838; Saml Bobbitt, bm.

Duke, Mark C. & Mrs. Elizabeth W. Powell, 10 Apr 1865; William A. White, clk, wit; m 4 May 1865 by Thos J. Pitchford, J. P.

Duke, Matthew & Frances Lanier, 29 Oct 1809; John Maclin, bm; M. Duke Johnson, C. C., wit.

Duke, Matthew (son of Matthew & Mary Eaton) (col) & Emily Cheek (dau of Chery Cheek), 28 Sept 1867; William A. White, clk, wit; 4 Oct 1867 by George M. Duke, M. G.

Duke, Myrick & Dolly Gunn, 9 Oct 1811; Thomas Davis, bm; Wm. Green, C. C. C., wit.

Duke, Ransom K. & Ann Ball, 25 aug 1846; Elijah W. Rudd, bm.

Duke, Richard & Tabitha Marshall, 28 Apr 1804; Reubin Coghill, bm; M. Duke Johnson, C. C., wit.

Duke, Samuel & Lucy G. Harris, 17 July 1819; Gideon Harton, bm; C. Drake, C. C., wit.

Duke, Simon G. & Ebeline Hawks, 24 Oct 1865; William P. Rose, bm; Wm A. White, clk, wit; m 25 Oct 1865 by Jno W. Pattillo, J. P.

Duke, Thomas K. & Hezey Bobbitt, 13 Mar 1820; Richard Duke, bm.

Duke, Thomas P. & Charity J. Paschall, 13 Apr 1846; M. W. Paschall, bm; M. J. Montgomery, wit.

Duke, Thomas S. & Parthena Omary, 19 Jan 1859; Robert W. Duke, bm; Jno W. White, clk, wit; m 27 Jan 1859 by L. C. Perkinson, M. G.

Duke, William & Elizabeth Pinix, 8 Jan 1782; Benjamin Duke, bm; Thos Machen, C. C., wit.

Duke, William & Amey Williams, 21 Mar 1797; john C. Green, bm; Sherwood Green, wit.

Duke, William & Frances Nuckles, 12 Oct 1853; Marion Coghill, bm; Jno W. White, clk, wit; m 12 Oct 1852 by Solon Southerland, J. P.

Duke, William C. & Sally C. Newman, 4 June 1847; George W. Omarry, bm; Edmd White, wit.

Duke, William C. & Obedience Cole, 12 Dec 1859; Robert W. Duke, bm; Jno W. White, clk, wit; m 14 Dec 1859 by Jas T. Russell, J. P.

Dun, James & Tamer Lamberd Pope, 17 Sept 1782; John Pope, bm; M. Duke Johnson, wit.

Duncan, Blanch & Nancy Smith (no date); John Watson, bm; M. D. Johnson, wit.

Duncan, James & Sally D. Twitty, 10 Dec 1850; Benjamin E. Cook, bm; Jno. W. White, wit.

Duncan, Jesse & Rebecah Riggan, 16 Oct 1791; Robert Williams, bm; M. Duke Johnson, C. C., wit.

Duncan, William & Elizabeth Vanlandingham, 3 Feb 1827; Charles Bennitt, bm; M. M. Drake, wit.

Dunkin, James & Peggy Cauthon (no date); Geo Vanlandingham, bm.

Dunkin, Willie & Sylvia Duke, 23 Nov 1800; Wiley Wood, bm; S. Johnson, wit.

Dunn, Thomas A. & Lucy Faulkner, 17 Dec 1853; C. H. Dunn, bm; m 21 Dec 1853 by A. G. Harris, M. G.

Dunsmore, Robert W. & Margaret Burcher, 21 Dec 1840; Thomas J. Judkins, bm.

Dunston, James & Sally Vaughan, 16 Aug 1858; Edward Haris, bm; Thos P. Paschall, wit; m 16 Aug 1858 by R. D. Paschall, J. P.

Dunston, Richard & Martha Guy, 26 Jan 1839; George Curtis, bm; Jno W. White, wit.

Durdin, Mills & Polley Lunsford, 20 Oct 1779; James Turner, bm; M. Duke Johnson, wit.

Durham, Charles & Mary Fortune, 10 Mar 1794; Randolph Row, bm; M. Duke Johnson, C. C., wit.

Durham, Haywood, & Laura Green, 23 Nov 1865; Wm. J. White, bm; William A. White, clk, wit; m 24 Nov 1865 by W. A. Brame.

Durham, James & Nancy Christian, 26 Aug 1783; Nath Thompson, Samuel Thompson, bm; M. Duke Johnson, wit.

Durham, James & Anney Balthrop, 18 May 1808; John Sims, M. Duke Johnson, C. C., wit.

Durham, James & _____, 6 Dec 1815; Benjamin Colclough, Stephen Hightower, bm; Will Green, C. C. C., wit.

Durham, James & Ollive Evans, 19 Mar 1840; Neverson Fortner, bm; Edwd W. Best, clk, wit.

Durham, James W. & Eliza A. Stainback, 10 July 1852; Benj F. Powell, bm; Jno W. White, wit.

Durham, John & Ann Center, 16 Aug 1797; Freeman Senter, bm; M. Duke Johnson C. C., wit.

Durham, Richard & Martha King, 18 Apr 1855; Jno W. White, bm; John Grant, wit.

Durham, Saml & Sally Reed, 24 Dec 1790; Joseph Johnson, bm; M. D. Johnson, C. C., wit.

Durham, Solomon & Nancy Durham, 30 Dec 1803; John Riggan, bm; M. D. Johnson, C. C., wit.

Durham, Thomas & Lucy Harris, 21 Nov 1854; Jas Meadows, bm; Jno W. White, C. C. C., wit; m 23 Nov 1854 by Thos J. Pitchford, J. P.

Durham, Wm. & Mary Haselwood (no date); Worwick Haselwood, bm.

Duty, Warren & Charlottee Dickoson, 19 Mar 1825; James Robertson, bm.

Dye, Avery & Salley Puckett, 23 May 1785; John White, bm; M. Duke Johnson, C. C., wit.

Dye, George W. & Nancy Green, 19 Dec 1813; Archabald Brown, bm; Wm. Green, C. C. C, wit.

Dye, Martin & Katey Mayfield, 22 July 1783; John White, bm; M. Duke Johnson ,C. C., wit.

Eadee, John & Susannah Wilson, 12 Oct 1852; David Coleman, bm; William A. White, wit.

Earl, Jesse & Dicey Lambert (no date); Lewis Patrick bm; M. D. Johnson, C. C., wit.

Earl, John & Zebiah Simms, 21 Jan 1780; Alexander Burnham, bm.

Earles, Frederick & Lucy Weaver, 10 Nov 1785; Thomas Earls, bm; M. D. J., wit.

Earles, William & Delila Macklin, 28 Mar 1839; James Macklin, bm; Burl Pitchford, J. P., wit.

Earls, George W. & Susan H. Regans, 15 Nov 1852; Daniel H. Byrd, bm; Thos P. Paschall, wit; m 16 Dec 1852 by Thos P. Paschall, J. P.

Early, John & Ann W. Jones, 17 Jan 1815; Clack Robinson, bm; W. Green, C. W. C. C., wit.

Eaton, Buckner & Ann Kearney, 3 Feb 1844; Wm. Eaton, Jr., bm.

Eaton, Charles R. & Catherine A. Eaton, 17 Oct 1831; Nathl T. Green, bm.

Eaton, James W. & Mary J. Davis, 14 Apr 1838; Joseph B. Somervell, bm.

Eaton, Samuel W. & Lucy F. Browne, 13 Jan 1860; Nathl R. Jones, bm; Jno W. White, clk, wit; m 17 Jan 1860 by Thos G. Lowe.

Eaton, William & Ceneora Macon, 19 Oct 1804; J. J. Daniel, bm; M. D. Johnson, C. C., wit.

Eaton, William & Martha Hickman, 20 Feb 1834; Caswell Drake, bm; E. D. Drake, clk, wit.

Eaton, Willis (col) (son of Adam Eaton & Polly Ross) & Kitty Webster (dau of Louis Webster & Rachel Palmer), 5 June 1867; William A. White, clk, wit; m 16 June 1867 by N. A. Purefoy, M. G.

Eaves, George & Nancy Duke, 24 Jan 1811; Benjamin Kimbell, bm; Jno C. Johnson, D. C. C., wit.

Eavins, Miles & Elizabeth Bell, 31 Jan 1839; Thomas James, bm; Edwd W. Best, clk, wit.

Edgerton, John & Parthena H. Cunningham, 1 Nov 1843; Henry H. Burwell, bm; M. J. Montgomery, wit.

Edmonds, Harrison & Anne Edmonds, 20 June 1832; James Edmonds, bm; Burl Pitchford, J. P., wit.

Edmons, Wm. H. & Harriet M. Wright, 28 July 1859; Jno D. Shearin, bm; William A. White, wit.

Edmonson, James W. & Martha Ann Johnson, 15 Oct 1844; Dry Gill, bm; M. J. Montgomery, wit.

Edmunds, Spencer & Sussan Huggan, 21 June 1832; John Vaughan, bm; Burl Pitchford, J. P., wit.

Edmunds, Thomas & Eliza Calais, 12 Jan 1829; Nicholas Winn, bm; E. D. Drake, wit.

Edmunds, William & Frances Callis, 25 June 1834; Thomas Edmunds, bm; Burl Pitchford, J. P., wit.

Edwardes, Devereaux & Mrs. Rebecca Edwards, 15 Oct 1866; James P. Satterwhite, bm; William A. White, wit.

Edwards, Anthony (col) & Dinah Russell, 2 Feb 1866; Edwin H. Russell, bm; William A. White, clk, wit; m 17 Feb 1866 by J. W. Wellons, M. G.

Edwards, Daniel & Lezy Allen, 17 May 1809; Allen Wren, bm; Jno C. Johnson, D. C. C., wit.

Edwards, J. G. E. & Darien Allen, 8 Dec 1866; William A. White, C. C., wit; m 11 Dec 1866 by P. H. Joyner.

Edwards, James & Mariam Carroll, 20 Sept 1813; James Robinson, bm; Jno H. Green, wit.

Edwards, Jeremiah & Delia Dickerson, 14 Dec 1793; Griffin Dickerson, bm; M. D. Johnson, C. C., wit.

Edwards, John & Sally Harris, 6 May 1821; James Ward, bm; Cas. Drake, clk, wit.

Edwards, John, Jr., & Martha Renn, 15 July 1844; Solomon Perdue, bm; M. J. Montgomery, wit.

Edwards, Jno. L. & Caroline S. Hodges, 8 Oct 1866; Charles W. Spruill, bm; William A. White, wit; m 9 Oct 1866 by William Hodges, rector Emmanuel Chh, Warrenton, N. C.

Edwards, Littleton & Mary Sims, 10 Mar 1800; Green Garrott, bm; M. Duke Johnson, C. C,. wit.

Edwards, Matthew & Elisabeth Parish, 9 Dec 1784; Ben King, bm; M. Duke Johnson, wit.

Edwards, Richard & Jane L. Rudd, 30 Dec 1856; Ford Falkner, bm; Jno W. White, clk, wit; m 4 Jan 1857 by Abner Steed, J. P.

Edwards, Samuel D. & Elizabeth G. Harris, 20 Dec 1847; Gideon V. Edwards, bm; Jno. W. White, wit.

Edwards, Washington (col) & Mary Paschall, 31 Mar 1866; William A. White, clk, wit; m 12 July 1866 by Jas T. Russell, J. P.

Edwards, Wilkins H. & Hannah B. Wilks, 27 May 1824; Nicholas E. Davis, bm; M. M. Drake, wit.

Edwards, William & Polley White (no date), John Brown, bm; M. Duke Johnson, C. C., wit.

Edwards, William E. & Mary Childres, 1 Feb 1855; H. L. Griffin, bm; Jno. R. Stewart, wit; m 1 Feb 1855 by Richd B. Robinson, J. P.

Edwards, Wm. Henry (son of William & Sally Ann Edwards) & Mrs. Adaline N. Wilson (dau of Lemuel P. & Harriet M. Johnson), 24 Sept 1857; William A. White, clk, wit; m 24 Sept 1867 by N. A. Purefoy, M. G.

Edwards, William J. & Louisa Haton, 25 Jan 1847; Thompson Harris, bm; Jno W. White, wit.

Edwards, William J. & Mary L. Vaughan, 16 Nov 1861; Richard Gibbs, bm; Jno W. White, clk, wit; m 17 Nov 1861 by Wm. Holmes.

Egerton, Benjamin L. & Emma R. Williams, 23 Apr 1850; Thomas S. Campbell, bm; William A. White, wit.

Egerton, Charles Jackson & Mary T. Pitchford, 12 Dec 1835; James A. Egerton, bm; E. D. Drake, clk, wit.

Egerton, Henry T. & Martha M. Kearney, 9 Dec 1850; Thomas J. Judkins, bm; Jno W. White, wit.

Egerton, Henry T. & Mrs. Bettie Powell, 4 Sept 1866; William A. White, wit; m 4 Sept 1866 by B. F. Long, M. G.

Egerton, James A. & Eliza H. Powell, 10 Nov 1836; John E. Brown, bm; E. D. Drake, clk, wit.

Egerton, James A. & Lucy J. Fleming, 10 Nov 1849; George W. Blacknall, bm; Jno. W. White, wit.

Egerton, Jno. J. & Nancy Harris, 21 Aug 1798; Wilmot E. Harris, bm; S. Green, wit.

Egerton, Joseph & Eliza Baker, 18 Jan 1851; Willis P. White, bm; Jno .W. White, wit.

Egerton, Moody & Martha Lancaster, 23 Aug 1827; John J. Harris, bm; M. M. Drake, wit.

Egerton, Thomas M. & Mary H. Fleming, 29 Nov 1853; M. W. Ransom, bm; Jno W. White, C. C. C., wit; m 7 [sic] Nov 1853 by N. A. Purefoy, M. G.

Egerton, Thomas M. & Nancy D. Fleming, 10 Dec 1866; William A. White, C. C. C., wit; m 13 Dec 1866 by N. A. Purefoy, M. G.

Egerton, Wilmot & Pricilla Riggan, 18 Apr 1808; Gilbert Grey Egerton, bm.

Egerton, Wilmot E. & Sally King, 19 Aug 1814; James Egerton, bm; W. Green, C. C., wit.

Elder, William & Ann Catherine Scott, 16 Mar 1795; Isaac Oslin, bm.

Elington, Steaphen & Frances Williams, 2 Aug 1800; Green B. Duke, bm; M. Duke Johnson, C. C., wit.

Ellenton, Daniel & S. Williams (no date); James Ellinton, bm; M. D. Johnson ,C. C, wit.

Ellington, Edward M. & Matilda C. Hilliard, 10 Feb 1853; Jno. W. White, clk, wit; m 9 Feb 1853 by Edmd White, J. P.

Ellington, Elijah & Catharine Rodwell, 17 Dec 1821; James Ellington, bm.

Ellington, James & Bettsey Wright, 29 Jan 1784; Philimon Hawkins, bm; M. D. Johnson, wit.

Ellington, James & Elizabeth Taylor, 18 Dec 1833; Daniel Taylor, bm; Burl Pitchford, J. P., wit.

Ellington, Joel & Sally Flemming, 17 Mar 1813; Elijah Ellinton, bm; Wm. Green, clk, wit.

Ellington, John & Betsey Rivers, 21 July 1834; James Talley, bm; Burl Pitchford, J. P.

Ellington, John & Elizabeth Clark, 12 Jan 1850; Thomas Vincent, bm; Jno. W. White, wit.

Ellington, Pleasant & Holly W. Burrow, 18 Feb 1831; James Burgess, bm; C. Drake, C. C., wit.

Ellington, Thomas & Frances Lancaster, 9 Oct 1849; John C. Overton, bm; Jno. W. White, wit.

Ellington, Thompson & Emely Rudd, 20 Sept 1830; Zachariah Wright, bm; C. Drake, C. C., wit.

Ellington, William & Martha Shearin, 19 Sept 1848; Thomas Ellington, bm; Jno. W. White, wit.

Elliott, Thomas M. & & Sarah Ann Black, 18 Nov 1822; John Robinson, bm; E. D. Drake, wit.

Ellis, Charles & Jinsey Shearrin, 16 Mar 1799; William Hicks, bm; S. Green, wit.

Ellis, Ephram & Sarah B. Davis, 18 Nov 1809; Eley Perkinson, bm; Jno. C. Johnson, D. C., wit.

Ellis, Hicks & Nancey Tilley, 10 Mar 1783; James Towns, bm.

Ellis, Hicks & Tabitha Gunn, 29 Aug 1810; Henry Fitts, bm; Jno C. Johnson, D. C., wit.

Ellis, Ira & Susan Parker, 24 Sept 1827; Jesse Myrick, bm; C. Drake, C. C., wit.

Ellis, James & Lewsey Ellington, 16 Sept 1797; James Ellinton, bm; Shd Green, wit.

Ellis, Jeremiah & Nancy Duke (no date); Joseph Ubanks, bm; M. D. Johnson, C. C., wit.

Ellis, John & Anne Gibson, 24 Nov 1779; William Park, bm; Thos Machen, wit.

Ellis, John H. & Frances Bell, 24 Dec 1811; Joseph Shearin, bm; P. R. Davis, wit.

Ellis, Joshua & Salley Perkinson, 24 Nov 1798; Jesse Perkinson, bm; M. Duke Johnson, clk, wit.

Ellis, Lewis & Nancy Bell, 1 Jan 1818; Wm. Hicks, bm; Wm. Green, wit.

Ellis, Michael & Elizabeth Murphy, 13 Oct 1779; Nelson Cole, bm; William Park, wit.

Ellis, Miles & Polly Bobbitt, 4 Feb 1813; Abraham Clanton, Thomas Allin, bm.

Ellis, Obadiah & Elizabeth Hicks, 10 Feb 1806; John Capps, bm; Jo Terrell, D. C., wit.

Ellis, Obadiah & Barshaba King, 2 Aug 1797; Richard Riggan, bm; Shd Green, wit.

Ellis, Sidney F. (son of A. D. & Louisa Ellis) & Mary E. Burrows (dau of William P. & Ann Burrows), 18 Dec 1867; William A. White, clk, wit; m 18 Dec 1867 by T. B. Kingsbury, M. G.

Ellis, Sims & Mary Bell, 1 Sept 1801; Major Neal, bm; S. Johnson, wit.

Ellis, Stephen & Salley Shell, 24 Nov 1778; Stephen Shell, bm; M. D. Johnson ,C. C., wit.

Ellis, Stephen & Cresey Ellis, 5 July 1799; Reubin Patrick bm; Shd Green, wit.

Ellis, Sumner J. & Murtilla King, 17 Dec 1844; John W. Hicks, bm; Jno W. White, wit.

Ellis, Thomas & Lucy Balthrop, 10 Aug 1802; John Balthrop, bm; Sugan Johnson, wit.

Ellis, William & Betsey Ellis (no date); Richard Ellis, bm; M. Duke Johnson, wit.

Ellis, William & Sarah Towns, 5 Aug 1806; Dickey Neal, bm; Jo Terrell, D. C., wit.

Ellis, Willie & Nancy Brown, 22 Oct 1798; Henry Foote, bm; S. Green, wit.

Ellis, Zachariah & Rebecah Hawkins, 5 Nov 1792; Daniel Fain, bm; M. Duke Johnson, C. C., wit.

Ellms, Charles & Rebecah Withers, 17 July 1785; Mills Bobbitt, bm; M. Duke Johnson, wit.

Ellums, James & Tamer Bennett, 21 Oct 1785; Darling Maddrey, bm; M. D. Johnson, wit.

Elmore, Edward G. & Desdemona V. Robins, 28 Feb 1842; Enes W. Parrish, bm; Burl Pitchford, J. P., wit.

Elms, James & Martha Capps, 19 Sept 1797; Clabon Harris, bm; Shd Green, wit.

Elton, William & Elizabeth B. Johnston, 4 March 1851; John White, bm; Jno W. White, clk, wit; m 6 Mar 1851 at 4 1/2 PM by Henry Harris, J. P.

Emerson, William T. & Amey Bobbit, 27 Nov 1792; Oliver Grissom. bm; M. Duke Johnson, C. C., wit.

Estes, Lyddal Bacon & Sally Alston Hunter, 15 Nov 1805; Patrick Connelly, bm; Jo. Terrell, D. C., wit.

Estes, Wiley & Milley Bagley (no date); Wm. Gwyn, bm; M. D. Johnson, wit.

Ethrage, Wilson & Rodah McFurson, 12 Jan 1854; S. B. Gills, bm; Jno W. White, clk, wit; m 12 Jan 1854 by Ph. W. Archer.

Evan, William & Jane Shell, 30 May 1821; Jno Ellis, bm; Frs. Jones, wit.

Evans, Alsa & Charlotte Scot, 3 Feb 1831; James Evans, bm; C. Drake, C. C., wit.

Evans, Archabald & Lucretia Green, 29 Dec 1823; Mins Guy, bm; C. Drake, C. C., wit.

Evans, Bowlin & Partheny Mushaw, 17 Nov 1852; John Burchette, bm; Thos P. Paschall, wit; m 17 Nov 1852 by Thos P. Paschall, J. P.

Evans, James & Martha Green, 31 Aug 1840; William Toney, bm; Edwd W. Best, clk, wit.

Evans, John & Lucy Shearin, 7 June 1803; Lewis Hazard, bm; M. Duke Johnson, wit.

Evans, John & Margarette Durham, 23 Dec 1852; Willis Kersey, bm; Thos P. Paschall, wit; m 23 Dec 1852 by J. H. Bullock, J. P.

Evans, John & Priscilla West, 3 Feb 1858; Hawood Cordle, bm; Jno W. White, wit; m 4 Feb 1858 by M. C. Duke, J. P.

Evans, John L. & Mary F. Myrick, 6 May 1847; Peter J. Evans, bm; Jno W. White, wit.

Evans, John W. (son of Thomas & Eliza Evans) & Parthenia G. Ellington (dau of James & Elizabeth Ellington, 14 Dec 1867; William A. White, clk, wit; m 18 Dec 1867 by J. W. Wellons, M. G.

Evans, Joseph & Susan Thomas, 5 Dec 1822; Kemp Plummer, bm; Cas Drake, wit.

Evans, Leaven & Hariot Scot, 18 Dec 1829; Thomas Edwards, bm; C. Drake, C. C., wit.

Evans, Miles W. & Scinnorey Mabry, 29 Nov 1853; C. M. Cook bm; Jno W. White, C. C. C., wit, m 1 Dec 1853 at Charles M. Cooks house by Henry Harris, J. P.

Evans, Nathaniel & Julia Guyan, 22 Dec 1848; Ebenezer Cyprus, bm; Jno W. White, wit.

Evans, Paul & Frances Ash, 28 Apr 1857; Azariah Smith, bm; Jno W. White, clk, wit; m 28 Apr 1857 by A. L. Steed, J. P.

Evans, Peter J. & Susan E. Turner, 13 Nov 1840; Bennett H. Stammire, bm; Edwd W. Best, wit.

Evans, Richard & Lucy Evans, 17 Dec 1793; Randolph Rowe, bm; M. D. Johnson, C. C., wit.

Evans, Thomas M. & Martha Hicks, 31 Dec 1866; William A. White, clk, wit; m 3 Jan 1867 by P. H. Joyner.

Evans, Thomas M. W. & Eliza Ann Paschall, 28 May 1841; Peter Evans, bm; Edwd W. Best, C. C., wit.

Evans, Thomas W. & Permelia A. Renn, 21 Apr 1867; P. J. Turnbull, bm; Jno W. White, clk, wit; m 22 Apr 1856 by P. H. Smith, M. G.

Evans, William & Mary Carter, 8 July 1850; Jos John Evans, bm; Jno. W. White, wit.

Evans, William J. & Ann J. Purdy, 1 Aug 1850; Robert Joyce, Jr., bm; James Perry, wit.

Exum, William J. & Mary A. Burt, 17 Apr 1854; Wm. J. Burt, bm; Jno W. White, C. C. C., wit; m 18 Apr 1854 by Henry Gray, M. G.

Ezard, Thomas & Elizabeth Harris, 20 Apr 1782; Benjamin Spain, bm; M. Duke Johnson, wit.

Fain, Charles (col) & Ginney Hendrick, 21 Aug 1865; Jno Read, bm; William A. White, clk, wit; m 26 Aug 1865 by Jas T. Russell, J. P.

Fain, Daniel & Nancy Hardridge, 13 Aug 1799; William Smith, bm; Shd Green, wit.

Fain, Joel & Susanah Dent, 16 Dec 1794; William Allen, bm; M. Duke Johnson, C. C. C., wit.

Fain, John & Martha Rainey, 18 Feb 1785; William Patrick, bm; M. Duke Johnson, C. C., wit.

Fain, John D. & Susan M. Hair, 4 Jan 1840; Jos S. Jones, bm.

Fain, Tyre & Aggey Smith, 21 July 1801; James Caller, bm; S. Johnson, wit.

Falconer, Alexander H. & Mary H. Eaton, 6 Sept 1828; Thomas White, bm.

Falkener, Bartholomew & Sally Clark, 7 July 1802; Charles Drury, bm; Sugan Johnson, wit.

Falkener, Edward (col) & Lizzie Hawkins, 14 Feb 1867; William A. White, clk, wit; m 17 Feb 1867 by L. C. Perkinson, M. G.

Falkener, Hardy & Mary Clark, 5 Jan 1807; James Harrison, bm; M. D. Johnson ,C. C., wit.

Falkener, Harry (col) & Jane Boyd, 12 Dec 1866; William A. White, clk, wit; m 16 Dec 1866 by L. C. Perkinson, M. G.

Falkener, Isaac (col) & Joanna Green, 23 May 1866; James Y. Christmas, bm; William A. White, clk, wit; m 23 May 1866 by William Hodges, M. G.

Falkener, John & Nancy Arnold, 14 July 1798; Solomon Arnold, bm; S. Green, wit.

Falkener, Sterling & Octavia D. Shearin, 18 Apr 1865; E. C. Waddill, bm; William A. White, wit.

Falkener, William & Ann Plummer, 17 July 1834; James Maxwell, bm; E. D. Drake, clk, wit.

Falkener, William A. K. & Elizabeth Johnson, 24 Sept 1807; Joel Terrell, Jr., bm; M. Duke Johnson, C. C., wit.

Falkner, Ford & Martha Rudd, 17 Jan 1852; Alpheus H. Ball, bm; Jno W. White, wit.

Falkner, John & Mary Riggan, 13 Dec 1853; Bnjn R. Browning, bm; Jno. W. White, C. C., wit; m 15 Dec 1853 by Nathl. Nicholson, J. P.

Falkner, John & Martha A. Rudd, 10 Nov 1857; A. H. Ball, bm; m 18 Nov 1857 by A. C. Harris, M. G.

Falkner, Littleton & Rosa Edwards, 9 Aug 1864; Jackson Pinnell, bm; William A. White, clk, wit; m 10 Aug 1864 by P. H. Joyner.

Fan, William & Dililah Langford, ___ Nov 1782; Jesse Fann, bm; M. D. Johnson, wit.

Fan, William & Polley Long, 1 Mar 1791; George Langford, bm; M. D. Johnson, C. C., wit.

Farrar, Jno. H. & Eliza R. Harris, 20 Nov 1817; Frs. D. Allen, bm; W. A. K. Falkener, bm.

Farrar, Jordon C. & Precilla Riggon, 28 Aug 1821; Matthew P. Johnson, bm.

Farrar, Joseph & Louisa Franklin, 6 Nov 1847; John J. Folks, bm; Jno. W. White, wit.

Farrar, Josiah & Eliza Macon, 12 Jan 1848; E. T. Rice, bm; Jno. W. White, wit.

Faulcon, Edward W. & Elizabeth W. Eaton, 14 Nov 1836; James Maxwell, bm; E. D. Drake, clk, wit.

Faulcon, Isaac N. & Martha W. Falkoner, 6 Oct 1823; Blake Baker, bm.

Faulcon, Jessee N. & Vesuvia Browne, 27 Oct 1856; L. O. Willcox, bm; Jno. W. White, wit.

Faulkes, John J. & Mary A. Traylor, 14 Aug 1843; Jacob W. Holt, bm; M. J. Montgomery, clk, wit.

Faulkner, John G. & Marilla Wright, 15 Feb 1866; John A. Macon, bm; William C. White, clk, wit; m 16 Feb 1866 by A. L. Steed, J. P.

Feild, Charles G. & Harriot B. Eaton, 20 Mar 1811; Thomas H. Person, bm; M. Duke Johnson, C. C., wit.

Feild, Eaton G. & Elizabeth M. K. Eaton, 8 Nov 1834; Zachariah Herndon, bm; E. D. Drake, clk, wit.

Feilds, Edmond S. & Mary A. Bugg, 9 Dec 1824; Thomas A. Langley, bm; Burl Pitchford, bm.

Felps, William & Emily Rudd, 28 Nov 1866; William A. White, clk, wit; m 28 Nov 1866 by P. H. Joyner.

Felts, Allen & Pattey Patterson, 2 Nov 1787; Francis Smith, bm; M. D. Johnson, clk, wit.

Felts, B. L. & Piety Painter, 16 Feb 1859; B. M. Darnell, bm; Jno. W. White, wit.

Felts, Benjamin & Polly Clardy, 15 Nov 1831; William H. Shearin, bm; C. Drake, C. C., wit.

Felts, Cary & Salley Foster (no date); Buckner Davis, bm.

Felts, Edward & Fanny Darnoll, 4 Dec 1832; Kinchen Felts, bm; C. Drake, Clk, wit.

Felts, Hardy & Nancy Edgerton, 26 Jan 1809; John Egerton, bm; J. C. Johnson, D. C. C., wit.

Felts, Henry & Nancy Stephens, 24 Dec 1806; Hardy Felts, bm; M. Duke Johnson ,C. C., wit.

Felts, James & Martha Dowlin (no date); Randolph Felts, bm.

Felts, James & Harriette Little, 2 Nov 1842; John Hardie, bm; M. J. Montgomery, wit.

Felts, James & Manerva Little, 30 Apr 1867; Benjamin P. Davis, bm; William A. White, clk, wit; m 2 May 1867 by Ridley Browne, J. P.

Felts, John & Polly Dowlin, 21 Dec 1805; William Felts, bm; Jo Terrell, D. C. C., wit.

Felts, John R. & Rebecca A. Bell, 20 June 1853; Robert Y. Tucker, bm; Jno. W. White, clk, wit; m 22 June 1853 by M. M. Drake, J. P.

Felts, Kinchin & Rebecca Dinkins, 1 Jan 1820; Thos Bell, bm; Cas Drake, C. W. C. C., wit.

Felts, Nathan & Betty Patterson, 26 Oct 1784; William Patterson, bm; M. D. Johnson, wit.

Felts, Nathaniel & Betsey Bostin, 23 Nov 1802; Warwick Hazelwood, bm; M. D. Johnson, C. C., wit.

Felts, Nathaniel & Jane Acre, 24 Dec 1818; John Jeffers, bm; W. A. K. Falkener, wit.

Felts, Ransom & Nancy Parish, 2 Nov 1816; Jacob Harris, bm; Wm Green, C. C. C., wit.

Felts, Rowland & Holley Hasilwood, 25 June 1782; Randolph Felts, bm; W. Duke Johnson, wit.

Felts, Rowland & Mary Durham, 18 Apr 1808; Warwick Hazelwood, bm; M. D. Johnson, C. C., wit.

Felts, Tilmon & Rebeca Ellis, 9 Sept 1802; Ralph Neal, Sr., bm; S. Johnson, wit.

Felts, William & Nancey Hollemon, 2 Dec 1788; Nathl Felts, bm; Wm. Johnson, wit.

Felts, William & Elizabeth Carter, 25 Jan 1806; Henry Felts, bm; Jo Terrell, D. C., wit.

Ferrall, Thomas & Mary W. Shearin, 23 Sept 1844; Joseph W. Harriss, bm; W. W. Vaughan, wit.

Ferrell, Micajah & Eliza Walker, 9 Aug 1816; Joel Harris, bm; Wm. Green, C. C. C., wit.

Finch, John H. & A. Johnson, 21 Dec 1863; J. H. Askew, bm; William A. White, clk, wit; m 5 Jan 1864 by P. H. Joyner.

Finch, Robert H. & Bettie L. Burney, 26 June 1860; E. H. Russell, bm; Jno. W. White, clk, wit; m 3 July 1860 by John D. Southall.

Finley, John & Mary Childress, 23 Dec 1790; James Dunn, bm; M. Duke Johnson, C. C. C., wit.

Fisher, John W. & Angelina Lancaster, 28 June 1853; Jacob August, bm; Jno. W. White, wit.

Fitts, Frank M. & Ann S. Thrower, 29 Nov 1864; Henry D. Milam, bm; William A. White, clk, wit; m 30 Nov 1864 by J. R. Finley, D. D.

Fitts, Henry G. & Minerva T. Jones, 29 Nov 1834; James Maxwell, bm; E. D. Drake, clk, wit.

Fitts, James & Rebecca Emily Alston, 25 June 1814; Robert Freeman, bm; W. Green, C. C., wit.

Fitts, James M. & Bettie T. Hunter, 6 Mar 1866; George W. Alston, bm; William A. White, wit; m 7 Mar 1866 by Robt O. Burton, M. G.

Fitts, Oliver & Peggy W. Dignall, 15 July 1813; Stephen Davis, bm; Wm. Green, C. C. C., wit.

Fitts, Oliver D. & Harriett A. E. Collins, 10 Apr 1828; Matthew M. Drake, bm; E. D. Drake, wit.

Fleming, Abbington K. & Mary C. Smith, 30 Dec 1854; Nathan S. Watkins, bm; Jno W. White, C. C. C., wit; m 31 Dec 1854 by Will Plummer, J. P.

Fleming, Charles J. & Winifred M. Paschall, 16 Oct 1855; Abington Fleming, bm.

Fleming, Jacob D. & Susanna D.Cole, 17 Dec 1861; Jessee J. Balthrop, bm; William A. White, wit, m; 18 Dec 1861 by J. N. Manning.

Fleming, Jessee P. & Sarrah Watkins, 5 Nov 1846; Charles E. Watkins, bm; Jno W. White, wit.

Fleming, John H. & Nancy Davis, 27 Oct 1838; George Fleming, Jr., bm.

Fleming, Leonard & Holley Smith, 21 Dec 179-; Duke Bennett, bm; Shd Green, wit.

Fleming, Peter & Betsey Fleming, 16 Dec 1791; Thomas Fleming, bm.

Fleming, (Dr.) R. D. & A. V. Watson, 13 Feb 1866; W. A. J. Nicholson, bm; William A. White, clk, wit; m 15 Feb 1866 by N. A. Purefoy, M. G.

Fleming, Reuben & Elizabeth Fleming, 12 Nov 1836; Henry Andrews, bm; E. D. Drake, clk, wit.

Fleming, Robert R. & Mrs. C. G. Daniel, 26 Feb 1867; Charles J. Fleming, bm; William A. White, wit.

Fleming, Solomon & Elizabeth Dowling, 6 Feb 1838; George Fleming, bm.

Fleming, Solomon & Elizabeth A. Johnson, 25 Nov 1847; Thomas J. Judkins, bm; Jno W. White, wit.

Fleming, Solomon & Maggie J. Watkins, 17 Dec 1866; William A. White, wit; m 18 Dec 1866 by J. W. Wellons, J. P.

Fleming, Thomas & Quinny Davis, 16 Dec 1817; David Dancy, bm; Wm. Green, wit.

Fleming, Thomas M. & Mary Ann Johnston, 26 Mar 1851; George R. Sledge, bm; Jno W. White, clk, wit; m 26 Mar 1851 by Chas Skinner, J. P.

Fleming, Thomas M. & Sallie A. Johnston, 15 Nov 1854; Thos J. Judkins, bm; Jno W. White, C. C. C., wit; m 15 Nov 1854 by H. J. Macon, J. P.

Fleming, Thomas T. & Leticia Regans, 5 Aug 1855; Robert H. Suit, bm; Thos P. Paschall, wit; m 8 Aug 1855 by Thos P. Paschall, J. P.

Fleming, W. B. & A. E. Duke, 24 Oct 1866; B. M. Nicholson, bm; William A. White, C. C., wit; m 31 Oct 1866 by J. W. Wellons, M. G.

Fleming, William & Elizabeth Riggon, 13 May 1801; James Clark, bm; M. Duke Johnson, C. C., wit.

Fleming, William & Sarah E. Webbster, 27 Sept 1862; H. Theodore Ellyson, D. S., & Jno M. Wilson, bm; Wm. A. White, wit

Flemmin, Simon & Nancy D. Davis, 14 Dec 1825; Matthew M. Drake, bm; C. Drake, C. C., wit.

Flemming, George & Betsey Reggin, 22 Dec 1801; Duke Bennett, bm; Sugan Johnson, wit.

Flemming, Richard & Polly Riggins, 29 Dec 1811; Thomas Fleming, bm; Wm. Green, C. C. C., wit.

Fletcher, Edward A. & Ann H. Robinson, 4 Feb 1832; Richard B. Robinson, bm; C. Drake, C. C. C., wit.

Fletcher, James & Elizabeth Wadkins, 5 Apr 1811; Joseph Watkins, bm; Jno C. Johnson, D. C. C., wit.

Fletcher, James A. & Levinia E. A. Cleaton, 28 Aug 1855; Alfred M. Tucker, bm; Jno. W. White, wit.

Fletcher, John & Elizabeth J. A. Tucker, 15 Sept 1830; Peyton Vaughan Duke, bm; Burl Pitchford, J. P., wit.

Fletcher, John & Candice Smith, 27 Mar 1844; Thomas J. Judkins, bm; M. J. Montgomery, wit.

Floyd, William F. & Mary Rose, 13 Aug 1858; Richard A. Davis, bm; Jno. W. White, wit.

Fluker, George & Elizabeth Matthews, 4 Sept 1781; George James, bm; Tho Machen, wit.

Foot, Henry, Jr., & Nancy D. Pitchford, 28 Aug 1832; Thomas J. Pitchford, Jr., bm; C. Drake, C. C., wit.

Foote, (Dr.) George A. & Sallie J. McDowell, 30 Nov 1863; Samuel N. Mills, bm; William A. White, wit; m 8 Dec 1863 by Henry Petty, M. G.

Foote, Henry & Polley Moss, 14 July 1800; Charles King, bm; M. D. Johnson, C. C., wit.

Foote, James S. & Pattie A. Bobbitt, 1 Dec 1863; Henry A. Foote, bm; William C. White, clk, wit; m 2 Dec 1863 by Lemmon Shell, M. G.

Foote, Jerry (col) & Mariah Goode, 24 Dec 1866; William A. White, clk, wit; m 26 Dec 1866 by J. M. Brame, J. P.

Foote, Joseph (col) & Frances Plummer, 14 July 1866; Dr. Geo A. Foote, bm; William A. White, clk, wit; m 15 July 1866 by N. A. Purefoy, M. G.

Foote, William & Elisabeth Barker, 16 May 1785; Moses Shearin, bm; M. Duke Johnson, wit.

Ford, James & Lucy Ellis (dau of Stephen Ellis), 6 July 1830; Fox Hunter, bm; C. Drake, C. C., wit.

Ford, Robert H. (of Virginia) & Mary A. E. Johnson, 14 Jan 1863; James A. Harrison, bm; W. A. White, clk, wit; m 14 Jan 1863 by Jno B. Williams.

Ford, William J. & Mary M. Manning, 26 Nov 1861; Thomas J. Judkins, Edmond H. Riggan, bm; Wm A. White, wit; m 4 Dec 1861 by James C. Robinson, J. P.

Forkner, Sugar & Priscilla Robertson, 6 Dec 1785; Moses Forkner, bm; M. D. J., wit.

Fortner, Benjamin & Rebecca Moore, 1 Jan 1827; Joseph P. Johnson, bm; M. M. Drake, wit.

Fortner, Edmund & Polly Grayard, 2 July 1831; Short Kimbell, bm; C. Drake, C. C., wit.

Fortner, Hardy & Nancy Wren, 1 Dec 1825; John V. Cawthorn, bm; C. Drake, C. C., wit.

Fortner, James R. & Elizabeth L. Fortner, 28 Dec 1839; William Pardue, bm.

Fortner, Joseph & Celia Fortner, 18 Aug 1836; Robert Harris, bm; E. D. Drake, clk, wit.

Fortner, Marcellas & Martha A. Clark, 10 Feb 1820; WM. H. Macon, bm; Cas. Drake, wit.

Fortner, Rufus H. & Margaret G. Rudd, 1 Jan 1861; James H. Ball, bm.

Fortner, Thomas & Sarah W. Fortner, 9 Oct 1848; Solomon G. Wortham, bm; Jno. W. White, wit.

Foster, Frederick & Nancy Swenney, 30 Nov 1806; Reubin Cawthon, bm; M. D. Johnson, C. C., wit.

Foster, Jordan H. & Lucy Ann Duke, 20 Dec 1865; Thomas A. Montgomery, bm; William A. White, clk, wit, m; 20 Dec 1865 by J. B. Solomon, M. G.

Foster, William B. & Pattie A. Southerland, 26 Aug 1857; Jordan H. Foster, bm; Jno. W. White, clk, wit; m 26 Aug 1857 by Wm. T. Brooks.

Fowler, Edmund F. & Susan D. Turner, 21 Jan 1836; George J. Rowland, bm; Benj. H. Cook, wit.

Fowler, H. G. W. & Sencord M. Shearin, 10 May 1828; Anderson Reese, bm; M. M. Drake, wit.

Fowler, James G. & Mary L. Walker, 4 May 1833; John Fletcher, bm; C. Drake, C. C., wit.

Fowler, Mason & Prudence Hill, 9 ___ 1799; Thomas Ferrell, bm; Shd. Green, wit.

Fowler, Pleasant & Salley Jenkins, 7 Nov 1799; John Macon, bm; Shd Green, wit.

Fowlkes, Kenner & Catharine Baldwin, 15 Dec 1819; William Tunstill, bm.

Frederick, John & Salley Stiles, 19 Sept 1783; Benjamin Stiles, bm; M. Duke Johnson, wit.

Freeman, John & Mrs. Mary Freeman, 2 Feb 1824; Robert R. Johnson, bm.

Freeman, John & Elizabeth Curtis, 24 Mar 1837; Samuel Huddgen, bm; Burl Pitchford, J. P., wit.

Fremon, James & Patsey Beard, 24 Feb 1831; Littleton Beard, bm; Burl Pitchford, J. P., wit.

Fulford, William J. & Josephine A. Harris, 1 Oct 1859; Saml Davis, bm; Jno W. White, clk, wit; m 12 Oct 1859 by Wm. C. Clanton, J. P.

Fuller, Augustus E. & Lucy R. Ball, 5 Jan 1860; Burwell & Parham [sic], bm; Jno W. White, clk, wit; m 11 Jan 1860 by L. K. Willie, M. G.

Furgason, Beryman & Martha Collier, 21 Oct 1818; Thomas Smith, bm.

Fussell, Harrison & Susannah Vaulx, 10 Nov 1803; James Harrison, bm; Gideon Johnson, wit.

Fussell, John & Sarah Hawks, 28 Nov 1795; James Moss, bm; Mark Harwell, wit.

Gale, John T. & Jane V. Keys, 13 May 1826; Saml Hillman, bm; M. M. Drake, wit.

Gardener, Thos & Polly Capps, 10 Aug 1800; William Madray, bm; R. R. Johnson, wit.

Gardner, Edward (col) & Kitty Boyd, 7 Apr 1866; Alfred Davis, bm; William A. White, clk, wit; m 7 Apr 1866 by Thos B. Ricks, M. G.

Gardner, John W. & Nancy Johnson, 25 Feb 1831; Jesse Myrick, bm; C. Drake, C. C., wit.

Gardner, Joseph & Catey Jones, 27 Feb 1799; Edmond Acock, bm; Shd Green, wit.

Gardner, Martin & Betsey Harper, 16 Jan 1807; Xanthus Snow, bm; M. Duke Johnson, wit.

Gardner, Thomas & Elizabeth Kirk, 14 Mar 1808; J. Read, bm; M. Duke Johnson, C. C., wit.

Gardner, Thos H. & Sally Fleming, 4 Dec 1843; Geo R. Sledge, bm; M. J. Montgomery, wit.

Gardner, Thomas P. & Finetto S. A. W. Myrick, 6 Mar 1848; George E. Johnson, bm; Jno W. White, wit.

Garland, David S. & Christian B. Garland, 28 Jan 1832; Joshua Davis, bm; C. Drake, C. C., wit.

Garland, Humphry & Elizabeth Blankinship, 11 Feb 1780; Mark Thornton, bm; Thos Machen, wit.

Garland, John & Susannah Nichols, 8 Aug 1781; Alexander Nicholson, bm.

Garland, John & Christian B. Boyce, 10 July 1819; Henry Fitts, bm.

Garnes, Berry & Winnifred H. Mewshaw, 8 Oct 1842; B. S. Montgomery, bm; M. J. Montgomery, wit.

Garnes, Isaac & Fanny Mayhaw, 17 Feb 1797; Eligah Garnes, bm; Shd Green, wit.

Garnes, John & Peggy Brannum, 8 Sept 1823; Benjamin Durom, bm; Edwin D. Drake, wit.

Garns, Elijah & Rhoda Mahoe, 5 Feb 1797; Charles Durham, bm; Cas Drake, C. C. C., wit.

Garratt, Joseph & Rebeccah Jeffreys (no date); John Thompson, bm; M. D. Johnson, wit.

Garrot, Green & Rebecca Sims, 15 Dec 1795; William Garrot, bm; M. Duke Johnson, C. C., wit.

Garrott, Abel & Nancy Sims, 27 Dec 1805; Reubin Coghill, bm; M. Duke Johnson, C. C., wit.

Garrott, James & Polly N. Abbott, 14 Apr 1836; James Edwards, bm; E. D. Drake, clk, wit.

Garrott, James & Mary Falkner, 2 July 1839; James Ball, bm; Edwd W. Best, clk, wit.

Garrott, Martin & Lucretia A. Burt, 17 Jan 1820; Henry Sims, bm; Cas Drake, C. C. C., wit.

Gase, Jonas & Cath Sherin, 26 Dec 1809; Joseph Sherin, bm; Jno C. Johnson, D. C. C., wit.

Gay, Carter H. & Rebecca Andrews, 30 Jan 1851; Jno C. Aycock, bm; Jno. W. White, clk, wit; m 30 Jan 1851 by J. Cheek, J. P.

Gee, Charles J. & Martha L. Williams, 28 Jan 1833; William M. Edwards, bm; C. Drake, C. C., wit.

Gee, John & _____ Pery (no date); Benja Ingram, bm.

Gee, Sterling H. & Mary T. Williams, 6 Nov 1828; William M. Edwards, bm; M. M. Drake, wit.

Gee, William & Prescilla Perry, 5 Mar 1794; Benjamin Ingram, bm; M. D. Johnson, C. C., wit.

George, Asa & Rebecca Archer, 29 May 1819; George Wortham, bm; Caswell Drake, wit.

George, Asa & Elizabeth King, 15 Dec 1851; Michael Riggan, bm; Jno W. White, clk, wit; m 15 Dec 1851 by M. Riggan, J. P.

George, Jeremiah R. & Sally Wright, 23 Mar 1831; M. N. Dunnavant, bm; C. Drake, C. C., wit.

George, Jno & Ann Crudwick, 10 Dec 1791; James Gordon, bm.

George, Marcus & Mary F. Campbell, 23 Apr 1807; Peter R. Davis, bm; John Norsworthy, wit.

Gibbs, Richard & Mary Ann Stainback, 7 Feb 1846; William J. Edwards, bm; M. J. Montgomery, wit.

Gill, Drury & Sinthea Perkinson, 22 Nov 1830; A. G. Elam, bm; Jno C. Johnson, wit.

Gill, James & Mary Burrow, 14 Jan 1780; David Gill, bm; Thos Machen, wit.

Gill, John & Betsey Mills, 29 Nov 1788; William Samford, bm; M. Duke Johnson, C. C., wit.

Gill, Phillip P. & Sarah E. Paschall, 12 Oct 1857; Thos W. White, bm; Jno W. White, clk, wit; m 22 Oct 1857 by N. A. Purefoy, M. G.

Gill, Samuel & Emily W. Arnold, 13 Dec 1853; A. A. Hudgins, bm; Jno W. White, clk, wit, m; 13 Dec 1853 by Ph. W. Archer, M. G. of M. E. Church, South.

Gille, Drury & Eliza B. Felts, 24 Sept 1866; James R. Daniel, bm; William A. White, clk, wit; m 30 Sept 1866 by T. Page Ricaud, M. G.

Gilrath, William & Sally Jones; 3 Dec 1779; James Jones, bm; Thos Machen, wit.

Glenn, James & Sally Barrow, 5 May 1797; G. Hunt Macon, bm; Shd Green, wit.

Glenn, John & Sarah Jones, 22 Sept 1804; Wm Balthrop, bm.

Glover, Charles & Lucy Sturdivant, 26 Dec 1791; Richd Glover, bm; M. D. Johnson, C. C., wit.

Glover, Darnel & Elizabeth Cannon, 30 Oct 1798; Charles Glover, bm; S. Green, wit.

Glover, Granderson F. & Arimenta Kidd, 22 June 1854; N. M. Thornton, bm; R. B. Robinson, wit; m 22 June 1854 by R. B. Robinson, J. P.

Glover, Henry & Rebecca Cannon, 19 Dec 1795; Peter Coleman, bm; M. D. Johnson ,C. C., wit.

Glover, John & Salley Jackson, 31 Jan 1785; Richard Thomas, bm; M. Duke Johnson, wit.

Glover, John & Betsey Thomas, 14 Jan 1790; Peter Thomas, bm; M. D. Johnson, C. C., wit.

Glover, Richard & Nancy Pope, 9 Nov 1805; Abraham Clanton, bm; Jo Terrell, D. C. C., wit.

Gober, John & Unity Wilson, 26 July 1798; Gray Mabry, bm; M. D. Johnson, C. C., wit.

Goebrel, Charles L. & Jane Thompson, 1 Sept 1855; John A. Hundley, bm; Jno W. White, wit.

Good, Joseph & Mary Lee, 15 Jan 1808; John M. Verell, bm; M. Duke Johnson, C. C., wit.

Goode, John C. & Mary Nuttall, 22 Feb 1819; Manson Williams, bm.

Goodloe, Henry G. & Indiana L. Duke, 11 Oct 1836; Richard Jordan, bm; E. D. Drake, clk, wit.

Goodman, Joel & Lucy Parish, 9 May 1803; Zachariah Rivers, bm; G. Johnson, wit.

Goodrich, John & Winney West, 21 Sept 1782; Samuel Willeford, bm; M. Duke Johnson, wit.

Goodrich, Matthias & Phebe Cheek, 1 Dec 1780; Darling Maddry, bm; M. D. Johnson, wit.

Goodson, James & Mrs. Martha Wiggins, 9 Sept 1865; Green R. Pinnell, bm; William A. White, clk, 13 Sept 1865 by W. A. Brame.

Goodwin, John & Nancy Ezard, 29 May 1793; Charles Marshall, bm; M. Duke Johnson, C. C., wit.

Goodwin, Thomas & Mary G. Harper, 5 July 1860; D. W. Harris, bm; Jno. W. White, clk, wit; m 5 July 1860 by Jno N. Andrews, M. G.

Goodwyn, George W. & Ann R. Burnett, 5 July 1838; Lazarus L. Burnett, bm; Benj E. Cook, wit.

Goodwyn, Capt. J. A. & Eugenia L. Feild, 2 July 1866; John T. Jones, bm; William A. White, clk, wit; m 5 Jul 1866 by W. Hodges, M. G.

Gordan, Randolph & Celia Williams, 28 July 1802; Robert Park, bm.

Gordon, James & Salley Caller, 23 June 1787; Laurence Richeson, bm; M. D. Johnson, C. C., wit.

Gordon, James & Elizabeth C. Jones, 10 Nov 1819; John M. Johnson, bm; Cas Drake, C. W. C. C., wit.

Gordon, Willie & Eveling Mayo, 12 Sept 1816; Isaac Mitchell, bm; Wm. Green, C. C., wit.

Graham, Hamilton C. & Minerva Little, 13 Dec 1832; Edward G. Benners, bm; C. Drake, C. C., wit.

Granger, Henry W. & Martha A. Wilson, 22 Nov 1859; Jno C. McCraw, bm; Jno W. White, clk, wit; m 22 Nov 1859 by R. G. Barrett, Clergyman.

Gray, Jackson & Eliza Trajetta, 19 Sept 1818; William Carr, bm.

Gray, Richard & Delilah Langford, 13 Mar 1812; John Darnell, bm; Wm. Green, C. C. C., wit.

Gray, William & Nancy Langford, 30 Aug 1805; Ezekiel Morey, bm; Jo Terrell, D. C. C., wit.

Greeley, Horace & Mary Y. Cheney, 5 July 1836; John G. Yancey, bm; E. D. Drake, clk, wit.

Green, Allan & Polley Taylour, 1 Aug 1797; Michal Haris, bm; Shd Green, wit.

Green, Allen & Fanny Evans, 24 Dec 1809; Kinchin Toney, Horrace Bell, bm; Jno C. Johnson, C. C., wit.

Green, George W. & Mary Cook, 14 Apr 1849; Saml Venis, bm; Jno. W. White, wit.

Green, Gideon M. & Francis L. Bullock, 12 Dec 1818; Joshua Davis, bm.

Green, Henry & Nancy Hawkins, 20 Dec 1858; James Green, bm; William A. White, wit; m 21 Dec 1858 by N. A. Purefoy, M. G.

Green, James & Priscilla McLamore, 5 Jan 1795; John Hazard, bm; M. Duke Johnson, C. C., wit.

Green, James & Nancy Power, 4 Mar 1797; Edmund Mayfield, bm; Shd Green, wit.

Green, James & Nancy Carter, 24 Dec 1847; Thos L. Twitty, bm; Jno W. White, wit.

Green, James & Bettie Mills, 25 May 1858; J. A. Macon, bm; Jno W. White, clk, wit; m 26 May 1858 by M. T. Hawkins, J. P.

67

Green, James T. (son of William & Mary Green) & Penina Copeland (dau of Benjamin & Frances Copeland), 7 Dec 1867; William A. White, clk, wit; m 19 Dec 1867 by M. P. Perry, J. P.

Green, John & Jane Christmas, 12 Oct 1805; Joel Terrell, Jr., bm; Jo Terrell, D. C., wit.

Green, John C. & Delia Martin Hawkins, 12 Apr 1801; Gedion H. Macon, bm; S. Johnson, wit.

Green, John C. & E. Macon, 18 Jan 1828; Bennett H. Stammire, bm; M. M. Drake, wit.

Green, John C., Jr., & Elizabeth Ann Bullock, 28 Mar 1853; Thos J. Judkins, bm; Jno W. White, wit; m 29 Mar 1853 by Edwin Hines, M. G.

Green, Joseph & Caty Day, 15 June 1809; George Norsworthy, bm; Jno C. Johnson, D. C. C., wit.

Green, Josepus & Polley Williams, 10 Dec 1780; John Oswald, bm.

Green, Robert & Elizabeth Evans, 22 Sept 1852; William A. White, bm; P. W. Mottley, wit.

Green, Samuel & Winney Thomas, 25 Nov 1862; Newsom Harris, bm; Wm. A. White, clk, wit; m 26 Nov 1862 by Saml Bobbitt, J. P.

Green, Simon (son of John and Peggy) & Phillis Goodrum (step dau of Ned & Emeline), 10 Aug 1867; Wm A. White, clk, wit; m 10 Aug 1867 by Thos A. Montgomery, J. P.

Green, Dr. Simon & Martha A. Jenkins, 5 Oct 1850; William A. Jenkins, bm; Jno. W. White, wit.

Green, Simon V. & Mary H. Macon, 26 Nov 1827; Henry G. Williams, bm; M. M. Drake, wit.

Green, Thomas & Prissilla Green, 6 Feb 1849; Peter R. Davis, bm; Jno. W. White, wit.

Green, Thomas (col) & Jacobine Vaughan, 25 Dec 1865; Geo R. Sledge, bm; William A. White, clk, wit; m 26 Dec 1865 by T. B. Kingsbury.

Green, Thomas E. & Ann Willis, 4 Aug 1823; Richard Davison, bm; Edwin D. Drake, wit.

Green, Thomas J. & Jane E. Wortham, 6 Sept 1860; Jno C. McCraw, bm; Jno. W. White, clk, wit; m 6 Sept 1860 by W. A. Dowtin, J. P.

Green, Wharton J. & Esther S. Ellery, 1 May 1858; M. R. Jones, bm; Jno. W. White, clk, wit; m 4 May 1858 by William Hodges, M. G.

Green, William & Ruthey Hunter, 14 June 1784; Samuel Person, bm; M. Duke Johnson, wit.

Green, William & Catharine Harriss, 15 Dec 1831; Robt F. Cheek, bm; M. M. Drake, wit.

Green, William A. & Mary P. Green, 14 Dec 1841; M. W. Williams, bm; M. J. Montgomery, wit.

Green, William T. & Martha O. Rowlette, 6 Nov 1847; Bushrod Carr, bm; Jno W. White, wit.

Green, Willis (col) & Ann Mayfield, 19 Jan 1866; Dr. W. J. Hawkins, bm; William A. White, clk, wit; m 24 Jan 1866 by T. Page Ricaud, M. G.

Gresham, James & Eliza Fraser, 21 Nov 1820; Peter Verell, bm; Frs. Jones, bm;

Griffice, Edward & Rebecca A. Thomas, 29 Dec 1852; James A. Taylor, bm; Jno. W. White, clk, wit; m 29 Dec 1852 by R. B. Robinson, J. P.

Griffin, Jeremiah & Jensy Solomon, 29 Dec 1817; Edmd Mayfield, bm; Wm. Green, wit.

Griffin, Jesse & Nancy Person, 24 June 1789; Peterson Person, bm.

Griffis, Lambert & Rebecca Moseley, 14 Nov 1826; Robert Cook, bm; M. M. Drake, wit.

Griggs, Rodam & Milley Bagley, 2 July 1784; John Estes, bm; M. Duke Johnson, wit.

Grison, Howel & Ginsey Newman, 29 May 1829; Thomas Newman, bm; Burl Pitchford, J. P.

Grist, Frederick & Susan Blount, 13 Aug 1845; William Grimes, bm; Jno. W. White, wit.

Guerrant, William P. (of Pittsylvania Co, VA) & Jane E. Greene, 17 Dec 1857; H. G. Goodloe, bm; Jno. W. White, clk, wit; m 17 Dec 1857 by John Tillett.

Gunn, Dudley G. & Angelica Matthews, 27 Mar 1822; Saunders Rooker, bm; Frs. Jones, wit.

Gunn, James W. & Olive K. Sallad, 2 Feb 1831; John Drinkwater, bm; M. M. Drake, wit.

Gunn, John & Theza Sims, 28 Mar 1799; Lewis Hazard, bm; S. Green, wit.

Gunn, William & Suzannah Clanton, 24 Mar 1782; William Clanton, bm; M. Duke Johnson, wit.

Gupton, Joseph & Mary Yarborough, 7 June 1836; James D. Yarbrough, bm; Benj. E. Cook, wit.

Gurkin, John & Janie Wilson, 6 Nov 1843; William P. Rose, bm; M. J. Montgomery, wit.

Guy, Asey & Nancy Robards, 8 Feb 1824; Hardaway Drew, bm; M. M. Drake, wit.

Guy, Baxter & Elizabeth Valentine, 21 Apr 1852; Charles Howell, bm; R. B. Robinson, wit; m 21 Apr 1852 by R. B. Robinson, J. P.

Guy, George & Nancy Hailstock, 20 July 1815; Frederick Harris, bm; W. Green, C. C. C., wit.

Guy, John & Sarrah E. Jones, 22 May 1847; Thos J. Judkins, bm; Jno W. White, wit.

Guy, Matthew & Surbrina Lowery, 10 Dec 1850; Woodson Hughes, bm; Jno. W. White, wit.

Guye, Hansel & Patsey Guye, 14 Dec 1826; Joseph Evans, bm; M. M. Drake, wit.

Guye, Mins & Theny Hawkins, 1 Jan 1825; John Wadkins, bm; C. Drake, C. C., wit.

Gwin, Elias & Rebecah Beckham, 21 Dec 1802; Charles Bennett, bm; Sugan Johnson, wit.

Gwinn, William & Nanney Childres, 29 Apr 1779; Benjamin Hawkins, bm; Thos Machen, wit.

Gworton, Richard & Nancy Steagall, 13 Dec 1818; Thomas Steagall, bm.

Hackney, John & Elizabeth Williams, 29 May 1805; Simon Williams, bm; Joel Terrell, D. C. C., wit.

Hagood, Howel & Elizabeth Burchett, 24 Dec 1807; Edward Burchett, bm; Jo Terrell, D. C. C., wit.,

Hagood, James W. & Elizabeth Gholson, 20 Jan 1855; Robert A. White, bm; Jno. W. White, wit.

Hagood, John & Mary Paschael, 3 Apr 1797; Elisha Paschal, bm; M. Duke Johnson, C. C., wit.

Hagood, John & Sabrina M. Harris, 7 Jan 1825; Jacob Davis, bm; Burl Pitchford, wit.

Hagood, John & Elizabeth Langford, 23 Nov 1846; John D. Tucker, Sr., bm.

Hagood, Lemuel P. & Sarah C. Burroughs, 38 Jan 1861; James W. Hagood, bm; Jno. W. White, clk, wit; m 31 Jan 1861 by R. D. Paschall, J. P.

Hagood, Ransom & _____ (no date); Matthews Goodrich, bm.

Hagwood, Turner & Fanny Colcly, 6 Jan 1838; Elijah W. Rudd, bm.

Hagwood, William & Silvia Davis, 15 Jan 1786; Moses Bennett, bm; M. Duke Johnson, wit.

Haithcock, Albert & Emeline J. Brack, 27 June 1844; James J. Vaughan, Jr., bm; W. W. Vaughan, wit.

Haithcock, Alfred L. & Joseph H. Bobbitt, 2 Apr 1867; Dr. Matthew W. Williams, bm; William A. White, wit; m 4 Apr 1867 at the residence of Mrs. Ann Bobbitt, by Thos J. Pitchford, J. P.

Haithcock, Grief & Nancy Thomas, 27 Jan 1846; Madison M. Haithcock, bm; M. J. Montgomery, wit.

Haithcock, Henry C. (son of Thomas & Matilda Haithcock) & Ange R. F. W. Conn (dau of Mary Capps), 15 Nov 1867; William A. White, clk, wit; m 17 Nov 1867 by George M. Darker, M. G.

Haithcock, Joseph J. & Susan Ann V. Lancaster, 20 July 1854; John Parris, bm; Jno W. White, C. C. C., wit; m 20 July 1854 by Saml Bobbitt, J. P.

Haithcock, Madison M. & M. L. Franklin, 16 Apr 1851; J. R. Johnson, bm; Jno W. White, wit.

Haithcock, Thomas & Matilda Capps, 1 Dec 1841; Jno W. White, bm; M. J. Montgomery, wit.

Haithcock, Thomas B. & Saluda Ann Patterson, 7 Aug 1846; Thomas Haithcock, bm; Jno. W. White, wit.

Hale, James D. & Elizabeth Roberson, 16 Feb 1848; Samuel Hale, bm; Jno W. White, wit.

Hale, Sterling & Ann Tucker, 19 Dec 1838; Rodon Parker, bm.

Hall, Miles & Elizabeth Kidd, 11 Oct 1850; Edrick H. Dugger, bm; Richd B. Robinson, wit.

Hall, Wesley (col) & Caroline Davis, 14 July 1866; Trim King, bm; William A. White, clk, wit; m 14 July 1866 by A. L. Steed, J. P.

Ham, Burton & Elizabeth Nuckals, 3 Aug 1849; William H. Nuckols, bm; Edwd J. Macon, wit.

Ham, Jeremiah & Orinda Ascue, 22 Jan 1827; John Ascue, bm; M. M. Drake, wit.

Hamilton, William & Sarah Tanner, 17 Sept 1808; Daniel Tucker, bm; M. D. Johnson, C. C. C., wit.

Hamlin, Robert P. & Penelope W. Bryan, 18 June 1844; K. P. Alston, bm; M. J. Montgomery, wit.

Hammond, Rawleigh & Mary Burford, 7 Aug 1781; John Rooker, bm; Thos Machen, wit.

Hammond, Saml & Francis Simms (no date); Rawleigh Hammond, bm; M. D. Johnson, C. C., wit.

Hancock, Clement & Rebecca Stanback, 6 Oct 1817; John Robinson, bm; W. Green, C. C., wit.

Haney, Madison & Plinny Mushaw, 4 June 1844; Jefferson Vaughan, bm; M. J. Montgomery, wit.

Hardaway, Joseph & Sarah Paine, 14 May 1799; Lewis Hazard, bm; M. Duke Johnson, C. C., wit.

Hardee, Curtiss & Dasey Harper, 11 Sept 1797; Sammul Harper, bm; Shd Green, wit.

Hardy, Henry & Susan Burrows, 13 Dec 1855; Jno S. Hardy, bm; Jno. W. White, wit.

Hardy, Samuel & Mary A. Shearin, 14 Feb 1826; Thomas Hardy, bm; M. M. Drake, wit.

Hardy, Samuel & Holly Harper, 30 Sept 1840; John Hardy, bm; Jno. W. White, wit.

Hardy, Stephen & Raney Shell, 5 Aug 1819; Richard Shell, bm; C. Drake, wit.

Hardy, Thomas & Mary Thompson, 21 Jan 1829; Edward Williams, bm; E. D. Drake, wit.

Hardy, Thomas & Wesley Harris, 12 Feb 1845; William Hardy, bm; Jno W. White, wit.

Hardy, Thomas & Matilda Nicholson, 5 Feb 1859; Francis M. Hardy, bm; Jno W. White, clk, wit; m 9 Feb 1859 by W. A. Dowtin, J. P.

Hardy, William & Cynthia Thompson, 18 Feb 1835; Banister R. Smith, bm.

Hare, John & Agness Bullock, 12 Aug 1799; Leonard Henderson, bm; Washington Latter, wit.

Hargrove, Bennit & Liddia Lambert, 20 Nov 1789; John Webb, bm; M. D. Johnson, C. C., wit.

Hargrove, Wesley & Martha Plummer, 20 Oct 1866; Dandridge J. Hilliard, bm; W. W. White, wit; m 20 Oct 1866 by W. W. White, J. P.

Hargrove, William & Holley Dodson, 12 Feb 1798; William Turner, bm; M. Duke Johnson, C. C., wit.

Haris, Archer & Eliza Edwards, 9 Nov 1779; Rowland Felts, bm.

Haris, Daniel & Elizabeth Harper, 11 Jan 1797; Alanson Nicholson, bm; Shd Green, wit.

Haris, Green H. & Margaret N. Harris, 24 Apr 1860; Jno W. White, bm; m 26 Apr 1860 by W. A. Dowtin, J. P.

Haris, Robert & Martha Ann Clark, 12 Nov 1842; John G. Mangrum, bm; M. J. Montgomery, wit.

Harper, Demise & Scithia Harris, 27 Dec 1827; Green Harris, bm; C. Drake, C. C., wit.

Harper, George W. & Winnefred Walker, 28 Jan 1850; James N. Harper, bm; Jno W. White, wit.

Harper, George W. & Elizabeth Minetree, 21 Aug 1858; D. W. Harris, bm; Jno W. White, clk, wit; m 22 Aug 1858 by L. C. Perkinson, M. G.

Harper, Hegdon & Polly Harton, 28 Jan 1797; William Johnson, bm; Shd Green, wit.

Harper, Henry & Martha Parrish, 25 Mar 1852; Jas N. Harper, bm; Jno W. White, clk, wit; m 25 Mar 1852 by N. Z. Graves.

Harper, John (son of Saml) & Lucy Morris, 13 June 1783; Samuel Harper, bm; M. D. Johnson, C. C., wit.

Harper, Joseph & Rebeccah Haselwood (no date); Worwick Haselwood, bm.

Harper, Kinchen & Frances Harris, 12 May 1825; Jno Pattillo, bm; M. M. Drake, wit.

Harper, Kinchen H. & Dolly Little, 29 Sept 1858; William H. Johnson, bm; Jno W. White, wit.

Harper, Pink & Frances Randolph, 24 Dec 1800; Jacob Bell, bm; M. D. Johnson, C. C., wit.

Harper, Samuel & Priscilla Sandifer, 4 Mar 1813; William Bennett, bm; Wm. Green, C. C., wit.

Harper, Samuel & Mary E. White, 13 Dec 1851; W. H. Furgurson, bm; Jno W. White, clk, wit; m 14 Dec 1851 by H. J. Macon, J. P.

Harper, Samuel & Elizabeth Moss, 30 Aug 1799; Joseph Harper, bm; Shd Green, wit.

Harper, William & Martha Yarbrough (no date); Wm Yarbrough, m; M. Yarbrough, wit.

Harper, William & Rebecca Bull, 24 Dec 1793; John Davis, bm.

Harper, William & Sarah Lancaster, 12 Feb 1829; Kinchen Harper, bm; E. D. Drake, clk, wit.

Harper, William & Mary Askew, 21 Nov 1834; Edward Harris, bm; E. D. Drake, clk, wit.

Harper, William H. & Sarah F. Aycock, 4 Jan 1855; J. M. Cook, bm; Jno W. White, wit.

Harper, Williamson & Rebecca Yarbrough, 10 Feb 1830; John Lucas, bm; C. Drake, clk, wit.

Harris-- see also Haris and Harriss

Harris, Alanson & Mary Riggon, 6 Dec 1821; Jiles Carter, bm.

Harris, Anderson & Elmina Lancaster, 23 Dec 1835; William C. Lancaster, bm; E. D. Drake, clk, wit.

Harris, Anderson R. & Nancy W. Harris, 31 Dec 1834; Raleigh Myrick, bm; E. D. Drake, clk, wit.

Harris, Archabald & Jincy Harris, 21 Aug 1820; Joel Harris, bm.

Harris, Arthur B. & Milly Thompson, 31 Jan 1824; Abner Aycock, bm.

Harris, Bedford & Priscilla Lancaster, 5 Dec 1811; Joel Harris, bm; Jo Terrell, D. C. C., wit.

Harris, Bedford & Catharine Saintsing, 22 Aug 1860; John Verser, bm; Wm. A. White, clk, wit; m 22 Aug 1860 by W. A. Dowtin, J. P.

Harris, Benjamin & Elizabeth Harris, 16 Dec 1835; Baker Pegram, bm; E. D. Drake, clk, wit.

Harris, Benjamin R. & Nancy T. Womble, 5 Sept 1854; Sol W. Stallings, bm; Jno W. White, C. C. C., wit; m 7 Sept 1854 by T. J. Pitchford, J. P.

Harris, Bennett & Amanda Wilson, 20 Mar 1852; William Matthews, bm; Jno W. White, wit.

Harris, Bennett & Rebecca Irby, 27 Nov 1852; N. M. Bobbitt, bm; Jno. W. White, wit.

Harris, Daniel & Mary Carter, 8 Apr 1802; Alanson Nicholson, bm; Gideon Johnson, wit.

Harris, Daniel & Polly Nicholson, 23 June 1811; Robert Harris, bm; Wm. Green, C. C., wit.

Harris, Daniel & Elizabeth Wammuth, 5 Jan 1833; George W. T. Blanch, bm; E. D. Drake, wit.

Harris, David W. & Susannah Taylor, 13 May 1837; Drury W. Harris, bm; E. W. Best, wit.

Harris, David W. & Betsey Mabry, 11 May 1843; Daniel Haithcock, bm; M. J. Montgomery, wit.

Harris, Doctor M. & Elizabeth Lancaster, 1 May 1845; Joseph J. Harris, M. J. Montgomery, wit.

Harris, Drewry & Lucy Wright, 9 June 1813; Jno Egerton, bm; Jno H. Green, wit.

Harris, Drewry W. & Nancy Harris, 20 Mar 1833; John P. Shearin, bm; C. Drake, C. C., wit.

Harris, Drury W. & Sarah Shearin, 30 Apr 1828; William Little, bm; M. M. Drake, wit.

Harris, Dudley W. & Mrs. Maggie A. Pegram, 14 Nov 1865; Jno W. Williams, bm; William A. White, clk, wit; m 15 Nov 1865 by Will H. Wheeler, D. C. M.

Harris, E. K. & Parmelia Plummer, 12 Feb 1865; Col. W. W. Wood, bm; William A. White, wit; m 21 Feb 1866 by Wm. H. Meade.

Harris, Edmund N. & Leah Lancaster, 13 Dec 1844; James J. Pegram, bm; M. J. Montgomery, wit.

Harris, Edward & Mary Nuckles, 29 Dec 1837; Kinchen Harper, bm; Edwd W. Best, clk, wit.

Harris, Edward & Rebecca F. Tucker, 27 Nov 1849; William R. Harris, bm; Jno W. White, wit.

Harris, Edwin & Mary Pattison, 14 Sept 1779; Rowland Felts, bm; Thos Machen, wit.

Harris, Elbert H. & Ann Riggan, 5 Dec 1848; James W. Harris, bm; Jno W. White, wit.

Harris, Elijah & Winnefred Meadows, 22 June 1830; Drewry Shearin, bm; C. Drake, C. C., wit.

Harris, George D. & Nancy Bennett, 19 Apr 1853; A. J. Johnson, bm; Jno W. White, wit; m 23 May 1853 by J. D. Solomon.

Harris, George W. & Sallie Harris, 15 Aug 1854; John L. Evans, bm.

Harris, Gideon & Elizabeth Ann Carter, 17 Jan 1826; Jacob Harriss, bm; M. M. Drake, wit.

Harris, Green & Betsey Harris, 16 Dec 1817; Henry Harris, bm; Wm Green, wit.

Harris, Green H. & Mary J. Harris, 5 Feb 1855; Isaac Harris, bm; Jno W. White, wit.

Harris, Guilford W. & Amanda OBryan, 6 May 1831; John H. Farrar, bm.

Harris, Hardy & Salley Harris, 31 Dec 1792; John Harris, bm; M. Duke Johnson, C. C., wit.

Harris, Harvel & Roxana Daniel 30 Sept 1844; James M. Daniel, bm; M. J. Montgomery, wit.

Harris, Henry & Nancy Nichols, 13 Jan 1798; Jno J. Egerton, bm; James Moss, wit.

Harris, Henry & Winifred Alston, 16 Aug 1819; Henry Dawson, bm; C. Drake, wit.

Harris, Henry & Lucretia Riggan, 14 Dec 1819; Joseph H. Riggan, bm; Cas Drake, clk, wit.

Harris, Henry Y. & Jane Lancaster, 23 Nov 1858; B. P. Harris, bm; Jno W. White, clk, wit; m 24 Nov 1858 by Saml Bobbitt, J. P.

Harris, Herbert & Polley West, 16 Feb 1796; Martin Smith, bm.

Harris, Isaac & Pattie A. Andrews, 7 Feb 1859; William A. White, bm; Jno W. White, wit; m 15 Feb 1859 by J. B. Solomon, Pastor of Baptist Church, Warrenton.

Harris, Isham & Betsey Banks, 14 Oct 1818; Brittan Harris, bm.

Harris, Jackson & Martha A. Baskervill, 31 May 1841; Peter Cain, bm; Burl Pitchford, J. P., wit.

Harris, Jacob & Eliza Parish, 10 Aug 1816; Robert Harris, bm; Wm. Green, C. C. C., wit.

Harris, Jacob & Sarah Egerton, 13 Dec 1827; Willie Harris, bm; M. M. Drake, wit.

Harris, James & Patience Wamoth, 28 Feb 1783; Robert Harris, bm; M. D. Johnson, wit.

Harris, James & Mary Smilling, 8 Oct 1784; Robert Haris, bm; M. Duke Johnson, wit.

Harris, James & Patsey Pegram, 29 Dec 1832; Burwell Harris, bm; C. Drake, C. C., wit.

Harris, James & Jane Andrews, 13 Nov 1836; Henry T. Allen, bm.

Harris, James & Elizabeth Brown, 15 Dec 1853; E. W. Best, bm; m 15 Dec 1853 by A. C. Harris, M. G.

Harris, James H. & Mary Davis, 4 Jan 1860; W. A. J. Nicholson, bm; Jno W. White, clk, wit; m 4 Jan 1860 by Thos J. Pitchford, J. P.

Harris, James H. & Mollie E. Shearin, 25 Apr 1865; Harry H. Harper, bm; William A. White, clk, wit; m 26 Apr 1865 by Chas M. Cook, J. P.

Harris, James P. & Dolly Shearin, 1 Jan 1825; Thomas Hardy, bm; C. Drake, C. C. C., wit.

Harris, James Y. & Ann Brown, 11 Jan 1826; Isham H. Davis, bm; M. M. Drake, wit.

Harris, John & Nanney Bartlet, 29 Mar 1791; Philip Harris, bm; M. D. Johnson ,C. C., wit.

Harris, John & Amey Crutchfield, 11 Sept 1816; Benjamin Pennington, bm; Wm. Green, C. C. C., wit.

Harris, John (col) & Lilly Hall, 3 March 1866; Walter A. Montgomery, bm; William A. White, clk, wit; m 3 Mar 1866 by W. Hodges, M. G.

Harris, John A. & Martha Elizabeth Lancaster, 6 Dec 1854; Isham H. Bennett, bm; William A. White, wit; m 8 Dec 1854 by Thos J. Pitchford, J. P.

Harris, John A. & Frances L. Carter, 22 Aug 1861; Z. W. Harriss, bm; Jno W. White, clk, wit; m 24 Aug 1861 by Nathl Nicholson, J. P.

Harris, John E. & Sally Bobbitt, 16 May 1795; John J. Egerton, bm; J. Moss, wit.

Harris, John E. & Nancy Parish, 30 Oct 1823; John Mealer, bm.

Harris, John J. & Nancy Lancaster, 30 Apr 1825; Green Harris, bm; M. M. Drake, wit.

Harris, John N. & Marina (or Ruina) A. Shearin, 7 Dec 1859; Z. W. Harriss, bm; Jno W. White, clk, wit; m 7 Feb 1859 by Nathl Nicholson, J. P.

Harris, John T. & Elizabeth Moore, 12 June 1855; Green R. Patterson, bm; Jno W. White, clk, wit; m 12 June 1855 by John S. Cheek, J. P.

Harris, John W. & Eveline Pegram, 20 Mar 1854; James H. Harris, bm; Jno W. White, C. C. C., wit; m 21 Mar 1854 by M. M. Drake, J. P.

Harris, Jones W. & Tabitha J. Riggan, 7 Jan 1858; Presley W. Harris, bm; Jno W. White, clk, wit; m 15 Jan 1858 by Saml Bobbitt, J. P.

Harris, Jordin & Salley Harvey, 7 Sept 1840; John Saintsing, bm; Burl Pitchford, J. P., wit.

Harris, Joseph (free col) & Sally Evans, 3 Feb 1853; Noah Evans, bm; Jno W. White, wit; m 4 Feb ___.

Harris, Jos. J. & Eliza Verser, 26 Mar 1852; Alfred A. Thompson, bm; Jno W. White, clk, wit; m 26 Mar 1852 by Saml Bobbitt, J. P.

Harris, Joseph J. & Mrs. Martha P. Ellington, 12 Jan 1860; Curtis Hardy, bm; Jno W. White, clk, wit; m 18 Jan 1860 by Wm. C. Clanton, J. P.

Harris, Joseph John, Jr., & Linny C. Riggan, 16 Mar 1852; Henry Hardy, bm; Jno W. White, clk, wit; m 17 Mar 1852 by Wm. C. Clanton, J. P.

Harris, Joshua & Jackuline E. Harris, 9 Sept 1834; Jacob Harris, bm; E. D. Drake, wit.

Harris, Joshua & Nancy Brame, 27 Oct 1835; Dudley Minga, bm; W. H. Foote, bm.

Harris, Kinchen & Marey Jones, 27 Oct 1824; Jacob Harriss, bm; E. D. Drake, wit.

Harris, Leonard & Polley Pike, 6 Aug 1801; Alanson Nicholson, bm; M. Duke Johnson, C. C. C., wit.

Harris, Nathaniel & Petty Ann Barker, 21 Dec 1847; F. A. Thornton, bm; Jno W. White, wit.

Harris, Nelson & Nancy Long, 30 Nov 1792; Jordan Harris, bm; M. D. Johnson ,C. C., wit.

Harris, Philemon & Daisy(?) Drew, 22 Jan 1816; Spious Bartlet, bm.

Harris, Pinkney N. & Rebecca Robertson, 2 July 1831; John Edwards, bm; C. Drake, C. C. C., wit.

Harris, Presley W. & Louiza H. Riggan, 7 Feb 1857; James W. Haris, bm; Jno W. White, clk, wit; m 12 Feb 1857 by Saml Bobbitt, J. P.

Harris, Pris & Hariot Jones, 30 Aug 1831; Joseph Evans, bm; C. Drake, C. C., wit.

Harris, Ransom & Eliza Davis, 11 Dec 1832; Richd Jordan, bm; C. Drake, C. C., wit.

Harris, Richard A. & Mary J. Pitchford, 22 Dec 1838; John E. Walker, bm.

Harris, Ridley L. & Lucy A. Pegram, 6 Oct 1864; B. F. Long, bm; Jno C. McCraw, wit; m 7 Oct 1864 by B. F. Long.

Harris, Robert & Tabbey Bobbit (no date); Simon Harris, bm.

Harris, Robert & Rachel Hollens, 23 Feb 1781; James Bennett, bm; Thos Machen, wit.

Harris, Robert (Robin) & Jane Lancaster, 5 Dec 1810; Robert N. Harris, bm; Jno C. Johnson, wit.

Harris, Robert & Martha Parish, 10 Mar 1812; Benjamin Nicholson, bm; Jno H. Green, wit.

Harris, Robert & Susan Durham, 4 Aug 1848; Henry Vaughan, bm; C. M. Cook, wit.

Harris, Robert M. & Elizabeth Duke, 13 Dec 1837; Drury A. Harris, bm; Edwd W. Best, wit.

Harris, Sampson W. & Mary F. Shearin, 17 Oct 1834; Gideon Harton, bm; E. D. Drake, clk, wit.

Harris, Samuel B. & Nancy J. Harris, 9 July 1849; Albert G. Jones, bm; Jno W. White, wit.

Harris, Sherwood S. & Sally Brame, 15 Feb 1837; David D. W. Dowtin, bm.

Harris, Simon & Martha Darden (no date); Robert Harris, bm.

Harris, Thomas & Winney Macklin, 28 Dec 1837; James Baskerville, bm; Burl Pitchford, J. P., wit.

Harris, Thomas E. & Mary T. Sledge, 13 Jan 1838; Doctor M. Harris, bm.

Harris, Thomas J. & Martha Hardy, 30 June 1856; R. K. Clanton, bm; Jno W. White, wit; m 1 July 1856 by Wm. C. Clanton, J. P.

Harris, Thomas W. & Martha H. Kearny, 8 May 1833; Benjamin T. Ballard, bm; C. Drake, C. C. C., wit.

Harris, Thompson & Elizabeth Smith, 22 Mar 1853; John D. Langford, bm; Jno W. White, wit; m 23 Mar 1855 by A. C. Harris, M. G.

Harris, Walter C. & Mary W. Southerland, 3 Feb 1866; R. E. Young, bm; William A. White, clk, wit; m 14 Feb 1866 by J. B. Solomon.

Harris, Wiley & Celey Harris, 24 Dec 1792; Silvanus Merritt, bm; M. D. Johnson, C. C., wit.

Harris, William & Patsy Wriggon, 19 Aug 1797; Alanson Nicholson, bm; Shd Green, wit.

Harris, William & Elizabeth Evans, 8 Oct 1858; John Stewart, bm; Jno W. White, clk, wit; m 14 Oct 1858 by A. L. Steed, J. P.

Harris, William A. & Adaline Pitchford, 16 Feb 1843; John F. Harris, bm; M. J. Montgomery, wit.

Harris, William F. & Mildred Pegram, 5 Aug 1831; Burwell Harris, bm; C. Drake, C. C., wit.

Harris, William F. & Nancy G. Parker, 16 May 1850; Newsom Harris, bm; Jno W. White, wit.

Harris, Wm. H. & Martha E. Wells, 5 Feb 1840; Edward Bowen, bm; Edwd W. Best, clk, wit.

Harris, William H. & Susan Sledge, 12 May 1842; Albert G. Jones, bm; Jno W. White, wit.

Harris, William H. & Martha A. B. Loyd, 19 Dec 1857; Green Harris, bm; Thos P. Paschall, wit; m 23 Dec 1857 by A. C. Harris, M. G.

Harris, William L. & Vermelia N. Harris, 30 Aug 1843; John Egerton, bm; M. J. Montgomery, wit.

Harris, William R. & Alpheus Ann Felts, 12 Apr 1851; Christopher N. Riggan, bm; Jno. W. White, clk, wit; m 16 Apr 1851 by Henry J. Macon, J. P.

Harris, Willie & Elizabeth Carter, 20 Dec 1824; Gideon Harris, bm; Jos A. Drake, wit.

Harris, Willis R. & Temperance Alston, 14 Mar 1821; Anthony Dowtin, bm; Cas Drake, C. C., wit.

Harris, Willson & Mary Anne King, 18 Sept 1813; Stephen H. Power, bm; Peter R. Davis, wit.

Harris, Wilmot E. & Catey Morris, 1 Jan 1799; Jeremiah Stephenson, bm; Shd Green, wit.

Harris, Yearba & Salley Egerton, 30 Jan 1804; Burwell Harris, bm; M. Duke Johnson, C. C., wit.

Harrison, Andrew & Frances Rittenbury, 11 Feb 1852; Alexander King, bm; R. B. Robinson, wit; m 11 Feb 1852 by Richard B. Robinson, J. P.

Harrison, Henry H. & Dollie Perdue, 6 Sept 1865; John R. Turnbull, bm; William A. White, clk, wit; m 7 Sept 1865 by R. B. Kingsbury, M. G.

Harrison, James & Hixcy Robertson, 11 Dec 1802; Charles Marshall, bm; S. Johnson, wit.

Harrison, John A. & Martha Ann Verell, 5 Oct 1849; William A. Jenkins, bm; Jno W. White, wit.

Harrison, Ned & Betsy Pitts, 1 July 1815; William Stokes, bm; W. Green, C. C. C., wit.

Harrison, Robert & Lucy Sims, 15 Dec 1795; William Garrot, bm; M. Duke Johnson, clk, wit.

Harrison, Robert W. & Julia Marie Haskins, 3 Feb 1845; Peter J. Turnbull, bm; M. J. Montgomery, wit.

Harrison, William & Betsey Ransom, 20 Dec 1780; Adkin McLamore, bm.

Harriss, Arthur & Molley Myrick, 4 Dec 1782; William Myrick, bm.

Harriss, Bennett & Lucy Dowden, 25 Sept 1810; John Lancaster, bm; Jno C. Johnson, D. C., wit.

Harriss, Gideon A. & Elizabeth F. Cook, 29 Apr 1844; Henry H. Burwell, bm; M. J. Montgomery, wit.

Harriss, Herbert & Betty Patterson, 23 Nov 1787; James Patterson, bm; M. Duke Johnson, C. C., wit.

Harriss, Howel & Tabitha Harris, 28 Dec 1811; Warwick Hazlewood, bm; Wm. Green, clk, wit.

Harriss, James H. & Sarah N. W. Egerton, 14 May 1855; R. D. Fleming, bm; Jno W. White, clk, wit; m 16 May 1855 by N. A. Purefoy, M. G.

Harriss, James P. & Mary Acre, 28 May 1864; William T. Thornton, bm; William A.White, wit.

Harriss, John A. & Sarah A. R. Nicholson, 8 Apr 1865; G. E. Shearin, bm; William A. White, wit.

Harriss, John C. & Nanny Harriss, 16 May 1856; Presley W. Harriss, bm; Jno W. White, clk, wit; m 18 May 1856 by Henry A. Foote, J. P.

Harriss, Jno P. & Mary A. R. Lancaster, 26 Feb 1848; Madison M. Haithcock, bm; Jno W. White, wit.

Harriss, Joseph A. & Nancy Harris, 31 Jan 1820; Anthony Dowtin, Jr., bm.

Harriss, Joseph J., Jr., & Mary Ann Hardy, 22 Mar 1864; Jos J. Harriss, Sr., bm; William A. White, clk, wit; m 23 Mar 1864 by C. M. Cook, J. P.

Harriss, Kinchen & Fanny Shearin, 16 Apr 1849; John L. Evans, bm; Jno W. White, wit.

Harriss, Kinchen H. & Sarah M. Lancaster, 10 Feb 1849; William R. Harriss, James E. Harriss, bm; Jno W. White, wit.

Harriss, Mordecai (col) (son of Chavis Harriss & Dilcey Rodwell) & Victoria Clanton (dau of Thomas & Lucy Hardy), 10 Aug 1867; William A. White, clk, wit; m 17 Nov 1867 by Saml Bobbitt, J. P.

Harriss, Nathaniel & Elizabeth A. Harriss, 22 Dec 1851; Michael Riggan, bm; Jno W. White, clk, wit; m 22 Dec 1851 by M. Riggan, J. P.

Harriss, Newsom & Nancy P. Pegram, 13 Dec 1843; Thos T. Davis, bm; M. J. Montgomery, wit.

Harriss, Randolph & Sarah Davis, 8 Nov 1809; John Mealer, bm; Jno C. Johnson ,D. C., wit.

Harriss, Reubin & Nancy Edwards, 14 Dec 1825; Pinckney N. Harriss, bm; M. M. Drake, wit.

Harriss, Robt G. & Jincey Walker, 23 Jan 1816; John J. Nicholson, bm; Will Green, C. C. C., wit.

Harris, Dr. Saml G. & Mary A. Plummer, 31 Dec 1857; R. L. Hendrick, bm; Jno W. White, wit.

Harriss, Thos P. & Martha Harriss, 23 Nov 1847; Saml B. Harriss, bm; Jno W. White, wit.

Harriss, Wm. H. & Mary E. A. Haggood, 13 Dec 1843; Thos T. Davis, bm; M. J. Montgomery, wit.

Hartien, John & Peggy _____, 9 Nov 1780; Robert Caller, bm.

Harton, Gideon & Dolly King Harriss, 27 July 1810; Jacob Stiner, bm; Jno C. Johnson, D. C. C., wit.

Harton, Hardaway & Amy Darden, 29 July 1796; Gideon Pegram; bm Shd Green, wit.

Harton, Robert P. & Priscilla J. Clark, 12 June 1852; Jas W. Jordan, bm; Jno W. White, wit; m 20 June 1852 by A. C. Harris, M. G.

Harton, Thomas, Jr., & Mary Wood, 24 Nov 1779; Blackmon Pardue, bm; Thos Machen, wit.

Harvey, George (col) & Sarah Garnes, 1 Apr 1867; P. J. Turnbull, bm; William A. White, clk, wit; m 3 Apr 1867 by Wm. Wallace White, J. P.

Harvey, Hilliard & Delia Ann Vaughan, 15 June 1852; Edward Harris, bm; Thos P. Paschall, wit; m 16 June 1852 by Edmd White, J. P.

Harvey, Nathl & Polly White, 24 Dec 1825; Henry Duncan, bm; C. Drake, clk, wit.

Harvey, Stephen A. & Martha Powell, 27 Nov 1839; William Mure, bm.

Harwell, James & Mary Nance, 30 Mar 1804; Wm. Malone, bm; M. Duke Johnson, C. C., wit.

Harwell, John H. & Rebecca Pettaway, 3 Mar 1800; Wm. Alexander, bm; M. Duke Johnson, C. C., wit.

Harwell, Thomas & Martha Smith, 5 Oct 1803; John Smith, bm;

Hase, James & Mary Jane Newman, 10 Feb 1866; Augustus A. Watkins, bm; William A. White, wit.

Hase, James M. & Sallie S. Stanback, 26 July 1866; John D. Langford, bm; William A. White, wit; m 28 July 1866 by Junius P. Moore, Elder.

Haslewood, W. G. & Virginia V. Perkinson, 13 Dec 1866; William A. White, clk, wit; m 13 Dec 1866 by Thos A. Montgomery, J. P.

Hatch, Cornelius & Sarah M. Smithwick, 5 June 1845; John R. Johnson, bm.

Hatch, George & Jane Wall, 28 Aug 1826; Phebey Wright, bm; Burl Pitchford, wit.

Hatchell, Elisha & Sarah Thomas, 7 Apr 1806; Samuel Paschall, bm; M. Duke Johnson, clk, wit.

Hathcock, John & Peggay Baker, 24 Jan 1804; Henry Capps, bm; M. Duke Johnson ,C. C., wit.

Hathcock, John & Amey Shearin, 5 Dec 1808; Benjamin Bradley, bm; M. Duke Johnson, C. C., wit.

Hathcoke, John & Betsey Bobbit, 19 Feb 1805; Higdon Moore, bm; M. Duke Johnson, clk, wit.

Haughan, John & Susannah Kinnamon, 4 Nov 1824; John Heavline, bm; E. D. Drake, wit.

Hawk, Frederick A. & Mrs. Martha E. White, 28 Aug 1866; William A. White, clk, wit; m 29 Aug 1866 by T. Page Ricaud, M. G.

Hawkins, Barney & Susanna Hawkins, 4 Nov 1833; William Hawkins, bm; Burl Pitchford, J. P.

Hawkins, Daniel (col) & Fanny Steed, 20 Apr 1867; Hugh J. Jones; bm; Jno C. McCraw, bm; m 20 Apr 1867 by A. L. Steed, J. P.

Hawkins, Edward (col) (son of Peter Hawkins & Caroline Little) & Sally Browne (dau of Sherrod & Phillis Browne) 22 June 1867; William A. White, clk, wit; m 22 June 1867 by N. A. H Goddin, M. G.

Hawkins, Francis & Lucy Ann Ward, 5 Jan 1850; James T. Alston, bm; Jno W. White, wit.

Hawkins, Jack (col) & Rosa Browne, 14 July 1866; Dr. Ridley Browne, bm; William A. White, clk, wit; m ___ July 1866 by Ridley Browne, J. P.

Hawkins, John & Holly Mills, 4 Dec 1850; William Kearsy, bm; C. Drake, C. C., wit.

Hawkins, John D., Jr., & Ann Clark, 30 June 1845; James B. Hawkins, bm; M. J. Montgomery, clk, wit.

Hawkins, John D., Jr. & Sallie Falkener, 2 Nov 1857; Kemp Plummer, Jr., bm; Jno W. White, clk, wit, m; 3 Nov 1857 by Robt B. Sutton, clergyman.

Hawkins, John F. & Rebecca T. Burrows, 28 Jan 1863; Wm. M. Watson, bm; Wm A. White, clk, wit; m 28 Jan 1863 by Jno B. Williams, M. G.

Hawkins, Joseph & Martha Alston, 2 Apr 1811; Philemon Hawkins, bm; Jno C. Johnson, wit.

Hawkins, M. T. & Mariah E. Baker, 13 Feb 1849; James W. Alston, bm; Jno W. White, wit.

Hawkins, Matthew & Aley Moosher, 26 Feb 1812; Frederick Parum, bm; Wm. Green, C. C., wit.

Hawkins, Micajah T. & Priscilla M. Moss, 20 Sept 1810; Seth Ward, bm; Jno C. Johnson, D. C., wit.

Hawkins, Nathaniel (col) & Patience Green, ____ 1863; [cohabitation bond acknowledged 1 Apr 1866]

Hawkins, Peter B. & Mary Eliz'th Williams, 14 June 1844; Joseph R. Hawkins, bm; M. J. Montgomery, wit.

Hawkins, Phil & _____, 28 May 1812; Wm. Green, bm; Wm. Green, C. C. C., wit.

Hawkins, Philemon & Mildred Twitty, 22 May 1780; John Scott, bm.

Hawkins, Philip & Elizabeth Moss, 13 May 1793; Wyatt Hawkins, bm; Richd Russell, wit.

Hawkins, Thomas (col) & Bettie Jones, 26 Dec 1865; Haywood Durham, bm; William A. White, wit.

Hawkins, William & Matilda Hill, 19 Dec 1825; Henry Shearin, bm; C. Drake, C. C. C., wit.

Hawkins, William J. & Mary A. Clark, 4 Jan 1833; James B. Hawkins, bm; M. J. Montgomery, wit.

Hawkins, Dr. Wm. J. & Lucy N. Clark, 24 Dec 1855; Phil B. Hawkins, bm; Jno W. White, clk, wit; m 27 Dec 1853 by L. L. Smith, M. G.

Hawkins, Willis A. & Leah T. Irwin, 3 Nov 1857; Alex B. Hawkins, bm; William A. White, wit; m 3 Nov 1857 by R. S. Mason, M. G.

Hawks, Anthony & Rebecca Duke, 21 Dec 1841; Peter D. Paschall, bm; M. J. Montgomery, wit.

Hawks, Benjamin & Sarah Beard, 22 Dec 1800; Devereux Mustian, bm; M. D. Johnson, C. C., wit.

Hawks, Benjamin & Rebecca Bartlet, 23 Aug 1832; James Hawks, bm; C. Drake, clk, wit.

Hawks, Benjamin & Mary C. Duke, 16 Nov 1843; James Hawks, bm.

Hawks, Erasmus (col) & Lucy Stewart, 30 June 1866; Gideon W. Nicholson, bm; William A. White, clk, wit; m 1 July 1866 by L. C. Perkinson, M. G.

Hawks, Fedrick & Nancy Robertson, 20 Oct 1798; James Ellis, bm; Shd Green, wit.

Hawks, Frederick & Susannah Perkinson, 6 Jan 1823; Churchwel Bartlet, bm; C. Drake, C. C. C., wit.

Hawks, James & Mary Wortham, 18 Dec 1832; Churchwel Bartlet, bm; C. Drake, C. C. C., wit.

Hawks, Jereman & Parthena Tally, 28 Mar 1854; John Hicks, bm; Jno W. White, C. C. C., wit; m 30 Mar 1854 by J. H. Hawkins, J. P.

Hawks, Jereman & Elizabeth Colemon, 21 Dec 1860; Frederick King, bm; Jno W. White, wit.

Hawks, Jermiah & Sally Hicks, 28 Oct 1796; Zachariah Ellis, bm; M. D. Johnson, C. C., wit.

Hawks, Jno & Elizabeth Smith, 13 May 1802; Brooks Neal, bm; Gideon Johnson ,wit.

Hawks, John W. & Polley Nuchcoals, 31 July 1834; Thomas A. Langley, bm; Burl Pitchford, J. P., wit.

Hawks, Nathaniel S. (son of Frederick & Susan Hawks) & Catharine W. Hicks (dau of John & Rowan Hicks), 22 Nov 1867; William A. White, clk, wit; m 27 Nov 1867 by L. C. Perkinson, M. G.

Hawks, Thomas & Sarah Ann Williams, 12 Mar 1824; William Andrews, bm; M. M. Drake, wit.

Haws, Henry H. & Synthia H. Jones, 4 Apr 1831; Thomas W. Pegram, bm; C. Drake, C. C. C., wit.

Hayes, Ezekel & Sally Cogwell, 25 Jan 1825; Zachariah Cogwell, bm.

Hayes, Hardy & Lucy Pendergrass, 14 July 1866; Peter R. Davis, bm; Wm. J. White, wit; m 14 __ 1866 by P. H. Joyner.

Hayes, James & Mary Jane Newman, 10 Feb 1866; William A. White, clk, wit; m 15 Feb 1866 by J. W. Wellons, M. G.

Hayes, Jno W. & Elizabeth J. Jones, 22 Dec 1852; A. H. Davis, bm; Jno W. White, clk, wit; m 12 Jan 1853 by N. F. Reid.

Hayes, Peter (col) & Louisanna Alston, 20 Feb 1867; William A. White, clk, wit; m 21 Feb 1867 by William Hodges, M. G.

Hayes, William & Martha Harrison, 6 Dec 1806; Lot Hazard, bm; Jo Terrell, D. C. C., wit.

Hayle, John & Elizabeth H. Vaughan, 20 Oct 1840; Samuel Edwards, bm.

Hayle, William J. & Mary K. Wright, 5 Dec 1866; Lewis P. Edwards, bm; Jord. H. Foster, wit; m 8 Dec 1866 by P. H. Joyner.

Haythcock, William & Nancy Capps, 23 Dec 1836; Henry D. Martin, bm; E. D. Drake, clk, wit.

Hazard, Lewis & Susanna Davis, 21 Dec 1799; Nathl Baxter, bm.

Hazard, Lott & Tabitha Tunstall, 22 Jan 1812; Lewis Hazard, bm; Jo Terrell, D. C. C., wit.

Hazelwood, Warwick & Mary Felts, 29 Dec 1783; Randolph Felts, bm; M. D. Johnson, wit.

Hearne, William & Eliza J. Cheek, 4 May 1865; Thomas D. Williams, bm; William A. White, clk, wit; m 7 May 1865 by John B. Williams, M. G.

Heathcock, George & Patsy Mardry, 24 Oct 1798; William Robertson, bm; S. Green, wit.

Heathcock, Peter & Susanna Moore, 28 Dec 1818; William Saintsing, bm.

Heathcotte, Alfred L. & Josephine H. Bobbitt, 2 Apr 1867; Dr. Matthew W. Williams, bm; William A. White, clk, wit; m 4 Apr 1867 by Thos J. Pitchford, J. P.

Heavilin, Benjamin & Mary Rose (no date); John Long, bm; M. D. Johnson, wit.

Helton, Joseph & Dison Benson, 2 Nov 1780; John Basford, bm.

Henderson, Archd G. & Ann Bullock, 28 Sept 1822; H. L. Plummer, bm.

Henderson, Joshua (col) & Sarah Sims, 17 Nov 1866; William A. White, clk, wit; m 17 Nov 1866 by Wm. Wallace White, J. P.

Henderson, Leonard & Lucy D. Hawkins, 17 May 1845; K. P. Alston, bm; M. J. Montgomery, wit.

Henderson, Leonard & Lizzie M. Green, 25 Aug 1863; Nathaniel R. Jones, bm; William A. White, wit; m 10 Sept 1863 by William Hodges, M. G.

Henderson, Oscar & Lizzie Bullock, 29 Dec 1866; William A. White, clk, wit; m 31 Dec 1866 by Wm Wallace White, J. P.

Henderson, William F. & Agnas F. E. Hare, 19 July 1838; Moses Neal, bm.

Hendrick, Alexander G. & Martha L. Harton, 27 Sept 1842; Joseph F. Allen, bm; M. J. Montgomery, wit.

Hendrick, Alexander W. & Isabella Rowland, 8 Dec 1859; Saml C. Harris, bm; Jno W. White, clk, wit; m 21 Dec 1859 by Charles J. Jones, J. P.

Hendrick, George J. & Eliza Harton, 12 Mar 1839; Guilford W. Harris, bm; Edwd W. Best, clk, wit.

Hendrick, John J. & Martha L. Harris, 18 May 1814; Gideon Harton, bm; M. J. Hawkins, wit.

Hendrick, Stephen & Molley Johnson, 16 May 1788; John Johnson, bm; M. Duke Johnson, C. C., wit.

Hendrick, Thomas R. & Catharine W. Mayfield, 8 July 1856; Jas T. Russell, bm; Jno W. White, wit; m 17 July 1856 by Thos G. Lowe, M. G.

Hendrick, Thomas R. & Mary J. Walker, 30 Jan 1860; James T. Russell, bm; Jno W. White, clk, wit; m 8 Feb 1860 by B. F. Long, M. G.

Hendrick, Wm. & Nancy T. Russell, 19 Nov 1817; Edward Cotten, bm; W. A. K. Falkener, wit.

Hewitt, Charles E. & Lucy Janis, 7 July 1859; Tippoo Brownlow, bm; Jno W. White, clk, wit; m 7 July 1859 by Chas Skinner, J. P.

Hicks, A. J. & Betsey R. Burchette, 17 Dec 1856; Edward Harris, bm; Thos P. Paschall, wit; m 17 Dec 1856 by Thos P. Paschall, J. P.

Hicks, Absalom & Sarahan Allen, 7 Dec 1809; Stephen Hester, bm; Jo Terrell, D. C., wit.

Hicks, Anthony (col) & Nancy Williams, 21 July 1866; W. A. J. Nicholson, bm; William A. White, clk, wit; m 22 July 1866 by James P. Moore, M. G.

Hicks, Benjamin & Nancy Fogg, 22 Apr 1834; Martin Fogg, bm; E. D. Drake, clk, wit.

Hicks, Benjamine S. & Nancy A. Bowdon, 28 Aug 1848; Jno White, bm.

Hicks, Charles & Susannah Bohanan, 4 Nov 1782; Samuel Rose, bm; M. D. Johnson, C. C., wit.

Hicks, Daniel & Temperance Parish, 23 Oct 1826; William Mustian, bm; M. M. Drake, wit.

Hicks, Daniel & Martha Stephenson, 11 Oct 1841; George Wortham, bm; M. J. Montgomery, wit.

Hicks, David & Mary M. Shearin, 8 May 1837; Nathan Milam, bm.

Hicks, Elza & Elizabeth Duke, 24 Jan 1838; Edward Power, bm.

Hicks, Isaac & Polley Werrel, 7 Mar 1829; John Paschall, bm; Burl Pitchford, J. P., wit.

Hicks, James & Suckey Hastings, 25 Nov 1785; Charles Hicks, bm; M. Duke Johnson, wit.

Hicks, John & Janney Semmons, 14 Jan 1782; Lewis Patterson, bm; Thos Machen, C. C., wit.

Hicks, John & Roan Paschall, 24 Nov 1840; James Samuel Walker, bm.

Hicks, John & Mary Harton, 5 Aug 1853; A. G. Hendrick, bm; Jno W. White, wit, m 17 Aug 1864 by A. G. Harris, M. G.

Hicks, John, Jr., & Patsey King, 18 May 1818; W. A. K. Falkener, bm; Wm. Green, C. W. C. C., wit.

Hicks, John B. & Betsey Marrable, 28 Oct 1817; Frs. D. Allen, bm; Wm. Falkener, wit.

WARREN COUNTY MARRIAGES

Hicks, Jno B. & Sally B. Montgomery, 18 June 1836; Richard Davison, bm; E. D. Drake, clk, wit.

Hicks, John W. & Mary S. Hicks, 11 Sept 1849; Aaron A. Hudgins, bm; Jno W. White, wit.

Hicks, Lewis & Mary S. Davis, 11 Dec 1840; John L. Foote, bm; Edwd W. Best, wit.

Hicks, Thomas & Sally E. Lewis, 7 May 1822; Thomas Organ, bm; Frs Jones, wit.

Hicks, Wiley & Lucy Carroll, 25 Nov 1823; Wm Mustian, bm; E. D. Drake, wit.

Hicks, William & Betsey Crutchfield, 18 Feb 1800; Jeremiah Hawkins, bm; M. D. Johnson, C. C. C., wit.

Hicks, William & Susanah Towns, 18 Jan 1809; Benjamin Johnson, bm; M. Duke Johnson, C. C., wit.

Hicks, William, Jr., & Sarah Robins, 11 __ June 1833; Baxter King, bm; E. D. Drake, clk, wit.

Hicks, Wm. F. & Mary Wynn, 2 May 1863; William T. Paschall, bm; Wm. A. White, wit; m 5 May 1863 by J. H. Wheeler.

Higgs, Allen H. & Eliza G. Sale, 9 Jan 1833; Edward W. Best, bm; C. Drake, C. C., wit.

Higgs, William H. & Everline Smith, 22 Dec 1854; Hames B. Lewis, bm; Wm. W. Daniel, clk, wit.

Higgson, William & Nancey Jenkins, 14 Sept 1779; John Jenkins, bm; Thos Machen, wit.

Hight, James B. & Melissa D. Duke, 18 Nov 1843; William Matthews, bm; M. J. Montgomery, wit.

Hill, Benjamin & Nancy F. Bobbitt, 29 June 1813; Drury Bobbitt, Jr., bm; Wm. Green, C. C. C., wit.

Hill, Hartwell (free col) & Mary Bishop, 30 Apr 1843; M. J. Montgomery, bm.

Hill, Henry & Winifred Alston, 10 May 1780; William Christmas, bm; Henry Pope, wit.

Hill, Robert & Martha Johnson, 6 Nov 1779; Thomas H. Hall, bm; Thos Machen, wit.

Hilliard, Dandridge B. & Annie E. Hilliard, 1 Oct 1857; Wm. F. Beckham, bm; Jno. W. White, wit.

Hilliard, John & Eliza Tunstall, 9 Dec 1806; Sugan Johnson, bm.

Hilliard, John & Polley Newman, 19 Dec 1827; Burrell Pitchford, Jr., bm; Burl Pitchford, wit.

Hilliard, John Jr. (son of John Sr. & Mary Hilliard) & Martha C. Cole (dau of Daniel & Catharine D. Cole), 17 Oct 1867; William A. White, clk, wit; m 23 Oct 1867 by J. W. Wellons, M. G.

Hilliard, Thos & Salley Bowdown, _____; Vincent Allen, bm.

Hilliard, Thomas D. & Eugenia A. Holloway, 19 Sept 1862; Thomas E. White, bm; Wm. A. White, clk, wit; m 22 Sept 1862 by Lemmon Shell, M. G.

Hindsman, John & Catharine Brown, 24 July 1808; William Brown, bm; M. Duke Johnson, C. C., wit.

Hines, Henry & Polley Evans, 9 Feb 1805; Jones Williams, bm; M. Duke Johnson C. C., wit.

Hines, Turner S. & Sarah A. Ogburn, 21 Jan 1853; Benja W. Hines, bm; Jno W. White, wit.

Hinton, David (of Wake Co.) & Mary B. Carr, 24 Mar 1852; J. Buxton Williams, bm; Jno W. White, wit; m 31 Mar 1852 by Robt O. Burton, M. G.

Hite, James L. & Mary Jane Moore, 30 Sept 1847; Thomas P. Walker, bm; Jno W. White, wit.

Hix, Little Bury & Margaret Smith, 15 Dec 1831; Richard Davis, bm.

Hix, Little Bury & Mary Walker, 1 Apr 1848; Henry H. Fitts, bm; O. D. Fitts, wit.

Hodge, William H. & Frances Boyd, 30 Dec 1828; Henry T. Clark, bm; E. D. Drake, wit.

Hogwood, James & Martha Davis, 31 Mar 1821; Edmd White, bm.

Hogwood, William & Mary Davis, 15 July 1798; John C. Green, bm; S. Green, wit.

Hohammer, Philip & Joice Pattershall, 31 Aug 1785; Richard Ellis, bm; M. Duke Johnson, wit.

Holden, Warren & Polly Beard, 29 Oct 1811; Samuel Holding, bm; Wm. Green, C. C., wit.

Holding, Samuel & Betsy Baird, 30 Nov 1809; William Baird, bm; Jno C. Johnson, D. C. C., wit.

Holliman, William & Rachel Coleman, 12 Dec 1783; William Felts, bm; M. Duke Johnson, wit.

Holloway, Daniel & Polly Hardy, 14 Jan 1817; Wm Hardy, bm; Wm. Green, C. C., wit.

Hooper, Dr. Wm. W. & Mary J. Kearney, 23 Dec 1852; J. C. Hooper, bm; Jno W. White, wit.

Hopkins, Henry L. (of Petersburg, VA) & Bettie M. Feild, 2 Apr 1866; William A. White, clk, wit; m 3 Apr 1866 by Churchill J. Gibson, M. G. of Petersburg, VA.

Hopkins, John & Sarah Alexander, 22 Dec 1785; James Caller, bm; M. D. Johnson, wit.

Horton, M. M. & Lucy A. Terrell, 27 Mar 1866; William A. White, clk, wit; m 29 Mar 1866 by T. B. Kingsbury, M. G.

House, Dudley, Jr., & Sarah Arnold, 5 Sept 1806; Dudley House, Sr., bm; Jo Terrell, D. C. C., wit.

House, Lott & Elisabeth Dent, 29 May 1792; Brittain Nicholson, bm.

House, William & Sarah Ann Harrison, 18 Dec 1801; Isham Robertson, bm; Sugan Johnson, wit.

Howard, Joseph (col) (son of Green Wall & Ellis Howard) & Mary Fitts (dau of Washington & Milly), 17 Aug 1867; William A. White, wit; m 18 Aug 1867 by L. C. Perkinson, M. G.

Howard, Peter (col) & Peggy Love, 21 Jan 1867; William A. White, clk, wit; m 2 Feb 1867 by L. C. Perkinson, M. G.

Howard, Waller (col) & Minerva Fitts, 4 June 1866; Edward H. Plummer, bm; William A. White, clk, wit; m 1 July 1866 by L. C. Perkinson, M. G.

Howard, William & Salley Childress, 19 Dec 1784; Charles Elams, bm; M. Duke Johnson, wit.

Howard, William & Ann E. Wilson, 18 Sept 1827; Thomas H. Brackett, bm; M. M. Drake, wit.

Howard, William E. & Arrena B. Maclin, 8 Aug 1854; Wm. H. Mayo, bm; Jno W. White, wit.

Howard, William T. & Lucy E. M. Fitts, 24 Dec 1850; George A. Howard, bm; Jno W. White, wit.

Howel, Charles & Delila Macklin, 31 Mar 1842; John Ciphers, bm; Burl Pitchford, J. P., wit.

Howell, Albert & Adeline Macklin, 19 Sept 1860; James Garns, bm; William A. White, wit.

Howell, John & Mary Perry, 28 Oct 1783; Joseph Darnall, bm; M. Duke Johnson, wit.

Howell, Paul & Elizabeth Thornton (no date); George King, bm; M. Duke Johnson, C. C., wit.

Howerton, John & Salley Key, 13 Jan 1806; Pleasant Wilson, bm; Jo Terrell, D. C. C., wit.

Howze, Isaac & Amey Robinson, 19 Sept 1780; William Wortham, bm; Thos Machen, wit.

Howze, Isaac & Sarah W. Ward, 17 Dec 1810; James K. Goodloe, bm; M. Duke Johnson, C. C., wit.

Howze, William & Burchet Robertson, 9 May 1785; William Johnson, Jr., bm; M. Duke Johnson, wit.

Hubbard, Henry (col) & Marinda Lester, 16 Aug 1866; William A. White, clk, wit; m 19 Aug 1866 by L. C. Perkinson, M. G.

Hubbard, John G. & Sarah E. Brickle, 16 July 1863; Jno C. McCraw, bm; Jno C. McCraw, wit, m; 16 July 1863 by N. A. Purefoy, M. G.

Hudgins, Aaron A. & Caroline J. Williams, 10 Feb 1858; Jno C. McCraw, bm; Jno W. White, clk, wit, m; 10 Feb 1858 by J. B. Solomon.

Hudson, Henry & Ann Green, 4 Aug 1782; John Scott, bm; M. Duke Johnson, wit.

Hudson, Henry & Tempy Gordon, 5 July 1797; William Thompson, bm; Shd Green, wit.

Hudson, John & Lucy Thompson, 12 Feb 1784; Thomas Hudson, bm; M. D. Johnson, wit.

Hudson, John & Elisabeth Goodrich, 10 Feb 1788; Jesse Acock, bm; M. Duke Johnson, C. C., wit.

Hudson, Joseph & Anne Russill, 15 Oct 1782; John Thompson, bm; M. D. Johnson, C. C., wit.

Hudson, Richard & Nancy Walker, 8 July 1810; Benja Ivey, bm; M. D. Johnson, C. C., wit.

Hudson, Thomas & Roday Acock, 12 Feb 1784; John Hudson, bm; M. Duke Johnson, wit.

Huff, George & Amey D. Bowles, _____ 179-; James Huff, bm; M. D. Johnson, C. C., wit.

Huff, James & Mary Barton, 26 May 1793; George Huff, bm; _____ Russell, wit.

Huff, Jno & Sarah Allen, 12 May 1780; William Allen, bm; Thos Machen, wit.

Huff, Reuben & Ann Allan, 3 Feb 1798; James Allen, bm; M. D. Johnson, C. C., wit.

Hughes, John & Mary Cyprous, 12 June 1850; Harrison Hicks, bm; Jno W. White, wit.

Hughes, William C. & Martha Ann Adams, 16 Dec 1828; Anthony Dowtin, bm; M. M. Drake, wit.

Hundeley, William A. & Elizabeth A. Lewis, 26 July 1831; Samuel W. Lafater, bm; C. Drake, C. C., wit.

Hundley, John & Eugenia Odam, 12 Jan 1858; J. A. Waddell, bm; Jno W. White, clk, wit; m 14 Jan 1858 by J. Tillett, M. G.

Hundley, William J. & Mahala W. Langford, 10 Mar 1838; Green D. Jenkins, bm.

Hunt, A. A. & Bettie Wilson, 13 Dec 1865; Revd. J. B. Solomon, bm; William A. White, wit; m 20 Dec 1865 by J. B. Solomon, M. G.

Hunt, Groves & Susan Laughter, 3 Oct 1811; Michael Hunt, bm; Wm. Green, C. C. C., wit.

Hunt, Lewis (col) & Rhoda Thornton, 28 Dec 1866; William A. White, clk, wit; m 31 Dec 1866 by R. S. F. Peete, J. P.

Hunt, Samuel & Babba Nichols, 12 Dec 1780; Julius Nichols, bm.

Hunt, Samuel R. & Indianah Harriss, 2 Oct 1850; P. R. Merryman, bm; Jno W. White, wit.

Hunt, Solomon & Sarah Jane Aikin, 6 Mar 1858; Anthony M. Bobbitt, bm; William A. White, wit; m 11 Mar 1858 by Saml Bobbitt, J. P.

Hunt, Thomas P. & Elizabeth Duke, 24 Sept 1802; Archibald Lytle, bm; Sugan Johnson, wit.

Hunter, Anderson & Martha C. Ward, 29 Sept 1813; Isaac Howze, Jr., bm; Jno H. Green, wit.

Hunter, Fox & Lucy W. Evans, 15 Sept 1831; Richard B. Robinson, bm; C. Drake, clk, wit.

Hunter, Dr. G. L. & Lucy Yancey, 21 Dec 1863; P. J. Turnbull, bm; William A. White, wit; m 23 Dec 1863 by William Hodges, M. G.

Hunter, H. Holmes & Mary H. Cheek, 15 Feb 1858; P. H. Joyner, bm; Jno W. White, clk, wit, m 16 Feb 1858 by P. H. Joyner.

Hunter, Henry B. & Mary Williams, 28 Jan 1813; Benjamin B. Hunter, John H. Hawkins, bm.

Hunter, Henry B., Jr., & Emma P. Jones, 25 June 1866; William J. White, bm; William A. White, clk, wit; m 27 June 1866 by J. P. Moore, M. G.

Hunter, John (col) (son of John Goodloe & Louisa Hunter) & Amy Watson (dau of Daniel Stainback & Sylvia Watson), 7 Dec 1867; William A. White, clk, wit; m 7 Dec 1867 by N. A. Purefoy, M. G.

Hunter, William & Sarah E. Jones, 6 Oct 1815; Seth Ward, Auguston Alston, bm; Will Green, C. C., wit.

Huskey, Nathaniel & Catey Coulclough, 2 Apr 1782; Richard Townes, bm; M. Duke Johnson, wit.

Hux, Malichi & Priscilla Cullum, 31 Dec 1830; H. Holt, bm; J. H. Harwell, wit.

Hyde, Charles P. & Eliza D. Allen, 29 May 1855; Will A. Jenkins, bm; Jno W. White, wit; m 31 May 1855 by N. Z. Graves.

Hyman, Francis M. & Ella S. Jones, 5 Oct 1865; Alex W. Waddell, bm; William A. White, clk, wit; m 6 Oct 1865 by J. R. Finley, D. D.

Iles, William & Lucy J. Bobbitt, 31 Jan 1848; William H. Bobbitt, bm; Jno. W. White, wit.

Ingraham, Henry (col) & Abby Christmas 20 Apr 1866; Weldon E. Davis, bm; William A. White, clk, wit; m 26 Aug 1866 b L. C. Perkinson ,M. G.

Ingram, Abram (col) & Julia Read, 24 Dec 1866; William A. White, clk, wit; m 26 Dec 1866 by Jno Watson, J. P.

Ingram, Benjamin & Letice Perry, 16 Nov 1781; Joshua Perry, bm.

Ingram, Presley C. & Eliza E. Bobbitt, 11 Apr 1857; Owen F. Myrick, Jr., bm; Jno W. White, clk, wit; m 15 Apr 1857 by P. H. Smith, M. G.

Ingram, Willis P. & Ann E. Ingram, 9 Oct 1829; Thomas J. Judkins, bm.

Isham, David & Rebecca Robberds, 7 Feb 1806; Philip Robberds, bm; Jo Terrell, D. C. C., wit.

Isles, David & Julia Ann Bobbitt, 6 Aug 1844; John R. Bobbitt, bm; M. J. Montgomery, wit.

Ivey, Charles E. & Sarah L. Harris, 23 May 1867; William A. White, clk, wit; m 26 May 1867 by P. H. Joyner.

Ivie, John (of Brunswick Co., VA) & Betsey M. Floyd, 17 Dec 1803; George Finch, bm; M. Duke Johnson, C. C., wit.

Ivie, Peter & Betsey Wills, 20 July 1786; Benjamin Ivie, bm; M. Duke Johnson, wit.

Jackson, F. S. & Caroline R. Gee, 18 May 1846; Peter J. Turnbull, bm; M. J. Montgomery, wit.

Jackson, John & Mary (or Amey) Brintle (no date); William Russel, bm; M. D. Johnson, wit.

Jackson, Leroy & Sarah A. C. Daniel, 8 Jan 1836; James M. Daniel, bm; E. D. Drake, clk, wit.

Jackson, Mark L. & Siller Rainey, 9 Dec 1784; John Langfurd, bm; M. Duke Johnson, wit.

Jackson, Solomon & ____ Bell, 3 Aug 1782; James Milam, bm; M. Duke Johnson, wit.

Jackson, William C. & Frances J. Tisdale, 26 Aug 1848; William R. Toone, bm; Jno W. White, wit.

Jackson, Wycke & Polly Dye, 28 Oct 1801; Abraham Mayfield, bm; Sugan Johnson, wit.

James, George & Salley Bohanan (no date); Daniel Duke, bm.

James, Henry L. & Emeline Harris, 27 Jan 1844; Henry M. Laughter, bm; M. J. Montgomery, wit.

James, Thomas, Jr., & Lucy T. Powell, 5 Jan 1858; A. A. Hudgins, bm; Jno W. White, wit, m 6 Jan 1858 by Thos J. Judkins, J. P.

Jeffers, James & Mary Acree, 24 Jan 1810; Thomas Bell, Sr., bm; Jno C. Johnson, D. C. C., wit.

Jeffers, John & Hannah Harrison, 24 Oct 1809; Thomas Bell, bm; Jno C. Johnson, D. C. C., wit.

Jefferson, Samuel & Martha Bowers, 1 Sept 1796; Lucas Gee, Alexr Falconer, bm; M. D. Johnson, C. C., wit.

Jeffres, Acrey & Salley Martin, 1 Aug 1799; John Randolph, bm; Shd Green, wit.

Jenkins, A. S. & Mrs. Martha E. Coleman, 3 Mar 1857; T. P. Walker, bm; William A. White, wit; m 5 Mar 1857 by Saml Bobbitt, J. P.

Jenkins, Belfield & Eliza Dobbins, 21 Dec 1838; Benjamin Jenkins, bm.

Jenkins, Green D. & Sarah L. Moseley, 16 Dec 1828; John V. Cawthorn, bm; M. M. Drake, wit.

Jenkins, John & Mary Wortham, 18 Dec 1841; Charles H. King, bm.

Jenkins, John (col) & Cornelia Green, 7 Mar 1866; Joseph Gholson, bm; William A. White, clk, wit; m 8 Mar 1866 by T. Page Ricaud, M. G.

Jenkins, Philip & Martha Wortham, 21 June 1825; Jordan H. Foster, bm; Matthew M. Drake, wit.

Jenkins, Thomas T. & Mary King, 28 Dec 1817; Wilmut E. Egerton, bm; Wm. Green, wit.

Jenkins, Thomas T. & Martha White, 24 Jan 1848; Michael Riggan, bm; Jno W. White, wit.

Jenkins, William (col) (son of William & Susan) & Elizabeth Drew (dau John & Ann), 2 Nov 1867; William A. White, clk, wit; m 3 Nov 1867 by Wm. Wallace White, J. P.

Jenkins, William F. & Caroline Shearin, 4 Dec 1832; George W. Shearin, bm; Jno W. White, wit.

Jiggits, Nicholas (col) & Polly Cole, 22 Dec 1865; James T. Russell, bm; William A. White, clk, wit; m 26 Dec 1865 by Jas. T. Russell, J. P.

Jiggitts, Anthony (col) & Frances Hunt, 9 May 1867; E. H. Plummer, bm; William A. White, clk, wit; m 12 May 1867 by L. C. Perkinson, M. G.

Jiggitts, Daniel (col) & Ann Hunt, 9 May 1867; E. H. Plummer, bm; William A. White, clk, wit; m 12 May 1867 by L. C. Perkinson, M. G.

Jinkings, Wilia & Nancy Tally, 14 Aug 1839; William Smith, bm; Burl Pitchford, J. P.

Jinkins, Green & Salley Green, 27 Dec 1802; Pleasant Fowler, bm; M. Duke Johnson, C. C., wit.

Jinkins, Willie & Febay Procter, 9 Dec 1799; John Smith, bm; Shd Green, wit.

Johns, William & Anne Beasly, 14 Oct 1795; Barnit Beasley, bm; J. Moss, wit.

Johnson, Andrew J. & Elizabeth Shearin, 2 Oct 1839; Alexander Nicholson, bm; Edwd W. Best, clk, wit.

Johnson, Benjamin & Nancy Robins, 2 Sept 1831; Benjamin Hawks, bm; C. Drake, C. C., wit.

Johnson, Benja., Jr., & Mary Duke, 21 Dec 1833; Gideon Harton, bm; E. D. Drake, clk, wit.

Johnson, Charles M. & Sally Myrick, 14 June 1815; John Sledge, bm; Jno H. Green, wit.

Johnson, Crawford & Susanah Willis (no date); Delk Mabry, bm; M. Duke Johnson, C. C., wit.

Johnson, Daniel & Rebeckah Wilson, 22 Dec 1795; Michael Johnson, bm; J. Moss, wit.

Johnson, Denis (col) & Mary Cheek, 2 Mar 1867; Wm. J. White, bm; William A. White, clk, wit; m 2 Mar 1867 by A. L. Steed, J. P.

Johnson, Ephraim & Mary L. Read, 29 Nov 1837; Micajah Hilliard, bm.

Johnson, Ephraim & Mrs. Sarah King, 13 June 1864; E. H. Russell, bm; William A. White, clk, wit; m 16 June 1864 by Jas T. Russell, J. P.

Johnson, Francis & Jeny Barner, 22 Jan 1817; David Dancy, bm; Wm. Green, C. C. C., wit.

Johnson, Gedion & Gilley Simms, 20 Apr 1783; John Sails, bm; M. Duke Johnson, C. C., wit.

Johnson, George E. & Lucy Askew, 26 June 1852; John J. Vaughan, bm; Jno W. White, clk, wit; m 7 July 1852 by J. S. Cheek, J. P.

Johnson, George T. & Susan Watkins, 27 Sept 1848; William Matthus, bm; Jno W. White, wit.

Johnson, Howell & Holley Crowder, 23 Nov ———.

Johnson, Jacob (col) & Rebecca Wright, 25 Oct 1865; James H. Mayfield, bm; William A. White, clk, wit; m 28 Oct 1865 by Jas T. Russell, J. P.

Johnson, Jacob & Sarah Carroll, 21 Feb 1867; William A. White, clk, wit; m 23 Feb 1867 by R. D. Paschall, J. P.

Johnson, James R. & Nancy Nuckerls, 1 Dec 1807; William Haygood, bm; Jo Terrell, C. C., wit.

Johnson, Jesse & Milley Ellis, 21 Dec 1805; Thomas Talley, bm; Jo Terrell, D. C. C., wit.

Johnson, Jesse & Martha Verser, 13 Oct 1828; Thomas J. Judkins, bm. M. M. Drake, wit.

Johnson, Jesse & Frances Gardner, 11 Jan 1834; William Meacham, bm; E. D. Drake, clk, wit.

Johnson, John & Betsey Williams, 17 Aug ____; Thomas Wms, bm; M. Duke Johnson, C. C., wit.

Johnson, John & Martha Newton, 14 July 1788; John Newton, bm; M. Duke Johnson, C. C., wit.

Johnson, John & Mary Dowtin, 5 July 1836; William Pardue, bm; E. D. Drake, clk, wit.

Johnson, John H. & Lucy Wilson, 1 Sept 1843; Thos H. Christmas, bm.

Johnson, John R. & Martha E. Bartholomew, 15 June 1859; Willoughby H. Stallings, bm; Jno W. White, clk, wit; m 15 June 1859 by William A. Dowtin, J. P.

Johnson, John W. & Rebeccah D. Davis, 11 Mar 1830; Jno Langley, bm;

Johnson, Joseph & Susanah Derham, 4 Mar 1791; James Baxter, bm.

Johnson, Joseph & Polley Thomas, 28 Mar 1800; Abner Mills, bm; Shd Green, wit.

Johnson, Joseph P. & Mary E. Beaman, 31 Dec 1833; Solomon Perdue, bm.

Johnson, Kemp & Nancy Pardue, 23 Oct 1802; Charles Bennitt, bm; M. D. Johnson, C. C., wit.

Johnson, Richard & Elizabeth Marshall, 31 July 1833; William E. Andrews, bm.

Johnson, Richard (col) & Ann Johnson, 21 Dec 1866; William W. White, clk, wit; m 21 Dec 1866 by Thomas J. Paschall, J. P.

Johnson, Robert R. & Ann Russell, 9 June 1826; Isham H. Daves, bm; M. M. Drake, wit.

Johnson, Terry & Susanah Turner, 23 Dec 1790; William Rivers, bm; M. D. Johnson, C. C., wit.

Johnson, Turner & Betsey Paschell, 20 Mar 1795; Samuel Paschall, bm; J. Moss, wit.

Johnson, William & Martha Person, 24 Nov 1779; Thomas Machen, bm; Nelson Cole, wit.

Johnson, William, Jr., & Martha Person, 24 Jan 1782; William Johnson, Sr., bm.

Johnson, William H. & Frances A. Parrish, 30 June 1853; James N. Harper, bm; Jno W. White, wit.

Johnson, William W. & Judith Chappell Reevis, 11 Mar 1802; Henry King, bm; M. D. Johnson, C. C., wit.

Johnston, Anthony M. & Nancy S. D. Newell, 15 Jan 1844; Richard M. Johnston, bm; M. J. Montgomery, wit.

Johnston, Anthony M. & Octavia D. Shearin, 28 Sept 1865; John W. Riggan, bm; William A. White, clk, wit, m 4 Oct 1865 by Chas M. Cook, J. P.

Johnston, Atherton & Elizth B. Shearin, 9 Dec 1843; Richd H. Johnson, bm; M. J. Montgomery, wit.

Johnston, Blake (formerly slave of A. M. Johnston) & Amanda Johnston (formerly slave of Jno P. Johnston), 5 Feb 1866; Anthony M. Johnson, bm; William A. White, clk, wit; m 5 Feb 1866 by C. M. Cook, J. P.

Johnston, Daniel (col) (son of James & Tiller) & Mariah Wilson (dau of Frank & Mariah), 16 Nov 1867; William A. White, clk, wit, m 17 Nov 1867 by Thos J. Pitchford, J. P.

Johnston, Doctor M. & Elizabeth Sledge, 30 Oct 1835; David W. Dowtin, bm.

Johnston, Judge Daniel (col) (son of Daniel & Nancy) & Sarah Powell (dau of Robert & Rainey), 26 Aug 1867; William A. White, clk, wit; m 27 Aug 1867 by Saml Bobbitt, J. P.

Johnston, Richard H. & Elizabeth King, 24 Oct 1851; Benjamin R. Harriss, bm; Jno W. White, clk, wit; m 27 Oct 1851 by Henry Harris, J. P.

Johnston, Sterling & & M. J. Johnston, 1 Dec 1839; William A. White, bm; Jno W. White, clk, wit; m 14 Dec 1859 by J. H. Northington, M. G.

Johnston, William E. & Elizabeth Willis, 30 July 1807; Robert Park, bm; Weldon Edwards, wit.

Johnston, Wm. L. & Martha W. Grant, 30 Apr 1849; A. B. Pierce, bm.

Joiner, Daniel & Eliza Evans, 3 Mar 1847; Moses Joiner, bm; Jno W. White, wit.

Jolliff, Davis & Averriller Hide, 25 Feb 1799; Presley C. Person, bm; Shd Green, wit.

Jolly, Thomas & Elizabeth Alford, 30 July 1807; Jacob Stiner, bm.

Jones, Albert C. & Ann Minge Baskerville, 27 Nov 1844; Geo D. Baskervill, bm.

Jones, Albert T. & Elizabeth H. Harris, 21 Nov 1832; John Verser, bm; C. Drake, wit.

Jones, Amis W. & Caroline Blanch, 24 Feb 1841; Jos Speed Jones, bm.

Jones, Amos (col) & Caroline Collins, 25 Dec 1865; James A. Cheatham, bm; L. H. Read, wit; m 25 Dec 1865 by T. Page Ricaud, M. G.

Jones, Edward C. & Jane B. Thomas, 7 Dec 1854; Charles Pennington, bm; Andrew J. Ellis, wit; m 7 Dec 1854 by R. B. Robinson, J. P.

Jones, Elijah & Martha Saunders, 21 Dec 1796; John Randolph, bm; M. D. Johnson, C. C., wit.

Jones, Epps & Polley Randolph, 5 Dec 1797; Peter Randolph, bm; Sherwood Green, wit.

Jones, Epps L. & Levina Harris, 8 Oct 1851; Thomas E. Harris, bm; C. Drake, C. C., wit.

Jones, Francis & Nancy Cyrus, 25 Jan 1818; F. W. Cyrus, bm.

Jones, Gabriel (col) & Fanny Wilson, 16 Feb 1867; William A. White, clk, wit, m 9 Mar 1867 by W. A. Brame, M. G.

Jones, Henry (col) & Olivia Edwards, 28 Dec 1866; William A. White, clk, wit; m 28 Dec 1866 by Jas. T. Russell, J. P.

Jones, Henry F. & Melissa Allen, 7 Dec 1842; Joseph J. Jones, bm; M. J. Montgomery, wit.

Jones, Henry G. & Mary E. Shearin, 24 Oct 1866; James W. Robertson, bm; William A. White, clk, wit; m 25 Oct 1866 by Ridley Browne, J. P.

Jones, Horace (col) & Henrietta Browne, 15 Sept 1866; William A. White, clk, wit; m 15 Sept 1866 by Thos A. Montgomery, J. P.

Jones, J. J., Jr., & Emma P. Williams, 4 May 1866; Phil K. Williams, bm; William A. White, clk, wit; m 8 May 1866 by B. F. Long.

Jones, James B. & Martha W. Newman, 27 Sept 1821; Bery Pearson, bm; Frs Jones, wit.

Jones, James W. & Dorathy (Dolly) Ann Duke, 27 Nov 1860; Alpheus Bobbitt, bm; William A. White, wit, m 12 Dec 1860 by John S. Cheek, J. P.

Jones, John C. & Nancy Moseley, 21 Feb 1810; John Milam, bm; Jno C. Johnson, D. C. C., wit.

Jones, Jno C. & Mary Ann Walker, 26 Sept 1822; Jesse Cole, bm.

Jones, John E. & India E. Royster, 18 Dec 1858; William D. Jones, bm; William A. White, wit; m 20 Dec 1858 by J. B. Solomon, M. G.

Jones, Joseph (col) (son of Caroline White) & Virginia Cawthorne (dau of Trim & Mary), 15 Oct 1867; William A. White, clk, wit; m 15 Oct 1866 by Edward Eagles, M. G.

Jones, Joseph B. & Lucy M. Plummer, 6 Oct 1862; Philip G. Alston, bm; William A. White, clk, wit; m 15 Oct 1862 by William Hodges, M. G.

Jones, Joseph J. & Jane E. Williams, 2 Nov 1847; Henry G. Goodloe, bm; Jno W. White, wit.

Jones, Latney & Francis Breedlove, 9 Feb 1836; James Robertson, bm; E. D. Drake, clk, wit.

Jones, Lewis (col) & Tempy Batchelor, 21 Mar 1866; William A. White, clk, wit; m 21 Mar 1866 by William Hodges.

Jones, Peter & Mary Hutson, 12 May 1812; Zachariah Milam, bm; Wm. Green, C. C., wit.

Jones, Phillip & Rhoda Cordle, 30 Aug 1838; J. Johnson, bm.

Jones, Robert & Anne Christmass, 18 Aug 1779; Thomas Machen, bm.

Jones, Robert (of Sussex Co., VA) & Elizabeth Jones, 22 Mar 1809; Hill Jones, bm; M. Duke Johnson, C. C., wit.

Jones, Seth & Sally B. Alston, 4 Apr 1812; Robert R. Cheek, bm; Jno H. Green, wit.

Jones, Sugars & Elisabeth Clinch, 1 Apr 1784; James Gray, bm; M. Duke Johnson, wit.

Jones, Taylor & Mary Beasley, 19 May 1809; Williamson Cannon, bm; Jno C. Johnson, D. C. C., wit.

Jones, Thomas B. & Martha R. Thomas, 28 July 1852; Edrick H. Dugger, bm; R. B. Robinson, wit; m 28 July 1852 by R. B. Robinson, J. P.

Jones, Col. Thomas M. & Mary C. London, 29 June 1864; E S. Jones, bm; William A. White, wit; m 29 June 1864 by W. Hodges, M. G.

Jones, W. D. & Rebecca F. Wood, 3 Nov 1854; Tippee Brownlow, bm; Jno W. White, C. C. C., wit; m 5 Nov 1854 by B. Eaton, J. P.

Jones, William & Betsy Ellis, 13 Oct 1797; Joseph Jones, bm; Sherwood Green, wit.

Jones, William & Lucinda Harris, 4 Oct 1826; William H. Shearin, bm; M. M. Drake, wit.

Jones, Wm D. & Angelina Fennell, 29 Aug 1833; Abner Steed, bm; C. Drake, wit.

Jones, William E. & Martha Green, 5 Oct 1848; Robert C. Pritchard, bm; Jno W. White, wit.

Jonnakin, James & Mrs. Ann Weldon, 28 Dec 1863; John W. Ham, bm; William A. White, clk, wit; m 30 Dec 1863 by Charles J. Jones, J. P.

Jordan, Archibald & Elisabeth Maurice, 26 Dec 1801; Richard Jordan, bm; M. D. Johnson, C. C., wit.

Jordan, Benja W. & Sally C. Cotten, 3 Sept 1823; Carter Nunnery, bm; C. Drake, C. C., wit.

Jordan, Christopher (col) & Tempey Brame, 27 Dec 1866; William A. White, clk, wit; m 28 Dec 1866 by P. H. Joyner.

Jordan, Hinton (col) & Martha Steed, 6 Apr 1867; Wm. J. White, bm; m 6 Apr 1867 by A. L. Steed, J. P.

Jordan, James W. & Ann M. Steed, 27 Apr 1857; Jno White, bm; Jno W. White, clk, wit; m 30 Apr 1857 by Thos S. Campbell, M. G.

Jordan, John & Polly Smith, 12 Nov 1821; Thomas Daniel, bm; Cas Drake, wit.

Jordan, Richard & Nancy Wilson, 7 Dec 1803; Benjamin Jordan, bm; Jo Terrell, D. C., wit.

Jordan, William H. & Ann W. Pope, 5 Jan 1854; E. T. Rice, bm; Jno W. White, wit; m 5 Jan 1854 by J. B. Solomon.

Joyner, Danl & Jane Hicks, 11 July 1845; Thos J. Judkins, bm; M. J. Montgomery, wit.

Joyner, William H. & Sarah Ann Clanton, 3 June 1845; Robert O. Burton, bm; T. J. Judkins, wit.

Judkins, Joseph (col) & Mary Boyd, 13 Oct 1866; D. Parrish, bm; William A. White, clk, wit; m 21 Oct 1866 by James C. Robinson, J. P.

Judkins, Peter (col) & Martha Miller, 7 Apr 1866; Samuel Bobbitt, bm; William A. White, clk, wit; m 7 Apr 1866 by Saml Bobbitt, J. P.

Keal, Saml & Salley Rosser (no date); Jonathan Salmon, bm; M. D. Johnson, C. C., wit.

Kearney, Anderson (col) & Ellen Williams, 26 Dec 1866; William A. White, clk, wit; m 2 Sept 1867 by John S. Cheek, J. P.

Kearney, Crawford & Mrs. Charity H Reavis, 13 Feb 1863; Wm. T. Vaughan, bm; William A. White, clk, wit; m 17 Feb 1863 by P. H. Joyner, M. G.

Kearney, Haywood (col) (son of Lewis & Nancy) & Charity Davis (dau of Wm Macklin & Annaca Davis), 14 Nov 1867; William A. White, clk, wit; m 7 Dec 1867 by John S. Cheek, J. P.

Kearney, Joseph (col) & Frances Jones, 28 Dec 1866; William A. White, clk, wit; m 28 Aug 1867 by John S. Cheek, J. P.

Kearney, Richard W. & Agnes Allen, 15 Dec 1837.

Kearney, Solomon (col) & Ann Newsom, 30 Oct 1866; William A. White, clk, wit; m 31 Oct 1866 by John S. Cheek, J. P.

Kearney, William T. & Jane Kearney, 16 Feb 1853; Jacob August, bm; Jno W. White, clk, wit; m 17 Feb 1853 by Henry Harris, J. P.

Kearny, Duncan (col) & Dolly Kearny, 28 Dec 1866; William A. White, clk, wit; m 31 Aug 1867 by John S. Cheek, J. P.

Kearny, Edward & Polly Davis, 5 June 1815; Doctor G. Williams, bm; Wm. Green, C. C., wit.

Kearny, James & Salley Mayfield, 23 Oct 1790; William Williams, bm; M. Duke Johnson, C. C., wit.

Kearny, John T. & Mary T. Williams, 1 July 1816; Wm. C. Clanton, bm; Wm. Green, C. C., wit.

Kearny, William K. & Benja. Hardy James Mariah Alston, 9 July 1810; Jno C. Johnson, bm; M. Duke Johnson, C. C., wit.

Kearsey, Hill & Martha Stewart, 20 Dec 1821; William Cearsey, bm.

Kee, Simeon M. & Joice Ann Daniel, 22 Jan 1838; James M. Daniel, bm.

Keele, Thomas P. & Elizabeth Moore, 10 Mar 1829; Benjamin Hawks, bm; E. D. Drake, wit.

Keen, John & Polley Towns, 28 Jan 1799; Zachariah Branscomb, bm; Shd Green, wit.

Kelley, Benjamin & Mary Williams, 22 Nov 1784; Nimrod Williams, bm; M. D. Johnson, wit.

Kelly, John & Mackarine R. Harris, 20 May 1847; Kinchen Harper, bm; Jno W. White, wit.

Kelly, Jno & Amanda Wilson, 8 Nov 1852; Joseph W. Harris, bm; Jno W. White, clk, wit; m 8 Nov 1852 by B. Eaton, J. P.

Kemp (Cemp), Stripplehill & Rebecca Johnston (no date); Francis Smith, bm.

Kendrick, James & Susan Green, 30 Aug 1827; Robert J. Williams, bm; M. M. Drake, wit.

Kendrick, Jno & Martha Dinkins (no date); John Smith, bm.

Kendricks, Isham & Elizabeth Tucker, 31 Oct 1781; Benjamin Tarver, bm; H. Machen, wit.

Kennedy, Charles & Martha Ann Rebecca Brodie, 7 Oct 1843; Thomas N. F. Alston, bm.

Kennedy, Hawkins & Rainey King, 21 Oct 1833; John Crowder, bm; Edwin D. Drake, clk, wit.

Kennedy, Hawkins & Holly Burrows, 10 Jan 1852; Marx Schloss, bm; Jno W. White, clk, wit; m 14 Jan 1852 by M. M. Drake, J. P.

Kersey, Benjamine & Elizabeth Epps Kersey, 17 Jan 1856; Wm. H. Lynch, bm; Thos P. Paschall, wit; m 17 Jan 1856 by Thomas P. Paschall, J. P.

Kersey, Edmund & Charity Mayhoe, 23 Jan 1834; Robert Day, bm; E. D. Drake, clk, wit.

Kersey, William J. & Elizabeth Burchette, 24 Jan 1856; Nowell Lynes, bm; Thomas P. Paschall, wit.

Kersey, Willis & Henrietta Seward, 29 Dec 1852; John Drew, bm; Thos P. Paschall, wit; m 29 Dec 1852 by John H. Bullock, J. P.

Kersey, Willis & Nancy Durham, 3 Nov 1856; Alexander Drew, bm; Thomas P. Paschall, wit.

Keuyne, William & Martha Stegall, 15 Oct 1838; Clack Robinson, bm.

Keyte, Walter E. & Rebecca Kippin, 10 Apr 1844; Edward Rice, bm; M. J. Montgomery, wit.

Kicker, Jarrel & Delila Capps, 16 Sept 1793; Joshua Bobbett, bm; Rd. Russell, wit.

Kid, Barlet M. & Virender Jones, 11 Aug 1853; G. F. Glover, bm; R. B. Robinson, wit; m 11 Aug 1853 by R. B. Robinson, J. P.

Kidd, James & Frankey Robertson, 16 Sept 1795; Simon Williams, bm; M. Duke Johnson, C. C., wit.

Kimbal, Short & Elizabeth Taylor, 21 Nov 1826; Matthew Marshall, bm; M. M. Drake, wit.

Kimball, Bartholomew & Winefred P. Davis, 13 Dec 1825; Burl Pitchford, wit.

Kimball, Durell B. & Aggie B. Watkins, 21 Dec 1858; Jno C. McCraw, bm; Jno W. White, clk, wit; m 19 Jan 1859 by A. C. Harris, M. G.

Kimball, James A. & Mary E. Watkins, 16 Jan 1852; E. T. Rice, bm; Jno W. White, clk, wit; m 20 Jan 1852 by Caswell Drake.

Kimball, Lewis & Francis Marshall, 26 Feb 1822; Will Williams, bm.

Kimball, Nathaniel & Mary Carroll, 19 Feb 1859; Joseph J. Haithcock, bm; Jno W. White, wit; m 20 Feb 1859 by J. B. Solomon, M. G.

Kimball, William J. & Elizabeth A. B. Watkins, 16 Jan 1852; E. T. Rice, bm; Jno W. White, clk, wit; m 20 Jan 1852 by Wm. A. Burwell, J. P.

Kimbell, Benjamin & Nancy Colclough, 14 Mar 1804; Solomon B. Williams, bm; M. Duke Johnson, C. C., wit.

Kimbell, Benjamin S. & Hannah Arnold, 3 Aug 1813; James Fletcher, bm; Wm. Green, C. C., wit.

Kimbell, Edmond & Elizabeth M. Tunstall, 1 Jan 1803; Sugan Johnson, bm; G. Johnson, wit.

Kimbell, Henly & Lotty Serug, 20 Nov 1826; Matthew Marshall, bm; C. Drake, C. C., wit.

Kimbell, James & Charlotte Smiley, 26 June 1827; Solomon G. Ward, M. M. Drake, wit.

Kimbell, Joseph & Elizabeth Davis, 24 Dec 1807; Ransom Kimbell, bm; Jo Terrell, D. C. C., wit.

Kimbell, Leonard & Prisilla Harris, 22 July 1780; Bedford Harris, bm.

Kimbell, Nathaniel & Nancy Lindsay, 8 Nov ____; Caleb Lindsey, bm; M. Duke Johnson, C. C., wit.

Kimbell, Peter & Ailcey Kimbell, 4 Sept 1782; William Allen, bm; M. Duke Johnson, C. C., wit.

Kimbell, Ransom & Elizh. Shearin, 14 Aug 1804; Xanthus Snow, bm; M. D. Johnson, C. C., wit.

Kimbell, Spell & Anne Harris, 18 May 1780; Christopher Blanton, bm; Thos Machen, wit.

Kimbell, William & Polley Harris, 16 Jan 1811; Robert Harris, bm; M. Duke Johnson, C. C., wit.

Kimbell, William & Polly Smith, 17 Dec 1817; John Mealer, bm.

King, Alexr W. & Graselda C. King, 10 Nov 1838; Alfred G. King, bm.

King, Alfred G. & Amanda M. King, 14 Dec 1835; Edward Davis, bm; E. D. Drake, clk, wit.

King, Allen & Temperance Acock, 24 Dec 1798; Henry Acock, bm; Shd Green, wit.

King, Allen & Mary Shearin, 9 Sept 1839; Drury Shearin, bm; Edwd W. Best, wit.

King, Anthoney & Mary Mory, 17 Oct 1785; Wood King, bm; M. Duke Johnson, wit.

King, Anthony, Jr., & Rainy Coleman, 13 Jan 1814; James White, bm; Jno H. Green, wit.

King, Armistead & Adeline Paschall, 15 Oct 1844; H. P. White, bm; M. J. Montgomery, wit.

King, Armistead & Lucy Hicks, 30 June 1860; Jereman Hawks, bm; Jno W. White, clk, wit; m 2 July 1860 by Thos J. Judkins, J. P.

King, Baxter & Martha Darrell, 13 Dec 1825; Hezekiah Coleman, bm; M. M. Drake, wit.

King, Benjamin & Hanah Davis, 21 Jan 1785; Robert Crow, bm; M. D. Johnson, wit.

King, Benjamin & Priscella F. Riggan, 23 Nov 1838; William H. Shearin, bm.

King, Benjamine & Rebecca Conn m 24 Feb 1852 by J. B. Solomon.

King, Berry & Rebecca Carter, 13 Dec 1858; W. A. J. Nicholson, bm; William A. White, wit; m 14 Dec 1858 by Nathl Nicholson, J. P.

King, Charles & Anne Duke, 18 Nov 1787; Jonathan King, bm; M. Duke Johnson, C. C., wit.

King, Charles & Rebecca Stanley, 14 Aug 1824; John Beasley, bm; C. Drake, C. C., wit.

King, Cudbarth & Jinsey Hasting, 1 Apr 1782; John Ballard, bm; M. Duke Johnson, wit.

King, David & Amey Ellington, 12 May 1783; Frederick Cook, bm; M. Duke Johnson, wit.

King, David & Abigal Young, 14 Dec 1788; Anthoney King, bm; M. Duke Johnson, C. C., wit.

King, David, Jr., & Henrietta Hawks, 8 Feb 1823; Joshua Rivers, bm; Edwin D. Drake, wit.

King, David S. & Sarah Hawks, 31 Dec 1823; John Darnol, bm; C. Drake, wit.

King, Durrell A. & Sarah E. Hawks, 11 June 1866; Simon G. Duke, bm; William A. White, clk, wit; m 12 June 1866 by Jno W. Pattillo, J. P.

King, Edward & Sally Bennett, 16 May 1823; James Martin, bm; Edwin D. Drake, wit.

King, Elbert & Martha Colemon, 11 Oct 1851; Wm. Matthews, bm; Jno W. White, clk, wit; m 15 Oct 1851 by C. D. Fitts, J. P.

King, Elijay & Lucy Tally, 28 Apr 1858; Joseph H. Parkinson, bm; m 19 Apr 1858 by J. B. Solomon, M. G.

King, Fain W. & Susan A. Perkinson, 24 Nov 1845; Alexander W. King, bm.

King, Frederick & Mary Mustian, 14 Dec 1844; Joseph King, bm; M. J. Montgomery, wit.

King, George G. & Martha E. Tutor, 17 Oct 1860; Jno. W. Pattillo, bm; Jno W. White, clk, wit; m 17 Oct 1860 by Jno W. Pattillo, J. P.

King, George R. & Mary King, 10 Dec 1857; Allen M. King, bm; Jno W. White, wit; m 10 Dec 1857 by Wm. C. Clanton, J. P.

King, George W. & Mary N. Carroll, 5 Apr 1860; Allen E. Rainey, bm; Jno W. White, clk, wit; m 5 Apr 1860 by N. A. Purefoy, M. G.

King, Henry & _____, 17 Apr 1799; Joseph King,, bm; M. Duke Johnson, C. C. C., wit.

King, Henry & Tabby Moseley, 16 Aug 1804; Gideon Johnson, bm; J. Malone, wit.

King, James & Nancy Davis, 25 Aug 1813; William Andrews, bm; Wm. Green, C. C. C., wit.

King, James & Nelly Wood, 21 Dec 1832; Joseph H. Aycock, bm; C. Drake, C. C.,wit.

King, James H. & Sarah A. Tally, 21 Dec 1859; John Hicks, bm; Jno W. White, clk, wit; m 22 Dec 1859 by Jas T. Russell, J. P.

King, James H. & Sallie King, 18 Oct 1866; A. M. King, bm; William A. White, C. C. C., wit; m 18 Oct 1866 by M. P. Perry, J. P.

King, James Y. & Elizabeth Harris, 17 Dec 1832; William Hicks, bm; C. Drake, C. C. C., wit.

King, John & Rebecca Foote, 22 Dec 1823; Jno W. Moseley, bm; Edwin D. Drake, wit.

King, John F. & Martha A. Hicks, 21 Aug 1865; Jno W. Pattillo, bm; William A. White, clk, wit; m 23 Aug 1865 by T. Page Ricaud, M. G.

King, Johnathan & Polly White, 15 Apr 1818; Mathew King, bm; Wm. Green, C. C., wit.

King, Jonathan or Joseph & Lizzie Coleman, 11 Nov 1793; Jonathan King or Joseph King, bm; Richd Russell, wit.

King, Jonathan & _____ Coleman (no date); Fredk Malone, bm; M. D. Johnson, wit.

King, Jonathan & Sally White, 21 Aug 1833; Charles C. King, bm; C. Drake, C. C., wit.

King, Joseph J. & Eliza Ann Mustian, 25 Nov 1851; Elbert King, bm; Jno W. White, clk, wit; m 27 Nov 1851 by Jas T. Russell, J. P.

King, Matthew & Elizabeth White, 5 June 1817; Jesse Milam, bm; Wm. Green, C. C., wit.

King, Matthew & Martha Mustian, 3 Dec 1836; Eli Perkinson, bm; E. D. Drake, clk, wit.

King, Medicus & Rebecca E. K. Vaughan, 20 Aug 1842; William W. Davis, bm; M. J. Montgomery, wit.

King, Miles & Amanda Hamlet, 17 Apr 1855; Allen M. King, Jr., bm; Jno W. White, wit.

King, Miles R. & Charity W. Paschall, 25 Jan 1861; B. R. Browning, bm; Jno W. White, clk, wit; m 30 Jan 1861 by N. A. Purefoy, M. G.

King, Nathaniel & Polly Kittrell, 7 Nov 1818; William C. King, bm.

King, Osmond E. & Harriot Blanton, 7 Sept 1830; Green Blanton, bm; C. Drake, C. C., wit.

King, Peter F. & Lucy D. Hicks, 24 Aug 1866; William A. White, clk, wit; m 5 Sept 1866 by Z. M. P. Cole, J. P.

King, Ransom & Elizabeth Darnold, 3 Nov 1824; James O'K. Mayfield, bm; E. D. Drake, wit.

King, Sampson & Elizabeth Young, 17 Dec 1790; John Hix, bm; Ja Turner, wit.

King, Saml & Mary Jane Harper, 9 Dec 1842; William Bennett, bm; M. J. Montgomery, wit.

King, Samuel D. (son of James Y. & Elizabeth King) & Sallie A. Walker (dau of Zachariah W. & Elizabeth Walker), 13 Nov 1867; William A. White, clk, wit; m 20 Nov 1867 by George M. Duke, M. G.

King, Samuel H. & Willy Overby, 28 Aug 1819; John Andrews, bm; C. Drake, C. W. C. C., wit.

King, Samuel W. & Mary A. Coleman, 28 Oct 1844; John L. Foote, bm; M. J. Montgomery, wit.

King, Tyra D. & Mary F. Hicks, 21 Dec 1857; Elley Jay King, bm; Jno W. White, clk, wit; m 23 Dec 1857 by M. M. Drake, J. P.

King, William & Minerva Carroll, 26 July 1823; John Gossee, bm; Edwin D. Drake, wit.

King, William & Caroline Harriss, 19 Dec 1848; John L. Evans, bm; Jno W. White, wit.

King, William W. & Sarah King, 24 Apr 1852; F. M. Tucker, bm; Jno W. White, clk, wit; m 25 Apr 1852 by J. H. Hawkins, J. P.

King, William Y. & Margaret J. Watkins, 16 Dec 1858; Isaac Harris, bm; William A. White, wit.

King, William Y. & Mary E. Shearin, 29 Dec 1860; Lewis B. Collins, bm; Jno W. White, clk, wit; m 2 Jan 1861 by·W. A. Dowtin, J. P.

King, Wood & _____ Childress (no date); Anthony King, bm; M. D. Johnson, C., C., wit.

King, Wood & Frances Duke, 19 Sept 1780; William Duke, bm; Thos Machen, wit.

King, Woodward & Elizabeth Capps (dau of Mary), 20 Dec 1822; Raibun Stegall, bm; Cas Drake, C. C., wit.

King, Wright (son of Frederick & Mary S. King) & Roan Rebecca King (dau of Armistead & Adaline King), 6 Dec 1867; William A. White, clk, wit; m 10 Dec 1867 by L. C. Perkinson, M. G.

Kinnaman, Samuel & Nancy Kinneman, 2 Oct 1799; John Gober, bm; M. D. Johnson, C. C. C., wit.

Kirby, John D. & Mrs. Eliza Ann Mason, 5 Feb 1835; Clack Robinson, bm; Wm. B. Wilkinson, R. B. Robinson, wit.

Kirkland, James M. & July Barner, 22 Feb 1836; Sterling H. Edmunds, bm; E. D. Drake, clk, wit.

Kirkland, John & Hariot Edmonds, 12 Aug 1831; Robert Cook, bm; C. Drake, C. C. C., wit.

Kittrell, Isham & Nancy Hunter, 16 Dec 1788; William Hunter, bm.

Kittrell, MickleJohn & Nancy Hunter, 19 Jan 1821; William H. Williamson, bm.

Kness, Henry & Mrs. Susan D. Stallings, 6 Nov 1866; Henry Harrison, bm; William A. White, C. C. C., wit; m 6 Nov 1866 by Ridley Browne, J. P.

Kurl, Abraham & Anny R. Duke, 12 May 1840; William P. Rose, bm.

Kyle, David & Lucy B. Robinson, 11 May 1833; John V. Cawthorn, bm; C. Drake, C. C., wit.

Lad, Jesse & Polley Ovebay, 22 Mar 1832; Wilkinsson, C. Harper, bm; Burl Pitchford, J. P., wit.

Lafater, Samuel W. & Mary Reynalds, 14 July 1831; Bennitt H. Stanmire, bm; C. Drake, C. C., wit.

Lambard, Edmund & Jane Thomas, 12 Jan 1815; Allen Thomas, bm; W. Green, C. C. C., wit.

Lamberd, David & Elizabeth Bolten, 11 Aug 1825; Joshua Young, bm; Burl Pitchford, wit.

Lamberd, Jabis & Judy Bolten, 8 May 1797; Corben Noles, bm; Thomas Malone, wit.

Lambert, Baxter & Martha Jones, 25 Sept 1830; Fox Hunter, bm; M. M. Drake, wit.

Lambert, John E. & Sarah A. J. Balthrop, 8 Jan 1844; James Shaw, bm; M. J. Montgomery, wit.

Lambert, Martin F. & Mary J. Carroll, 10 Dec 1836; Jurdan W. Carroll, bm; E. D. Drake, clk, wit.

Lambert, Samuel & Rebecca Hall (or Hale), 10 Mar 1785; Wm Blanton, bm; M. D. Johnson C. C., wit.

Lamburt, Thomas & Juda Moon, 11 Nov 1797; Jaba Lamburt, bm; Sherwood Green, wit.

Lamburt, William & Sarah Jones, 10 Aug 1798; Fedrick Hawks, bm; S. Green, wit.

Lamkin, James B. E. & Maria L. Laughter, 17 Nov 1856; Person Duncan, bm; Thomas P. Paschall, wit; m 3 Dec 1856 by Thos J. Judkins, J. P.

Lampkin, George W. & Obedience Wood, 17 Apr 1824; Benjamin Lamkin, bm.

Lampkin, Matthew & Rebecca George, 19 Feb 1824; Green Judkins, bm; C. Drake, C. C., wit.

Lancaster, Alfred & Elizabeth Aycock, 6 Dec 1839; Samuel Lancaster, bm; Edwd W. Best, clk, wit.

Lancaster, James B. & Angeline C. Pegram, 14 Jan 1867; Gordan C. Duncan, bm; William A. White, clk, wit; m 17 Jan 1867 by Samuel W. Dowtin, J. P.

Lancaster, John & Ann Forrester, 16 Dec 1800; Sugan Johnson, bm; M. D. Johnson, C. C., wit.

Lancaster, John & Amy Bobbitt, 17 Feb 1813; Peter R. Davis, bm; Jno H. Green, wit.

Lancaster, John & Polly Bennett, 23 Dec 1813; John Mealer, bm; Wm. Green, C. C., wit.

Lancaster, John & Winefred Harris, 24 Dec 1828; Green Harris, bm; E. D. Drake, wit.

Lancaster, Larkin & Dela Lankester, 26 Oct 1797; Lawrence Lancaster, bm.

Lancaster, Lawrence R. & Rebecca Prior, 3 Aug 1815; John B. Hicks, bm; Will Green, C. W. C. C., wit.

Lancaster, Lemuel & Suzan Ayecocke, 10 Dec 1821; Anthony Dowtin, bm.

Lancaster, Micajah & Elizabeth Lancaster, 21 Apr 1802; Robert Crocker, bm; Gideon Johnson, wit.

Lancaster, Moses & Martha Harris, 7 Dec 1779; Lawrence Lancaster, bm.

Lancaster, Samuel B. & Leah Martin, 27 May 1844; T. J. Judkins, bm; M. J. Montgomery, wit.

Lancaster, William & Jane Jemmerson, 1 Oct 1781; Lawrence Lancaster, bm; Thos Machen, wit.

Lancaster, William & Martha Bennett, 5 Jan 1816; Lewis Patrick, bm.

Lancaster, William & Elizabeth B. Cunningham, 31 Aug 1819; Willie Lancaster, bm.

Lancaster, William C. & Mary Kimball, 15 Feb 1826; William Lancaster, bm; M. M. Drake, wit.

Lancaster, Willie & Prudence Bennett, 9 Jan 1799; Jeremiah Stephenson, bm; Shd Green, wit.

Lane, Joel H. & Mary A. G. Freeman, 4 Jan 1815; John Snow, Stephen Davis, bm; Wm. Green, C. C. C., wit.

Langford, George & Pattsy Mallary, 5 Sept 1781; Thomas Poythress, bm; Thos Machen, wit.

Langford, George & Winny Fletcher, 5 Dec 1844; James Paschall, bm; M. J. Montgomery, wit.

Langford, Green & Ibey Thomas, 20 Nov 1824; Anderson Sturdivant, bm; E. D. Drake, wit.

Langford, Hardy & Bashy Capps, 24 May 1814; William Darnell, bm; W. Green, C. W. C. C., wit.

Langford, Joab & Betsey White, 22 Nov 1790; Thomas Paschal, bm; M. Duke Johnson, C. C., wit.

Langford, John & Polly Bennett, 2 Aug 1811; William Andrews, bm; Wm. Green, C. C. C., wit.

Langford, John D. & Martha E. Steed, 15 Mar 1837; Henry T. Allen, bm; E. W. Best, wit.

Langford, Raleigh, Jr., & Polly Moore, 5 Oct 1821; Raleigh Langford, Sr., bm; Cas Drake, C. C. C., wit.

Langford, Rolley & Elizabeth World, 15 Jan 1820; Littleberry Andrews, bm.

Langford, William & Suasan Omary, 4 Aug 1841; Robert D. Paschall, bm; Burl Pitchford, J. P., wit.

Langford, William & Ann Langford, 3 Jan 1848; Michl W. Paschall, Jr., bm; Jno W. White, wit.

Langfurd, John & Patsey Duke, 25 July 1787; William Beckham, bm; M. Duke Johnson, wit.

Langley, Thomas A. & Polley Matthews, 10 Feb 1834; John Hawks, Jr., bm; Burl Pitchford, J. P., wit.

Langley, William B. & Jane Sims, 1 Sept 1804; Leonard H. Sims, bm; J. Malone, wit.

Lanier, Lewis & Rebecca Duke, 4 May 1785; Thomas Christmass, bm; M. Duke Johnson, C. C., wit.

Lankester, Irey & Mary Johnson, 16 Nov 1796; Rob Crocker, bm; M. Duke Johnson, C. C., wit.

Lankford, George & Mary Fain, 16 July 1783; Joel Fain, bm; M. Duke Johnson, wit.

Lankford, Rawleigh & Betsey Wheeler, 4 July 1785; William Beckham, bm; M. D. Johnson, wit.

Lashley, Howell & Silvey Estes (no date); J. Barrow, bm.

Laughter, Robert W. & Elizabeth P. Bartlett, 19 Dec 1836; William Wortham, bm; E. D. Drake, clk, wit.

Laughter, Robert W. & Nancy Evans, 12 Jan 1841; Matthew M. Drake, wit.

Lee, Edward & Sally Hardy, 20 Jan 1840; James Felts, bm; Edwd W. Best, clk, wit.

Lee, Israe (Ezra) & Nancy Hamlet, 14 Nov 1855; Edward Hardy, bm; Jno W. White, wit; m 15 Nov 1855 by Wm. C. Clanton, J. P.

Lee, Micajah (col) & Maggie Daniel, 24 Dec 1866; William A. White, clk, wit; m 25 Dec 1866 by Ridley Browne, J. P.

Leftwich, Robert & Priscilla Thamar Jones, 13 June 1806; Peter R. Davis, bm; Duke Johnson, C. C., wit.

Lemont, John & Betsey Murrah (no date); Chas Marshall, bm; B. Davis, wit.

Lesher, Jacob & Patsey Laughter, 27 Apr 1795; William Rooker, bm; J. Moss, wit.

Levister, Thomas P. & Frances S. Robertson, 14 Nov 1854; Jno Stallings, bm; Jno W. White, wit; m 15 Nov 1854 by Thos J. Pitchford, J. P.

Lewis, David, Jr., & Lucy Floyd, 9 Aug 1779; Thomas Fussell, bm; Thos Machen, wit.

Lewis, Edward S. & Martha Vick, 28 June 1821; Frs Jones, bm; Frs A. Thornton, wit.

Lewis, Freemond & Elizabeth Wright, 12 June 1821; Amos P. Sledge, bm.

Lewis, Jno & Frances Hodge, 23 Oct 1837; John C. Green, wit.

Lewis, John H. & Rowena F. Robinson, 9 Jan 1838; William E. Hinton, bm.

Lewis, Richard (col) (son of William Simms & Martha Morgan) & Keziah Watson (dau of Austin Jones & Fanny Johnston), 2 July 1867; William A. White, clk, wit; m 2 July 1867 by William Hodges, M. G.

Lewis, Samuel H. & Henrietta Mabrey, 4 July 1818; Thomas Pitchford, bm.

Lewis, William & Elizabeth Samuel, 17 June 1805; Lot Hazard, bm; Jo Terrell, D. D., wit.

Lewis, Wm. Henry (col) & Frances Elizabeth Allgood, 18 May 1866; William A. White, clk, wit; m 21 May 1866 by N. A. Purefoy, M. G.

Lewsey, Thomas & Mrs. Mary Goodwin, 28 Nov 1865; Kinchen Harper, bm; William A. White, clk, wit;m 28 Nov 1865 by Will H. Wheeler, V. D. M.

Liles, Robert S. & Sarah E. Riggan, 1 Apr 1867; Jeremiah F. Riggan, bm; Wm. A. White, clk, wit; m 4 Apr 1867 by Ridley Browne, J. P.

Linch, Charles & Rebecca Drummons, 7 Jan 1825; Benjamin Linch, bm; E. D. Drake, wit.

Lindsay, Jno & Sarah Kerney, 9 Nov 1796; H. G. Kearny, bm; Shd Green, wit.

Lindsey, Caleb & Temperance House, 28 June 1803; Sugan Johnson, bm; M. Duke Johnson, C. C., wit.

Lindsey, W. J. & Annie E. Hornfleur, 1 July 1865; John Sexton, bm; William A. White, wit.

Little, Isaac & Haney Mabry, 4 Feb 1803; Gardener Shearin, bm; M. Duke Johnson, C. C., wit.

Little, Isaac & Sally Dowtin, 21 Dec 1842; Wm. L. Harriss, bm; M. J. Montgomery, wit.

Little, Isaac & Sarah A. D. Stallings, 24 Jan 1860; Samuel W. Dowtin, bm; Jno W. White, clk, wit; m 25 Jan 1860 by W. A. Dowtin, J. P.

Little, Lewis & Rosa Shearin, 4 Feb 1846; Thomas A. Little, bm; M. J. Montgomery, wit.

Little, Louis (formerly slave of Thomas P. Little) & Sylvia Ashe, 21 May 1866; Mary A. Mosby, bm; C. M. Cook, wit; m 21 May 1866 by Chas M. Cook, J. P.

Little, Thomas & Polley Thomas, 22 Jan 1800; William Thomas, bm; Shd Green, wit.

Little, Thomas A. & Elizabeth Riggan, 1 Feb 1848; James Felts, bm; Jno W. White, wit.

Little, William & Lucy Shearin, 18 Nov 1811; Robert Harris, bm; Jno. H. Green, wit.

Littlejohn, Joseph B. & Sallie Jones Field, 11 Oct 1852; Wm. H. Bobbitt, bm; Jno W. White, clk, wit; m 13 Oct 1852 by Jos Blount Cheshire, Rector of Calvary Church, Tarboro, NC.

Livingston, Timothy & Adeline C. Parsons, 16 June 1846; Daniel Turner, bm; H. C. Lucas, wit.

Locke, George & Fanny H. Macay, 21 Dec 1822; George Anderson, bm.

Loftis, Archibald & Susanna Paschall, 2 Jan 1782; William Paschall, bm; Thos Machen, C. C., wit.

Loftis, Martin & Phereba Pascal, 19 Oct 1790; John Pascal, bm.

Long, B. F. & Rebecca Brame, 16 Jan 1860; R. G. Moore, bm; William A. White, wit; m 18 Jan 1860 by Ira T. Wyche.

Long, John J. & Melisa Williams, 14 Sept 1837; N. M. Long, bm.

Long, John S. & Nancy Green, 10 May 1811; Dennis O'Bryan, bm; M. D. Johnson, C. C., wit.

Long, Nicholas M., Jr., & Sallie Hawkins Williams, 19 Dec 1859; W. J. Squiggins, bm; Jno W. White, clk, wit; m 21 Dec 1859 by Jos Blount Cheshire.

Long, Zant (colored) & Mary Williams, 27 Jan 1866; Osborn Williams, bm; T. P. Alston, wit; m 20 Feb 1866 by C. M. Cook, J. P.

Longwith, Reubin & Nancy Hathcock, 8 Sept 1796; John Hathcock, bm; M. D. Johnson, C. C., wit.

Lott, Elisha & Elizabeth J. Jean, 13 Aug 1831; B. H. Stanmire, bm; M. M. Drake, wit.

Loughlin, J. J. & Lucy A. Johnson, 26 Dec 1865; Robt H. Ford, bm; William A. White, clk, wit; m 27 Dec 1865 by T. B. Kingsbury.

Love, Lewis (col) & Fanny Mabry, 26 Dec 1866; William A. White, clk, wit; m 26 Dec 1866 by Thomas P. Paschall, J. P.

Lowery, Willie & Winnie Tann, 16 Jan 1860; Matthew Guy, bm; John W. White, clk, wit; m 16 Jan 1860 by N. A. Purefoy, M. G.

Lowry, Samuel & Pricilla Green, 28 Jan 1826; Moses Wadkins, bm; M. M. Drake, wit.

Lowwell, Samuel & Betsey Foote, 17 July 1797; Benjamin Bell, bm; M. Duke Johnson, clk, wit.

Loyd, George W. & Elizabeth Tunstall, 8 Dec 1858; Lewis B. Collins, bm; Jno W. White, clk, wit; m 22 Dec 1858 by A. L. Steed, J. P.

Loyd, Joseph & Elizabeth Johnson, 22 Apr 1828; William G. Wilson, bm; M. M. Drake, wit.

Loyd, Thomas & Nancy Coleman, 3 Oct 1780; Phileman Hilliard, bm; Thos Machen, wit.

Loyd, Thompson & Polly Bennitt, 20 June 1832; William G. Wilson, bm; C. Drake, C. C., wit.

Loyd, William & Rebecca Clark, 1 Jan 1817; James Clark, bm.

Loyd, William, Jr., & Lucy Rowland, 22 Nov 1831; James Robertson, bm; C. Drake, C. C., wit.

Loyde, Stephen & Elisa Cogwell (no date); James Cogwell, bm; M. D. Johnson, wit.

Lucas, John & Martha Yarborough, 30 Mar 1830; Williams Moss, bm; C. Drake, C. C,. wit.

Lynch, John H. & Mary J. Nanny, 18 June 1860; James B. Mosely, bm; Jno W. White, clk, wit.

Lynch, Robert & Lucy Tunk alias Evans, 24 Aug 1849; Thomas J. Judkins, bm; Jno W. White, wit.

Lyne, George & Harriet L. Jones, 11 Nov 1826; James Somerville, bm; M. M. Drake, wit.

Lyne, Henry (of Granville Co.) & Mary Plummer, 16 Aug 1782; John Pann (of Granville Co.), bm; M. Duke Johnson, wit.

Lyne, Nowell & Mary G. Harris, 15 Dec 1862; Badger Mushaw, bm; Thos P. Paschall, bm; m 17 Dec 1862 by Thos P. Paschall, J. P.

Lynes, Norvel (col) & Sally Birchett, 8 Dec 1866; William A. White, clk, wit; m 12 Dec 1866 by Thos P. Paschall, J. P.

Mabery, Frederick & Elisabeth Watkins, 24 Mar 1790; Richard Watkins, bm; M. D. Johnson, C. C., wit.

Mabry, Branch M. & Catharine Langford, 6 Jan 1824; Jones Mabry, bm; Edwin D. Drake, wit.

Mabry, Charles & Elizabeth Cole, 26 Jan 1826; Daniel Cole, bm; Burl Pitchford, wit.

Mabry, Hartwell & Polly Tilman Williams, 15 Feb 1815; William Paschall, bm; W. Green, C. W. C. C., wit.

Mabry, John & Rosey Sherrin, 24 Dec 1824; Robert Nicholson, bm; Jos A. Drake, wit.

Mabry, John & Martha Cowley, 13 Jan 1851; James H. Moore, bm; R. A. Ezell, wit.

Mabry, Jones & Nancy Reaves, 18 Apr 1810; Joab Langford, bm; M. Duke Johnson, C. C., wit.

Mabry, Kinchen & Martha Riggans, 9 Apr 1822; Luke H. Paschall, bm; Peter R. Davis, bm, wit.

Mabry, Matthew & Sarah Long, 23 Oct 1783; Benjamin Bradley, bm; M. Duke Johnson, wit.

Mabry, Seth W. & Nancy Walker, 24 Nov 1840; Jos Speed Jones, bm.

Mabry, Stephen G. & Martha R. Tunstall, 16 Apr 1850; Henry Turner, bm; Jno W. White, wit.

Mabry, Stephen G. & Lucy M. Best, 29 June 1861; Thomas R. Tunstall, bm; Jno W. White, clk, wit; m 30 June 1861 by A. L. Steed, J. P.

Mabry, William & Pricella Shearin, 1 Dec 1808; Guardner Shearin, bm; J. C. Johnson, D. C. C., wit.

McClenahan, John & Judith Waddy, 6 Aug 1792; Benjamin Waddey, bm; M. D. Johnson, C. C., wit.

McCraw, Alexander C. & Sarah T. (Sallie) Waddill, 21 Nov 1854; E. T. Rice, bm; Jno W. White, wit; m 22 Nov 1854 by J. B. Solomon.

McDowell, Jno M. & Martha P. Washington, 9 June 1863; Jno C. McCraw, bm; Wm. A. White, clk, wit; m 9 June 1863 by Henry Petty, M. G.

McGehee, Solomon & Henry Judson [sic], 30 Nov 1797; Henry Hudson, bm; Shd Green, wit.

McKinney, Samuel & Elizabeth Newman, 14 Jan 1808; William Jones, bm; M. Duke Johnson, C. C., wit.

McKinny, Jordan & Elizabeth Blankenship, 9 Dec 1810; Darnel Glover, bm; Jno C. Johnson, wit.

Macklin, George & Marey Gui, 16 Jan 1840; Richard Drew, bm; Burl Pitchford, J. P., wit.

Macklin, Matthew & Salley Jones, 9 Nov 1787; Isaac Evans, bm; M. D. Johnson, C. C., wit.

Macklin, Nathaniel & Frances Duglass, 5 Oct 1861; Ephraim Macklin, bm; Jno W. White, wit.

McLaren, James & Lucy Nicholson, 16 May 1823; Lemuel P. Nicholson, bm; Edwin D. Drake, wit.

Maclin, Durell & Catharine Duglas, 16 June 1857; Jame Algood; bm; Jno W. White, wit.

Maclin, Henry H. & Jane Netherry, 17 Mar 1835; John Egerton, bm; E. D. Drake, clk, wit.

Maclin, James & Thursy Cypress, 14 Mar 1864; John E. Boyd, bm; William A. White, clk, wit; m 16 Mar 1864 by T. B. Ricks.

Maclin, Thomas & Polly Rottenberry, 9 Mar 1838; William Chandler, bm.

Macon, Albert G. & Mary H. Davis, 29 Sept 1824; John V. Cawthorn, bm; Gordan Cawthorn, wit.

Macon, Arthur & Martha H. Hawkins, 7 Oct 1828; George Cawthorn, bm; M. M. Drake, wit.

Macon, Gabriel L. & Burchet T. Jordan, 22 June 1816; John C. Green, bm; Wm. Green, C. C., wit.

Macon, George W. & Elizabeth Kimbell, 24 Oct 1807; Joel Terrell, Jr., bm; M. Duke Johnson, C. C., wit.

Macon, Dr. Gid. H. & Lou Jenkins, 1 June 1857; Will A. Jenkins, bm; Jno W. White, clk, wit; m 9 June 1857 by N. Z. Graves.

Macon, Gideon Hunt & Mary Green, 26 July 1779; Wm. Christmas, bm.

Macon, John C. & Ann Gordan, 1 Feb 1830; William F. Tucker, bm; C. Drake, C. C., wit.

Macon, John C. & Indianna Askew, 30 Apr 1864; H. G. Goodloe, bm; William A. White, clk, wit; m 12 May 1864 by Solon. Southerland, J. P.

Macon, Jno T. & Elizabeth R. Willis, 1 Jan 1823; Robert Ransom, bm; C. Drake, C. C., wit.

McRorie, William & Mary Best, 30 Oct 1794; Benjamin Moss, bm; Richd Russell, wit.

McSparren, John & Elizabeth Kimbell, 30 Oct 1799; Dancy Standley, bm; M. Duke Johnson, C. C., wit.

Maddra, Darling & Mary Gwinn, 18 Aug 1783; Charles Ellums, bm; M. D. Johnson, wit.

Maddra, John & Cloey Saintsing, 17 July 1782; Darling Maddra, bm; M. Duke Johnson, wit.

Maddry, Robert & Jeane Duncan, 12 June 1803; Milley Smith, bm; M. Duke Johnson, C. C,. wit.

Madray, William & Millender Saintsing, 21 Feb 1784; James Saintsing, bm; M. Duke Johnson, wit.

Magers, William & Minerva Derby, 18 Oct 1825; William W. Brick, Thos Jefferson Green, bm; M. M. Drake, wit.

Mallory, Francis & Sally P. Vaughan, 4 Apr 1855; Wm. L. Harris, bm; Jno W. White, wit.

Malone, John & Nancy Earles, 17 Sept 1787; James Hutchison, bm; M. D. Johnson, wit.

Malone, William & Poly Baxter, 17 Aug 1795; William Colclough, bm; J. Moss, wit.

Mangham, Solomon & Elizabeth Hays, 9 June 1820; Gideon Harton, bm; Cas Drake, C. C. C., wit.

Mangum, James & Susanna Harris, 26 Jan 1796; Joseph Mangum, bm; Richd Russell, wit.

Mangum, Samuel & Catey Harris, 3 Jan 1807; Isham Harris, bm; W. R. Johnson, wit.

Mangum, William & Polley Wren, 20 Feb 1800; Allen Wren, bm; Shd Green, wit.

Mann, Benjamin (of Nash Co.) & Caroline M. T. Williams, 27 Dec 1852; P. D. Powell, bm; Jno W. White, clk, wit; m 4 Jan 1853 by Thos G. Lowe, M. G.

Marks, Peter & Araminta Valentine, 19 Nov 1851; Beverly Valintine, bm; E. Dromgoole, wit; m 19 Nov 1851 by Richd B. Robinson, J. P.

Marlow, Allin C. & Maria Hill, 6 May 1829; Richard Davis, bm; C. Drake, C. C., wit.

Marlow, Middleton & Ann Acre, 4 Feb 1822; Edward Pattillo, bm; Cas Drake, C. C., wit.

Marrow, James A. & Ellen M. Taylor, 8 Sept 1865; S. W. Jones, bm; T. G. Burwell, wit; m 8 Sept 1865 by T. B. Kingsbury, M. G.

Marshal, Wm & _____ Wortham (no date); John Wortham, bm.

Marshall, Charles & Elizabeth Arrington, 21 Feb 1807; Stephen Marshall, bm; Jo Terrell, D. C., wit.

Marshall, David & Patsey Hamlet, 7 May 1795; William Person, bm; J. Moss, wit.

Marshall, David & Patience Evans, 25 June 1823; Isaac Mitchell, bm; Edwin D. Drake, wit.

Marshall, David & Caroline Pegram, 11 Apr 1838; Joseph H. Riggan, bm.

Marshall, Eleazar & Polley Tucker, 9 July 1793; William Allen, bm; Richd Russell, wit.

Marshall, Eli B. & Henney Reter Wood, 7 Oct 1830; John D. Langford, bm; Burl Pitchford, J. P., wit.

Marshall, Hary & Nancy Andrews, 22 Nov 1841; Wm. D. Jones, bm; M. J. Montgomery, wit.

Marshall, Isaac & Mary Foote, 11 June 1785; William Beckham, bm; M. D. Johnson, wit.

Marshall, Jessee & Rebecca King, 1 Nov 1859; Gideon Hamlin, bm; Jno W. White, clk, wit; m 2 Nov 1859 by Wm. C. Clanton, J. P.

Marshall, John H. & Sally D. Christmas, 11 May 1818; Wm. Green, bm.

Marshall, Josiah & Nancy Dowlen, 11 Aug 1803; Saml Marshall, bm; M. Duke Johnson C. C., wit.

Marshall, Matthew & Rebecca Kimball, 21 Dec 1815; Archibald Brown, bm; Sh Green, wit.

Marshall, Matthew & Polly Smiley, 25 Sept 1831; James Vincent, bm; C. Drake, C. C., wit.

Marshall, Thomas D. & Jane Hawks, 7 June 1824; Ransom King, bm; M. M. Drake, wit.

Marshall, William H. & Sally Hazard, 12 Nov 1821; Amos P. Slege, bm; Cas Drake, wit.

Marshall, William R. & Rebecca Moss, 25 Nov 1806; John Owen, bm; Jo Terrell, D. C. C., wit.

Martin, Henry D. & Sarah Bennett, 16 Dec 1833; James Maxwell, bm; E. D. Drake, wit.

Martin, James & Elizabeth Bennett, 31 Aug 1805; Micajah Walker, bm; Jo Terrell, D. C., wit.

Martin, James & Leoa Cunningham, 13 June 1839; John W. White, bm.

Martin, John & Parmelia Duke, 15 Dec 1829; Isham H. Davis, bm.

Martin, Robert & Rhoda Mason, 13 Nov 1828; Richard Evans, bm; M. M. Drake, wit.

Mason, Henry & Harriett Evans, 12 Apr 1834; Griffin Evans, bm; E. D. Drake, clk, wit.

Mason, Henry & Betsey Hamilton, 18 Apr 1843; James Burroughs, bm; M. J. Montgomery, wit.

Mason, Jefferson & Henrietta Hicks, 28 Jan 1854; Solomon Pettyfoot, bm; Jno W. White, wit.

Mason, John & Clary Mason, 10 Dec 1827; Joseph T. Daniel, bm; M. M. Drake ,wit.

Mason, John & Eliza Durham, 14 Sept 1844; James Burroughs, bm; M. J. Montgomery, wit.

Mason, John (col) & Chany Clark, 29 May 1866; James W. Jordan, bm; William A. White, clk, wit; m 31 May 1866 by A. L. Steed, J. P.

Mason, Joshua & Fanny Pettefoot, 16 Dec 1828; Daniel Joiner, bm; E. D. Drake, wit.

Massenburg, Nicholas & Lucy Davis, 5 Nov 1831; Edward Alston, bm.

Mathis, Hopkins & Betsy Langford, 16 Aug 1812; Tilmon Felts, bm; Wm. Green, C. C. C., wit.

Matthews, Hopkins & Susanah Mardray, 13 Feb 1794; Asa Forster, bm; M. Duke Johnson, C. C., wit.

Matthews, Hopkins & Susanah Tanner, 30 Sept 1800; Abner Sears, bm; M. D. Johnson, C. C., wit.

Matthews, Samuel J. & Jane King Bragg, 27 Sept 1865; Sterling Falkener, bm; William A. White, clk, wit; m 8 Oct 1865 by S. P. J. Harris, M. G.

Matthews, William & Sarah J. Duke 18 Nov 1843; John C. Paschall, bm; M. J. Montgomery, wit.

Matthus, William J. & Victoria J. Powell 24 Mar 1847; Mark Matthus, bm; Jno W. White, wit.

Maxwell, James & Virginia Nunnery, 27 Apr 1836; Weldon Hall, bm; E. D. Drake, clk, wit.

May, Chas Oliver & Sallie Shearin, 5 Dec 1865; Thomas C. May, bm; William A. White, clk, wit; m 6 Dec 1865 by B. F. Long, M. G.

May, Enoch & Elizabeth Willson, 1 Jan 1802; Joseph Shearin, bm; Sugan Johnson, wit.

May, Julius & Matilda Myrick, 18 Oct 1824; Henry Talley, bm; E. D. Drake, wit.

Mayfield, Abraham & Mary White, 11 June 1798; Joseph M. Myers, bm; S. Green, wit.

Mayfield, Abraham & Franky Shearrin, 28 Dec 1801; William Mayfield, bm; S. Johnson, wit.

Mayfield, Edmond & Catey Dye, 20 July 1787; Martin Dye, bm; M. Duke Johnson, wit.

Mayfield, Simon (col) & Martha Bellamy, 22 Dec 1866; William A. White, clk, wit; m 23 Dec 1866 by L. C. Perkinson, M. G.

Mayfield, Thomas (col) & Rhoda Wright, 31 Aug 1866; William A. White, clk, wit; m 16 Sept 1866 by L. C. Perkinson, M. G.

Mayfield, William & Elizabeth Shearrin, 7 Nov 1797; Mayfield Bell, bm; Shd Green, wit.

Mayho, Hinton & Mary Drew, 8 Dec 1843; Abraham Seaward, bm; Jas L. Duke, wit.

Mayho, Jesse & Sarah Smith, 20 Jan 1863; James Valentine, bm; William A. White, wit.

Mayhoe, Henry & Nancy Smith, 5 June 1848; George Grain, bm; Jno W. White, wit.

Mayhoe, Jubiter & Rebecca Pettiford, 29 Oct 1809; Jacob Davis, bm; M. Duke Johnson, C. C., wit.

Mayo, Edward & Betsey Mayo, 25 Feb 1832; Hardaway Drue, bm; Burl Pitchford, J. P., wit.

Mayo, Henry & Margarett Guarns, 17 Oct 1809; Richard Russell, bm; M. Duke Johnson, C. C., wit.

Mayo, Isham & Martha Chavis, 26 Nov 1857; Edward Harris, bm; Thomas P. Paschall, J. P., wit; m 26 Nov 1857 by Thomas P. Paschall, J. P.

Mayo, Jeremiah & Betsy Pettyford, 8 Dec 1813; David Burton, Peter R. Davis, bm; Wm. Green, C. C. C., wit.

Meadows, Elijah & Lucy Ann Thomasson, 19 July 1855; William H. Minor, bm; Jno W. White, wit.

Meadows, James & Mary Robertson, 21 Apr 1843; William L. Harriss, bm; M. J. Montgomery, wit.

Meadows, Thomas P. & Ann Durham, 3 Feb 1840; Jos S. Jones, bm.

Mealer, James & Saly Haris, 3 Jan 1778; Fredrick Harris, bm; John Parrish, wit.

Medlin, Asa & Harriet Allgood, 24 Aug 1841; Edward Power, bm.

Melvin, G. W. & Mary E. Thompson, 22 Dec 1864; John Burroughs, bm; William A. White, clk, wit.

Merritt, John & Rebecah Patterson, 25 Mar 1785; Thomas Merritt, bm; M. Duke Johnson, wit.

Merritt, Silvanus & Mary Carter, 14 June 1795; John Merritt, bm; M. D. Johnson, C. C., wit.

Merritt, Thomas & Rebecca Riggon, 24 Oct 1783; James Myrick, bm; M. Duke Johnson, wit.

Merryman, P. R. & Mrs. Mary Davis, 4 Sept 1851; Saml R. Hunt, bm; Jno W. White, wit; m 9 Sept 1851 by A. C. Harris, M. G.

Milam, Cyrus (col) & Sally Garnes, 19 Apr 1867; John O. Drake, bm; Jno C. McCraw, wit; m 21 Apr 1867 by N. A. Purefoy, M. G.

Milam, Drury & Rebeccah Short, 3 Feb 1789; Lawrence Knoles, bm; M. Duke Johnson, C. C., wit.

Milam, Ellick (col) & Louisa Shearin, 7 Apr 1866; Frank M. Fitts, bm; William A. White, clk, wit; m 8 Apr 1866 by Thos B. Ricks, M. G.

Milam, James & Rebecca Jackson, 4 Jan 1780; Solomon Jackson, bm; Thos Machen, wit.

Milam, John & Elizabeth Short, 22 Dec 1782; James Milam, bm.

Milam, John & Susanah Ellis, 30 Dec 1802; Daniel Pegram, bm; M. Duke Johnson, C. C., wit.

Milam, Nathan & Elizabeth Fitts, 22 Aug 1827; Matthew M. Drake, bm; Thos S. Twitty, wit.

Milam, Rowland & Liddia Jackson, 4 Jan 1785; James Milam, bm; M. Duke Johnson, wit.

Milam, Zachariah & Mary Fitts, 14 Aug 1819; Thos Bragg, bm; C. Drake, C. C., wit.

Milles, Abner & Patsey Harper, 25 Aug 1801; Warwick Doyal, bm; M. D. Johnson, C. C., wit.

Mills, Daniel & Mary Good, 2 Aug 1791; Benjamin Bradley, bm; M. Duke Johnson, C. C., wit.

Mills, Major & Rody Carter, 7 Oct 1856; William Mitchell, bm; Jno W. White, wit.

Mills, Samuel M. & Lucy Ann Foote, 9 Dec 1845;; Jacob W. Holt, bm; M. J. Montgomery, wit.

Mills, Solomon & Martha Colclough, 12 July 1865; Redding McGee, bm; William A. White, clk, wit; m 12 July 1865 by T. B. Kingsbury, M. G.

Mils, Abner & Rebecca Dickens, 24 June 1809; William Price (of Halifax Co.), bm; M. D. Johnson, C. C., wit.

Minge, Alexander & Loisa Shearin, 12 Sept 1832; Jesse Pittard, bm; C. Drake, C. C., wit.

Minge, Jesse (col) & Mariah Williams, 26 Dec 1866; William A. White, clk, wit; m 19 Dec 1866 by Saml Bobbitt, J. P.

Mingo, Richard & Sarah Rodwell, 27 July 1836; James A. Egerton, bm; E. D. Drake, clk, wit.

Mingo, Williamston & Martha Egerton, 22 May 1834; Jesse Pittard, bm.

Mise, William J. & Elizabeth C. Richardson, 9 Jan 1850; William V. Mabry, bm; Richd B. Robinson, wit.

Mitchel, William P. & Amelia W. Martin, 31 July 1850; Philip T. Norwood, bm; Jno W. White, wit.

Mitchell, Henry & Eliza Lankford, 8 Mar 1853; Tippoo Brownlow, bm; John W. Paschall, wit; m 17 Mar 1853 by B. Eaton, J. P.

Mitchell, Henry & Mary E. Ashe, 3 Feb 1858; George J. Hendrick, bm; Jno W. White, clk,wit; m 6 Feb 1858 by A. L. Steed, J. P.

Mitchell, Hilliard (col) & Rhoda Birchett, 10 Aug 1864; Stephen G. Cawthorn, bm; William A. White, clk, wit; m 24 Dec 1865 by Wm. Wallace White, J. P.

Mitchell, John & Edith Shearin, 13 Dec 1792; John Brown, bm; M. D. Johnson, C. C., wit.

Mitchell, John & Susan Burton, 26 Feb 1829; Thomas G. Watkins, bm; E. D. Drake, wit.

Mitchell, Peter & Elizabeth H. Person, 14 Oct 1824; Thomas White, bm.

Monger, Henry & Alsey Jones, 29 Oct 1803; Joseph Gardner, bm; Gideon Johnson, wit.

Montford, Thos J. & Ceiley Bobbett, 8 Oct 1822; Kinchen Harris, bm; Cas Drake, C. C., wit.

Montgomery, Benjamin S. & Caroline Daly, 18 June 1846; Thomas A. Montgomery, wit.

Montgomery, Marcellus J. & Mary A. L. Johnson, 18 Dec 1847; Philemon Jinkens, bm; Jno W. White, wit.

Montgomery, Thomas A. & Darica D. Cheek, 25 Oct 1843; Kemp P. Alston, bm; M. J. Montgomery, wit.

Montgomery, Thomas A. & Sarah H. Dowtin, 11 July 1853; Will A. Jenkins, bm; Jno W. White, wit; m 13 July 1853 by Robt O. Burton, M. G.

Montgomery, William & Charlot H. Jordan, 6 Jan 1809; David Terry, bm; J. C. Johnson, D. C., wit.

Moody, James & Rebeccah Wilson, 15 Jan 1804; Samuel Wren, bm; M. Duke Johnson, C. C., wit.

Moody, William A. & Nancy H. Barner, 16 Dec 1818; W. A. K. Falkener, bm.

Moor, John & Sally Sturdevant, 6 June 1832; John Darnol, bm; C. Drake, C. C., wit.

Moor, Thomas & Salley Shell (no date); William Shell, bm.

Moore, David & Mary Howard, 27 Aug 1784; Thomas Washington, bm; M. Duke Johnson, wit.

Moore, Edward & Decy Mangum, 1 Nov 1820; Bartholomew Fortner, bm; Cas Drake, C. C., wit.

Moore, Elijah & Thamar Rosser, 4 Jan 1802; Richard Towns, bm; M. Duke Johnson, C. C., wit.

Moore, Higdon & Betty Bennitt, 30 Dec 1783; John Bobbitt, bm; M. D. Johnson, wit.

Moore, Higdon & Nancy Terry, 28 July 1810; Robert Moore, bm; Jno C. Johnson, C. C., wit.

Moore, James B. & Quinny Bennett, 26 Nov 1849; Thomas Haithcock, bm; Jno W. White, wit.

Moore, James C. & Cynthia Bell, 7 Jan 1828; Carter Nunnery, bm; M. M. Drake, wit.

Moore, John (son of Mark Moore) & Rebecca _____lly, 12 June 1780; Mark Moore, bm.

Moore, John & Elizabeth Felts, 24 Dec 1832; Jno P. Beasley, bm; C. Drake, C. C., wit.

Moore, Dr. John & Lucy Burgess (dau of Jno Burgess), 10 June 1851; A. Alston, bm; Jno W. White, wit, m 11 June 1851 by Robt O. Burton.

Moore, Jordan & Nancy Parish, 26 May 1825; Isham H. Davis, bm; C. Drake, C. C. C., wit.

Moore, Lewis & Hannah Moore, 9 May 1831; Plummer More, bm; C. Drake, C. C., wit.

Moore, Plummer & Nancy Moore, 6 Dec 1834; Lewis Moore, bm; E. D. Drake, clk, wit.

Moore, Robert & Hicksey Bobbitt, 19 Nov 1817; Wm. B. Clark, bm; W. A. K. Falkener, wit.

Moore, Thos & Vesta Myrick, 16 Dec 1795; Daniel Vaulx, bm; M. D. Johnson, C. C., wit.

Moore, Wm. B. & Barsha Bennett, 24 Feb 1817; John Allen, bm; Wm. Green, C. C., wit.

Moran, William & Delila Mann, 25 Aug 1780; Aaron Sparks, bm.

Mordecai, Jacob & Rebecca Myers, 20 Mar 1798; Joseph M. Myers, bm; James Moss, bm.

More, Robert & Polley Hathcock, 7 Mar 1805; Anthony Dowtin, bm; M. D. Johnson, C. C., wit.

Morey, James & Mary Sturdivant, 9 Nov 1796; David Moss, bm; S. Green, wit.

Morey, Jeremiah & Betsey Sturdivant, 22 Apr 1799; David Thomas, bm; M. D. Johnson, C. C., wit.

Morey, John & Salley Hamilton, 15 July 1825; John Darnal, bm; Burl Pitchford, wit.

Morgin, Mark & Elizabeth Good, 5 Mar 1793; Daniel Mills, bm; M. Duke Johnson, C. C., wit.

Morris, John & Caty Wilson, 24 Nov 1798; Daniel Mills, bm; M. Duke Johnson, C. C., wit.

Morris, Lewis & Dolly Wallace, 26 Dec 1810; Mark Ward, bm; Jno C. Johnson, D. C., wit.

Morriss, Isham & Polly Harris, 30 Dec 1801; Wilmot E. Harris, bm; Sugan Johnson, wit.

Morriss, John & Mary Haney, 7 Jan 1825; Joseph Carter, bm; E. D. Drake, wit.

Morriss, Marculandus & Theopatra Shearin, 28 June 1838; N. N. Southall, bm.

Mosby, Richard H. & Mary A. Little, 9 Feb 1826; Robert R. Johnson, bm; M. M. Drake, wit.

Mosby, Robert & Adalene Johnston, 14 Feb 1866; Mary A. Mosby, bm; C. M. Cook, wit; m 14 Feb 1866 by C. M. Cook, J. P.

Mosee, Mason Godfry & Mary Williams, 23 Apr 1792; William Weaver, bm; M. Duke Johnson, wit.

Moseley, Abner & Sarah Kirkland, 20 Dec 1832; Bennitt H. Stanmire, bm; C. Drake, C. C., wit.

Moseley, Benjamin & Sousan Singleton, 25 May 1850; Joseph Clay, bm; James E. Crichton, wit.

Moseley, Hardaway & Harriet Richardson, 6 Apr 1822; Francis Jones, bm.

Moseley, James & Patsey Archer, 20 Dec 1799; John Colclough, bm; Shd Green, wit.

Moseley, James & Mrs. Ann Turner, 18 Feb 1867; William A. White, clk, wit; m 18 Feb 1867 by Jno W. Pattillo, J. P.

Moseley, Jesse & Jane Edmonds, 17 Jan 1799; Martin Smith, bm; Shd Green, wit.

Moseley, John & Delila Wall, 5 Feb 1805; Drury Jones Barner, bm; M. Duke Johnson, C. C., wit.

Moseley, John & Nancy Waller, 24 Feb 1806; James Fain, Jr., bm; Jo Terrell, D. C. C., wit.

Moseley, John W. & Sarah L. Coleman, 10 May 1824; Robert R. Johnson ,bm; M. M. Drake, wit.

Moseley, Nathan S. & Mary J. Woodson, 28 Feb 1866; Jno M. Waddill, bm; William A. White, C. C. C., wit; m 1 Mar 1866 by T. B. Kingsbury.

Moseley, Nicholas (col) & Mary Jane Thornton, 19 May 1866; Robt B. Thornton, bm; Wm. H. Shaw, wit; m 19 May 1866 by R. S. F. Peete, J. P.

Mosely, Andrew J. & Margaret C. Barner, 2 Apr 1856; Benja W. Ivie, bm; H. T. Brown, bm; m by Rich B. Robinson, J. P.

Mosely, Hartwell & Martha Carroll, 26 Dec 1831; James Maxwell, bm; E. D. Drake, wit.

Mosley, John & Lucy Carroll, 24 Dec 1830; John Kirkland, bm; C. Drake, C. C., wit.

Moss, Barrot & Ann Merrit, 15 Apr 1811; John Southall, bm; M. Duke Johnson, C. C., wit.

Moss, Benjamin & Ann W. Harris, 29 Nov 1814; Gideon Harton, bm; W. Green, C. C., wit.

Moss, Bennet & Nancy Vaughan, 27 May 1809; Benjamin Jordan, bm; M. Duke Johnson, C. C., wit.

Moss, David & Lucy Twitty, 18 Nov 1793; Philip Hawkins, bm; M. Duke Johnson, C. C., wit.

Moss, H. R., Jr., & Robert A. Fleming, 18 June 1865; John R. Talley, bm; William A. White, wit.

Moss, Howell & Nancy Daniel, 28 Jan 1791; John Daniel, bm.

Moss, Howell R. & Mrs. Mary A. Duke, 18 May 1864; I. J. Moss, bm; William A. White, clk, wit; m 19 May 1864 by Jas T. Russell, J. P.

Moss, Iry & Rebecca Moss, 11 Nov 1858; Leonard T. Mabry, bm; Jno W. White, clk, wit; m 24 Nov 1858 by Jas T. Russell, J. P.

Moss, James & Priscilla M. Macon, 9 July 1807; M. Duke Johnson, bm; Jo Terrell, C. C. C., wit.

Moss, James F. & Elizth R. Cale, 28 Nov 1843; William G. Watkins, bm; M. J. Montgomery, wit.

Moss, Richard & Dionitia Davis, 20 June 1840; James M. Williams, bm.

Moss, Samuel & Elizabeth Loyl, 30 July 1806; Henry Foote, bm; M. D. Johnson, C. C., wit.

Moss, Wilkins & Elizabeth Hasilwood, 8 Jan 1780; Warwick Hasilwood, bm; Thos Machen, wit.

Moss, William & Rebecca Robertson, 28 Sept 1798; William Burrow, bm.

Moss, William Daniel & Amanda Cale, 29 Nov 1842; William G. Watkins, bm.

Moss, Williams & Sally Reeves, 16 Dec 1816; Benjamin Moss, bm; Wm. Green, C. W. C. C., wit.

Mounger, Spell & Rhody Cogwell, 27 Feb 1799; Atkins McLamore, bm; Shd Green, wit.

Munford, Edward J. H. & Virginia A. Andrews, 12 Nov 1832; Littleberry Andrews, bm; C. Drake, C. C., wit.

Munford, James H. & Elizabeth R. Power, 29 Sept 1807; Thomas Power, bm; Jo Terrell, D Clk, wit.

Mure, William & Eliza Hardy, 20 Feb 1840; John Hardy, bm; Edwd W. Best, clk, wit.

Murphey, George & Polly Kimbell, 13 Oct 1806; Jacob Hunter, bm.

Murphy, John & Delilah M. Flemming, 1 Nov 1841; Robert Watkins, bm; Benj E. Cook, wit.

Murrah, Ambrose & Barbary Fleming, 12 Oct 1808; John C. Green, bm; J. C. Johnson, D. C., wit.

Murrah, Thaddeus & Caty Allen, 14 Dec 1793; Matthew Marshal, bm; Richd Russell, wit.

Mushaw, Badger & Frances Harris, 12 Feb 1856; Jno W. Paschall, bm; Thomas P. Paschall, wit; m 13 Feb 1856 by Thos P. Paschall.

Mushaw, Benjamin & Nancy Hicks, 5 Nov 1845; William J. Edwards, bm; M. J. Montgomery, wit.

Mushaw, Louis & Quientiny Vaughan, 22 June 1856; Alex Chavis, bm; Thos P. Paschall, wit.

Mustain, Lewis & Sarah Bolton, 10 Nov 1855; Jno C. McCraws, bm; Jno W. White, clk, wit; m 11 Nov 1855 by Robt D. Paschall, J. P.

Mustain, Deborix & Francis Loyd, 24 Dec 1802; Daniel Fain, bm; S. Johnson, wit.

Mustain, Deborux & Sarah Loyd, 2 Feb 1811; Lewis Christmas, bm; Jno C. Johnson, D. C., wit.

Mustian, Jesse & Tabatha Hicks, 18 July 1808; Robt R. Johnson, bm; Wm. R. Johnson, wit.

Mustian, John & Mary Wilson, 15 Aug 1848; James Saintsing, bm; Jno W. White, wit.

Mustian, Jno S. & Elizabeth Mustian, 3 Feb 1862; James S. Walker, bm; Jno W. White, clk, wit; m 5 Feb 1862 by Jno W. Pattillo, J. P.

Mustian, Lewis & Mary C. Whitton, 11 Dec 1851; Frederick King, Alfred W. Smith, bm; William A. White, wit; m 18 Dec 1851 by O. D. Fitts, J. P.

Mustian, Williby & Elizabeth Paschall, 16 Nov 1809; George Wilson, bm; Jno C. Johnson, D. C., wit.

Mustian, Willoughby & Lucy Hawks, 15 Dec 1835; Churchwell Bartlett, bm; E. D. Drake, clk, wit.

Mustin, John C. & Eveline King, 11 Nov 1840; Charles B. Thompson, bm; Edwd W. Best, clk, wit.

Mustion, William J. & Susannah B. Whitlow, 18 Dec 1852; Frederick King, bm; Jno W. White, clk, wit; m 19 Dec 1852 by O. D. Fitts, J. P.

Myrick, Benjamin H. & Elizabeth Pearson, 24 Dec 1841; Hardy Myrick, bm.

Myrick, Charles & Martha Ray, 28 Nov 1792; James Myrick, bm.

Myrick, Charles & Mary Hyde, 1 Dec 1818; W. A. Falkener, bm.

Myrick, Giles (col) & Rachael Green, 14 Dec 1865; LaFayette B. Myrick, bm; William A. White, clk, wit; m 19 May 1866 by B. F. Long, M. G.

Myrick, Hardy & Ann F. Hill, 22 Jan 1831; Jesse Myrick, bm.

Myrick, James & Mary F. Shearin, 16 Feb 1835; Amiel Camp, bm.

Myrick, James C. & Mary E. Shearin, 19 Nov 1866; Robert Y. Tucker, bm; J. H. Bennett, wit; m 21 Nov 1866 by John M. Brame, J. P.

Myrick, James Maddison & Mary Shearin, ____ 1842; William H. Bobbitt, bm; M. J. Montgomery, wit.

Myrick, Jesse & Rachel E. Bobbitt, 2 Apr 1821; Charles Myrick, bm; Cas Drake, C. C., wit.

Myrick, John C. & Sarah Nicholson, 19 Nov 1852; J. W. Balthrop, bm; Jno W. White, wit.

Myrick, John H. & Winnefred Stephenson, 28 Nov 1854; W. E. Nicholson, bm; Wm. A. White, wit; m 28 Nov 1854 by H. A. Foote, J. P.

Myrick, LaFayette B. & Mrs. Virginia R. Shearin, 8 Mar 1867; John Collins, bm; William A. White, clk, wit; m 14 Mar 1867 by B. F. Long, M. G.

Myrick, Manuel (col) & Nancy Thornton, 18 Dec 1865; John Collins, bm; William A. White, clk, wit; m 19 Nov 1865 by James C. Robinson, J. P.

Myrick, Moses & Susanah Little, 31 Jan 1791; Philemon Hawkins, Jr., bm; M. Duke Johnson C. C., wit.

Myrick, Moses & Lucretia Brack, 16 Apr 1844; James M. Myrick, bm; M. J. Montgomery, wit.

Myrick, Oran F. & Mary Robarson, 4 Dec 1821; Charles M. Johnson, wit.

Myrick, Owen & Mary Green, 18 Feb 1804; Jordan Worsham, bm; M. D. Johnson ,C. C., wit.

Myrick, Rodolphus & Doritha Mabrey, 2 Jan 1851; Robert Harris, bm; Wm. Green, C. C. C., wit.

Myrick, Thomas & Nisha Omary, 22 Jan 1861; Simon G. Duke, bm; Jno W. White, clk, wit; m 23 Jan 1861 by Jno W. Pattillo, J. P.

Myrick, Thomas H. & Rebecca L. Allen, 11 Sept 1816; Dorrel F. Harris, bm; Wm. Green, C. W. C. C., wit.

Myrick, William & Rebecah Newell, 22 Oct 1786; William Newell, bm; M. Duke Johnson, wit.

Myrick, Wm. Henry (col) & Lizzie Williams, m 26 Jan 1867 by Thos J. Pitchford, J. P.

Myrick, William W. & Susan S. Shearin, 8 Nov 1856; Jarratt H. Shearin, bm; Jno W. White, wit.

Myrick, Willis (col) & Lucinda Browne, 12 Dec 1866; W. A. J. Nicholson, bm; William A. White, wit.

Nance, John & Catharine Harper, 27 Aug 1842; John V. Cawthorn, bm; E. W. Best, wit.

Nanney, George W. & Eliza Paschall, 16 Jan 1844; Howel B. H. Taylor, bm; M. J. Montgomery, wit.

Nanney, Henry L. & Mary Ledbetter, 28 Dec 1835; John Turner, bm; E. D. Drake, clk, wit.

Nanney, John G. & Elizabeth Ellington, 17 Dec 1838; Thomas P. Paschall, bm; Burl Pitchford, J. P., wit.

Neal, Brooks & Betsey Wright, 15 Apr 1797; John Wright, bm; M. Duke Johnson, C. C., wit.

Neal, Cud & Lucy Robertson, 15 Oct 1807; Modicus Robertson, bm; Jo Terrell, D. C. C., wit.

Neal, Dudley S. & Leacy Lancaster, 15 Feb 1826; Thomas Hardy, bm; M. M. Drake, wit.

Neal, Jack & Syntha Shearin, 17 Nov 1801; Charles Crutchfield, bm; Sugan Johnson, wit.

Neal, John L. & Ann P. Rodwell, 26 Dec 1853; H. T. Duke, bm; Jno W. White, wit; m 27 Dec 1853 by Wm. C. Clanton, J. P.

Neal, Joseph H. & Caroline T. Harris, 16 May 1857; Jones W. Harris, bm; Jno W. White, clk, wit; m 17 May 1857 by William A. Dowtin, J. P.

Neal, Major & Nancy Mayfield, 15 Dec 1801; Abraham Mayfield, bm; Sugan Johnson, wit.

Neal, Richard & Nancy Towns, 28 July 1801; Major Neal, bm; S. Johnson, wit.

Neal, Stephen & Sealy Patterson, ____ 1792; Archd Brown, bm; M. Duke Johnson, C. C., wit.

Neal, Thomas H. & Martha J. Harris, 31 July 1851; J. H. B. Reid, bm; Jno W. White, clk, wit; m 1 Aug 1851 by Wm. C. Clanton, J. P.

Neal, Thomas S. & Nancy Thompson, 23 Dec 1822; Abner Aycock, bm; C. Drake, C. C., wit.

Neal, William & Martha Rudd, 10 May 1838; John Rudd, bm; Burl Pitchford, J. P., wit.

Neal, William W. & Martha L. Bobbitt, 22 Dec 1854; Joseph H. Neal, bm; Jno W. White, clk, wit; m 24 Dec 1854 by Thos J. Pitchford, J. P.

Neal, Wm. W. & Delia Harris, 27 May 1860; Joseph H. Neal, bm; Jno W. White, clk, wit; m 29 May 1860 by W. A. Dowtin, J. P.

Neale, Moses & Betsey Gill, 22 Jan 1785; Isaac Gill, bm; M. D. Johnson, wit.

Neathery, Robert S. & Mouring Hendrick, 30 Mar 1835; Geo W. Barnes, bm.

Nelms, Noyal & Nancy Ransom, 29 Dec 1784; Atkin Mclemore, bm; M. Duke Johnson, wit.

Netherly, Thomas T. & Nancy K. Bennett, 4 Oct 1835; Allen T. Meacham, bm.

Netherry, James & Elizabeth Hendrick, 16 Dec 1829; Thomas Neathery ,bm; E. D. Drake, wit.

Newby, Henry & Frances W. Smith, 27 Mar 1846; Churchwell Curtis, bm; M. J. Montgomery, wit.

Newby, Wm. H. & Elizabeth J. Newby, 2 July 1854; H. G. Goodloe, bm; John J. Brame, wit.

Newell, Alexander D. & Nancy Bobbitt, 5 July 1817; Willis Read, bm; W. Green, C. C., wit.

Newell, Andrew (col) (son of Jefferson & Penny) & Caroline Williams (dau of Harry & Lila) 5 Dec 1867; William A. White, clk, wit; m 7 Dec 1867 by George M. Duke, M. G.

Newell, David & Nancy Cheek, 25 May 1802; Wm Newell, bm; M. Duke Johnson, C. C., wit.

Newell, Edwd & Salley Moody, 19 June 1797; William Newell, bm; Shd Green, wit.

Newell, John D. & Emily Brame, 14 Feb 1854; Jacob August, bm; Jno W. White, clk, wit; m 15 Feb 1854 by Thos J. Pitchford, J. P.

Newell, Matthew L. & Olive Capps, 15 Dec 1804; James Capps, bm; M. Duke Johnson, C. C., wit.

Newell, Peter & Susanah Hail, 9 Nov 1795; David H. Newell, bm.

Newell, Thomas & Elisabeth Daniel, 6 Nov 1782; John Newell, bm.

Newell, William P. & Mary A. T. Powell, 12 May 1824; Isham H. Davis, bm.

Newman, Amacy J. & Mary E. Duty, 28 May 1857; James W. Paschall, bm; Jno W. White, clk, wit; m 28 May 1857 by Thomas P. Paschall, J. P.

Newman, Austin & Lucretia Mabry, 10 Dec 1839; Jno W. White, bm; Edwd W. Best, clk, wit.

Newman, Avery & _____ Wittason (no date); Avery Due, bm.

Newman, Bartlett H. & Ellen R. Wilson, 8 Dec 1843; Richard Omery, bm; M. J. Montgomery, wit.

Newman, Daniel & _____ White, 24 Nov 1790; John White, bm; M. Duke Johnson, C. C. C., wit.

Newman, George & Mary Tucker, 15 Dec 1827; John W. White, bm; M. M. Drake, wit.

Newman, James L. & Martha N. Watkins, 15 Dec 1838; Daniel Taylor, bm; Burl Pitchford, J. P., wit.

Newman, Joseph & Prudence Swinney ,4 Dec 1802; Pleasant Baskett, bm; M. D. Johnson, C. C., wit.

Newman, Macon G. & Althier O. Tucker, 6 Dec 1853; Nathan S. Watkins, bm; Jno W. White, C. C. C., wit; m 14 Dec 1853 by Caswell Drake, M. G.

Newman, Martin & Sally Certin, 7 Sept 1811; Bird Ellington, bm; Wm. Green, C. C. C., wit.

Newman, Reuben & Elizabeth Carrol, 18 July 1822; Edmond Carrol, bm; Cas Drake, C. C., wit.

Newman, Thomas & Nancy Pardue, 5 Dec 1784; James Burk, bm; M. D. Johnson, wit.

Newman, Thomas & Judy Lankford, 23 Dec 1813; William White (son of Jno), bm; Jno H. Green, wit.

Newman, Wiley J. & Martha Towns, 14 Jan 1833; Burwell Pitchford, Jr., bm; Burl Pitchford, J. P., wit.

Newman, William & Catharine Cole, 27 Jan 1821; Thomas Pitchford, bm; Caswell Drake, wit.

Newman, Wm. A. & Mary E. Newman, 20 July 1866; Wm. D. Newman, bm; William A. White, clk, wit; m 22 July 1866 by T. Page Ricaud, M. G.

Newman, William D. & Rhoda C. Moss, 14 Dec 1866; William A. White, C. C. C., wit; m 19 Dec 1866 by Jas T. Russell, J. P.

Newsom, Eaton & Mary Harris, 28 Dec 1824; Silas Tarver, bm; C. Drake, C. C., wit.

Newsom, J. V. & Nancy Nicholson, 18 Oct 1855; S. E. Vaughan, bm.

Newsom, John B. & Elizabeth Nicholson, 26 Nov 1836; Edwin D. Drake, bm; E. D. Drake, clk, wit.

Newsom, John S. & Clarisa A. Rooker, 5 May 1860; James J. Lancaster, bm; Jno W. White, clk, wit; m 8 May 1860 by Nathl Nicholson, J. P.

Newton, Green & Lucy Twisdale, 16 Dec 1828; John G. Chapman, bm.

Newton, Hailey & Polley Taylor, 28 Jan 1830; Howel B. A. Taylor, bm; Burl Pitchford, J. P., wit.

Newton, Henry A. & Mary D. Newton, 29 Nov 1853; W. H. Harris, bm; Jno W. White, wit.

Newton, James G. & Lucy J. Newton, 28 Feb 1853; Richard Nicholson, bm; Wm. A. White, wit; m 1 Mar 1855 by Jas. T. Russell, J. P.

Newton, John B. & Harret E. Newton, 2 Feb 1842; John Langley, bm; Burl Pitchford, J. P., wit.

Newton, John G. & Sarah E. Rudd, 11 Feb 1857; J. S. Bridgers, bm; Jno W. White, clk, wit; m 11 Feb 1857 by A. L. Steed, J. P.

Newton, Joseph & Lucey Taylor, 21 Dec 1826; Howel Taylor, bm.

Newton, Richd G. & Eliza Brown, 18 Feb 1833; William Pearce, bm; C. Drake, C. C. C., wit.

Newton, William & Elizabeth Hargroves, 21 Nov 1822; Haley Newton, bm; E. D. Drake, wit.

Nicholson, Adkin & Mary J. Harris, 1 Dec 1851; Jeremiah McCormick, bm; Jno W. White, clk, wit; m 3 Dec 1851 by Saml Bobbitt, J. P.

Nicholson, Alexander & Molley Fann, 13 Apr 1780; Wm. Noyall Norsworthy, bm; Thos Machen, wit.

Nicholson, Benjamin & Martha Pegram, 17 Mar 1812; George Pegram, bm; Wm. Green, C. C. C., wit.

Nicholson, Brittain & Molly Harris, 18 Apr 1792; Archer Nicholson, bm; M. Duke Johnson, C. C., wit.

Nicholson, Davis & Mary Mabrey, 28 May 1793; William E. Johnson, bm; B. Davis, wit.

Nicholson, Gideon W. & Nancy T. Hicks, 28 Nov 1836; Michael Riggan, bm; E. D. Drake, clk, wit.

Nicholson, James & Martha Shearin, 28 Feb 1831; David Shearin, bm; C. Drake, C. C. C., wit.

Nicholson, John & Nancy Freeman, 22 Feb 1794; Benjamin Freemund, bm; M. Duke Johnson, C. C., wit.

Nicholson, John H. & Bettie R. Shearin, 13 Oct 1857; M. A. J. Nicholson, bm; Jno W. White, clk, wit; m 15 Oct 1857 by N. A. Purefoy, M. G.

Nicholson, John J. & Sally Shearin, 23 Jan 1816; Robt G. Harris, bm; Wm. Green, C. W. C. C., wit.

Nicholson, Macklen & Citha Acrey, 25 May 1824; George Pegram, bm; M. M. Drake, wit.

Nicholson, Nathaniel & Catharine Riggan, 4 May 1841; Benjamin Nicholson, bm.

Nicholson, Nathaniel & Amarellas Shearin, 4 Jan 1838; John W. Riggan, bm; Jno W. White, wit.

Nicholson, Osborn P. & Sackey Hunter, 9 Oct 1799; William P. Little, bm; Sh Green, wit.

Nicholson, Richard & Martha D. White, 20 Dec 1838;' William U. Meacham, bm; Burl Pitchford, J. P., wit.

Nicholson, Solomon (col) & Betsey Cole, 14 Oct 1865; William A. White, clk,wit; m 15 Oct 1865 by Jno W. Pattillo, J. P.

Nicholson, William A. J. & Bettie E. Williams, 31 Oct 1859; Thomas J. Foote, bm; Jno W. White, wit; m 1 Nov 1859 by J. B. Solomon, M. G.

Nicholson, Wyatt & Mary Hazlewood, 20 Dec 1823; Benja Nicholson, bm.

Nicholson, Wyat E. & Mary Pegram, 11 Feb 1848; Benjamin Nicholson, bm; Jno W. White, wit.

Nicolson, Benjamin C. & Mary Thomas, 31 July 1856; E. P. Shearin, bm; Jno W. White, clk, wit; m 31 July 1857 [sic] by Nathl Nicholson, J. P.

Noles, Corban & Sewsy Bell, 18 Feb 1797; John Tansil, bm; Shd Green, wit.

Nolly, George & Lethe Bobbitt, 5 Apr 1831; James F. Rose, bm; C. Drake, C. C., wit.

Nolly, James & Sally Fowler, 13 July 1831; George W. Barnes, bm; C. Drake, C. C., wit.

Norfleet, Stephen A. & M. Louisa Spruill, 22 Aug 1860; Chas W. Spruill, bm; Jno W. White, clk, wit; m 23 Aug 1860 by Wm. Hodges, M. G.

Norman, Samuel & Hanah Roberts, 25 Apr 1791; William Mitchel, bm; M. D. Johnson, C. C., wit.

Norsworthy, Willis & Partheny Balthrop, 2 Mar 1798; Jas Frances, bm; M. D. Johnson, C. C., wit.

Norton, Thomas & Sarah Cousins (no date); George Allen, bm; M. D. Johnson, wit.

Norwood, Benjamin, Jr., & Temperance D. Davis, 28 Nov 1826; Sherwood Green, bm; C. Drake, C. C., wit.

Norwood, P. T. & Rebecca Turner, 3 Sept 1851; Richard C. Pope, bm; Jno W. White, clk, wit; m 10 Sept 1851 by Clemment McRae, M. G.

Nuckals, James & Winnifred Hicks, 23 Sept 1843; M. L. Perdue, bm; M. J. Montgomery, wit.

Nuckles, James H. & Sarah Rudd, 22 Jan 1856; W. V. Allen, bm; Jno W. White, wit.

Nuckles, Jas H. & Elizabeth M. Chapman, 12 Aug 1856; T. M. Parrish, bm; Jno W. White, wit.

Nuckles, Joseph W. & Pink Vaughan, 26 Dec 1857; Edward Harris, bm; Tho P. Paschall, wi;t m 28 Dec 1857 by R. D. Paschall, J. P.

Nuckles, Thomas & Jane Renn, 19 Dec 1846; James Nuckles, bm; Jno W. White, wit.

Nuckles, Thomas & Elizabeth Bobbitt, 12 June 1854; Wm. V. Allen, bm; Jno W. White, wit.

Nuckols, John & Elizabeth Lambert, 2 June 1812; James R. Johnson ,bm; Wm. Green, clk, wit.

Nuckols, Silvester & Salley Sails, 29 Sept 1791; Beavel Pardue, bm; M. Duke Johnson, C. C., wit.

Nuckols, William & Nancy Parish, 17 Feb 1834; Lewis Turner, bm.

Nunn, Thomas & Nancy Dowtin, 30 Jan 1828; Bennett Harriss, bm.

Nunnery, Carter & Priscilla J. Macon, 25 Apr 1815; Madison J. Hawkins, bm; W. Green, C. C., wit.

Nuttall, Alexander H. & Mateld C. Hawkins, 9 Nov 1830; Zachariah Herndon, bm; C. Drake, C. C., wit.

Oathworth, Thomas & Sarah Lampkin, 10 Dec 1823; George W. Macon, bm;

O'Bryan, Dennis & Polly Green, 21 June 1811; Stephen Davis, bm; Wm. Green, C. C. C., wit.

Ogburn, Charles W. & Fluoy Gill, 13 Dec 1853; Cs. R. Edmonson, bm; Jno W. White, clk, wit; m 13 Dec 1853 by P. A. March.

Oliver, Asa & Charlotte Webb, 12 June 1790; George Webb, bm; M. Duke Johnson, C. C., wit.

Olmstead, James & Lucretia E. Riggan, 20 Jan 1844; Michl Riggan, bm; M. J. Montgomery, wit.

Omarey, George W. & Ellendar Langford, 6 Mar 1840; Robert D. Paschall, bm; Burl Pitchford, J. P., wit.

Omary, Rhoda & Hollon Paschall, 1 Dec 1831; Richard Omary, bm; C. Drake, C. C., wit.

Omary, Richard & Irenie Paschall, 21 May 1819; Thomas Omary, bm; C. Drake, C. W. C. C., wit.

Omary, Rodolphus & Patience Bartlett, 9 Dec 1841; Green B. Paschall, bm; M. J. Montgomery, wit.

Omary, Weldon & Permelia J. Bolton, 4 Oct 1851; Rodolphus Omary, bm; Jno W. White, clk, wit; m 13 Oct 1851 by Jas T. Russell, J. P.

Omerry, Thomas & Rilly Paschall, 12 Feb 1817; Thomas Nuckols, bm; Wm. Green, C. W. C. C., wit.

Oslin, David & Elizabeth O. Oslin, 7 Nov 1845; Peter J. Turnbull, bm; M. J. Montgomery, wit.

Ostwalt, Henry & Betsey Williams, 25 Nov 1780; Thomas Machen, bm.

Overton, John C. & Lucy Southall, 24 Aug 1847; William Joyner, bm; Jno W. White, wit.

Overton, Moses & Mary A. J. Vaughan, 7 Nov 1837; James Garrett, bm; E. W. Best, clk, wit.

Owen, Hugh B. & Ann E. Davis, 28 Dec 1840; James T. Walker, bm; Burl Pitchford, J. P., wit.

Owen, John & Nancy Cocke, 29 July 1811; Halcot Terrell, b; Wm. Green, C. C., wit.

Owen, Philip & Polley Brown, ___ 1798; John Owen, bm; John Moore, wit.

Owens, John & Polly Williams, 25 Mar 1800; Povy Carter, bm; S. Johnson, wit.

Ownley, John & Elizabeth Jones, 17 May 1824; Henry H. Maclin, bm.

Ozburn, John & Obedience Kendrick (no date); James Kendrick, bm; M. Duke Johnson, C. C., wit.

Pace, William A. & Mariah E. Farrer, 30 May 1853; J. Alex Pace, bm; Jno W. White, clk, wit; m 30 May 1853 by N. A. Purefoy, M. G.

Paine, Jas & Mary W. Alexander (no date); John Norsworthy, bm; Wm. R. Johnson, wit.

Paine, Thomas & Cynthia F. Power, 9 Feb 1813; Micajah T. Hawkins, bm; Jno H. Green, wit.

Painter, Thomas & Frances Ellington, 12 Sept 1857; Armistead King, bm; Jno W. White, clk, wit; m 14 Sept 1857 by H. J. Macon, J. P.

Palmer, Amasa D. & Elizabeth Rooker, 20 Mar 1826; Anthony Davis, bm.

Palmer, Charles & Polly Cole, 1 Nov 1813; Smith Palmer, bm; Wm. Green, C. C. C., wit.

Palmer, Elihu J. & Doritha Sutton, 29 July 1813; William Marshall, bm; Wm. Green, C. C. C., wit.

Palmer, Horace & Caroline Fitts, 19 May 1838; James O'K. Mayfield, bm; Edwd W. Best, clk, wit.

Palmer, Horace, Jr., & Sallie E. Milam, 12 Apr 1855; James C. Robinson, bm; Jno W. White, clk, wit; m 18 Apr 1855 by T. G. Lowe, M. G.

Palmer, Isaac (col) (son of Thomas Hinton and Patsey Palmer) & Salinda Moseley (dau of Squire Moseley & Jane Moseley), m 9 Nov 1867 by Jas C. Robinson, J. P.

Palmer, Jacob M. & Bettie F. Rodwell, 9 Aug 1853; Jas T. Russell, bm; William A. White, wit; m 17 Aug 1853 by Thos G. Lowe, M. G.

Palmer, Jacob M. & Sophie George Finley, 28 Feb 1865; Maj. Wm. C. Drake, bm; William A. White, clk, wit; m 1 Mar 1865 by J. R. Finley, D. D.

Palmer, Paul & Bettie Twitty, 14 Jan 1867; Wm. H. Palmer, bm; William A. White, clk, wit; m 16 Jan 1867 by James P. Moore, M. G.

Palmer, Robt (col) & Jinsey Ann Allgood, 15 Dec 1866; William A. White, clk, wit; m 27 Dec 1866 by R. S. F. Peete, J. P.

Palmer, Smith & Elizabeth Mayfield, 18 Feb 1811; Reuben Wright, Jr., bm; Wm. Green, C. C. C., wit.

Palmer, Thomas & Polly Mayfield, 28 Aug 1806; Thomas H. Davis, bm; M. Duke Johnson, C. C., wit.

Palmer, Wm. H. & Alice F. Scoggins, 5 Dec 1865; Jacob M. Palmer, bm; William A. White, wit.

Pardue, Daniel A. & Mary Beckham, 1 July 1807; Robert Pardue, bm; Jo Terrell, D. C. C., wit.

Pardue, Joel & Sarah Weaver, 14 Dec 1802; Sylvester Nuccols, bm; Sugan Johnson, wit.

Pardue, John & Nancy Rowland, 20 Feb 1787; Patram Pardue, bm; M. D. Johnson, C. C., wit.

Pardue, John & Clarimon Cooper, 23 Feb 1791; Cannon Cooper, bm; M. Duke Johnson, C. C., wit.

Pardue, John & Elizabeth Godfrey, 21 Dec 1802; Sylvester Nucchols, bm; Sugan, Johnson, wit.

Pardue, John & Elby Duty, 26 Aug 1813; William Smith, bm; Wm. Green, C. C. C., wit.

Pardue, Morriss & Molley Jenkins, 7 Sept 1781; Patram Purdue, bm; Thos Machen, wit.

Pardue, Patram & Nancy Flemming, 29 Nov 1811; Pleasant Baskett, bm; Jo Terrell, D. C. C., wit.

Pardue, Philemon & Liza Allen, 24 May 1810; James Ball, bm; Jno C. Johnson, D. C. C., wit.

Pardue, Pleasant & Sally Tucker, 29 May 1811; John Perdue, bm; Wm. Green, C. C. C., wit.

Pardue, Solomon & Sarah C. Harton, 12 Dec 1826; Joseph P. Johnson, bm; M. M. Drake, wit.

Pardue, Thomas & Sally Godfrey, 10 Aug 1802; James Clark, bm; Sugan Johnson, wit.

Pardue, William & Jane Savage, 13 June 1807; Patram Pardue, bm;

Pardue, William & Blancket Tucker, 22 Dec 1809; Aaron Fussill, bm; M. Duke Johnson, C. C., wit.

Pardue, William & Mildred Fortner, 7 Feb 1831; Gideon Harton, bm; C. Drake, C. C., wit.

Parham, Henry Gee & Susan J. Deloney, 26 Dec 1843; B. H. Stammire, bm; M. J. Montgomery, wit.

Parham, John & Deliley Williams, 31 Mar 1799; Pleasant Baskett, bm; Shd Green, wit.

Parham, Samuel & Nancy Garrott, 28 Nov 1797; Daniel Duke, bm; Shd Green, wit.

Parham, Samuel J. & Maria L. Southerland, 23 Jan 1866; Rev. T. B. Kingsbury, bm; William A. White, clk, wit; m 24 Jan 1866 by T. B. Kingsbury.

Parham, Smith, & Harriet G. Blan, 20 Dec 1826; Tyre B. Jackson, bm; Burl Pitchford, wit.

Parham, William & Rebecah Rains, 4 Dec 1800; William Lesslie, bm; J. Moore, wit.

Parham, William A. & Hannah J. Turnbull, 5 Aug 1850; Peter J. Turnbull, bm; Jno W. White, wit.

Parish, Banister & Hannah Foster, 20 Dec 1823; Thomas Allen, bm; Edwin D. Drake, wit.

Parish, Edward & Sally Green, 21 Dec 1821; Churchwell Bartlet, bm; Cas Drake, wit.

Parish, Edwd & Nancy Tanner, 25 Feb 1823; William Tanner, bm; C. Drake, C. C., wit.

Parish, Hutson & Druscilla Sturdivant, 5 Apr 1814; Anderson Sturdivant, bm; M. J. Hawkins, wit.

Parish, Joel & Nancy Shearin, 27 July 1811; Robert Hariss, bm; Jno H. Green, wit.

Parish, John & Isabella Hicks, 27 Nov 1838; Solon Southerland, bm.

Parish, Stephen S. & Elizabeth Jackson, 23 Aug 1831; Michael Riggan, bm; M. M. Drake, wit.

Parish, William & Eliza Jane Wilson, 17 Dec 1839; Thos Wilson, bm; Edwd W. Best, wit.

Park, Edward (col) (son of Rebecca Park) & Harriet Moss (dau of Nelson & Oney), 4 July 1867; William A. White, clk, wit; m 6 July 1867 by James C. Robinson, J. P.

Park, William (col) (son of Edward & Sarah) & Betty Cheek (dau of John Eaton & Elvira Cheek), 20 July 1867; William A. White, clk, wit; m 20 July 1867 by John S. Cheek, J. P.

Parker, Francis & Nancy Little, 10 Aug 1799; John Randolph, bm; Shd Green, wit.

Parker, Jacob & Bettie K. Kearney, 20 Nov 1855; Fran M. Hyman, bm; Jno W. White, clk, wit; m 21 Nov 1855 by W. H. Jordan.

Parker, Rodon & Sarah M. Langford, 8 Jan 1839; William P. Rose, bm.

Parrish, J. G. & Elizabeth J. Harris, 31 Aug 1859; Godfrey Augustin, bm; William A. White, wit; m 14 Sept 1859 by Saml Bobbitt, J. P.

Parrish, John & Elizabeth Lancaster, 12 Jan 1813; M. Duke Johnson, bm; Wm Green, C. C. C., wit.

Parrish, William D. & Nancy Ellis, 8 Nov 1848; John S. Mustian, bm; Jno W. White, wit.

Paschael, John & Mary Robertson, 26 Nov 1783; William Paschael, bm; M. D. Johnson, wit.

Paschael, Robert & Lucy Todd, 27 Aug 1787; Phil Hawkins, bm.

Paschal, James & Maryann Burchitt, 4 Feb 1783; James Burchitt, bm; M. Duke Johnson, wit.

Paschal, James & Rachel Willson, 24 Dec 1802; Richard Wadkins, bm; Sugan Johnson, wit.

Paschal, John & Patsy Wilson, 15 Dec 1798; Wm Malone, bm; Sherwood Green, wit.

Paschal, William H. & Salley Perkinson, 18 May 1831; Peyton V. Duke, bm; Burl Pitchford, J. P., wit.

Paschall, Anderson & Sally Twitty, 26 Apr 1795; Jordan Worsham, bm; J. Moss, wit.

Paschall, Beckham (col) & Ann Carroll, 20 Dec 1866; William A. White, clk, wit; m 26 Dec 1866 by R. D. Paschall, J. P.

Paschall, Edmund & Nancy Wilson, 27 May 1814; Edward Burchett, bm; W. Green, C. C. C., wit.

Paschall, George & Viny Rivers, 21 Oct 1841; Thomas P. Walker, bm; M. J. Montgomery, wit.

Paschall, Green B. & Marey Perkinson, 20 Feb 1829; John Paschall, bm; Burl Pitchford, J. P., wit.

Paschall, Hansel & Polly Smith, 8 Jan 1823; Green B. Langford, bm; C. Drake, C. C., wit.

Paschall, Henry & Polley Capps, 27 Feb 1811; William R. Johnson ,bm; M. D. Johnson, C. C., wit.

Paschall, J. Wm. Henry & Mrs. Sarah E. Gill, 23 Apr 1866; John R. Turnbull, bm; William A. White, clk, wit; m 25 Apr 1866 by L. C. Perkinson, M. G.

Paschall, James & Dolley Hamilton, 31 Dec 1835; Samuel E. Phillips, bm; Burl Pitchford, J. P., wit.

Paschall, John & Rody Pitchford, 11 Feb 1807; George Smith, bm; Jo Terrell, D. C. C., wit.

Paschall, John C. & Jacky P. L. Laughter, 23 Dec 1843; Peter D. Paschall, bm; M. J. Montgomery, wit.

Paschall, John T. (col) & Virginia Russell, 21 Dec 1865; Thomas P. Paschall, bm; William A. White, clk, wit; m 26 Dec 1865 by Jas T. Russell, J. P.

Paschall, John W. & Martha A. Paschall, 19 Mar 1857; T. P. Walker, bm; Jno W. White, clk, wit; m 19 Mar 1857 by Wm. A. Burwell, J. P.

Paschall, Joshua & Lucy Hicks, 4 Jan 1809; Samuel Paschall, bm; J. C. Johnson, D. C. C., wit.

Paschall, Joshua & Suassan Langford, 17 Nov 1824; John Hawgood, bm; Burl Pitchford, wit.

Paschall, Luke & Ellin Burrows, 22 Feb 1823; Francis Tucker, bm; Edwin D. Drake, wit.

Paschall, Mark & Sarah Burchett, 14 Feb 1807; Charles Bennitt, bm; Jo Terrell, D. C. C., wit.

Paschall, Michael W. & Frances R. Ellington, 14 Dec 1865; Samuel Bobbitt, bm; William A. White, clk, wit; m 19 Dec 1865 by J. W. Wellons, M. G.

Paschall, Michael W., Jr., & Hester Ann Paschall, 26 Oct 1835; Nathaniel D. Brickle, bm; E. D. Drake, clk, wit.

Paschall, Michael Wood & Elizabeth Wood, 4 Jan 1811; James Darnall, bm; Jno C. Johnson, D. C. C., wit.

Paschall, Phinawel J. & Nancy A. O. Buchannon, 9 Dec 1835; William F. Hilliard, bm; E. D. Drake, clk, wit.

Paschall, Robert & Nancy D. Hagwood, 24 Feb 1816; Jesse Walker, bm; Will Green, C. C. C., wit.

Paschall, Robert A. & Martha D. Roberson, 1 Dec 1858; Warren H. Cappas, bm; William A. White, wit; m 7 Dec 1858 by Wm. A. Burwell, J. P.

Paschall, Robert D. & Mary E. Walker, 16 Sept 1848; John Hicks, bm; Jno W. White, wit.

Paschall, Robt H. M. & Melissa A. Twisdale, 29 May 1860; Samuel Harper, bm; Jno W. White, clk, wit; m 31 May 1860 by B. F. Long.

Paschall, Robert W. & Lucy N. Paschall, 20 Apr 1852; Thomas P. Paschall, bm; Daniel Burckett, wit; m 21 Apr 1852 by Caswell Drake.

Paschall, Samuel & Dizzy Long, 21 Feb 1793; Anderson Paschal, bm.

Paschall, Samuel A. & Nancy King, 10 Nov 1858; Thomas P. Walker, bm; William A. White, wit; m 10 Nov 1858 by L. G. Perkinson, M. G.

Paschall, Thomas & Salley Mabry, 17 Dec 179_ (1795-8, admn of Gov. Samuel Ashe); Richard Wadkins, bm; Sherwood Green, wit.

Paschall, Thomas M. & Mahala G. Lambkin, 4 Sept 1840; Jno W. White, bm.

Paschall, Thomas P. & Elizabeth Andrews, 25 July 1861; D. B. Kimball, bm; R. D. Paschall, wit; m 25 July 1861 by R. D. Paschall, J. P.

Paschall, Ward & Elizabeth Wilson, 15 Aug 1806; John Paschall, bm; M. Duke Johnson, C. C., wit.

Paschall, Wesley G. & Sarah H. Harper, 21 Jan 1850; George W. Harper, bm; Jno W. White, wit.

Paschall, William & Martha Wittson, 12 May 1807; Henry Paschall, bm; W. R. Johnson, wit.

Paschall, William E. & Suasan Dowland, 29 Nov 1838; Daniel Taylor, bm; Burl Pitchford, J. P., wit.

Paschall, William E. & Martha A. Riggans, 9 Dec 1843; John N. Turner, Jr., bm.

Paschall, William T. & Lucy D. Hagood, 4 Sept 1847; William Matthus, bm; Jno W. White, wit.

Paschall, William W. & Martha Bartlette, 16 Dec 1828; John Andrews, bm; Burl Pitchford, wit.

Paschall, Willie & Polly Wilson, 24 Nov 1819; Hansel Paschall, bm; Cas Drake, C. C. C., wit.

Paterson, Jordan & Elizabeth Reed, 30 Nov 1799; Thomas Reed, bm; Shd Green, wit.

Patrick, John & Charlot Harris, 23 Apr 1805; Lewis Patrick, bm; M. Duke Johnson, C. C., wit.

Patrick, Lewis & Tabby Lewiston(?), 30 Mar 1807; John Capps, bm; John P. Johnson, wit.

Patrick, Reuben & Elizabeth Allen, 12 Dec 1783; Georg Allen, bm; M. D. Johnson, wit.

Patrick, Reubin & Elisabeth Allen, 4 Feb 1785; Lewis Patrick, bm; M. D. Johnson, wit.

Patrick, William & Polley Cole, 13 Jan 1792; Lewis Patrick, bm.

Patterson, Burrel & Tabby Finch, 11 Aug 181; James H. Highs, bm; Wm. Green, C. C. C., wit.

Patterson, Calloway & Nancy Ragsdale (no date); Littleberry Patterson, bm; M. D. Johnson, C. C. C., wit.

Patterson, George & Rebecca Falkner, 10 Oct 1822; Edward Tillet, bm.

Patterson, Green & Quinney Moore, 17 May 1855; Fleming Thompson, bm; Wm. A. White, wit; m 18 May 1855 by John S. Cheek, J. P.

Patterson, Henry & Temperance Haythcock, 10 Feb 1825; Myrick Duke, bm; E. D. Drake, wit.

Patterson, Isham & Nancy Young, 29 Nov 1785; William Patterson, bm; M. Duke Johnson, wit.

Patterson, James & Betty Hightower, 1 Feb 1782; Presly Thorn, bm.

Patterson, James & Polley Morris, 19 Oct 1789; Herbert Harris, bm; M. D. Johnson, C. C., wit.

Patterson, Jno & Sarah Parish (no date); John Featherston, bm; M. D. Johnson, C. C., wit.

Patterson, John & Nancy J. Carroll, 4 May 1813; Charles Palmer, bm; Jno H Green, wit.

Patterson, Littlebury & Elisabeth Ragsdale (no date); Isham Patterson, bm; M. Duke Johnson, C. C., wit.

Patterson, William & Betsy Crowder, 9 Oct 1789; John Featherston, bm; M. Duke Johnson, C. C., wit.

Patterson, William & Anne Cunningham, 26 Oct 1818; John Andrews, bm.

Pattillo, Augustin C. & Mrs. Judith Johnson, 20 Sept 1825; Robert Cook, bm; Joseph A. Drake, wit.

Pattillo, Edward & Nancy Mayfield, 7 Apr 1814; William Green, bm.

Pattillo, George G. & Elizabeth Moseley, 14 Nov 1826; Robert Cook, bm; M. M. Drake, wit.

Pattillo, Israel (col) & Violet Green, 28 Dec 1866; William A. White, clk, wit; m 31 Dec 1866 by Jno W. Pattillo.

Pattillo, James E. & Winnefred Kimball, 29 Dec 1840; Thomas A. Montgomery, wit.

Pattillo, James H. & Louiza J. Land, 4 Sept 1849; Charles M. Pattillo, bm; Jno W. White, wit.

Pattillo, John W. & Mary S. Hicks, 3 Feb 1861; Richd A. Davis, bm; Jno W. White, clk, wit; m 13 Feb 1861 by Lemmon Shell, M. G.

Pattillo, John W. & Mary A. Cole, 26 Sept 1865; Thomas E. White, bm; William A. White, clk, wit; m 1 Oct 1865 by T. Page Ricaud, M. G.

Pattillo, Williamson & Mary M. White, 24 May 1831; John E. Walker, bm; C. Drake, C. C., wit.

Payne, Robert & Betsey Williams, 25 Apr 1804; Alanson Williams, bm; M. Duke Johnson, C. C., wit.

Peagram, Daniel & Permelia Bennitt, 20 Dec 1824; Gideon Harris, bm; Jos A. Drake, wit.

Pearce, John & Rebecca Allen, 16 Oct 1800; Edwd Kimbell, bm; M. D. Johnson, C. C., wit.

Pearce, John W. & Martha S. B. Williams, 13 May 1845; Peter D. Powell, bm.

Pearcy, James & Susan Paschall, 18 Jan 1867; William A. White, clk, wit; m 19 Jan 1866 by Jno W. Pattillo, J. P.

Pearcy, Joshua & Ann Perry, 1 Dec 1860; Barnet L. Felts, bm; John W. White, wit.

Pearcy, William & Pollen Fletcher, 15 Jan 1819; Matthew Boulton, bm; Cas Drake, C. C. C., wit.

Pearsey, William & Nancy Nicholson, 12 May 1827; John Smith, bm; Burl Pitchford, wit.

Pearsey, William & Mary Rivers, 17 Dec 1835; Joshua Rivers, bm; E. D. Drake, wit.

Pearson, Charles H. & E. Matilda Burgess, 5 Mar 1860; W. A. Dowtin, bm; Jno W. White, clk, wit; m 7 Mar 1860 by Robt O. Burton, M. G.

Pearson, Paschall & Sarah Pearson, 7 Oct 1823; James Johnston, bm.

Peebles, Plummer & Jenney Asque, 23 Feb 1831; John Asque, bm; C. Drake, C. C., wit.

Peebles, Robert R. & Elizabeth Brewer, 24 Dec 1827; Jno E. Twitty, bm; M. M. Drake, wit.

Peegram, George H. & Ann Mary Laughter, 14 Feb 1838; Benjamin W. Andrews, bm.

Peeples, Anderson & Elizabeth Knight, 15 May 1813; Jacob Stiner, bm; Wm. Green, C. C. C., wit.

Peete, R. S. F. & Mary A. Davis, 22 Oct 1860; Joseph Peete, bm; Jno W. White, clk, wit; m 24 Oct 1860 by T. G. Lowe, M. G.

Pegram, Allen & Mary Shearin, 9 Sept 1839; Drury Shearin, bm; Edwd W. Best, wit.

Pegram, Baker & Eliza B. Andrews, 21 Mar 1836; E. James H. Munford, bm.

Pegram, Daniel & Lucy Milam, 10 Dec 1800; Gideon Pegram, bm; S. Johnson, wit.

Pegram, Edward & Patty Jean, 23 Aug 1779; William Jean, bm; Thos Machen, wit.

Pegram, George & Clary Lancaster, 14 Dec 1803; William Pegram, bm; M. Duke Johnson, C. C., wit.

Pegram, Harris & Nancy Harris, 18 Mar 1799; Wiley Harris, bm; S. Green, wit.

Pegram, Henry & Hariot Baker, 17 May 1833; John Harvey, bm; C. Drake, C. W. C. C., wit.

Pegram, Henry & Mary Elizabeth Harriss, 22 Dec 1842; Xanthus Snow, bm; M. J. Montgomery, wit.

Pegram, James B. & Magia Alston Patton, 2 Nov 1859; A. S. Jenkins, bm; Jno W. White, wit.

Pegram, John L. & Martha Jane Robertson, 19 Dec 1854; John H. Nicholson, bm; Jno W. White, clk, wit; m 21 Dec 1854 by Saml Bobbitt, J. P.

Pegram, M. S. & Bettie Duncan, 17 Sept 1866; William A. White, C. C. C., wit; m 18 Sept 1866 by J. M. Brame, J. P.

Pegram, Robert B. & Martha A. Pegram, 5 June 1860; William T. Pegram, bm; Jno W. White, clk, wit; m 6 June 1860 by Saml Bobbitt, J. P.

Pegram, Thomas & Elizabeth Riggan, 8 May 1811; Joseph Walker, bm; J. C. Johnson, D. C. C., wit.

Pegram, Thomas & Martha A. Vaughan, 14 June 1827; Benjamin Nicholson, bm; M. M. Drake, wit.

Pegram, William & Nancy Riggan, 28 Jan 1808; George Pegram, bm; J. C. Johnson, wit.

Pegram, William T. & B. M. Hilliard, 11 May 1861; A. S. Jenkins, bm; William A. White, wit; m 14 May 1861 by Wm. Holmes, M. G.

Pegram, Zachariah & Sintha Lancaster, 1 Jan 1824; Jacob Harriss, bm.

Pelham, Jesse & Elizabeth Faulcon, 4 July 1815; John M. Walker, bm; W. Green, C. C. C., wit.

Pemberton, Jesse & Sally Ellis, 1 June 1797; Joseph Jones, bm; Shd Green, wit.

Pendergrass, Daniel & Nancy Weldon, 8 Jan 1821; Isaac Pendergrass, bm; Cas Drake, C. W. C. C., wit.

Pendergrass, Jesse & Rachel Vigors, 8 Aug 1784; Jno Norman, bm; M. Duke Johnson, wit.

Pendergrass, Jesse C. & Matilda Coghill, 7 Aug 1844; James Edwards, bm; M. J. Montgomery, wit.

Pendergrass, Jordan & Mary Jane Coley, 23 Nov 1865; J. M. Dickerson, bm; William A. White, C. C. C., wit; m 24 Nov 1865 by P. H. Joyner.

Pendergrass, Robert & Elizabeth Perdue, 12 Dec 1860; Jno W. White, clk, wit; m 12 Dec 1860 by A. L. Steed, J. P.

Pendergrass, Thomas & Sallie Nuckles, 1 Apr 1859; Jas S. Bridgers, bm; Jno W. White, clk, wit; m 1 Apr 1859 by C. J. Jones, J. P.

Pendergrass, William & Mrs. Sarah Pendergrass, 8 Dec 1865; R. J. Pendergrass, bm; J. H. Bennett, D. C., wit; m 10 Dec 1865 by P. H. Joyner.

Pendleton, Richard & Althea Paschall, 20 Nov 1841; John P. Rose, bm; M. J. Montgomery, wit.

Pennell, Albert & Henrietta Duke, 25 Nov 1853; M. R. Pennell, bm; Jno W. White, C. C. C., wit; m 30 Nov 1853 by P. H. Smith, M. G.

Perdue, Joseph H. & Indeanah Allen, 30 Oct 1856; Jos R. Smithwick, bm; Jno W. White, clk, wit; m 31 Oct 1856 by N. A. Purefoy, M. G.

Perdue, Robert & Martha Perdue, 3 Nov 1807; William Perdue, bm; Jo Terrell, D. C. C., wit.

Perdue, Robert & Elizabeth Perdue, 12 Dec 1860; William N. Robards, bm; William A. White, wit.

Perdue, Thomas & Martha E. Young, 19 Dec 1842; Macon L. Perdue, bm; M. J. Montgomery, wit.

Perkerson, Eli & Sally Ellis, 4 July 1798; Thomas Ellis, bm.

Perkins, Julian V. & Lucy F. Alston, 4 Nov 1859; N. F. Alston, bm; Jno W. White, clk, wit; m 8 Nov 1859 by R. G. Barrett, Clergyman.

Perkinson, Anderson & Jacoba Walker, 19 Aug 1818; Guilford Talley, bm; Wm. Green, wit.

Perkinson, Benjamin L. & Ann B. Twisdale, 29 Aug 1843; Jas Robt Smithwick, bm; M. J. Montgomery, wit.

Perkinson, Ely & Susannah Rivers, 25 Nov 1817; Jas Talley, bm.

Perkinson, Geo W. & Rosa A. Smelley, 13 Dec 1866; William A. White, C. C. C., wit; m 13 Dec 1866 by Thos A. Montgomery, J. P.

Perkinson, James R. & Martha Smith, 23 aug 1832; William U. Meacham, bm; C. Drake, C. C. C., wit.

Perkinson, Jeremiah & Sophia Talley, 10 Sept 1822; Jesse C. Perkinson, bm.

Perkinson, Jeremiah & Cynthia Walker, 17 Oct 1838; Thomas C. King, bm.

Perkinson, Jessee & Frances Shearin, 23 June 1828; Wesley Perkenson, bm; E. D. Drake, wit.

Perkinson, Jessey & Nancy Smelly, 31 Jan 1800; Levi Perkinson, bm; Wm. R. Johnson, wit.

Perkinson, Joel & Henrietta Langford, 30 Dec 1844; Travis Talley, bm; M. J. Montgomery, wit.

Perkinson, Joseph H. & Syntha Talley, 15 Nov 1851; William P. Rose, bm; Jno W. White, clk, wit; m 19 Dec 1851 by O. D. Fitts, J. P.

Perkinson, Levi & Nancy Walker, 21 Dec 1796; Jesse Perkinson, bm; M. Duke Johnson, C. C., wit.

Perkinson, Levi G. & M. E. Hicks, 9 Apr 1855; E. T. Rice, bm; Jno W. White, clk, wit; m 11 Apr 1855 by N. A. Purefoy, M. G.

Perkinson, Moses (col) & Esther Hicks, 13 Apr 1866; Levi Tally, bm; William A. White, clk, wit; m 18 Apr 1866 by L. C. Perkinson, M. G.

Perkinson, Nathanil & Cealy E. Smithwick, 12 Nov 1840; Joshua Paschall, bm; Edwd W. Best, clk, wit.

Perkinson, Peter (col) & Rebecca Palmer, 25 Dec 1866; William A. White, clk, wit; m 26 Dec 1866 by L. C. Perkinson, M. G.

Perkinson, Robert J. & Susan A. Talley, 13 June 1854; W. R. Perkinson, bm; Jno W. White, C. C. C., wit.

Perkinson, Robt J. & Emma M. Perkinson, 15 Dec 1866; William A. White, C. C. C., wit; m 20 Dec 1866 by N. A. Purefoy, M. G.

Perkinson, Seth & Mary Williams, 31 Oct 1827; Jesse C. Perkinson, bm; M. M. Drake, wit.

Perkinson, Travis & Cintha Walker, 1 Oct 1811; Eli Perkinson, bm; Wm. Green, C. C. C., wit.

Perkinson, W. W. & Amanda F. Lambert, 29 May 1860; Robt J. Perkinson, bm; Jno W. White, clk, wit; m 30 May 1860 by L. C. Perkinson, M, G.

Perkinson, Wesley & Nancy D. Robins, 5 Sept 1832; William Falkener, bm; C. Drake, C. C., wit.

Perkinson, Wesley & Sarah Duke, 25 Oct 1851; Robert J. Perkinson, bm; Jno W. White, clk, wit; m 27 Oct 1851 by Jas T. Russell, J. P.

Perkinson, Zachariah & Ann E. Vaughan, 13 June 1850; Willis P. White, bm; Jno W. White, wit.

Perry, Allen (col) & Merina Williams, 24 Dec 1866; William A. White, clk, wit; m 26 Dec 1866 by J. Buxton Williams.

Perry, Elijah & _____, 8 June 1818; W. A. K. Falkener, bm.

Perry, Elijah B. & Sallie Burgess, 18 June 1853; P. S. Norwood, bm; Jno W. White, wit; m 22 June 1853 by Ro. O. Burton, M. G.

Perry, Green & Margt Johnson, 10 Oct 1821; Thomas White, bm.

Perry, Henry & Elizabeth Green, 13 Feb 1812; William Brown, bm; Wm. Green, C. C. C., wit.

Perry, John & Elizabeth E. Sledge, 4 Nov 1856; Alpheus Bobbitt, bm; Jno W. White, wit; m in Nov 1856 by Saml Bobbitt, J. P.

Perry, Joseph (col) (son of Dennis Alston and Harriet Perry) & Cynthia Williams (dau of Osborne and Cherry Williams), m 16 Nov 1867 by M. P. Perry, J. P.

Perry, Joshua & Betsey Kearney, 17 Dec 1802; William Denson, bm; M. Duke Johnson, C. C., wit.

Perry, Joshua (of Franklin Co.) & Elizabeth H. Gee, 26 July 1851; R. W. Hyman, bm; William A. White, wit; m 29 July 1851 by William Arendell, Elder.

Perry, Samuel & Elizabeth Williams, 5 June 1815; William Hunter, bm; W. Green, C. C. C., wit.

Perry, Solomon W. & Sallie D. Stamper, 7 June 1859; J. Thomas Cook, bm; Jno W. White, wit; m 9 June 1859 by R. G. Barrett.

Person, Peterson & Elisabeth Yarbrogh, 1 Jan 1789; Wm. Yarbrough, bm; M. D. Johnson, C. C., wit.

Person, Peterson & Prisilla Persons, 21 Dec 1801; Joel Randolph, bm; Sugan Johnson, wit.

Person, Robert (col) & Malinda Tillman, 26 Dec 1866; William A. White, clk, wit; m 31 Dec 1866 by R. S. F. Peete, J. P.

Person, Samuel & Tabitha Powell, 25 Mar 1789; Peterson Person, bm.

Person, Turner & Martha Sledge, 6 Nov 1821; Amos P. Sledge, bm.

Pettway, Mark H. & Marina C. Williams, 25 or 26 May 1824; Kemp Plummer, bm.

Pettyfoot, Wesley & Rachal Mason, 22 July 1831; Griffin Evans, bm; C. Drake, C. C., wit.

Phillips, Samuel E. & Mary P. Holaway, 19 June 1828; John W. White, bm; Burl Pitchford, wit.

Phillips, Samuel E. & Susan K. Walker, 19 Jan 1832; William Davis, bm; Benj E. Cook, bm.

Pickerell, Walker & Mary Hudson, 22 Jan 1793; James Walker, bm; Richd Russell, wit.

Pike, Edward & Sarah Jane Lancaster, 9 Dec 1858; David C. Reid, bm; Jno W. White, clk, wit; m 15 Dec 1858 by Nathl Nicholson, J. P.

Pike, Joshua & Patsey Harris, 27 Dec 1803; Leonard Harris, bm; M. D. Johnson, C. C,. wit.

Pike, Lewis & Ann Harriss, 25 Dec 1848; Albert Shearin, bm; Jno W. White, wit.

Pike, Lewis & Dolly Parrish, 15 Mar 1853; Guilford Duke, bm; Benj F. Powell, wit; m 17 Mar 1853 by J. Buxton Williams, J. P.

Pike, Samuel & Mary Shearin, 11 Jan 1826; Henry Shearin, bm; M. M. Drake, wit.

Pike, Saml & Winey Shearin, 6 Jan 1845; Weldon E. Carter, bm; M. J. Montgomery, wit.

Pinnell, Jackson & Frances A. Loyd, 30 Oct 1851; Green Pinnell, bm; Jno W. White, wit.

Pitchford, Aaron (col) & Sarah Alston, 18 Apr 1866; T. J. Pitchford, bm; William A. White, wit; m 21 Apr 1866 by J. Buxton Williams, J. P.

Pitchford, Aaron H. & Wilkey B. Paschall, 29 May 1830; Burrell Pitchford, Jr., bm; Burl Pitchford, J. P., wit.

Pitchford, Allen B. & Lucy Lett, 1 Oct 1839; Daniel Cole, bm; Burl Pitchford, wit.

Pitchford, Armistead (col) & Martha Alston, 2 Feb 1867; Phil K. Williams, bm; William A. White, wit; m 3 Mar 1867 by Thos J. Pitchford, J. P.

Pitchford, Burwell, Jr., & Scintha Pitchford, 15 Jan 1833; Allen B. Pitchford, bm; Burl Pitchford, J. P., wit.

Pitchford, Elijah & Martha Hardridge, 25 Oct 1805; Jno M. Johnson, bm; Jo Terrell, D. C. C., wit.

Pitchford, Hezekiah & Sally Johnson (no date); Michael Johnson, bm; A. Paschall, wit.

Pitchford, James A. & Sallie A. Davis, 16 Aug 1859; Isham H. Davis, bm; Jno W. White, clk, wit; m 17 Aug 1859 by John S. Cheek, J. P.

Pitchford, Peter (son of Plummer Davis & Amy Pitchford) & Millie Little (dau of Peter & Caroline) 1 Aug 1867; William A. White, clk, wit; m 4 Aug 1867 by N. A. H. Goddin, M. G.

Pitchford, Sterling & Betsey Davis, 4 Sept 1809; William G. Macon, bm; M. D. Johnson, C. C., wit.

Pitchford, Thomas & Martha Pitchford, 23 Mar 1826; Wesley B. Pitchford, bm; Burl Pitchford, wit.

Pitchford, Thomas & Matilda Cheek, 20 Mar 1833; John A. Burt, bm; C. Drake, C. C.,wit.

Pitchford, Thomas J. & Pattie B. Plummer, 21 Dec 1863; P. J. Turnbull; bm; Charles Price, wit; m 23 Dec 1863 by William Hodges, M. G.

Pitman, John B. & Frances Snow, 5 Sept 1840; Henry T. Doles, bm; Edwd W. Best, clk, wit.

Pitman, Merrit & Priscilla Lancaster, 6 Sept 1831; Bennett Harriss, bm.

Pittard, Jesse & Eliza A. Minge, 31 Mar 1830; Thomas Harris, bm; C. Drake, C. C., wit.

Pittillo, Augustin (of Mecklenburg Co., VA) & Elizabeth Moseley, 18 Sept 1782; Jesse Moseley, bm; M. Duke Johnson, wit.

Pittillo, James H. & Lucy B. Hicks, 6 Dec 1820' George W. T. Blanch, bm; Frs. Jones, wit.

Pittman, Thomas H. & Sarah Elizabeth Kearney, 1 Apr 1842; Xanthus Snow, bm; M. J. Montgomery, wit.

Pitts, James & Polley Stiles, 8 Aug 1785; John Frederick, bm; M. Duke Johnson, wit.

Pleasants, Thomas & Dicy Stewart, 13 July 1830; Samuel Edwards, bm.

Plummer, Edward H. & Sallie D. Fitts, 30 June 1863; Jos B. Batcheler, bm; Wm. A. White, wit; m 1 July 1863 by William Hodges, M. G.

Plummer, Henry L. & Sarah D. Falkener, 3 June 1828; Benjamin E. Person, bm.

Plummer, James K. & Mary B. Henderson, 25 Sept 1866; H. C. Hendrick, bm; William A. White, clk, wit; m 3 Oct 1866 by Joseph W. Murphy, M. G.

Plummer, John Love (col) & Ara Burwell, 17 Nov 1865; David Parrish, bm; William A. White, clk, wit; m 18 Nov 1865 by L. Henderson, J. P.

Plummer, Ralph (col) & Rela Plummer, 26 Dec 1865; W. A. K. Felkener, bm; William A. White, clk, wit; m 27 Dec 1865; by T. Page Ricaud, M. G.

Plummer, Thomas (col) & Susan Jerman, 25 Dec 1865; Austin Plummer, bm; William A. White, clk, wit; m 29 Dec 1865 by T. Page Ricaud, M. G.

Plummer, Thomas G. & Aera M. Hunter, 13 Nov 1835; Kemp Plummer, bm; E. D. Drake, clk, wit.

Plummer, William (col) & Catharine Bowser, 14 July 1866; Thos G. Plummer, bm; William A. White, clk, wit; m 14 July 1866 by T. B. Kingsbury.

Plummer, William (col) (son of Benjamin & Lucy Ann) & Ary Hawkins (dau of Pattie Hawkins), 16 Nov 1867; William A. White, clk, wit; m 16 Nov 1867 by R. D. Paschall, J. P.

Plunkett, Achelles & Caroline Mordecai, 18 Dec 1820; John D. Plunkett, bm; Cas Drake, C. C. C., wit.

Poe, Hasten & Eliza Paine, 18 Sept 1804; Robert Fleming, bm; M. Duke Johnson, C. C., wit.

Poe, Jacob F. & Rebeca Paine, 17 Nov 1806; James Paine, Jr., bm; Jo Terrell, D. C. C., wit.

Polk, Wm H. & Lucy E. Williams, 13 July 1854; Wm. T. Alston, bm; Jno W. White, wit.

Pool, Wm & Mary E. Stewart, 30 May 1866; Jno E. Dugger, bm; William A. White, clk, wit; m 30 May 1866 by W. Hodges, M. G.

Poole, Jno W. & Georganna Williams, 23 Apr 1862; Jno E. Dugger, bm; Wm. C. Poole, Jr., wit.

Pope, Humphrey & Elisa Bell, 21 Dec 1787; John Pope, bm; M. D. Johnson, C. c., wit.

Pope, James T. & Mariam G. Tunstall, 2 June 1849; John V. Cawthorn, bm; Jno W. White, wit.

Pope, Manuel Wright (col) & Henrietta Powell, 21 Mar 1866; M. C. Batchelor, bm; William A. White, clk, wit; m 21 Mar 1866 by William Hodges.

Pope, Philip C. & Mary D. Cothran, 6 Apr 1813; Thomas B. Gloster, bm; Wm. Green, C. C. C., wit.

Postell, E. C. (of Iredell Co, NC) & A. E. Collins, 2 Nov 1857; Henry Fitts, bm; John W. White, clk, wit; m 3 Nov 1857 by J. Tillett, M. G.

Powell, Abner & Dicey Brintle, 22 Mar 1782; John Ballard, bm; M. Duke Johnson, C. C., wit.

Powell, Andrew (col) & Esther Powell, 9 Apr 1867; Benj F. Powell, bm; William A. White, clk, wit; m 14 Apr 1867 by Thos J. Pitchford, J. P.

Powell, Cader & Frances Foote, 3 June 1782; William Foote, bm; M. Duke Johnson, wit.

Powell, Henry & Martha Francis Robertson, 13 July 1863; Nathaniel G. Robertson, bm; William A. White, clk, wit; m 23 July 1863 by S. P. J. Harris, M. G.

Powell, James & Priscilla Sledge, 19 Dec 1815; John Powell, bm; Will Green, C. W. C. C., wit.

Powell, Jeff (col) (son of Jordan Davis & Rachael Powell) & Martha Davis (dau of Nelson & Margaret), 21 Sept 1867; William A. White, clk, wit; m 28 Sept 1867 by Thos J. Pitchford, J. P.

Powell, Jefferson (col) & Anna Watson, 21 July 1866; P. J. Tunstall, bm; William A. White, clk, wit.

Powell, John B. & Nancey Davis, 14 Feb 1804; Richard K. Bennitt. bm; M. Duke Johnson, C. C., wit.

Powell, Jno B. & Caroline Egerton, 12 Dec 1846; Benjamin F. Powell, bm; Jno W. White, wit.

Powell, Jno C. & Bettie A. Cheek, 1 Apr 1859; C. M. Farris, bm; Jno W. White, clk, wit; m 6 Apr 1859 by Chas M. Cook, J. P.

Powell, Judge & Mary Garrott, 11 May 1835; Abel Garrott, bm.

Powell, Lemuel B. & Martha J. Williams, 13 May 1848; John White, bm; Jno W. White, wit.

Powell, Marquis & Sarah Harwill, 15 Sept 1821; Thos S. Harwell, bm.

Powell, Nichlis & Milley Smith (no date); Obed Green, bm; M. D. Johnson, wit.

Powell, Peter D. & Elizabeth W. Williams, 15 Dec 1838; Kemp P. Alston, bm.

Powell, Robert J. & Bettie D. Cheek, 1 May 1858; J. C. Powell, bm; Jno W. White, clk, wit; m 4 May 1858 by R. G. Barrett, M. G.

Powell, S. & Bettie Ball, 18 Jan 1866; Geo C. Clark, bm; William A. White, clk, wit; m 18 Jan 1866 by S. P. J. Harris.

Powell, Sandy (col) & Mary Jane Williams, 22 Dec 1866; William A. White, clk, m 27 Dec 1866 by John S. Cheek, J. P.

Powell, Sandy (col) (son of Orran & Matilda) & Emmaline Alston (dau of King & Lucinda), 19 Oct 1867; William A. White, clk, wit; m 3 Nov 1867 by Thos A. Montgomery, J. P.

Powell, Thomas & Sarah Gardner, 14 Nov 1797; Caleb Capps, bm; Shd Green, wit.

Powell, Thomas & Louise P. Person, 19 Nov 1829; John S. Smith, bm.

Powell, Wm & Jane Davis, 29 Oct 1811; Robert R. Ruffin, bm; Wm. Green, C. C. C., wit.

Powell, William & Ann Renn, 24 Dec 1857; A. C. Harris, bm.

Powell, William M. & Maria Johnston, 10 Nov 1823; Gordon Cawthorn, bm.

Powell, William Morgan & Martha P. Baker, 5 Feb 1833; William C. Williams, bm; C. Drake, clk, wit.

Powell, William Morgan & Mary A. C. Trewaller, 15 Aug 1849; Jeremiah McCormick, bm.

Powell, William Morgan & Emily T. Kearney, 27 Oct 1858; Henry T. Egerton, bm; Jno W. White, wit; m 4 Nov 1858 by Wm. C. Clanton, J. P.

Power, Nathl. C. & Nancy M. Marshall, 5 Nov 1822; Jno W. Mayfield, bm; Cas Drake, wit.

Power, Richard & Polly G. Christmas, 28 Oct 1811; Lewis Christmas, bm; Wm. Green, C. C. C., wit.

Power, Samuel D. & Martha A. Ward, 10 Nov 1819; A. P. Sledge, bm; Cas Drake, C. C. C., wit.

Power, Thomas & Alice D. Christmas, 2 Sept 1807; Edward Wortham, bm; Jo Terrell, D. C. C., wit.

Poynor, John & Nancy Davis, 15 Apr 1799; Benjamin Moss, bm; M. Duke Johnson, C. C., wit.

Poythress, David & Sally Dortch, 15 Mar 1848; George S. Moss, bm; Jno W. White, wit.

Poythress, Joshua L. & Elizabeth J. Crowder, 30 Sept 1852; John J. Rainey, bm; R. B. Robinson, wit; m 30 Sept 1852 by R. B. Robinson.

Price, John & Betsey Kendrick, 10 Oct 1787; William Moss, bm; M. D. Johnson, C. C., wit.

Price, John M. & Martha Reynolds, 21 May 1839; Henderson C. Lucas, bm.

Price, Josiah L. & Matilda Kearney, 15 Dec 1854; Henry J. Macon, bm; Jno W. White, wit.

Price, William & Frances Graves, 1 Nov 1784; Ephraim Price, bm; M. Duke Johnson, C. C., wit.

Price, William & Nancy Smelly, 15 Sept 1810; Randolph Harriss, bm; Jno C. Johnson, wit.

Price, Williamson & Lucy Harton (no date); Gideon Pegram, bm; M. Duke Johnson, C. C., wit.

Priddy, Thos & Sally Rice, 8 Nov 1819; James Bell, bm; Cas Drake, wit.

Primrose, Capt John W. & Mary S. Twitty, 14 Nov 1865; Wm. J. White, clk, wit; m 14 Nov 1865 by Jas A. Duncan, M. G.

Pritchard, R. C. & Anna Jones, 13 Feb 1846; M. J. Montgomery, wit.

Proctor, Richard & Lucretia Mabry, 7 Jan 1780; Joshua Mabry, bm; Thos Machen, wit.

Pryor, Ezra & Milly Pryor, 5 Feb 1810; William Rodwell, bm; Jno C. Johnson, D. C. C., wit.

Puckett, Abraham & Elizabeth Beasley, 27 May 1805; James Kidd, bm; M. Duke Johnson, C. c., wit.

Puckett, Arthur & Lucy Smith, 14 June 1802; Lewis Hazard, bm; Gid. Johnson, wit.

Puckett, Benjamin & Salley Hansell, 13 May 1785; Thomas Buttrill, bm; M. Duke Johnson, wit.

Pugh, Francis, Jr., & Dianna Hazard, 8 Dec 1816; Joseph J. Hawkins, bm.

Pugh, Francis, Sr., & Letha Smith, 1 Nov 1822; Drury Andrews, bm.

Pumfrey, John & Elisa Parker, 13 May 1803; William A. K. Falkener, bm.

Purdue, Patram & Elisabeth Pardue, 29 Oct 1782; Phillimon Beckham bm; M. Duke Johnson, wit.

Purefoy, Nicholas A. & India F. Watson, 15 Oct 1850; John Watson, bm;

Purnell, Marian & Narcissa Duke, 5 Mar 1847; Zedikiah Edwards, bm; Jno W. White, wit.

Qualls, Henry & Tempy Hamlet, 8 May 1867; John Wood, bm; William A. White, clk, wit; m 8 May 1867 by M. P. Perry, J. P.

Quincy, William A. & Mary T. Fleming, 22 May 1843; Jeremiah M. Fleming, bm; M. J. Montgomery, wit.

Radcliff, John W. & Jaquilin Pace, 13 Par 1826; Robt D. Starke, bm; M. M. Drake, wit.

Ragsdale, Jones & Salley Todd, _____ 179-; Claton Bobbitt, bm.

Ragsdale, Samuel & Annis Ussiry, 20 Mar 1788; Nathaniel Chambles, bm; M. D. Johnson, C. C., wit.

Ragsdil, William & Polley Bell, 20 Apr 1793; Thomas Bell, bm; Richd Russell, wit.

Rainey, Isaac & Rebecca L. Carrol, 26 Feb 1814; Thomas Carrol, bm; Wm. Green, wit.

Rainwater, Gilliom & Nancy Christmas, 7 Nov 1787; Wiley Goodwin, bm; M. Duke Johnson, C. C., wit.

Rainy, William H. & Mary T. Crutchfield, 7 Sept 1852; B. B. Vaughan, bm; Jno W. White, clk, wit; m 7 Sept 1852 by R. B. Robinson, J. P.

Ramy, Govan (col) (son of John & Rosetta) & Margaret Fitts (dau of Collin & Ermy), 27 Nov 1867; William A. White, clk, wit; m 27 Nov 1867 by R. D. Paschall, J. P.

Randolph, Joel & Huldy Yarborough, 21 Dec 1802; James Kearny, bm; Sugan Johnson, wit.

Randolph, John & Morgiana M. Goosley, 19 Sept 1845; John F. Jordan, bm; M. J. Montgomery, wit.

Randolph, Peter & Patsey Pace, 24 Dec 1799; John Randolph, bm; Shd Green, wit.

Raney, Thomas H. & Elizabeth Gray, 2 Feb 1808; Joseph Bradley, bm; Rob R. Johnson, wit.

Ransdell, James P. & Margaret B. Kettrell, 15 Nov 1830; Lemuel Potter, bm; C. Drake, C. C., wit.

Ransom, Marcellus & Lucy Snow, 24 Aug 1855; William Mitchell, bm; B. Eaton, wit.

Ransom, Stephen (col) & George Anna Southerland, 31 Dec 1866; William A. White, clk, wit; m 1 Jan 1867 by A. L. Steed, J. P.

Ransom, William T., Jr., & Milly Robertson, 31 Mar 1814; William Ransom, Sr; W. Green, C. C., wit.

Ratican, Michael & Sarah Bragg, 15 Mar 1832; George Vokes, bm; C. Drake, C. C. C., wit.

Read, James & Sarah Carrall, 11 Nov 1798; Hillery Capps, bm; M. D. Johnson, clk, wit.

Read, James & Mary Eliza Spears, 8 Jan 1854; James B. Read, bm; Jno W. White, wit.

Read, John & Fanny Basket, 1 Apr 1795; Pleasant Baskett, bm.

Read, John & Prudence Huddleston, 30 May 1805; John Paschall, bm; Jo Terrell, D. C., wit.

Read, John & Sally Parish, 6 Oct 1837; James T. Browne, bm.

Read, Lewis & Polly Fain, 14 Sept 1819; William Johnson, bm.

Read, Robert H. & Pattie A. Patterson, 26 Sept 1864; Lewis H. Newman, bm; William A. White, clk, wit; m 29 Sept 1864 by John H. Bullock, J. P.

Read, Thomas, Jr., & Martha Ann Read, 1 May 1845; Wm. C. Clanton, bm; M. J. Montgomery, wit.

Read, William H. & Martha T. Turner, 11 May 1832; Jno Langley, bm; C. Drake, clk, wit.

Read, Willie & Priscilla Jane Stokes, 2 Feb 1836; Richard H. Johnston, bm.

Reavis, George W. & Martha Ann Harris, 7 Apr 1846; William H. D. Stanton, bm; M. J. Montgomery, wit.

Reavis, Samuel & Patsey Harris, 21 July 1801; Reuben Smith, bm; S. Johnson, wit.

Reavis, Thomas C. & Eliz W. Best, 26 Nov 1860; Nathaniel C. Tunstall, bm; William A. White, wit; m 5 Dec 1860 by N. A. Purefoy, M. G.

Redd, Gardner & Harriet Hawkins, 7 May 1850; Ezekiah Copelin, bm; Jno W. White, wit.

Reed, Benjamin & Charity Vaughan, 17 Dec 1792; Robert Walden, bm; M. D. Johnson, C. C., wit.

Reed, James & Brind Green, 29 Aug 1807; Allen Green, bm.

Reed, Leonard & Betsey Sainsing, 5 Jan 1801; Matthew Duke, bm; M. Duke Johnson, clk, wit.

Reed, Thomas & Lucy Hilton, 1 Jan 1808; John Lancaster, bm; M. Duke Johnson, clk, wit.

Reed, Willis & Polley Lancaster, 16 Nov 1802; Lawrence Lancaster, bm; M. D. Johnson, C. C., wit.

Rees, Matthew & Nancy Roberds, 23 July 1836; William Nash, bm; Burl Pitchford, J. P., wit.

Regan, Matthew & Jenny Flemming, 1 Jan 1800; Richard Short, bm.

Regan, Richard J. & Margaret F. Lamkins, 27 Dec 1855; William E. Paschall, bm; Thomas P. Paschall, wit.

Regans, Charles D. & Mary A. Watkins, 5 Mar 1855; John Dowling, bm; Thos P. Paschall, wit; m 5 Mar 1855 by Thomas P. Paschall, J. P.

Regans, Peter F. & Elizabeth Tisdale, 5 May 1826; James H. Bouchier, bm; M. M. Drake, wit.

Reid, J. A. Bineum & Nancy Lilly Neal, 10 Nov 1852; G. B. Alston, bm; C. M. Cook, wit.

Reid, James L. & Sarah Ann Stacy, 22 Sept 1830; Jno T. Kearny, bm; C. Drake, C. C., wit.

Ren, Harmon & Tabitha Beckham, 3 Apr 1806; Solomon Beckham, bm; Jo Terrell, D. C. C., wit.

Renn, Henry & Elizabeth Robertson, 3 Oct 1837; James Clark, bm; E. W. Best, wit.

Renn, J. J. & Susan W. Twisdale, 21 Dec 1865; Joseph E. Drake, bm; William A. White, clk, wit; m 24 Dec 1865 by S. P. J. Harris, M. G.

Renn, James & Elizabeth Vaughan, 6 May 1840; Thomas M. Renn, bm.

Renn, James R. & Henrietta Alley, 19 Dec 1848; Jno M. Wilson, bm; Jno W. White, wit.

Renn, William G. H. & Delila Bowdon, 16 Feb 1849; Harmon H. Renn, bm; Jno W. White, wit.

Reynolds, Thomas & Martha Pergeson, 2 Jan 1807; Jo Terrell, Jr., bm; M. Duke Johnson, clk, wit.

Rhee, Andrew & Francis H. Slade, 20 Sept 1817; M. Duke Johnson, bm; W. Green, wit.

Rice, Francis & Rebecca Arrington, 30 Sept 1822; Willis Arrington, bm.

Rice, Harness & Nancy Short, 15 June 1798; Edmond Smith, bm. J. Moss, wit.

Rice, M. V. & Mrs. Mary L. Brinkley, 16 May 1857; E. T. Rice, bm; Jno W. White, clk, wit; m 17 May 1857 by J. B. Solomon.

Richardson, Faulcon (col) & Rebecca Alston, 1 May 1866; George W. Davis, bm; William A. White, clk, wit; m 2 May 1866 by M. P. Perry, J. P.

Richardson, Isham (col) & Betsy Richardson, 7 Oct 1865; Cofield Richardson, bm; William A. White, clk, wit.

Richardson, Nathan (col) & Martha Birchett, 18 May 1867; William A. White, clk, wit; m 21 May 1867 by Thomas P. Paschall, J. P.

Richardson, Presley & Rody Richardson, 14 Nov 1855; Jessee Richardson, bm; Jno W. White, wit; m 16 Nov 1855 by Wm C. Clanton, J. P.

Richardson, Robert & Jenkins Richardson, 28 Nov 1856; Hardy Richardson, bm; Jno W. White, clk, wit; m 18 Nov 1856 by Wm C. Clanton, J. P.

Richardson, Thomas M. & Nelly Moseley, 17 Dec 1851; Edmond Shell, bm; William A. Robinson, wit; m 17 Dec 1851 by R. B. Robinson, J. P.

Richison, Laurence & Martha Russill, 12 Nov 1782; Joshua Mabry, bm; M. Johnson, wit.

Rickman, Mark & Mary Harper (no date); William Storey, bm; M. D. Johnson, wit.

Ricks, Thomas B. & Elizabeth Brame, 8 Nov 1847; William Tell Skelton, bm; Jno B. White, wit.

Riddick, Willice F. & Addie B. Currier, 29 Oct 1866; John Collins, bm; William A. White, clk, wit; m 5 Nov 1866 by William Hodges, M. G.

Rideout, James V. & Rebecca Epps, 3 Dec 1833; Frederick Rideout, bm; C. Drake, D. C., wit.

Rideout, John J. & Mary W. Jones, 29 Aug 1831; Zachariah Jones, bm; C. Drake, clk, wit.

Rideout, Thomas & Mary Thomas, 4 Sept 1844; John Collins, bm; M. J. Montgomery, wit.

Ridout, John J. & Ann Hall, 12 Apr 1841; Ransom Harris, James D. Ridout, bm; Edwd W. Best, clk, wit; m 14 Apr 1841 by E. Chambers, M. G.

Ridout, Robert B. & Martha F. Wiggins, 20 Jan 1858; David Wiggins, bm; William A. White, wit; m 20 Jan 1858 by R. D. Paschall, J. P.

Riggan, Bille Pegram & Mary Cranshaw, 16 Nov 1787; Francis Riggan, bm; M. Duke Johnson, C. C., wit.

Riggan, C. S. & Alice F. Pegram, 23 Mar 1867; Wm. H. Johnson, bm; Wm A. White, clk, wit; m 28 Mar 1867 by Ridley Browne, J. P.

Riggan, Daniel & Frances Harper, 30 Jan 1798; Francis Riggan, Jr., bm; James Moss, wit.

Riggan, Daniel R. & Virginia Ann Wright, 15 Nov 1854; Lewis B. Collins, bm; Jno W. White, C. C. C., wit; m __ Nov 1854 by M. M. Drake, J. P.

Riggan, Edward D. & Sally Harris, 6 Apr 1830; Jacob J. Riggan, bm.

Riggan, Francis & Ann Harris, __ Apr 1789; Robt Harris, bm; M. D. Johnson, C. C., wit.

Riggan, Francis B. & Elizabeth Pegram, 7 Oct 1816; William Riggan, bm; Wm. Green, C. C., wit.

Riggan, Gideon B. & Loucinda Jane Harriss, 19 Dec 1848; James E. Harriss, bm; Jno W. White, wit.

Riggan, Isham S. & Sarah Stephens, 19 Jan 1847; Christopher N. Riggan, bm; Jno W. White, wit.

Riggan, Jacob J. & Jane Cambress, 20 Dec 1834; John H. Riggan, bm; E. D. Drake, clk, wit.

Riggan, James & Patsey Nicholson, 15 Mar 1819; Michael Riggan, bm.

Riggan, James & Elizabeth Raney, 22 Mar 1830; Michael Riggan, bm.

Riggan, Jeremiah & Elizabeth N. Egerton, 23 Mar 1814; John Riggan, bm; Wm Green, C. C. C., wit.

Riggan, Jeremiah & Mary Johnson, 5 Feb 1839; Washington L. Barnes, bm.

Riggan, Jerry & Carolina Riggan, 20 Nov 1866; E. H. Harris, bm; William A. White, wit.

Riggan, John & Jesibel Durham (no date); Zachariah Shearin, bm; M. D. Johnson, C. C., wit.

Riggan, John & Mary Durham, 17 Feb 1836; James T. Brown, bm; E. D. Drake, clk, wit.

Riggan, John H. & Adelia A. Separk, 12 Sept 1854; John W. Fisher, bm; Jno W. White, clk, wit; m 12 Sept 1854 by N. A. Purefoy, M. G.

Riggan, John W. & Sarah B. Vaughan, 9 June 1851; C. N. Riggan, bm; Jno W. White, clk, wit; m 12 June 1851 by B. Eaton, J. P.

Riggan, John W. & Mrs. Elizabith Fleming, 9 Nov 1863; Zachariah Perkinson, bm; William A. White, clk, wit; m 12 Nov 1863 by Thos J. Judkins, J. P.

Riggan, Joseph & Polly D. Harris, 1 Jan 1821; John Riggan, bm; Cas Drake, C. C., wit.

Riggan, Joseph H. & Elizabeth S. Marshall, 28 Feb 1834; Littleton F. Riggan, bm; E. D. Drake, clk, wit.

Riggan, Joseph L. & Mary Night, 22 Dec 1819; Randolph Smith, bm.

Riggan, Littleton F. & Rebecca Shearin, 19 Dec 1825; Henry Harris, bm; C. Drake, C. C., wit.

Riggan, Matthew M. & L. E. H. Lampkin, 23 Jan 1857; Richd J. Riggan, bm; Jno W. White, wit; m 29 Jan 1857 by J. B. Solomon, M. G.

Riggan, Michael & Rebecca Shearin, 2 Aug 1815; William W. Riggan, bm; W. Green, C. C. C., wit.

Riggan, Michael & Maria A. Raney, 7 Feb 1823; William W. Riggan, bm.

Riggan, Peter & Nancy Cauthon, 19 Nov 1800; Caleb Lindsey, bm; M. D. Johnson, C. C., wit.

Riggan, Peter R. & Elizabeth Verser, 21 Mar 1853; M. W. Duke, bm; Jno W. White, wit.

Riggan, Richard & Martha Riggan, 20 Nov 1866; E. H. Harris, bm; William A. White, clk, wit; m 18 Dec 1866 by Ridley Browne, J. P.

Riggan, Shugar A. & S. A. Shearin, 31 Dec 1846; Gideon W. Nicholson, bm; Jno W. White, wit.

Riggan, Wm. D. & Elizabeth Raney, 19 Dec 1831; M. Riggan, bm; M. M. Drake, wit.

Riggan, William W. & Elizabeth Nicholson, 2 Oct 1805; William Miller, bm; Jo Terrell, D. C. C., wit.

Riggan, William W. & Elizabeth Riggan, 17 Mar 1812; Gideon Pegram, bm; Wm. Green, C. C., wit.

Riggin, Nauy(?) & Sally Beckham, 13 May 1795; William Short, bm; J. Moss, wit.

Riggon, Joel & Nancy Carter, 15 Feb 1785; Jacob Ragon, bm; M. Duke Johnson, C. C., wit.

Rigons, Saml & Polley Lucas, 26 Dec 1804; John Burges, bm.

Rigons, Richard & Fanney King (no date): Zachariah Hasting, bm.

Rittenberry, Baxter M. & Nancy Wood, 17 Dec 1829; John Writtenbury, bm; C. Drake, C. C., wit.

Rittenberry, James & Lucinda Wood, 27 Feb 1833; John Solmon, bm; E. D. Drake, wit.

Rivers, John & Sally Ellington, 9 Jan 1838; John Paschall, bm; John V. Cawthorne, wit.

Rivers, John & Elizabeth Collins, 11 Nov 1862; George W. Harper, bm; William A. White, clk, wit; m 11 Nov 1862 by N. A. Purefoy, M. G.

Rivers, Joshua & Rebecca Glover, 29 June 1805; Willis Cannon, bm; M. Duke Johnson, clk, wit.

Rivers, Joshua & Susannah Nicholson, 17 Dec 1835; Edwin D. Drake, bm.

Rivers, Joshua & Elizabeth R. Tally, 24 Oct 1854; Jesse C. Perkinson, bm; Wm. H. White, wit; m 25 Oct 1854 by John H. Hawkins, J. P.

Rivers, Richard & Lucy B. Gibbs, 19 Apr 1808; Willis Arrington, bm; M. Duke Johnson, clk, wit.

Rivers, Zacharias & Sarah Paschall, 22 Mar 1802; John Patrick, bm; M. Duke Johnson, C. C., wit.

Rives, Edmund & _____, 24 Feb 1798; Green Duke, bm; Sherwood Green, wit.

Rives, Stephen & Sophia Cannon, 18 Dec 1815; Jones Mabry, bm; Wm Green, C. C. C., wit.

Rives, William & Mary Turner, 5 Jan 1788; Presley Thorn, bm; M. D. Johnson ,C. C., wit.

Robards, Jessee W. & Elizabeth Crow, 15 Dec 1851; Wm Matthus, bm; Jno W. White, clk, wit; m 15 Dec 1851 by J. H. Bullock, J. P.

Robards, Samuel & Sally Spurlock, 8 Mar 1817; Zach Spurlock, bm; Wm Green, clk, wit.

Robards, Wilson & Nancy Freeman, 23 Jan 1832; Lewis Payne, bm; Burl Pitchford, J. P., wit.

Robbins, Howel & Sally Robins, 22 Mar 1811; Reuben Hawkins, bm; Jno C. Johnson, D. C. C., wit.

Roberds, Philip & Nancy Brannum, 4 May 1797; Jeremiah George, bm; Shd Green, wit.

Roberson, Christopher & Salley Hawgood, 21 Dec 1831; Joseph Newton, bm; Burl Pitchford, wit.

Roberson, David & Sallie Clark, 6 Jan 1859; Rufus H. Falkner, bm; Jno W. White, clk, wit; m 12 Jan 1859 by Alexr L. Steed, J. P.

Roberson, J. M. & M. A. Harriss, 11 May 1864; M. Z. Beckham, bm; William A. White, wit; m 12 May 1864 by N. A. Purefoy, M. G.

Roberson, James & Martha Brown, 28 Jan 1852; William G. Renn, bm; Jno W. White, clk, wit; m by Abner Steed, J. P.

Roberson, Nathaniel J. & Rebecca Falkner, 23 Dec 1850; B. E. Cook, Jr., bm; Jno W. White, wit.

Roberts, James & Sarah M. Harper, 21 Apr 1852; Isham E. Rook, bm; R. B. Robinson, wit; m 21 Apr 1852 by R. B. Robinson, J. P.

Roberts, James W. & Mary Eliza Dickerson, 3 Feb 1863; Thomas Stainback, bm; Wm. A. White, clk, wit; m 4 Feb 1863 by S. P. J. Harris, M. G.

Roberts, John J. & Mary Jane Evans, 24 Dec 1847; E. T. Rice, bm; Jno W. White, wit.

Robertson, Allen P. & Mildred J. Myrick, 2 Jan 1844; Merritt Pittman, bm; M. J. Montgomery, wit.

Robertson, Archer F. & Francis B. Foulkes, 18 Oct 1813; Robert W. Winfree, bm; W. Green, C. C. C., wit.

Robertson, Arthur & Temperence Topp, 8 Apr 1826; Gideon Coghill, bm; M. M. Drake, wit.

Robertson, Arthur & Sally Beckam, 21 Oct 1840; W. Hudgins, bm.

Robertson, Benjamin & Betsy Riggans, 9 Dec 1812; Francis Riggan, bm; Wm Green, C. C. C., wit.

Robertson, Christopher & Nancy House, 21 July 1787; James House, bm.

Robertson, Claiborn & Nancy Thornton, 21 Dec 1791; Jesse Lain, bm.

Robertson, Haily & Patsey Stone, 13 Dec 1832; John Edwards, bm; C. Drake, C. C., wit.

Robertson, Henry & Polly Dawson, 11 Apr 1801; John Gardner, bm; S. Johnson, wit.

Robertson, Henry & Caroline Perdue, 30 Nov 1836; John Edwards, bm; E. D. Drake, clk, wit.

Robertson, Henry C. & Sally Foster, 8 Nov 1824; Alexander H. Falconer, bm; C. Drake, wit.

Robertson, Henry C., Jr., & Eliza Falkner, 23 Dec 1857; R. H. Hawkins, bm; m 23 Dec 1857 by A. C. Harris, M. G.

Robertson, Isham & Patty Peebles, 9 Dec 1779; John Wortham, bm; Thos Machen, wit.

Robertson, J. H. & Mary A. Johnson, 6 Jan 1862; John R. Rivers, bm; Jno. W. White, clk, wit; m 8 Jan 1862 by Jno Watson, J. P.

Robertson, Jas & ___cy Newton (no date); Thos Newton, bm; B. Davis, wit.

Robertson, James & Elizabeth Clark, 31 Jan 1812; Nathan Turner, bm; Jo Terrell, D. C., wit.

Robertson, James & Martha Jones, 4 Mar 1828; Benjamin Felts, bm; M. M. Drake, wit.

Robertson, James & Susan W. Robertson, 16 Oct 1866; T. G. Robertson, bm; William A. White, wit; m 17 Oct 1866 by Saml Bobbitt, J. P.

Robertson, James W. & Mary E. Kearney, 5 Oct 1865; Thomas J. Pitchford, bm; William A. White, clk, wit; m 11 Oct 1865 by Chas M. Cook, J. P.

Robertson, Jeremiah & Peggey Layhead, 6 Feb 1797; Young Dickoson, bm; Shd Green, wit.

Robertson, John (col) & Susan Syrus, 26 Feb 1867; Henry G. Jones, bm; William A. White, clk, wit; m 28 Feb 1867 by Dick Alston, M. G.

Robertson, John F. & Susan Mitchell, 6 Apr 1840; Joseph Coly, bm; Edwd W. Best, clk, wit.

Robertson, John P. & Jackey Reynolds, 15 Aug 1812; Modicus Robertson, bm; Wm Green, C. C., wit.

Robertson, LittleBerry & Mrs. Priscilla Person, 3 Oct 1818; John Sledge, bm.

Robertson, Littleberry & Sally Shearin, 8 Nov 1820; John H. Mulholland, bm.

Robertson, Littleberry L. & Sally Robertson, 9 Sept 1825; Samuel Hardie, bm.

Robertson, Littleton & Sally Emberson, 5 July 1815; Lewis Bobbitt, bm; W. Green, C. C. C., wit.

Robertson, Littleton & Martha Felts, 14 Dec 1824; Thomas Hardy, bm; E. D. Drake, wit.

Robertson, Marcus A. & Maranda Bennett, 19 Mar 1823; Jacob Harris, bm; E. D. Drake, wit.

Robertson, Modicus & Sally Arrington, 15 Dec 1813; Amos P. Sledge, bm; Wm. Green, C. C. C., wit.

Robertson, Newell & Rebecca Little, 13 Feb 1827; James Y. Harriss, bm; M. M. Drake, wit.

Robertson, Phil & Amey Clark, 30 Oct 1817; Harden Falkener, bm; W. A. K. Falkener, wit.

Robertson, Pompey (col) & Nancy Richardson, 8 May 1867; A. S. Webb, bm; William A. White, clk, wit; m 9 May 1867.

Robertson, Tho B. & Emily Thompson, 24 Nov 1840; Henry J. Macon, bm.

Robertson, Thomas P. & Lucy Ann T. Smith, 3 Oct 1840; Henry J. Macon, Henry A. Kearny, bm; Benj E. Cook, wit.

Robertson, Weldon E. & Martha Bobbitt, 14 Dec 1836; Claiborn Shearin, bm; E. D. Drake, clk, wit.

Robertson, William & Urkey Beckham, 1 Jan 1800; Stephen Beckham, bm; Shd Green, wit.

Robertson, William & Frances Thompson, 18 Feb 1862; Henry T. Egerton, bm; Jno W. White, clk, wit; m 18 Feb 1862 by Chas M. Cook, J. P.

Robins, William & Nancy White, 28 Nov 1808; Thomas Stackhouse, bm; J. C. Johnson, D. C. C., wit.

Robinson, Anthony (col) (son of Anthony Robinson & Venus Pearson) & Sylvia Twitty (dau of Charles Thrower & Cherry Collins), 2 May 1868; William A. White, clk, wit; m 3 May 1868 by L. C. Perkinson, M. G.

Robinson, Archer (col) & Matilda Palmer, m 30 Dec 1867 by R. S. F. Peete, J. P.

Robinson, Blanch (col) (son of Hubbard & Flora) & Harriet Scoggins (dau of James & Sally), 2 Nov 1867; William A. White, clk, wit; m 9 Nov 1867 by J. M. Brame, J. P.

Robinson, Edward (col) (son of Anthony & Lizzie Robinson) & Zilphy Cheek (dau of James & Adaline), 15 Nov 1867; William A. White, clk, wit; m 23 Nov 1867 by John S. Cheek, J. P.

Robinson, George W. & Sarah S. Boyd, 26 Oct 1855; James C. Robinson, bm; Jno W. White, wit; m 31 Oct 1855 by Robt O. Burton, M. G.

Robinson, Hartwell & Sarah T. Paschall, 9 Sept 1854; John L. Burchett, bm; Jno W. White, clk, wit; m 27 Sept 1854 by J. J. Bullock, J. P.

Robinson, James C. & Rebeca M. Palmer, 16 June 1848; H. G. Goodloe, bm; Jno W. White, wit.

Robinson, John P. & Cynthia J. Sledge, 5 Feb 1814; Asa G. Sledge, bm.

Robinson, Remus (col) & Eliza Boyd, 14 Aug 1866; William A. White, clk, wit; m 19 Aug 1866 by L. G. Perkinson, M. G.

Robinson, Robert J. & Louisa J. Bickanan, 7 Feb 1859; R. H. H. Paschall, bm; Thomas P. Paschall, wit; m 8 Feb 1859 by Thomas P. Paschall, J. P.

Robinson, Russell (col) & Jane Stewart, __ Feb 1855; Cohabitation bond acknowledged 3 Apr 1866.

Robinson, William & Lucy Ann Hawkins, 31 Jan 1855; E. W. Best, bm; Jno W. White, clk, wit; m 1 Feb 1855 by Will Plummer, J. P.

Rodgers, John W. & Mary J. Cole, 6 Dec 1859; Alexander Bennett, bm; Jno W. White, clk, wit; m 7 Dec 1859 by N. A. Purefoy, M. G.

Rodwell, Gideon (col) & Susan Bobbitt, 10 Mar 1866; William A. White, clk, wit; m 11 Mar 1866 by Thos B. Ricks, M. G.

Rodwell, Hardy W. & Caroline Jones, 27 Dec 1819; John Rodwell, bm.

Rodwell, James & Nancy Shearin, 13 Oct 1803; John Balthrop, bm.

Rodwell, John & Priscilla Harris, 14 June 1817; Benjn Colclough, Wm. Green, bm.

Rodwell, John J. & Mary P. Rodwell, 5 Apr 1858; Thos D. Rodwell, bm; Jno W. White, wit; m 12 Apr 1858 by J. B. Solomon.

Rodwell, John M. & Elizabeth Rodwell, 13 Apr 1840; Nathan Milam, bm.

Rodwell, Joseph L. & Sallie Allen, 19 Dec 1859; Thos B. Fleming, bm; Jno W. White, clk, wit; m 21 Dec 1859 by N. A. Purefoy.

Rodwell, Kelly (col) & Mariah Watson, 1 Apr 1867; W. P. Watson, bm; William A. White, clk, wit.

Rodwell, Robert & Franky Milam, 7 Feb 1814; William R. Johnson, bm; Jno H. Green, wit.

Rodwell, Robert & Elizabeth Milam, 4 Feb 1830; William D. Jones, bm; E. D. Drake, wit.

Rodwell, Thomas D. & Annie F. Rodwell, 17 Feb 1866; John J. Rodwell, bm; William A. White, clk, wit; m 21 Feb 1866 by T. B. Kingsbury.

Rodwell, Wm. B. & Mary D. Egerton, 4 Sept 1851; J. J. Rodwell, bm; Jno W. White, clk, wit; m 10 Sept 1851 by W. Hudgins.

Rodwell, William H. & Ann M. Hudgins, 29 Aug 1851; William A. White, bm; Jno W. White, wit.

Rogers, George & May P. Milam, 3 Mar 1823; Jno E. Twitty, bm; C. Drake, C. C., wit.

Rogers, George O. & Mary A. Drake, 22 May 1850; Wm. T. Howard, bm; Jno W. White, wit.

Ronald, Hugh & Mrs. Catharine Baker, 21 May 1862; H. H. Harper, bm; Jno W. White, clk, wit; m 22 May 1862 by William Hodges, M. G.

Rooker, James P. & Martha Riggan, 24 Dec 1832; John R. Shearin, bm; C. Drake, C. C., wit.

Rooker, James T. & Sallie M. Thompson, 12 Dec 1859; Wm J. Burt, bm; Jno W. White, clk, wit; m 15 Dec 1859 by Chas M. Cook, J. P.

Rooker, John & Anna Hawkins, 15 Apr 1780; Rawleigh Hammond, bm; Thos Machen, wit.

Rooker, Presley & Martha Stanback, 9 Jan 1797; William Rooker, bm; Shd Green, wit.

Rooker, Presley & Nancy Pegram, 19 July 1832; Bennitt H. Stammire, bm.

Rooker, Thomas & Elizabeth Pegram, 31 Dec 1845; Wm. W. Daniel, Sr, bm; M. J. Montgomery, wit.

Rooker, Thomas W. & Mary Jane Moody, 31 Dec 1845; Wm. W. Daniel, bm; M. J. Montgomery, wit.

Rooker, William & Nancy White, 5 May 1803; William Neal, bm; Wm. Falkener, wit.

Rooker, William & Francis Riggan, 15 Feb 1819; Daniel Riggan, bm; W. A. K. Falkener, wit.

Rooker, William T. & Almeda Newman, 7 Nov 1865; Wm. H. White, bm; William A. White, wit; m 15 Nov 1865 by Jno W. Pattillo, J. P.

Roper, John & Frances D. Jolly, 6 June 1837; Michael Ratican, bm.

Rose, George A. & Lucy Ann Tunstall, 31 May 1854; Jas T. Wiggins, bm; Jno W. White, wit.

Rose, John E. & Ellen Burroughs, 15 Oct 1856; Nathl McLean, bm; Jno W. White, wit.

Rose, John E. & Rebecca Twisdale, 18 Dec 1858; George A. Rose, bm; William A. White, wit; m 24 Nov 1858 by P. H. Joyner.

Rose, John P. & Mary H. Langford, 26 Oct 1819; Robert Paschall, bm.

Rose, Robert F. & Bettie P. Duke, 21 Nov 1857; William P. Rose, bm; Jno W. White, clk, wit; m 26 Nov 1857 by J. Tillett.

Rose, William J. & Julia A. Turner, 1 Feb 1853; John E. Rose, bm; Jno W. White, clk, wit; m 1 Feb 1853 by Edmd White, J. P.

Rose, William P. & Dellah Langford, 23 Oct 1819; John King, bm; Cas Drake, wit.

Rose, William P. & Ann W. Collins, 5 July 1854; Thos E. Wilson, bm; Jno W. White, wit.

Rottenberry, Samuel & Polley Neal, 9 Apr 1833; James Huddgins, bm; Burl Pitchford, J. P., wit.

Rottenberry, William B. & Annee Shell, 4 Oct 1810; James Carroll, bm; Jno C. Johnson, D. C., wit.

Rottenbery, John & Alander Jones, 24 Dec 1827; Henry Fitts, bm.

Rottenbury, Daniel & Mildred Douglass, 19 Apr 1810; Matthew Bolton, bm; M. Duke Johnson, C. C., wit.

Rottenbury, Isham H. & Sarah W. Jones, 23 Dec 1828; Zachariah Jones, bm; E. D. Drake, wit.

Rowe, Randolph & Susanah Stewart, 17 Dec 1793; Richard Evans, bm; M. Duke Johnson, C. C., wit.

Rowland, Burch & Polley Bartholomew, 3 Nov 1801; Wm. Rowland, bm; M. Duke Johnson, C. C., wit.

Rowland, Thaddeus B. & Mary T. Davis, 17 Sept 1829; John Wiggins, bm; E. D. Drake, wit.

Rowland, Thaddeus P. (of Granville Co.) & Hixey J. Vanlandingham, 19 Dec 1857; Jas R. Watkins, bm; Thos P. Paschall, wit; m 23 Dec 1857 by J. Tillett, M. G.

Rowland, Thomas & Hannah H. Harris, 29 Nov 1824; Jno H. Farrow, bm.

Rudd, George D. & Martha A. Falkner, 11 Oct 1854; Ford Falkner, bm; Jno W. White, wit; m 11 Oct 1854 by A. C. Harris, M. G.

Rudd, James C. & Emma R. Loyd, 15 Dec 1853; James R. Renn, bm; Jno W. White, wit; m 22 Dec 1853 by A. C. Harris, M. G.

Rudd, James G. & Nancy Turner, 24 Sept 1828; Nathaniel Brown, bm; M. M. Drake, wit.

Rudd, John & Jane Nicholson, 30 Nov 1821; John Johnson, bm; Cas Drake, wit.

Rudd, John H. & Martha Jordan, 29 Sept 1810; William McRorie, bm; M. Duke Johnson, clk, wit.

Rudd, William Lee & Hannah Hoyle, 27 July 1825; James G. Rudd, bm; M. W. Drake, wit.

Russell, Anderson (col) & Sylvia Russell, 22 Dec 1866; William A. White, clk, wit; m 28 Dec 1866 by Jas T. Russell, J. P.

Russell, Henry (col) & Winny Johnson, 18 Dec 1865; James T. Russell, bm; William A. White, clk, wit; m 23 Dec 1865 by Jas T. Russell, J. P.

Russell, James & Mary Ann Palmer, 21 July 1841; James S. Walker, bm.

Russell, Kit & Rosa White, 10 Feb 1866; R. A. White, bm; m 15 Feb 1866 by Jno W. Pattillo, J. P.

Russell, Richard & Rebecah Mayfield, 2 Nov 1797; Sherwood, bm; Shd Green, wit.

Russell, Thomas T. & Frances M. Clanton, 21 Nov 1831; William C. Clanton, bm.

Sail, William & Polley Towns, 26 Mar 1796; Beavel Pardue, bm; M. Duke Johnson, C. C., wit.

Sailes, Robt & Fanney Talley, 31 Jan 1797; Silvester Nuccols, bm; Shd Green, wit.

Sainsing, William & Mary Ostwall, 12 July 1804; James Capps, bm; M. Duke Johnson, wit.

Sainsing (Senseng), William & Jenny Lamkin, 28 Dec 1810; Matthew Lamkins, bm; M. Duke Johnson, C. C., wit.

St. John, William & Catherine Loyd, 14 June 1786; James Gray, bm; M. D. Johnson, wit.

St. John, William E. & Priscilla Morriss, 16 Oct 1827; Edmund Adams, bm.

Saintsing, George W. & Alice A. Lamkin, 20 Dec 1854; David Collins, bm; Jno W. white, wit.

Saintsing, Jacob & Catharine Ostwall, 23 June 1804; John Randolph, bm; M. Duke Johnson, C. C., wit.

Saintsing, James & Holley Capps, 20 Nov 1784; John Capps, bm; M. Duke Johnson, C. C., wit.

Saintsing, James & Ann Wilson, 19 Oct 1830; John P. Rose, bm; C. Drake, C. C., wit.

Saintsing, James & Lucy Ann Clark, 21 Dec 1860; David Collins, bm; William A. White, wit; m 23 Dec 1860 by A. L. Steed, J. P.

Saintsing, John & Suasan Wilson, 31 Jan 1839; John Hagood, bm; Burl Pitchford, J. P., wit.

Saintsing, John & Winifred Hicks, 26 Oct 1856; Somerville Saintsing, bm; Jno W. White, clk, wit; m 29 Oct 1856 by Robert D. Paschall, J. P.

Saintsing, Somerill & Matilda Wilson, 28 Nov 1843; James Saintsing, bm; M. J. Montgomery, wit.

Saintsing, Washington & Charlotte Kimbell, 24 Dec 1829; John Saintsing, bm; C. Drake, C. C., wit.

Sale, Anthony & Peggey Williams, 5 June 1799; Alanson Williams, bm; M. D. Johnson, clk, wit.

Salmon, Henry & Susan Langford, 13 July 1850; Jno Smith, bm; Jno W. White, wit.

Salmon, John & Mary B. Wood, 30 July 1823; Guilford Talley, bm.

Salmon, Jonathan & Rebecah Glover, 19 Nov 1803; Willis Cannon, bm; Gideon Johnson, wit.

Salmon, Jonathan & Jincy Goodman, 28 Dec 1816; John Howerton, bm; Wm Green, C. C., wit.

Salmon, Reuben & Harriet Darnell, 1 Oct 1842; Frederick King, bm; M. J. Montgomery, wit.

Salmon, William & Rebecca Childress, 17 Aug 1807; Jonathan Salmon, bm; Jo Terrell, D. C., wit.

Samford, John & Mary Jeane Mills, 1 Mar 1786; Anthony Dowden, bm; M. Duke Johnson, wit.

Sammon, Robert & Sarah Patterson, 2 Nov 1791; Lewis Paterson, bm.

Sampson, William & Altona Alston, 11 June 1847; Oscar F. Alston, bm; Jno W. White, wit.

Samuel, Andrew & Elisabeth Murphy, 8 Oct 1789; Henry Fitts, bm; M. Duke Johnson, C. C., wit.

Sandefur, James & Ann Hammock, 13 Jan 1796; Philip Kinnamon, bm; M. Duke Johnson, C. C. C., wit.

Sanders, Richard & Elizabeth Marshall (dau of John), 18 Nov 1780; Charles Dixon, bm; Thos Machen, wit.

Sandeson, James & Eliza Durham (no date); William Durham, bm; M. D. Johnson ,C. C., wit.

Schloss, Marx & Mary E. Burrows, 5 Oct 1854; W. P. White, bm; Jno W. White, clk, wit; m 5 Oct 1854 by H. J. Macon, J. P.

Scoggin, James L. & Ann E. Fitts, 18 Apr 1842; Henry G. Fitts, bm; M. J. Montgomery, wit.

Scot, Isaac & Agnis Mayo, 27 Mar 1839; Bowling Evans, bm; Burl Pitchford, J. P., wit.

Scott, Ellington & Mariah Toney, 3 Sept 1863; Newsom Harris, bm; William A. White, clk, wit; m 2 Dec 1863 by Ridley Browne, J. P.

Scott, Isaac & Anna Drew, 9 Apr 1849; Jesse Garnes, bm; Jno W. White, wit.

Scott, Julius & Frances J. Porter, 28 June 1861; Julius Wilcox, bm; Jno W. White, clk, wit; m 29 June 1861 by Drury Lacy.

Scott, Samuel & Mary Watson, 27 July 1809; Isaac Watson, bm; M. Duke Johnson, C. C., wit.

Scott, Theoderick & Polley Scott, 8 Nov 1792; Admiral White, bm; M. Duke Johnson, C. C., wit.

Scott, William W. & Mary L. Bowers, 31 Mar 1858; E. A. Drumright, bm; William A. White, wit.

Scribler, David & Judith Holliday, 5 Oct 1781; William Coggin, bm; Thos Machen, wit.

Searcy, William H. & Darcas Lindsey, 24 Dec 1805; Atkins McLemore, bm; Jo Terrell, D. C. C., wit.

Searcy, William Wms & Betsey Harris (no date); Enos Scott, bm; M. Duke Johnson, C. C., wit.

Sears, Abner & Nancy Marks (no date); William Smith, bm; M. D. Johnson, clk, wit.

Seat, Emanuel & Cusiah Talley, 29 Aug 1787; Lewis Shearin, bm; M. Duke Johnson, C. C., wit.

Sensing, John & Amey Powell, 26 Oct 1785; Charles Sensing, bm; M. Duke Johnson, wit.

Senter, Buckner & Fanny Bell, 24 Feb 1801; Ezekiel Marshall, bm; Wm. Robards, wit.

Sentill, Freeman & Betsey Coleclough, 15 May 1795; Ezekiel Marshall, bm; J. Moss, wit.

Seward, Abram & Chatharine Durham, 25 Oct 1853; Badger Mushaw, bm; Thos P. Paschall, wit; m by J. H. Bullock, J. P.

Seward, Jacob (col) & Ella Russell, 13 Nov 1865; Howell R. Moss, bm; William A. White, clk, wit; m 19 Nov 1865 by Jas. T. Russell, J. P.

Seward, Mecdoland & Eliza Joiner, 4 Feb 1852; Willis Kersey, bm; Thos P. Paschall, wit; m 4 Feb 1852 by John H. Bullock, J. P.

Shaw, Alexander W. & Felicia M. Hill, 15 Mar 1836; Jesse Myrick, bm; E. D. Drake, clk, wit.

Shaw, Guilford & Susan Stacy, 22 Dec 1832; James L. Reid, bm; C. Drake, C. C., wit.

Shaw, James & Elizabeth Balthrop, 16 June 1835; Charles Myrick, bm; E. D. Drake, clk, wit.

Shaw, Jessee & Temperance D. Bobbitt, 29 Nov 1854; T. P. Walker, bm; W. A. White, wit.

Shaw, Wm. H. & Rebecca H. Shearin, 12 Feb 1867; William A. White, clk, wit; m 14 Feb 1867 by N. A. Purefoy, M. G.

Shearin, Aaron & Cathorin Foote, 20 June 1799; Moses Shearin, bm; M. D. Johnson, wit.

Shearin, Abner & Patsey Meadows (no date); John Reed, bm.

Shearin, Abner & Cinthia Riggins, 20 Dec 1825; Jno Bobitt, bm; M. M. Drake, wit.

Shearin, Abner & Nancy W. Harris, 7 Jan 1844; Wm. H. Egerton, bm; M. J. Montgomery, wit.

Shearin, Albert & Malissa Shearin, 26 Dec 1848; Henry G. Goodloe, bm; Jno W. White, wit.

Shearin, Claibourn & Martha Fleming, 7 Dec 1840; Thomas J. Judkins, bm.

Shearin, Daniel & Elisabeth Rodwell, 7 Aug 1797; Thomas Rodwell, bm; M. D. Johnson, C. C., wit.

Shearin, Elishea & Nancy Rodwell, 24 Nov 1813; John J. Nicholson, bm.

Shearin, Federick J. & Judah Hutson, 23 Dec 1847; Eaton Wilson, bm; Jno W. White, wit.

Shearin, Frederick & Mary Walker, ____ 1785; Moses Shearin, bm; M. D. Johnson, wit.

Shearin, Frederick & Nelly Ellis, 18 Oct 1816; Lewis Ellis, bm; Wm. Green, C. C., wit.

Shearin, Gardener & Judith Williams, 12 Oct 1792; William Shearin, bm; M. D. Johnson, C. C., wit.

Shearin, Gardner & Emily Crowder, 30 Jan 1850; Albert Shearin, bm; Jno W. White, wit.

Shearin, Gardner & Lucy J. Pegram, 29 Mar 1859; W. A. J. Nicholson, bm; William A. White, wit; m 30 Mar 1859 by Saml Bobbitt, J. P.

Shearin, Henry & Nancy Oswald, 14 Dec 1811; Robert Harris, bm; Jno H. Green, wit.

Shearin, Henry & Fanny Riggan, 24 Sept 1816; Wm. W. Riggan, bm; Wm Green, C. C., wit.

Shearin, Henry & Amanda Johnson, 20 Jan 1828; John Bobbitt, Jr., bm; M. M. Drake, wit.

Shearin, Henry & Anyrelous Bobbitt, 26 Aug 1839; Joseph Speed Jones, bm; Edwd W. Best, wit.

Shearin, Henry W. & Mary M. Minge, 25 Sept 1832; William T. Minga, bm; C. Drake, C. C. C., wit.

Shearin, Isam & Nancy Riggon, 17 Dec 1783; Jacob Riggan, bm; M. Duke Johnson, wit.

Shearin, J. R. & Catharine Thompson, 4 Sept 1865; Gardner E. Shearin, bm; William A. White, clk, wit; m 5 Sept 1865 by Chas M. Cook, J. P.

Shearin, J. R. & Rosanna Thompson, 31 Aug 1866; William A. White, clk, wit; m 5 Sept 1866 by J. M. Brame, J. P.

Shearin, Jacob J. & Cynthia Shearin, 5 May 1851; Weldon E. Carter, bm; Jno W. White, clk, wit; m 5 May 1851 by H. J. Mason, J. P.

Shearin, James & Dolley Carter, 19 June 1803; John Riggan, bm; M. Duke Johnson, C. C., wit.

Shearin, James & Delia King, 2 Oct 1844; Michl Riggan, bm; M. J. Montgomery, wit.

Shearin, Jarriot & Mary Yarbrough, 29 Nov 1848; Lewis B. Collins, bm; Jno W. White, wit.

Shearin, John & Rebecah Walker (no date); John Reed, bm.

Shearin, John & Elizabeth Burrow (no date); Shd Green, bm; M. Duke Johnson, C. C., wit.

Shearin, John & Ruth Powell, 22 May 1793; James Cannon, bm; Richd Russell, bm.

Shearin, John & Nancy Shearin, 2 Aug 1834; John Egerton, bm; E. D. Drake, clk, wit.

Shearin, John & Susan Verser, 7 Jan 1863; Joseph C. Harris, bm; William A. White, wit.

Shearin, John Daniel & Fanny A. Watkins, 1 Dec 1860; Robt A. Shearin, bm; William A. White, wit; m 6 Dec 1860 by C. F. Harris.

Shearin, John P. & Elizabeth M. Kearny, 8 Sept 1837; John E. Browne, bm.

Shearin, John R. & Charlotte Daniel, 9 Dec 1834; Drury S. Wright, bm; E. D. Drake, clk, wit.

Shearin, John W. & Lucy W. Clark, 9 Apr 1859; A. H. Ball, bm; Jno W. White, clk, wit; m 20 Apr 1859 by A. L. Steed, J. P.

Shearin, Joseph & Lucy Bell, 5 Feb 1801; Jesse Bell, Jr., bm; M. D. Johnson ,C. C., wit.

Shearin, Joseph & Polly Hardrige, 7 June 1802; David Asslin, bm; Sugan Johnson, wit.

Shearin, Joseph & Cealia Ellis, 20 Jan 1804; Henry Foote, bm; M. Duke Johnson, C. C., wit.

Shearin, Joseph & Mary Evans, 3 Oct 1856' John Hardy, bm; Jno W. White, wit.

Shearin, Joseph H. & Nancy T. Hicks, 19 Dec 1837; John A. Davis, bm.

Shearin, Leonidas S. & Mary M. A. Lewis, 10 Mar 1855; R. G. Newsom; bm; Jno W. White, clk, wit; m 12 Mar 1855 by B. Eaton, J. P.

Shearin, Lewis & Susan Meadows, 1 May 1779; James Moseley, bm; M. D. Johnson, wit.

Shearin, Lewis & Jacobina Robinson, 10 Aug 1816; Henry Shearin, bm; Wm. Green, D. C., wit.

Shearin, Mark H. & Sabrina Burrow, 20 Dec 1820; Jesse Myrick, bm; J. M. Johnson, wit.

Shearin, Nathaniel & Martha E. Marshall, 13 Jan 1857; Furney Southall, bm; William A. White, wit; m 15 Jan 1857 by J. Buxton Williams, J. P.

Shearin, Nathaniel M. & Elizabeth Bobbitt, 9 Jan 1828; Kinchen Bobbitt, bm; M. M. Drake, wit.

Shearin, Nathaniel M. & Elizabeth Marshall, 23 Mar 1853; Marx Schloss, bm; Jno W. White, wit.

Shearin, Nathaniel W. & Mrs. Mary C. Sledge, 12 May 1860; W. A. J. Nicholson, bm; Jno W. White, clk, wit; m 13 Mar 1860 by Nathl Nicholson, J. P.

Shearin, Nicholas & Elizabeth J. Harris, 11 Dec 1850; Newsom Harris, bm; Jno W. White, wit.

Shearin, Nicholas & Malissa Shearin, 7 Jan 1852; Edward Sherin, bm; Jno W. White, clk, wit; m 8 Jan 1852 by William C. Clanton, J. P.

Shearin, Oliver & Fanny Brack, 19 Mar 1845; James M. Myrick, bm; M. J. Montgomery, wit.

Shearin, Richard & Martha Clanton, 7 Oct 1811; Jesse Milam, bm; Wm Green, clk, wit.

Shearin, Richard & Maria Jones, 19 Dec 1818; Willis R. Harris, bm; W. A. K. Falkener, wit.

Shearin, Richard & Rebecca Reid, 23 Dec 1852; J. C. Hooper, bm; Jno W. White, clk, wit; m 28 Dec 1852 by Henry Harris, J. P.

Shearin, Sebastian C. & Mary C. Marshall, 24 apr 1866; A. M. Johnston, bm; William A. White, clk, wit; m 10 May 1866 by Chas M. Cook, J. P.

Shearin, Starling & Anne Williams, 10 Oct 1788; Allan Williams, bm; M. Duke Johnson, C. C., wit.

Shearin, Thomas & Mary Durham, 5 Apr 1806; John Patrick, bm; Jo Terrell, D. C., wit.

Shearin, Thomas & Sarah Mayfield, 21 Mar 1810; Benjn Colclough, bm; Jno C. Johnson, D. C., wit.

Shearin, Thomas & Susan Myrick, 13 Dec 1858; W. A. J. Nicholson, bm; William A. White, wit; m 15 Dec 1858 by Nathl. Nicholson, J. P.

Shearin, Thomas W. & Cynthia Bartlett, 6 Feb 1866; Jacob J. Shearin, bm; William A. White, clk, wit; m 8 Feb 1866 by Jno W. Pattillo, J. P.

Shearin, William & Elizebeth Balthrope, 20 May 1799; Willis Norsworthy, bm; Sherwood Green, wit.

Shearin, William, Jr., & Rebeca Shearin, 14 Nov 1827; Henry Shearin, bm; M. M. Drake, wit.

Shearin, William H. & Mary Ann Fleming, 8 Nov 1837; John P. Shearin, bm.

Shearin, Zachariah & Mary Bobbit, 6 Jan 1804; Joseph Shearin, bm; M. Duke Johnson, C. C., wit.

Shearin, Zachariah & Ann Myrick, 25 Feb 1830; Joseph Shearin, bm.

Shearin, Zachariah T. & Eliza R. Johnson, 30 Mar 1865; George R. Sledge, bm; William A. White, clk, wit; m 31 Mar 1865 by Henry Harris, J. P.

Shell, John B. & Tabitha Carrol, 17 Jan 1826; Thomas Carrol, bm; M. M. Drake, wit.

Shell, John Lemmon & Dorithey Clanton, 14 Mar 1792; Stephen Shell, bm; M. Duke Johnson, C. C., wit.

Shell, Oliver P. & Mary C. Turnbull, 1 Nov 1858; Alfred Alston, bm; Jno W. White, clk, wit; m 2 Nov 1858 by William Hodges, M. G.

Shell, Thomas (col) (son of Thomas Poythress & Louisa Perceval) & Nannie Robinson (dau of Hubbard & Flora), 13 July 1867; William A. White, clk, wit; m 13 July 1867 by B. F. Long, M. G.

Sheppard, Egbert & Mary T. Johnson, 19 Feb 1822; George Anderson, bm; Cas Drake, C. C., wit.

Sherin, Gardner, Jr., & Elizabeth Rodwell, 9 Jan 1821; Danl B. Allen, bm; Cas Drake, clk, wit.

Sherrin, Charles & Nancy Nichols, 6 June 1804; Simon Kimbell, bm; Gideon Johnson, wit.

Sherrin, John & Mary U. Cliborne, 14 Dec 1852; Will H. Clibourn, bm; Jno W. White, clk, wit; m 15 Dec 1852 by T. B. Ricks.

Sherrin, William & Tabitha Wilson, 11 Feb 1843; William S. Ransom, bm.

Sherrod, James & Rebecca Perry, 9 Dec 1793; Jeremiah Perry, bm; M. D. Johnson, clk, wit.

Short, Federick & Eliza C. Goode, 6 Dec 1823; Samuel Simmons, bm.

Short, John & Cinthia Harthorn, 30 July 1807; William Miller, bm; M. Duke Johnson, wit.

Short, Richard & Agness Wriggan, 19 Oct 1797; Caleb Lindsey, bm; Shd Green, wit.

Short, Theophilas & Fanny Boyd, 20 Nov 1860; Jas W. Adkins, bm; Jno W. White, clk, wit; m 22 Nov 1860 by A. L. Steed, J. P.

Shroyer, Edward & Frances M. Powell, 29 June 1855; Jno A. Waddill, bm; Jno W. White, clk, wit; m 2 July 1855 by T. B. Ricks, clergyman.

Shroyer, Edward & Mary P. Powell, 12 May 1860; George W. Harper, bm; Jno W. White, clk, wit.

Shuck, L. H. & M. A. Parrish, 18 June 1856; J. W. Mitchell, bm; Jno W. White, clk, wit; m 19 June 1856 by N. Z. Graves, M. G.

Sigrus, Theophilus & Armed Kersey, 1 Sept 1836; John Stewart, bm; Burl Pitchford, J. P., wit.

Silver, John & Martha Harris, 3 Jan 1837; Richard Davis, bm.

Simes, James G. & Polly Frances Hicks, 23 Jan 1866; John R. Byrum, bm; William A. White, clk, wit; m 25 Jan 1866 by T. Page Ricaud, M. G.

Simes, John & Nancy Hendrick, 15 Dec 1810; Reubin Coghill, bm; Jno C. Johnson, D. C. C., wit.

Simmons, Abijah & Elizabeth Desch, 19 May 1838; Thomas J. Judkins, bm.

Simmons, William G. & Mary E. Foote, 29 Aug 1853; Jas A. Egerton, bm; William A. White, wit; m 1 Sept 1853 by John B. White, M. G.

Simms, Christopher T. & Dorothy Milam, 8 Jan 1840; Anderson F. Brame, bm.

Sims, Benjamin & Holley Duke, 9 Mar 1805; Philemon Hawkins, bm.

Sims, Benjamin & Mary Sims, 23 Feb 1809; William Howard, bm; J. C. Johnson, D. C., wit.

Sims, Briggs & Fanny Duke, 25 Feb 1796; Frances Gill, bm.

Sims, Chesley & Polley Brown, 30 Nov 1799; L. Saunders Sims, bm; Shd Green, wit.

Sims, Henry & Sally Burt, 29 Nov 1813; Amos P. Sledge, bm; Wm. Green, C. C., wit.

Sims, James & Martha Bowdon, 8 Dec 1834; James Cooper, bm; E. D. Drake, clk, wit.

Sims, Joseph & Catharine Bullock, 18 May 1822; David Dancy, bm.

Sims, Leonard H. & Elizabeth Vaughan, 19 Aug 1804; Robert Temple, bm; Gideon Johnson, wit.

Sims, Leonard S. & Sally G. Jones, 2 Aug 1837; Jno White, bm.

Sims, Mattathias & Sally Wilson, 5 Feb 1801; Julius Sims, bm; S. Johnson, wit.

Sims, Richard & Harriet W. B. Sims, 7 July 1841; L. S. Sims, bm.

Singleton, John D. & Nancy Wall, 22 Oct 1836; James Hugens, bm; Burl Pitchford, J. P., wit.

Singleton, William & Caroline Evans, 9 June 1860; Jos Egerton, bm; Jno W. White, clk, wit; m 9 June 1860 by Jno N. Andrews, M. G.

Skinner, Charles & Susan E. Little, 21 May 1835; Richard H. Mosby, bm.

Skinner, Micajah (col) & Ann Shearin, 28 Mar 1867; P. J. Turnbull, bm; William A. White, clk, wit; m 28 Mar 1867 by Wm. Hodges, M. G.

Slade, Thomas P. & Eliza Gordan, 28 Oct 1830; Edwin E. Slade, bm; C. Drake, clk, wit.

Sledd, R. N. & Fannie C. Green, 25 Aug 1855; W. T. Bailey, bm; Jno W. White, wit.

Sledge, Adolfus & Martha A. Crowder, 23 Feb 1847; James U. Nicholson ,bm.

Sledge, Alfred A. & Mary B. Burgess, 18 Dec 1845; Jno W. White, bm; M. J. Montgomery, wit.

Sledge, Amos P. & Nancy L. Pitchford, 17 March 1824; Carter Nunnery, bm; E. D. Drake, wit.

Sledge, Asa G. & Elizabeth A. Stewart, __ Nov 1842; Edward J. Mason, bm; M. J. Montgomery, wit.

Sledge, Geo R. & Nancy D. Fleming, 22 Oct 1845; Joseph J. Harris, bm; M. J. Montgomery, wit.

Sledge, Hubbard A. & Eliza Bobbitt, 20 Dec 1831; William Pearce, bm; E. D. Drake, wit.

Sledge, Isam & Tabitha Myrick, 20 June 1782; Daniel Sledge, bm; M. Duke Johnson, wit.

Sledge, James J. & Susan Ann King, 18 Feb 1839; Thomas Reynolds, bm.

Sledge, John W. & Mariah Davis, 14 Dec 1822; Amos P. Sledge, bm; E. D. Drake, wit.

Sledge, Maclin & Francis M. Clanton, 6 June 1825; Mark Clanton, bm; M. M. Drake, wit.

Sledge, Mark W. & Mary C. Crowder, ____ 1843; H. Gee Parham, bm.

Sledge, Robert & Francis J. Wortham, 25 July 1836; Joseph S. Jones, bm; E. D. Drake, clk, wit.

Sledge, Sherwood & Susanah Myrick, 20 Oct 1792; Charles Myrick, bm; M. D. Johnson, C. C., wit.

Sledge, Turner & Tabathy Davis, 26 July 1809; John Williams, bm; Jno C. Johnson, D. C. C., wit.

Sledge, Wm. S. & Elizabeth Shearin, 26 Nov 1839; Jno P. Shearin, bm.

Smartt, Elisha & Martha Skelton, 18 Feb 1825; Griffin King, bm.

Smartt, Francis & Martha Cheek, 29 Dec 1784; Randolph Cheek, bm; M. Duke Johnson, wit.

Smiley, Jackson & Amelia G. O'Bryan, 19 Dec 1845; John R. Johnson, bm; M. J. Montgomery, wit.

Smiley, Jackson & Sally M. Roberson, 13 Oct 1847; Henry G. Goodloe, bm; Jno W. White, wit.

Smiley, Joseph & Nancy Patterson, 27 Mar 1824; Solomon Fleming, bm; C. Drake, C. C., wit.

Smiley, Robert & Henrietta Emeline Harris, 16 Dec 1848; Harry Harper, bm; Jno W. White, wit.

Smiley, Wm. Henry & Minerva Burchett, 20 Dec 1842; Christopher Robertson, bm; M. J. Montgomery, wit.

Smilly, Jno & Frances Todd, 6 May 1788; Geo Nicholson, bm; M. D. Johnson, C. C., wit.

Smilly, William & Martha Pennington, 27 Oct 1817; Ely Perkinson, bm; W. A. K. Falkener, wit.

Smilly, Willis & Nancy Ellis (no date); C. Nicholson, bm.

Smily, James & Ann Adams, 15 Aug 1832; Carter Nunnery, bm; C. Drake, clk, wit.

Smith, A. W. & Susan A. Coleman, 27 Nov 1866; William A. White, clk, wit; m 12 Dec 1866 by Ira T. Wyche, M. G.

Smith, Arrow & Rowena Thomerson, 8 Mar 1850; Wm. E. Lancaster, bm; Jno W. White, wit.

Smith, Arthur & Polley Duffey, 27 Nov 1780; James Willson, bm; William Green, wit.

Smith, Asa G. & Rebecca H. Griffice, 2 Jan 1850; Abner Mosely, bm; Richd B. Robinson, wit.

Smith, Bannister & Polly Fleming, 23 Nov 1818; John Fleming, bm; Wm. Green, C. C., wit.

Smith, Baxter & Agness Ellis, 17 Dec 1842; James Tally, bm; M. J. Montgomery, wit.

Smith, Baxter & Jane Ellis, 8 Apr 1847; William Smith, bm; Jno W. White, wit.

Smith, Bennett & Nancy Smith, 4 Feb 1799; Tyre Fain, bm; Shd Green, wit.

Smith, Bourbon & Margaret Robertson, 12 Feb 1840; John M. Price, bm.

Smith, Charles & Rebecca Mayfield, 18 Apr 1809; Joel Smith, bm; M. Duke Johnson, clk, wit.

Smith, Daniel & Elisabeth Daniel (no date); Samuel Smith, bm.

Smith, David L. & Catherine Parish, 10 Jan 1826; Banister B. Smith, bm; M. M. Drake, wit.

Smith, Edmond & Sarah B. Judd, 26 July 1820; Benjamin H. Bass, bm; Frs Jones, wit.

Smith, Edward & Martha Blount, 30 Sept 1806; Willis Arrington, bm; Jo Terrell, D. C. C., wit.

Smith, Edward & Frances Daniel, 30 Dec 1808; Thomas Daniel, bm; M. D. Johnson, C. C., wit.

Smith, Edward & Elizabeth Cox, 16 Dec 1821; Henry Smith, bm; Frs Jones, wit.

Smith, Elihu & Dicey Hilton, 27 Feb 1792; S. Davis, bm; M. Duke Johnson, C. C., wit.

Smith, Francs & Fanny Howard (no date); Archd Brown, bm.

Smith, George & Mary Paschall, 3 Feb 1802; Jno Smith, bm; M. Duke Johnson, C. C., wit.

Smith, Geo & Henrietta Darnald, 20 Aug 1844; Littleberry Smith, bm; M. J. Montgomery, wit.

Smith, George & Eleanor Langford, 16 Mar 1851; John P. Beasly, bm; Jno W. White, clk, wit; m 17 Mar 1851 by O. D. Fitts, J. P.

Smith, George S. & Dionesia S. Vaughan, 1 Nov 1841; Edward M. Steed, bm; M. J. Montgomery, wit.

Smith, Henry & Mary Butler, 27 Nov 1865; Jos J. Haithcock, bm; William A. White, clk, wit; m 27 Nov 1865 by T. B. Kingsbury, M. G.

Smith, Isaiah & Polly Cogwell, 20 Nov 1822; Thomas Coghill, bm; Cas Drake, wit.

Smith, Jack & Mary Denkins, 17 Sept 1785; Daniel Smith, bm.

Smith, James & Salley Acree, 11 Jan 1786; John Mosely, Jr., bm.

Smith, James & Mary Thomas, 5 Nov 1808; John Darnol, bm; M. Duke Johnson, C. C., wit.

Smith, James & Martha Alston, 10 Feb 1829; Gordon Cawthorn, bm; E. D. Drake, wit.

Smith, James & Abbey Mushtin, 22 Jan 1841; Samuel Huggens, bm; Burl Pitchford, J. P., wit.

Smith, James L. & Poly Darnald, 29 Dec 1818; Richard O'Mara, bm.

Smith, John & Mary Myrick, 20 Mar 1789; John Paine, bm; M. Duke Johnson, C. C., wit.

Smith, John & Nancy Ellis, 15 July 1794; John Hicks, bm; M. D. Johnson, C. C., wit.

Smith, Jno & Arreney Thomas, 23 May 1799; William Hicks, bm; M. D. Johnson ,C. C., wit.

Smith, Jno & Betsey Greyard, 12 Aug 1796; Jno Hicks, bm; M. Duke Johnson, C. C., wit.

Smith, John & Jincy Archer, 28 Aug 1821; Benjamin Johnson, bm.

Smith, John & Lucy Nicholson (dau of Nancy), 24 Jan 1823; William Johnson, bm.

Smith, John & Tabitha Moore, 11 June 1824; Edward Moore, bm; M. M. Drake, wit.

Smith, John A. & Martha C. Jones, 7 Oct 1830; James Somervell, bm; C. Drake, C. C., wit.

Smith, John H. & Cora Morton 14 Apr 1849; D. P. Taylor, bm; Jno W. White, wit.

Smith, John J. & Lucy J. Moseley, 24 Aug 1863; Robt E. Mosely, bm; William A. White, clk, wit; m 2 Sept 1863 by A. F. Davidson (in Mecklenburg Co., VA).

Smith, Joshua & Polly Green Malone, 7 July 1808; Archibald Thomas, William Ross, bm; Wm. R. Johnson, wit.

Smith, Lewis F. & Olive A. Sims, 12 Dec 1826; John Bowdon, bm; M. M. Drake, wit.

Smith, Mical & Betsy Marshall, 17 Jan 1797; Saml Marshall, bm.

Smith, Patrick H. & Mary Edwards, 25 July 1834; Samuel Edwards, bm; E. D. Drake, clk, wit.

Smith, Richard H. & Sarah Hall, 12 Nov 1833; John V. Cawthorn, bm; E. D. Drake, clk, wit.

Smith, Robert & Elizabeth Bowdon, 21 Jan 1829; James Loyd, bm; E. D. Drake, wit.

Smith, Robert B. & Emma J. Mitchell, 26 Sept 1853; J. H. Wallace, bm; Chas M. Smith, wit; m 26 Sept 1853 by R. B. Robinson, J. P.

Smith, Samuel R. & Mary Jane Pattillo, 28 Nov 1839; Francis McHenry, bm.

Smith, Solomon W. & Martha Kearney, 14 May 1850; H. J. Macon, bm; Jno W. White, wit.

Smith, Solomon W. & Martha B. Snow, 26 Jan 1852; Henry J. Macon, bm; William A. White, wit; m 26 Jan 1852 by H. J. Macon, J. P.

Smith, William & Polly Tally, 27 Apr 1831; John Smith, bm; C. Drake, C. C., wit.

Smith, Wm. H. & Julia A. Spruill, 1 Dec 1853; R. W. Hyman, bm; Jno W. White, C. C,. wit. m 1 Dec 1853 by Jos Blount Cheshire, M. G.

Smith, Wm. H. & Amarillis Williams, 10 Apr 1858; Wm. D. Harris, bm; William A. White, wit; m 10 Apr 1858 by J. B. Solomon.

Smith, Williamson & Suckey Dowell 9 June 1809; Jacob Coleman; Jno C. Johnson, D. C. C., wit.

Smith, Willie & Lewsy Rawyster, 16 Mar 1797; Richard Daniel, bm; Shd Green, wit.

Smithwick, James R. & Frances A. Allen, 14 Dec 1850; Alexr L. Steed, bm; Jno W. White, wit.

Snow, John & Maria L. A. Freeman, 30 Sept 1812; Peter R. Davis, bm; Jno H. Green, wit.

Snow, John & Caroline Harper, 6 Feb 1850; Thos A. Montgomery, wit; Jno H. Green, wit.

Snow, Premus (formerly slave of Elizabeth Elton) Annis Williams (formerly slave of S. A. Williams), 6 Feb 1866; Saml A. Williams, bm; C. M. Cook, wit; m 6 Feb 1866 by C. M. Cook, J. P.

Snow, Xanthus & Polly Kearney, 13 Jan 1814; Thomas Bragg, bm; Jno H. Green, wit.

Somervell, James & Catharine Volkes, 24 Mar 1806; Joel Terrell, Jr., bm; Jo Terrell, D. C. C., wit.

Somervell, John B. & E. M. Kearney, 17 May 1830; E. D. Drake, bm.

Somerville, Boson (col) (son of James Beasley & Henrietta Somerville) & Charlotte Carroll (dau of Joe Watkins & Betty Carroll), 9 Nov 1867; William A. White, clk, wit; m 16 Nov 1867 by R. D. Paschall, J. P.

Somerville, Matthew (col) & Dorsey Crossan, 24 Jan 1867; William A. White, clk, wit; m 26 Jan 1867 by J. M. Brame, J. P.

Somerville, Solomon (col) & Louisa Cawthorn, 20 Feb 1867; William A. White, clk, wit; m 20 Feb 1867 by William Hodges, M. G.

Somerville, William (col) & Indiana Hill, 20 Apr 1867; Wm H. Bobbitt, Jr., bm; William A. White, clk, wit; m 20 Apr 1867 by Wm. Hodges, M. G.

Sommervell, Sandy (col) & Priscilla Somervell, 4 July 1866; James B. Somerville, bm; William A. White, clk, wit; m 7 July 1866 by Thos A. Montgomery, J. P.

Southall, Henry & Mary Arrington, 28 July 1798; Henry Arrington, bm; S. Green, wit.

Southall, Holmon & Rebecca Reaves, 4 Dec 1829; Gordon Cawthorn, bm; C. Drake, C. C., wit.

Southall, James & Ann B. Harper, 14 Dec 1824; Alexander H. Falconer, bm.

Southall, John & Patsey Drewry, 26 Sept 1822; Alexander Crossland, bm; Cas Drake, C. C., wit.

Southall, Pherney & Rose Ann Edwards, 18 Dec 1835; Drewry Shearin, bm; E. C. Drake, clk, wit.

Southerland, Simmons B. & Elizabeth A. Ward, 11 Sept 1821; Wm. H. Marshall, bm; Cas Drake, C. C. C., wit.

Soward, John J. & Ann Kersey, 7 Jan 1841; Anthony L. Soward, bm; Burl Pitchford, J. P., wit.

Sparks, Thos & Jane Hogwood (no date); Ben Kelley, bm.

Spears, John & Tempy Reed, 1 Aug 1835; Anthony M. Johnson, bm.

Spratley, John W. & Sarah Jane Jones, 10 June 1847; James Shaw, bm; Jno W. White, wit.

Springer, John & Ann Green, 9 Dec 1783; William Green, bm; M. Duke Johnson,m wit.

Sprunt, James & Milley Duncan, 23 Dec 1783; Jos Lunsford, bm; M. Duke Johnson, wit.

Spurlock, Zachariah & Eley Hendrick, 26 Mar 1809; Benjamin Johnson, bm; Jno C. Johnson, D. C. C., wit.

Stainback, James H. & Lucy Griffin, 13 Jan 1812; Harrison Fussell, bm; Wm. Green, C. C. C., wit.

Stainback, John O. & Susan Allen, 14 Jan 1822; George W. Tunstall, bm; Cas Drake, wit.

Stainback, Thomas W. & Martha A. Lankford, 8 Mar 1836; Robert Bowdon, bm; William A. White, wit; m 12 Mar 1856 by A. L. Steed, J. P.

Stainback, William R. & Mary C. Mason, 3 Jan 1841; William C. Snead, bm; John J. Vaughan, wit.

Stainback, William H. & Sarah Coghill, 16 Dec 1815; Reubin Coghill, bm; Will Green, C. C. C., wit.

Stallings, Hilliard & Emily A. Daniel, 15 Jan 1834; James M. Daniel, bm; E. D. Drake, clk, wit.

Stallings, James & Caroline Verser, 18 Dec 1848; Petter J. Turnbull, bm; Jno W. White, wit.

Stallings, James & Lucy J. Harriss, 3 Oct 1866; David Parrish, bm; William A. White, clk, wit; m 11 Oct 1866 by Ridley Browne, J. P.

Stallings, John & Eveline Verser, 20 Dec 1855; Henry A. Foote, bm; Jno W. White, wit.

Stallings, John & Lucy A. Womble, 21 Dec 1864; Isaac Harris, bm; William A. White, clk, wit; m 22 Jan 1864 by M. C. Duke, J. P.

Stallings, John A. & Sarah A. Robertson, 5 Dec 1859; Jno C. McCraw, bm; Jno W. White, clk, wit; m 15 Dec 1859 by Saml Bobbitt.

Stallings, Joseph & Lucy Hazilwood, 1 Nov 1784; William Madra, bm; M. Duke Johnson, C. C., wit.

Stallings, Josiah & Mariah Dowten, 17 Dec 1816; Roderick Bigelow, bm; Wm. Green, D. C. C., wit.

Stallings, Solomon & Thamer Davis, 3 Sept 1822; Josiah Stallings, bm; Cas Drake, wit.

Stallings, Solomon & Elizabeth Turner, 9 Feb 1848; Archibald H. Davis, Jr., bm; Jno W. White, wit.

Stallings, Solomon P. & Sarah A. Stallings, 18 Oct 1865; T. P. Alston, bm; T. P. Alston, wit; m 18 Oct 1865 by T. P. Alston, J. P.

Stallings, Solomon W. & Susan D. Harriss, 1 May 1855; Jas A. Egerton, bm; Jno W. White, clk, wit; m 2 May 1855 by Saml Bobbitt, J. P.

Stallings, Theopilus & Martha Brame, 7 Sept 1852; Jno C. McCraw, bm; Jno W. White, wit; m 8 Sept 1862 by Robt O. Burton, M. G.

Stallings, William P. & Eliza J. Pegram, 26 Jan 1847; John Verser, bm; Jno W. White, wit.

Stallins, William & Elizabeth Dowtin, 28 Apr 1830; Isham H. Davis, bm.

Stammire, Bennett H. & Elizabeth Henry Powers, 13 Nov 1827; Green D. Jenkins, bm; M. M. Drake, wit.

Stamper, Jacob (col) & Julia Brame, 26 Feb 1867; Dr. V. O. Thompson, bm; William A. White, clk, wit; m 2 Mar 1867 by P. H. Joyner.

Stamper, James & Sally Southerland, 14 May 1834; Richard Jordan, bm;

Stanback, George W. & Sally Pendergrass, 12 Apr 1836; Samuel Edwards, bm; E. D. Drake, clk, wit.

Standley, Dancy & Priscilla Wood, 1 Feb 1796; Daniel Newman, bm.

Stansbury, William & Rebecca Walker, 8 Jan 1823; John Neal, bm.

Stark, Richard L. & Ann E. Reid, 19 July 1830; Burwell Starke, bm; Benj E. Cook, wit.

Stark, William H. & Mary Jane Moseley, 15 Oct 1861; Jordan H. Foster, bm; Jno W. White, clk, wit; m 11 Dec 1861 by Nathl Nicholson, J. P.

Steagall, Jesse & Elizabeth Brooks, 6 Jan 1818; Thos Carrol, bm; Wm. Green, wit.

Steed, Abner & Patsy C. Allen, 29 Jan 1813; Henry Allen, bm; Wm. Green, C. C. C., wit.

Steed, Alexander L. (son of Abner & Martha C. Steed) & Elizabeth L. Phipps (dau of James N. & Mary E. Phipps), 29 July 1867; William A. White, clk, wit; m 30 July 1867 by Will H. Wheeler, M. G.

Steegall, Willis & Nancy Thomas, 26 Dec 1823; John Heavlin, bm; C. Drake, clk, wit.

Stegall, James & Martha Gordin, 28 Dec 1829; Willis Stegall, bm; Burl Pitchford, J. P., wit.

Stegall, John W.& Sarah J. Newton, 25 Nov 1846; John G. Nanney, bm; Jno W. White, wit.

Stegall, Raibun & Polly Hawks, 23 Feb 1824; Hopkins Matthews, bm; C. Drake, C. C., wit.

Stegall, Richard (col) & Margaret Mayho, 16 June 1863; Albert Howell, bm; William A. White, clk, wit.

Stegall, Thomas & Catharine Carrington, 12 Jan 1826; Willis Stegall, bm; Burl Pitchford, wit.

Stegall, William & Lucy Newton, 2 Dec 1851; James F. Moss, bm; Jno W. White, clk, wit; m 3 Dec 1851 by Jas T. Russell, J. P.

Stephens, Asa & Susan Turner, 1 Jan 1817; Stephen Rives, bm; Wm. Green, C. C. C., wit.

Stephens, James C. & Mary Manier, 10 Jan 1822; Richd Allen, bm.

Stephens, John & Cusiah Kendrick, 11 Jan 1791; Nathl Mason, bm; M. Duke Johnson, C. C.,wit.

Stephenson, Jeremiah & Salley Harris, 27 Jan 1799; Wilmot E. Harris, bm; Shd Green, wit.

Stephenson, Richard & Mary Patterson, 19 Apr 1864; Matthew M. Drake, bm.

Stephenson, Saml & Gean Allen, 19 Aug 1790; Reuben Smith, bm; Ja Turner, wit.

Stevens, John & Betty Wadkins, 30 Sept 1796; Richd Wadkins, bm; M. Duke Johnson, C. C., wit.

Stevenson, Richard & Priscilla Darnell, 4 Feb 1834;. Green D. Jenkins, bm; E. D. Drake, clk, wit.

Steverson, John D. & Julia D. James, 15 June 1857; Jas A. Egerton, bm; Jno W. White, wit; m 15 June 1857 by Thos J. Judkins, J. P.

Steward, John & Emily Evans, 8 Feb 1843; Wesley Pettiford, bm; M. J. Montgomery, wit.

Steward, Stanfield & Nancy Mills, 15 July 1846; Alexander Steward, bm; J. J. Anderson, wit.

Stewart, Andrew & Ann Ash, 5 July 1858; John Stewart, bm; Jno W. White, wit.

Stewart, Benja & Susanah Evans (no date); Eaton Walden, bm; M. Duke Johnson, C. C., wit.

Stewart, Charles & Rebecah Myrick, 19 May 1799; Jos Johnson, wit; Shd Green, wit.

Stewart, James & Salley Evans, 2 May 1791; Eaton Walden, bm; M. D. Johnson ,C. C., wit.

Stewart, James & Rosey Stewart, 27 Sept 1824; Robert Smith, bm; M. M. Drake, wit.

Stewart, James & Nancy Maclin, 3 Nov 1849; James E. Augood, bm; Jno W. White, wit.

Stewart, James W. & Mary E. Daly, 15 Nov 1849; George W. Robinson, bm; Jno W. White, wit.

Stewart, John & Sarah Kearsey, 25 Aug 1840; Edmund Kersey, bm; Edwin D. Drake, C. C. C., wit.

Stewart, John & Eliza Cyprus, 19 Feb 1833; James Algood, bm; Jno W. White, wit.

Stewart, Matthew & Casiah Drew, 20 June 1804; Stanfield Drew, bm; M. D. Johnson, C. C., wit.

Stewart, Standfield & Mary Brewer, 27 Jan 1848; Alexander Stewart, bm; Jno W. White, wit.

Steward, William & Lilly T. Robinson, 8 Jan 1834; Richard B. Robinson, bm; E. D. Drake, clk, wit.

Stiles, Belfield & Anne E. Jenkins, 20 Feb 1841; Jas J. Sledge, bm.

Stiner, Jacob & Nancy Balthrop, 28 Feb 1809; Joel Terrell, Jr., bm; J. D. Johnson, D. C. C., wit.

Stokes, William & Lucy Dean, 21 Dec 1808; William Wootton, bm; M. D. Johnson, C. C., wit.

Stone, James T. & Mary W. Bledsoe, 19 Nov 1841; Thomas Coghill, bm; M. J. Montgomery, wit.

Stone, Macon & Patsey Cogyhill, 8 Jan 1822; Thomas Cogwell, bm; Cas Drake, wit.

Stone, Merideth & Elizabeth Garret, 7 Feb 1826; Ch Haskins, Jr., bm; Burl Pitchford, wit.

Stroud, Richard & Matilda E. King, 15 May 1833; William Blanton, bm; Burl Pitchford, J. P., wit.

Strum, William & Nancy L. Sledge, 26 Nov 1836; Jacob Davis, bm; Burl Pitchford, J. P., wit.

Strum, William & Mary Harris, 12 Dec 1853; A. G. Hendrick, bm; Jno W. White, wit; m 14 Dec 1853 by A. C. Harris, M. G.

Sturdivant, Anderson & Theney Riggans, 17 Nov 1821; John Heavlin, bm.

Sturdivant, Benjamin & Rebecca Kimbell, 5 Feb 1805; William Newell, bm; M. D. Johnson, C. C., wit.

Sturdivant, William & Martha Arrington, 14 Apr 1835; Benjn Kimbell, bm; E. D. Drake, clk, wit.

Suit, Ralph & Nancy Wetherington, 10 Mar 1797; Anthony Beard, bm; Thomas Malone, wit.

Suit, Robert & Elizabeth Riggan, 1 Oct 1849; Jeremiah M. Fleming, bm; Jno W. White, wit.

Suit, William H. & Elener Duncan, 16 Jan 1830; Len H. Bullock, bm.

Sullivan, Colgate W. & Mary L. Minor, 7 Nov 1849; Lewis McGee, bm; Thos P. Paschall, wit.

Sullivant, Jesse & Catey Pope, 11 Feb 1791; Jas Dunn, bm; M. Duke Johnson, C. C., wit.

Sullivante, Russell & Mary Bush, 6 Feb 1792; John Bush, bm; M. Duke Johnson, C. C., wit.

Sully, Thomas & Sarah Sully, 27 June 1806; Sugan Johnson, bm; M. Duke Johnson, C. C., wit.

Sutherland, Jno & Anne Alston, 27 Aug 1805; Anthony Sale, bm; Jo Terrell, D. C. C., wit.

Sutherland, Solon & Ann C. Wortham, 25 Jan 1853; Jno W. White, clk ,wit; m 25 Jan 1853 by N. A. Purefoy, M. G.

Sutton, Richard & Elisabeth Ellenton, 5 July 1788; John Power, Jr, bm; M. Duke Johnson, C. C. C., wit.

Sutton, William & Elisabeth Jackson, 5 Sept 1789; Martin Dye, bm; M. Duke Johnson, C. C., wit.

Sylver, Henry (col) & Lucy Richardson, 1 Nov 1865; Cofield Richardson, bm; William A. White, clk, wit.

Talley, Branch & Nancey Posey, 23 Nov 1797; John Sheless, bm; Sherwood Green, wit.

Talley, Frederick & Mimy Perkinson, 1 Oct 1812; Henry Talley, bm; Jno H. Green, wit.

Talley, Guilford & Martha P. Gardner, 11 Jan 1826; Matthew M. Drake, bm.

Talley, Guilford & Nancy P. Southerland, 11 June 1830; Willoughby Huggins, bm.

Talley, Guilford, Jr., & Suasan Whitlow, 22 Dec 1835; Alexander King, bm; Burl Pitchford, J. P., wit.

Talley, Henry & Tabitha Ellice, 7 Nov 1803; Joel Tally, bm; Gideon Johnson, wit.

Talley, Joel & Nancy Perkinson, 12 Sept 1797; Seth Perkinson, bm; M. Duke Johnson, C. C., wit.

Talley, Levi, Jr., & Mary F. Perkinson, 16 June 1852; Robt D. Paschall, bm; Jno W. White, clk, wit; m 16 June 1852 by J. H. Hawkins, J. P.

Talley, Starling & Martha Ellis, 17 Mar 1786; William Ellis, bm.

Talley, Solomon (col) & Evaline Jefferson, 17 Nov 1866; P. R. Perkinson, bm; William A. White, clk, wit; m 25 Nov 1866 by L. C. Perkinson, M. G.

Talley, Thomas & Betsey Johnson, 22 Sept 1804; Henry Talley, bm; M. Duke Johnson, C. C., wit.

Talley, Travis & Salley Wright, 15 Feb 1850; Jeremiah Perkerson, bm; Burl Pitchford, J. P., wit.

Tally, Henry & Susan Shearin, 13 June 1818; James Talley, bm.

Tally, Joel & Vina Coleman, 7 Jan 1815; Anderson Sturdivant, bm; W. Green, C. C., wit.

Tannahill, Robert & Sallie Sims, 3 Oct 1860; Tippoo S. Brownlow, bm; Jno W. White, clk, wit; m 4 Oct 1860 by Wm. Hodges.

Tannahill, Stephen (col) & Nancy Fitts, 4 June 1866; Edward H. Plummer, bm; William A. White, clk, wit; m 1 July 1866 by L. C. Perkinson, M. G.

Tanner, Edwd & Nancy Christmas, 20 Mar 1797; Shd Green, bm; Shd Green, wit.

Tanner, Edward & Nancy Smith, 11 Aug 1823; Hopkins Matthews, bm; E. D. Drake, wit.

Tanner, John & Tabitha Weldon, 16 Nov 1824; John D. Langford, bm.

Tanner, Joseph & Tabitha B. Hightower, 11 Dec 1808; Jo Terrell, Jr., bm; M. Duke Johnson, C. C., wit.

Tanner, Joseph & Elizabeth Gardener, 15 Jan 1812; Joel Terrell, Jr, bm; Jo Terrell, D. C. C., wit.

Tanner, Wm. & Viney Rivers, 13 Nov 1811; Jack Jeffers, bm; Wm. Green, C. C. C., wit.

Tansel, Lot & Parthenia Tansel, 2 May 1831; James Brame, bm; C. Drake, C. C., wit.

Tarry, Barnaby (col) (son of Andrew & Netty) & Ellen Barnes (dau of Sandy & Betsey), 6 Sept 1867; William A. White, clk, wit; m 7 Sept 1867 by Jas. T. Russell, J. P.

Tarry, Edward & Lucy Little, 8 Apr 1821; James Somervell, bm; Cas Drake, C. C., wit.

Tarry, Ellick (col) (son of Autaway & Cloye Farrar) & Eliza Davis (dau of Lisbon & Angeline), 6 Sept 1867; William A. White, clk, wit; m 7 Sept 1867 by Jas. T. Russell, J. P.

Tarry, James P. & Amanda C. Collins, 21 July 1858; Thos C. Collins, bm; Jno W. White, clk, wit; m 23 July 1858 by John Tillett, M. G.

Tarver, Silas & Nancy A. Harris, 24 Dec 1822; John C. Baker, bm; C. Drake, C. C., wit.

Tate, John G. & Sarah Falkner, 18 Apr 1848; John D. Vaughan, bm; Jno W. White, wit.

Tate, Robert W. E. & Frances E. Renn, 13 Dec 1856; James Stainback, bm; Jno W. White, clk, wit; m 16 Dec 1856 by P. H. Smith, M. G.

Tatem, Richard (col) (son of Charles Allen & Betsey Bowden) & Eliza Pritchard (dau of Lot & Hannah Aven), 21 Oct 1867; William A. White, clk, wit; m 22 Oct 1867 by R. D. Paschall, J. P.

Tatum, Frank W. & Harriet Plummer, 5 Nov 1853; Will A. Jenkins, bm; Jno W. White, wit; m 7 Nov 1853 by L. L. Smith, clergyman.

Taylor, Francis & Martha Thorp, 6 Apr 1785; John Willis, bm; M. Duke Johnson, wit.

Taylor, Howel B. A. & Hapsey Ann Paschall, 3 June 1830; Daniel Taylor, bm; Burl Pitchford, J. P., wit.

Taylor, James & Holly B. Davies, 18 July 1809; John Alston, bm; Jno C. Johnson, D. C., wit.

Taylor, James & Mary Dowlin, 21 Nov 1829; Thomas G. Watkins, bm; E. D. Drake, wit.

Taylor, John & Elizabeth Nanny, 18 Dec 1832; Howel B. A. Taylor, bm; C. Drake, C. C., wit.

Taylor, John Y. & Martha Alexander, 21 Dec 1811; Henry Fitts, bm; Sd Green, wit.

Taylor, Kinchen & Betsey Harris, 18 Nov 1830; John Colely, bm; C. Drake, C. C., wit.

Taylor, Montgomery L. & Rebecca Ann Barnett, 4 Jan 1843; Samuel Hudgins, bm; M. J. Montgomery, wit.

Taylor, Nathaniel & Mary Story, ____ 1793; Philemon Morris, bm; M. Duke Johnson, C. C., wit.

Taylor, Oliver P. & Catharine L. Bullock, 12 Mar 1857; D. B. Kimball, bm; William A. White, wit; m 18 Mar 1857 by N. Z. Graves.

Taylor, Robert & Martha Griffis, 26 Aug 1841; Samuel Griffis, bm; Burl Pitchford, J. P., wit.

Taylor, Samuel (col) (son of Isaac Taylor) & Cora Hawkins (dau of John Hawkins), 9 Nov 1867; William A. White, clk, wit; m 9 Nov 1867 by R. D. Paschall, J. P.

Taylor, Wm. A. & Sarah A. Jones, 20 July 1825; Z. Herndon, bm; M. M. Drake, wit.

Taylor, Wm Barzillai & Elizabeth Ward, (no date); John Ward, bm; M. Duke Johnson, C. C., wit.

Taylor, William H. B. & Mary P. J. Jones, 1 May 1858; A. G. Jones, bm; Jno W. White, wit; m by J. B. Solomon, M. G.

Terrell, Halcot & Martha Cook, 28 Aug 1811; Wm. Green, bm; Wm. Green, C. C. C., wit.

Terrell, James & Polley House, 23 Nov 1802; Richard Jordan, bm; M. D. Johnson, C. C., wit.

Terrill, Richmond & Sarah Martin, 22 May 1786; Wm. Rush, bm; M. Duke Johnson, wit.

Terry, David & Nancy Jordan, 11 Nov 1807; Joel Terrell, Jr., bm; M. Duke Johnson, C. C., wit.

Terry, Jason & Hannah Wright, 19 Dec 1812; John Wright, bm; Wm. Green, C. C. C., wit.

Thomas, Charles L. & Mildred J. Nicholson, 12 June 1844; Gideon W. Nicholson, bm; M. J. Montgomery, wit.

Thomas, Charles W. & Mary R. Person, 10 Nov 1852; James A. Taylor, bm; Jno W. Seward, wit; m 10 Nov 1852 by Richd B. Robinson, J. P.

Thomas, David & Marey King (no date); Richd Riggan, bm; M. Duke Johnson, C. C., wit.

Thomas, David & Susanah Watson, 19 Sept 1786; Jno Thomas, bm; M. Duke Johnson, wit.

Thomas, David & Betsey Childress, 17 June 1800; Thomas Paschall, bm; M. D. Johnson C. C., wit.

Thomas, David & Mary Ann Southall, 17 Sept 1859; N. M. Arrington, bm; Jno W. White, clk, wit; m 18 Sept 1859 by R. G. Barrett, clergyman.

Thomas, James G. & Bettie W. Bobbitt, 31 Aug 1865; Austin W. Green, bm; William A. White, clk, wit; m 12 Sept 1865 by Thos P. Alston, J. P.

Thomas, John & Phillis Mills (no date); Thos E. Milles, bm; M. D. Johnson, wit.

Thomas, John & Mary Cuningham, 18 Feb 1783; David King, bm; M. Duke Johnson, wit.

Thomas, John & Nancey Gotney, 7 Oct 1830; Jesse Stegall, bm; Burl Pitchford, J. P., wit.

Thomas, John E. & Martha A. Hughes, 27 Dec 1832; Washington Branch, bm; C. Drake, C. C., wit.

Thomas, Jno T. & Annie B. Bullock, 29 Aug 1853; W. K. Plummer, bm; William A. White, wit; m 1 Jan 1855 by Edward Hines, M. G.

Thomas, Richard & Mary Glover, 3 Oct 1783; David Thomas, bm; M. D. Johnson, wit.

Thomas, Stephen & Lucy King, 6 May 1811; Zachariah Burlock, bm; Jno C. Johnson, D. C., wit.

Thomas, Taylor & Margaret Burton, 8 June 1837; Allen B. Pitchford, bm; Burl Pitchford, J. P., wit.

Thomas, William & Nancy Jackson, 7 July 1803; William Rooker, bm; Gideon Johnson, wit.

Thomas, William B. & Louisa J. Taylor, 7 Dec 1853; William L. Taylor, bm; E. H. Riggan, bm; m 7 Dec 1853 by Richd B. Robinson, J. P.

Thomasson, George & Parthena G. Basket, 20 Aug 1840; T. A. Montgomery, bm.

Thomasson, William H. & Harriet P. Bowdon, 29 Dec 1845; John White, bm; M. J. Montgomery, wit.

Thompson, Dr. A. J. & Rebecca F. Brown, 30 Nov 1859; T. J. Foote, bm; Jno W. White, wit; m 1 Dec 1859 by J. B. Solomon, M. G.

Thompson, Alfred & Harriet Felts, 24 Feb 1830; Benj Thompson, bm; M. M. Drake, wit.

Thompson, Arthur & Arrena Askew, 3 Oct 1856; Jas A. Egerton, bm; Jno W. White, clk, wit; m 9 Oct 1856 by John Watson, J. P.

Thompson, Benjamin & Jane Capps, 31 July 1823; Daniel Pegram, bm; Edwin D. Drake, wit.

Thompson, Benjamin W. & Susan Ann Hicks, 17 Dec 1850; Michl Riggan, bm; Jno W. White, wit.

Thompson, Charles B. & Winnefred L. Coleman, 5 Nov 1841; Robt D. Paschall, bm; M. J. Montgomery, wit.

Thompson, Christopher T. & Arametta Jackson, 2 May 1853; E. H. Dugger, bm; Jno W. White, clk, wit; m 5 May 1853 by R. B. Robinson, J. P.

Thompson, Drury & Eliza Shearin, 19 Dec 1837; Gardner Sherin, bm.

Thompson, Drury, Jr., & Anna Parish, 18 Apr 1815; Turner Jinkins, bm; W. Green, C. C., wit.

Thompson, Edmund A. & Lucy Ann Tucker, 8 Aug 1839; Benjamin E. Cook, bm; Edwd W. Best, wit.

Thompson, Fleming & Ann Smith, 27 Feb 1855; James Shearin, bm; W. A. White, wit; m 27 Feb 1855 by N. A. Purefoy, M. G.

Thompson, Fredk & Mary Wilson, 25 Apr 1787; William Foote, bm; M. D. Johnson, wit.

Thompson, Harrod & Frances Little, 31 Jan 1837; Francis Little, bm; E. W. Best, wit.

Thompson, Henderson & Mary A. Tucker, 1 Oct 1816; Daniel Tucker, bm; Wm. Green, C. C., wit.

Thompson, Herod & Rebecca Shearin, 22 Dec 1800; Nathl Baxter, Jr., bm; S. Johnson, wit.

Thompson, James & Mary Person, 17 Mar 1830; William Rodwell, bm; C. Drake, C. C., wit.

Thompson, James & Lucy H. Thompson, 19 Dec 1865; Kinchen Harper, bm; William A. White, wit.

Thompson, Lewis & Sue Alston, 14 Dec 1865; George W. Alston, bm; William A. White, clk, wit; m 20 Dec 1865 by R. J. Carson, M. G.

Thompson, Littleton & Sarah Patterson, 20 Oct 1851; Wm Morgan Powell, bm; William A. White, wit; m 21 Oct 1852 by John S. Cheek, J. P.

Thompson, Randolph & Amelia S. George, 3 Apr 1817; John Minor, bm; Wm. Green, C. C., wit.

Thompson, Richard & Emily Pitchford, 14 Mar 1866; William A. White, clk, wit; m 15 Mar 1866 by Jas T. Russell, J. P.

Thompson, Dr. V. O. & L. D. Joyner, 13 Dec 1866; William A. White, C. C., wit; m 20 Dec 1866 by J. P. Moore, M. G.

Thompson, William & Elizabeth Bennett, 14 May 1822; Thomas Edwards, bm; Cas Drake, C. C., wit.

Thompson, William & Mary Wortham, 16 Feb 1850; Benjamin F. Wortham, bm; Jno W. White, wit.

Thompson, William D. & Sarah A. Cole, 15 Nov 1841; Charles B. Thompson, bm.

Thompson, William G. & Nancy Perkinson, 6 Sept 1848; Hilliard G. Colclough, bm; Jno W. White, wit.

Thomson, Joseph & Nancy Evans, 27 Apr 1842; Lucindy Mayo, bm; Burl Pitchford, J. P., wit

Thomson, William & Nancy Taylor (no date); Saml Taylor, bm; M. D. Johnson, wit.

Thorn, Thomas & Abigal Duke, 18 Dec 1804; Daniel Duke, bm; M. Duke Johnson, C. C., wit.

Thorne, Presley & Anne Williams, 17 Dec 1783; Nimrod Williams, bm; M. Duke Johnson, wit.

Thorne, William H. & Martha J. Alston, 13 Oct 1856; N. F. Alston, bm; Jno W. White, clk, wit; m 15 Oct 1856 by Robt O. Burton, M. G.

Thornton, Francis A. & Ann S. Boyd, 19 Apr 1822; Gordon Cawthorn, bm; Cas Drake, C. C. C., wit.

Thornton, Granderson (col) & Jane Shaw, 30 June 1866; Robt B. Thornton, bm; William A. White, wit.

Thornton, John (col) & Esther Peete, 19 May 1866; Robert B. Thornton, bm; W. H. Shaw, wit; m 19 May 1866 by R. S. F. Peete, J. P.

Thornton, Kitter (col) (son of Alonzo & Martha) & Caroline Branch (dau of Charles & Arilla), 20 June 1867; William A. White, clk, wit; m 20 June 1867 by William Hodges, M. G.

Thorton, Moses & Salley Turner, 23 Dec 1800; Wm. Turner, bm; M. D. Johnson, C. C., wit.

Thornton, Rowland & Elizabeth Turner, 18 Dec 1797; William Rives, bm; M. Duke Johnson, C. C., wit.

Thornton, William R. & Isabella F. Clanton, 1 Mary 1850; Jas P. Alston, bm; Jno W. White, wit.

Thorton, Willis (col) (son of Samuel & Nancy Rowe) & Mary Dowtin (dau of Solomon Brown & Francis Dowtin), 5 Nov 1867; William A. White, clk, wit; m 9 Nov 1867 by R. S. F. Peete, J. P.

Thrift, A. E. & Mrs. Joanna Jamison, 21 July 1863; T. A. Wainwrith, bm; William A. White, clk, wit; m 21 July 1863 by John B. Williams, M. G.

Thrift, William & Salley Kearney, 2 May 1820; Wm. C. Clanton, bm; Cas Drake, C. C. C., wit.

Thrower, Christopher & Polley Barrow, 29 Apr 1797; Henry Drake, bm; Shd Green, wit.

Thrower, Edward & _____ Robertson, 8 Nov 1788; Isham Rainey, bm.

Thrower, Sterling P. & Ann S. Twitty, 6 Dec 1820; Clack Robinson, bm; Cas Drake, C. C. C., wit.

Thrower, William E. & Harriet Fitts, 1 Aug 1845; Henry F. Twitty, bm.

Thurmon, Benjamin & Milley Lensey, 13 June 1790; Caleb Lindsay, bm; M. Duke Johnson, C. C., wit.

Timberlake, David & Sally Hill, 26 Jan 1807; Richard Moore, bm; Jo Terrell, D. C. C., wit.

Todd, George & Polly Waller, 2 Aug 1802; John Rodwell, bm; S. Johnson, wit.

Toler, Jechonias & Mary Simmons, 24 Oct 1786; William Blanton, bm; M. Duke Johnson, wit.

Tomlinson, James E. & Mary Newell, 7 June 1816; Doctor G. Williams, bm; Wm Green, C. C. C., wit.

Toney, Matthew & Celia Evans, 22 Dec 1808; Allen Green, bm; M. D. Johnson ,C. C., wit.

Tony, William & Jane Evans, 6 Dec 1841; Edward Green, bm; M. J. Montgomery, wit.

Toone, Harbert J. L & Elizabeth White, 21 Apr 1831; Lewis G. Meacham, bm; Burl Pitchford, J. P., wit.

Toone, Tavener & Ann Elizer Amos, 17 Aug 1827; Thomas Johnson, bm; Burl Pitchford, wit.

Topp, Richard L. & Christanner Elizabeth Elenton, 24 Dec 1866; William A. White, clk, wit; m 17 Dec 1866 by P. H. Joyner.

Towlers, James W. & Elizabeth J. Avret, 18 Mar 1825; James Garrotts, bm; Burl Pitchford, wit.

Townes, Halcott & Mary Williams, 22 Dec 1799; Leonard Henderson, bm.

Townes, Harbert T. & Polly Bill, 17 Nov 187; Richd Shearin, bm; W. A. K. Falkener, wit.

Townes, James & Elizabeth Buchanan, 20 Mar 1780; Richard Ellis, bm; John Scott, wit.

Townes, Richard & Joice King Rosser, 25 Sept 1795; Benjamin Ellis, bm; M. D. Johnson, C. C., wit.

Towns, David & Martha Marshall, 5 Feb 1811; Dickey Neal, bm; Jno C. Johnson, wit.

Towns, Edmund & Polley Ellis, 8 Mar 1802; Wm Sailes, bm; M. D. Johnson, C. C., wit.

Towns, Elisha & Ankey Bell (no date); John Mayfield, bm.

Towns, John & Frances Simms, 24 Oct 1780; Elisha Townes, bm; Thos Machen, wit.

Towns, Peter & Polley Willis, 23 Jan 1780; William Stanfield, bm; M. D. Johnson, C. C., wit.

Travis, Edward & Lucy Worsham, 13 Feb 1804; Philip Williams (of Brunswick Co, VA), bm; M. Duke Johnson, clk, wit.

Traylor, Thomas & Rebecca Cabaness, 11 Nov 1811; Robert Jones, bm; Jno H. Green, wit.

Tripp, William (col) (son of Thomas & Chloe Tripp) & Louise Skinner (dau of Ezekiel Eaton & Julia Robinson), 10 June 1867; William A. White, clk, wit; m 11 June 1867 by William Hodges, M. G.

Trisvan, Jordon & Sally Evans, 23 Sept 1835; Joshua Mason, bm; E. D. Drake, clk, wit.

Trotter, James & Betsey Malory, 4 Oct 1802; Wyatt Williams, Wm Newell, bm.

Trotter, Thomas R. & Mary L. Mitchell, 2 Feb 1843; William H. Boyd, bm.

Trotter, William Edwin & Caroline Walker, 8 Aug 1830; Harwood A. Lockett, bm.

Tucker, Allen & Mary Ann Southall, 21 Dec 1836; Dixon Conn, bm; Benj. E. Cook, wit.

Tucker, Anderson & Lusey Sims, 7 Jan 1797; L. Sanders Sims, bm; Shd Green, wit.

Tucker, Benjamin & Mary Powell, 13 Sept 1807; Pleasant Ellington, bm; M. Duke Johnson, C. C., wit.

Tucker, Charles S. & Matilda F. Myrick, 11 June 1859; Alfred M. Tucker, bm; Jno W. White, clk, wit; m 22 June 1859 by R. Browne, J. P.

Tucker, Daniel & Jane White, 14 Aug 1805; John Tucker, bm; Jo Terrell, clk, wit.

Tucker, Eley & R. Thompson, 19 Aug 1812; Joseph Anstead, bm; Wm Green, C. C. C., wit.

Tucker, Francis J. & Sarah J. Perkinson, 20 Dec 1865; G. W. S. Tucker, bm; William A. White, clk, wit; m 21 Dec 1865 by N. A. Purefoy, M. G.

Tucker, Francis M. & Elizabeth King, 10 May 1824; Wm. C. Clanton, bm.

Tucker, George W. & Martha M. Stokes, 9 Dec 1850; Edward H. Conn, bm; Jno W. White, wit.

Tucker, Henry & Mary Francis Southall, 19 Aug 1844; Allen Tucker, bm; M. J. Montgomery, wit.

Tucker, John & Lissay Tucker, 11 Apr 1788; Laurence Richeson, bm; M. Duke Johnson, C. C., wit.

Tucker, John & Elizebeth Marks, 15 Dec 1798; William Short, bm; Shd Green, wit.

Tucker, John D. & Mary D. Hagood, 10 June 1841; Jno C. Johnson, bm.

Tucker, John D. & Frances A. Wakins, 20 Dec 1841; James L. Newman, bm.

Tucker, John D. & Eliza M. Parish, 11 Oct 1853; Caswell Drake, bm; m 13 Oct 1853 by Caswell Drake.

Tucker, John D., Jr., & Lucy Ann Colemon, 17 Nov 1849; C. M. Cooke, bm; Jno W. White, wit.

Tucker, Lewis (col) & Amy Pritchard, 25 Dec 1866; William A. White, clk, wit; m 27 Dec 1866 by J. M. Brame, J. P.

Tucker, Richard & Susan Harriss, 21 Dec 1841; John Verser, bm; M. J. Montgomery, wit.

Tucker, Taylor & Amanda Burrows, 26 Dec 1861; Ira Finch, bm; Jno W. White, clk, wit; m 26 Dec 1861 by Jno Watson, J. P.

Tucker, William & Elizabeth Mayfield, 10 Mary 1797; Francis Tucker, bm; Thomas Malone, wit.

Tucker, William F. & Nancy B. Rose, 29 May 1821; John Andrews, bm; Cas Drake, C. C. C., wit.

Tunstall, George W. & Lucy Brown, 30 Mar 1820; Wm. H. Marshall, bm; Cas Drake, C. C. C., wit.

Tunstall, George W. & Frances Smithwick, 7 July 1851; Jno M. Wilson, bm; Jno W. White, wit.

Tunstall, George W. & Susan Turner, 15 Sept 1851; William M. Wilson, bm; Jno W. White, wit.

Tunstall, George W., Jr., & Margaret A. Turner, 29 Oct 1861; Thomas R. Tunstall, bm; Jno W. White, wit.

Tunstall, Thomas R. & Elizabeth J. Mabry, 15 Nov 1851; Joseph H. Perdue, bm; Jno W. White, clk, wit; m 16 Nov 1851 by Caswell Drake.

Tunstall, Thomas R. & Francis C. Mabry, 20 Feb 1855; Stephen G. Mabry, bm; Jno W. White, wit; m 27 Feb 1855 by A. C. Harris, M. G.

Tunstall, Thomas R. & Lucy A. Young, 17 Nov 1856; A. C. Harris, bm; m 18 Nov 1856 by A. C. Harris, M. G.

Tunstall, William B. & Angelica J. Mabry, 29 Sept 1847; Thomas Stanback, bm; Jno W. White, wit.

Turnbull, Jno R. & Bettie M. Eaton, 24 Feb 1866; Nathaniel R. Jones, bm; William
A. White, clk, wit; m 27 Feb 1866 by Chas M. Cook.

Turnbull, Robert & William Walker [sic], 25 June 1795; William J. Walker, bm.

Turner, Hamner & Bathena Sims, 19 Mar 1806; Chesley Sims, bm; Jo Terrell, D. C.,
wit.

Turner, Henley & Elizabeth Duke, 17 Feb 1810; Stephen Turner, bm; Jno C.
Johnson, C. C., wit.

Turner, Henry & Ann M. E. Darnall, 19 Dec 1854; Thos H. White, bm; Jno W. White,
wit.

Turner, Henry H. & Ellen Mabry, 1 Jan 1844; John Stainback, bm; M. J.
Montgomery, wit.

Turner, Isaac (col) & Ann Stallings, 19 May 1866; Alfred Davis, bm; William A.
White, clk, wit; m 19 May 1866 by T. B. Kingsbury.

Turner, James & Molley Allen, 14 Jan 1799; George Allen, bm; Shd Green, wit.

Turner, James & Elizabeth Sims, 9 Feb 1801; William Rives, bm; M. Duke Johnson,
C. C., wit.

Turner, James & Elizabeth Johnston, 21 July 1810; Thomas B. Gloster, bm; Jno C.
Johnson, wit.

Turner, James & Ann S. Hawkins, 10 Dec 1842; Daniel Turner, bm; M. J.
Montgomery, wit.

Turner, James (col) & Rachel Hicks, 24 Aug 1867; William A. White, clk, wit; m
25 Aug 1867 by R. D. Paschall, J. P.

Turner, John & Peggy Baskett, 5 Feb 1813; Thomas M. White, bm; Wm. Green, C. C.
C., wit.

Turner, John & Sarah P. Buchannon, 27 July 1839; Jno W. White, bm.

Turner, Nathan & Elizabeth Lewis, 1 May 1790; Benja Kimbell, bm; Jas Turner,
wit.

Turner, Solomon (col) & Catharine Baker, 7 Jan 1867; William A. White, clk, wit;
m 8 Jan 1867 by William Hodges, M. G.

Turner, Thomas & Sarah Pattillo, 16 Feb 1822; Edward Pattillo, bm; C. Drake, C.
C., wit.

Turner, Thomas R. & Suasan M. Newman, 15 Dec 1837; Daniel Taylor, bm; Burl
Pitchford, J. P., wit.

Twisdale, James & Tabitha Baskett, 21 Mar 1835; Henry G. Fitts, bm; E. D. Drake,
clk, wit.

Twisdale, John & Sally Baskett, 15 Oct 1835; Henry T. Allen, bm.

Twisdale, John & Martha Stainback, 1 Apr 1841; Daniel Bowdon, bm.

Twisdale, John L. & Agness Watkins, 2 Dec 1843; J. Speed Jones, bm; M. J.
Montgomery, wit.

Twittey, James T. & Caroline C. Cheek, 6 May 1836; Richd B. Robinson, bm; E. D.
Drake, clk, wit.

Twitty, Henry & Martha Foote, 30 Mar 1853; Theos. Stallings, bm; Jno W. White,
clk, wit; m 6 Apr 1853 by N. A. Purefoy, M. G.

Twitty, Joe (col) & Fanny Stewart, 31 Mar 1866; Jno C. McCraw, bm; William A. White, clk, wit; m 1 Apr 1866 by James C. Robinson, J. P.

Twitty, Jno E. & Susan Fitts, 15 Dec 1821; Amos P. Sledge, bm.

Twitty, John E. & Sallie D. Drake, 29 Dec 1863; Henry F. Twitty, bm; William A. White, clk, wit; m 31 Dec 1863 by Rev. Lemmon Shell.

Twitty, Jno E. & Caroline Nicholson, 4 Jan 1866; Joseph S. Jones, bm; William A. White, clk, wit; m 15 Jan 1866 by T. B. Ricks, M. G.

Twitty, Robert C. & Sallie F. Palmer, 28 May 1860; M. M. Ward, bm; Jno W. White, clk, wit; m 30 May 1860 by Rev. Thos. G. Lowe.

Twitty, Thomas T. & Eveline Fitts, 13 Dec 1827; Jno E. Twitty, bm; M. M. Drake, wit.

Upshur, Littleton & Frances E. Macon, 14 Oct 1855; M. W. Ransom; bm; Jno W. White, wit; m 15 Oct 1855 by N. Z. Graves.

Upshur, T. W. & Mary E. Upshur, 12 Sept 1862; John D. Alston, bm; Wm. A. White, wit.

Urls, Obediah & Joice Cuningham, 21 Oct 1782; Thomas Urls, bm; M. Duke Johnson, wit.

Utley, Gabriel & Letsy Twisdale, 28 June 1841; Wm. H. Bobbitt, bm.

Uzzel, Henry T. & Susan Wilson, 28 Nov 1848; William B. Uzzel, bm; Jno W. White, wit.

Vallaningham, Thomas & Susan Baskett, 19 Dec 1835; Reuben Flemming, bm.

Vandyck, John & Elizabeth M. Sledge, 1 Oct 1821; John C. Green, bm; Cas Drake, C. C. C., wit.

Vanlandingham, George (col) & Delia Vanlandingham, 14 Dec 1865; Robert Vanlandingham, bm; William A. White, clk, wit; m 26 Dec 1865 by T. Page Ricaud, M. G.

Vanlandingham, Henry & Betsey Paschall, 24 Jan 1787; John Williams, bm; M. Duke Johnson, wit.

Vanlandingham, Richd & Jeane Riggon, 1 Jan 1803; William Burroughs, bm; M. D. Johnson, C. C., wit.

Vanlandingham, Richard & Mary Bartlett, 23 Jan 1854; E. W. Best, bm; Jno W. White, wit.

Vanlandingham, Solomon (col) (son of Peter & Chloe) & Manerva Holley (dau of Nelson & Harriet), 31 Oct 1867; William A. White, clk, wit; m 2 Nov 1867 by R. D. Paschall, J. P.

Vanlandingham, William & Hariet Burroughs, 28 June 1842; Jno C. Johnson, bm; M. J. Montgomery, wit.

Vanlandingham, William & Sarah Bowden, 21 Mar 1864; Nathl R. Jones, bm; William A. White, clk, wit; m 31 Mar 1864 by R. D. Paschall, J. P.

Vaughan, Alexander & Rebecca Vaughan, 2 Sept 1838; William A. Dortch, bm; Burl Pitchford, J. P.,, wit.

Vaughan, Alfred & Rebecca Beasley, 17 Nov 1814; William Insco, bm; W. Green, C. C. C., wit.

Vaughan, Beins & Susan Patterson, 1 Apr 1814; Hardy Patterson, bm; W. Green, C. C. C., wit.

Vaughan, Beverly B. & Ester W. Drumwright, 14 Sept 1853; J. W. Ezell, bm; Jno W. White, clk, wit; m 14 Sept 1853 by N. A. Purefoy, M. G.

Vaughan, Burwell & Polly P. Coleman, 29 July 1818; Henry B. Vaughan, bm.

Vaughan, Frederick C. & Martha F. Gholdson, 27 Mar 1834; W. M. Wilson, bm; Jno W. White, wit; m 29 Mar 1854 by A. C. Harris, M. G.

Vaughan, James J. & Esther R. Johnson, 16 Jan 1821; Francis Mallory, bm; Cas Drake, wit.

Vaughan, James J. & Elizabeth W. Johnson, 13 July 1847; Thomas J. Judkins, bm; Jno W. White, wit.

Vaughan, Jefferson H. & Nancy Nuckals, 1 June 1831; Jesse Garns, bm; C. Drake, C. C., wit.

Vaughan, John & Caroline Mayo, 27 Nov 1851; Edward Harris, bm; Thos P. Paschall, wit; m 28 Nov 1851 by J. H. Bullock, J. P.

Vaughan, John D. & Elizabeth F. Duke, 11 June 1849; John D. Hoyle, bm; Jno W. White, wit.

Vaughan, John J. & Mary A. Allen, 21 Mar 1845; M. J. Montgomery, bm.

Vaughan, John W. & Adeline King, 24 Jan 1840; John Ellis, bm; Burl Pitchford, J. P., wit.

Vaughan, N. D. & Mary E. Poythress, 17 May 1861; B. D. Williams, bm; Jno W. White, clk, wit; m 17 May 1861 by Thos A. Montgomery, J. P.

Vaughan, Nathan & Polley Harris, 25 July 1810; Henry Wilson, bm; M. D. Johnson, C. C., wit.

Vaughan, Peyton & Betsey Pegram, 20 Apr 1809; Ozborn Vaughan, bm; M. D. Johnson, C. C., wit.

Vaughan, Ransom (col) (son of Sophia Vaughan) & Caroline Richardson (dau of Allen & Mary), 10 Aug 1867; William A. Whitek, clk, wit; m 13 July 1867 by Thomas P. Paschall, J. P.

Vaughan, Robert S. & Mary Eliza Clarke, 3 Jan 1848; Thompson Harris, bm; Jno W. White, wit.

Vaughan, William & Mary Pattison, 21 Feb 1809; William Pattison, bm; J. C. Johnson, D. C. C., wit.

Vaughan, William & Mariah Dortch, 22 Sept 1841; Beverley B. Vaughan, bm; Burl Pitchford, J. P., wit.

Verell, Robert N. & Nancy Reynolds, 18 June 1828; Allen M. Cawben (Corbin), bm; M. M. Drake, wit.

Verell, William & Tabitha Johnson, 1 Nov 1780; James Johnson, bm; Thos Machen, wit.

Verser, Daniel & Susan Brack, 27 Mar 1845; Oliver Shearin, bm; W. W. Vaughan, bm.

Verser, John & Sally Harris, 17 June 1818; Willis R. Harris, bm; Wm. Green, wit.

Verser, John & Agatha Nicholson, 10 Mar 1830; David W. Dowtin, bm; C. Drake, C. C., wit.

Verser, John & Emily Sally Harris, 1 Jan 1845; William C. Clanton, bm.

Verser, Nathan & Winnifred Dowten, 22 Dec 1813; John Verser, bm; Wm. Green, C. C. C., wit.

Vincent, James & Holly Harris, 2 Sept 1819; Bennett Harris, bm; C. Drake, C. C. C,. wit.

Vincent, Thomas E. & Mary Ann Clarke, 3 May 1845; Harmon H. Renn, bm; William Vincent, bm.

Volentine, James (col) & Nancy Catharine Overby, 14 Feb 1867; William A. White, clk, wit; m 14 Feb 1867 by J. P. Moore, M. G.

Waddell, Henry (col) & Phillis Dowtin, 16 June 1866; Ed W. Best, bm; William A. White, clk, wit; m 16 June 1866 by B. F. Long, M. G.

Waddill, Henry & Mary Ann Short, 1 Feb 1830; Gordon Cawthorn, bm.

Wade, Michael O. & Mildred A. Cook, 13 June 1837; Robert A. Jenkins, bm; E. D. Drake, clk, wit.

Wade, Thomas W. & Permelia P. Golson, 26 Feb 1861; Jerreman Hawks, bm; Jno W. White, clk, wit; m 28 Feb 1861 by Lemmon Shell, M. G.

Wade, William F. & Jane Lambert, 21 Jan 1832; John J. Thomas, bm; C. Drake, C. C., wit.

Wadkins, Manning & Jane Flemming, 20 Nov 1797; John Wadkins, bm; Sh Green, wit.

Wadkins, Richard & Nancy Paschael, 30 Sept 1796; John Stevens, bm; M. Duke Johnson, C. C., wit.

Wainwright, John & Phoebe W. Harper, 8 Oct 1806; George Rogers, bm; M. Duke Johnson, C. C., wit.

Walden, John & Edey Harriss, 23 Apr 1809; Terisha Turner, bm; Jno C. Johnson D. C., wit.

Walden, Thomas & Rebecca Day, 17 Mar 1818; John M. Johnson, bm.

Walker, Burney (col) & Isabella Bottom, 12 Dec 1866; William A. White, clk, wit; m 19 Dec 1866 by Jas T. Russell, J. P.

Walker, Christopher & Parthena Paschall, 2 Oct 1865; Thomas T. James, bm; William A. White, clk, wit; m 5 Oct 1865 by Jno W. Pattillo, J. P.

Walker, Freeman & Parthena T. Newman, 18 July 1826; James W. Wilson, bm; M. M. Drake, wit.

Walker, George (col) & Isabella Hargrove, 30 Jan 1867; William A. White, clk, wit; m 1 Feb 1867 by L. Henderson.

Walker, Henry & Nancy Pike, 27 May 1828; Daniel Shearin, bm; C. Drake, C. C., wit.

Walker, James & Tabitha Harris, 21 Aug 1785; Wm Rooker, bm; M. D. Johnson, wit.

Walker, James J. & Lutitia Paschall, 2 Oct 1862; P. J. Turnbull bm; William A. White, clk, wit; m 2 Oct 1862 by N. A. Purefoy, M. G.

Walker, James T. & Elizabeth W. Odum, 27 Dec 1852; William P. Rose, bm; Jno W. White, wit.

Walker, Jeremiah G. & Ailsey T. Langford, 30 Dec 1842; Rodon Parker, bm; M. J. Montgomery, wit.

Walker, Jesse & Patsey Haithcock, 28 May 1803; Reuben Longwith, bm.

Walker, Jesse & Permelia Smith, 4 May 1821; John Andrews, bm.

Walker, John & Elizabeth Finch, 16 Oct 1805; Peter Mounger, bm; Jo Terrell, D. C. C., wit.

Walker, John E. & Sally C. Palmer, 16 Sept 1828; William E. Mayfield, bm.

Walker, John M. & Martha Faulcon, 16 Jan 1811; John Falcon, Jr., bm; M. Duke Johnson, C. C., wit.

Walker, Joseph & Rebecca Riggin, 29 Oct 1811; Joel Harris, bm; Wm. Green, C. C. C., wit.

Walker, Joseph & Parthenia Acre, 5 Feb 1834; Edmond D. Riggan, bm.

Walker, Levi & Patience E. Paschall, 23 May 1860; Wm. H. Bennett, bm; Jno W. White, clk, wit; m 24 May 1860 by L. C. Perkinson, M. G.

Walker, Micajah & Pietta Bennett, 17 Oct 1803; Isham Bennett, bm; Gideon Johnson, wit.

Walker, Micajah & Rebecca Bennitt, 25 Mar 1814; Willie Lancaster, bm; Jno H. Green, wit.

Walker, Peter & Amey Bennett, 16 July 1796; Joshua Capps, bm; Shd Green, wit.

Walker, Pleasant H. & Tabitha Allen, 25 Nov 1809; Rowland Betty, bm; M. Duke Johnson, C. C., wit.

Walker, Ransome & Martha Paschall, 13 Apr 1809; Benjamin Davis, bm; Jno C. Johnson D. C., wit.

Walker, Robert & Winnefret Ellms, 30 Oct 1785; Wm Beckham, bm; M. Duke Johnson, wit.

Walker, Samuel & Ann Newton, 31 Dec 1835; John E. Walker, bm; Burl Pitchford, J. P., wit.

Walker, Saunders & Rosa Pike, 28 Oct 1857; Weldon E. Carter, bm; Jno W. White, wit.

Walker, William & Charity Newton, 22 Dec 1802; William Newton, bm; M. D. Johnson, C. C. C., wit.

Walker, William & Betsey B. Caps, 27 May 1830; Thomas J. Judkins, bm; C. Drake, C. C., wit.

Walker, William & Sarah Stevenson, 26 Feb 1856; Wm. W. King, bm; Wm. A. White, wit.

Walker, William H. & Anna J. Harris, 6 Jan 1858; Nathl McLean, bm; Jno W. White, wit.

Walker, Wm Ransom & Jane Omary, 30 Dec 1857; J. G. Walker, bm; Jno W. White, clk, wit; m 30 Dec 1857 by Jas T. Russell, J. P.

Walker, Zachariah & Elizabeth Little, 24 Mar 1849; Zachariah Perkinson, bm; Jno W. White, wit.

Wall, Burgess T. & Sarah Tucker, 29 Jan 1809; Lewis P. Duke, bm; J. C. Johnson, D. C., wit.

Wall, John H. & Tabitha Thomas, 16 Sept 1834; Henry L. Bradley, bm.

Wall, Thomas M. T. & Elizabeth H. Clack, 22 Mar 1837; John Mabry, bm; E. W. Best, wit.

Wallace, Enoch & Dolley Colclough, 14 July 1792; Edward Clanton, bm.

Waller, Robert & Dilley Sledge, 22 July 1783; John Rodell, bm; M. Duke Johnson, C. C., wit.

Waller, William R. & Adaline M. Harvel, 27 Feb 1855; A. J. Mosely, bm; Wm. A. White, wit.

Wallice, Samuel & Mary Trowler, 28 Aug 1834; Thomas Edmunds, bm; Burl Pitchford, J. P., wit.

Ward, Eli W. & Cynthia Little, 5 June 1824; Joseph E. May, bm; M. M. Drake, wit.

Ward, Gilbard & Pattsey Tucker, 30 Sept 1784; Theophilus Burk, bm; M. Duke Johnson, wit.

Ward, Hiram P. & Emma M. Hammond, 5 Mar 1860; William Hodges, bm; Jno W. White, clk, wit; m 26 Mar 1860 by Wm. Hodges.

Ward, James & Rebecca Duke, 24 Mar 1802; Robert H. Jones, bm; Sugan Johnson, wit.

Ward, James & Mary Woodward, 30 June 1810; Joseph Anstead, bm.

Ward, Seth & Sarah Green, 15 Nov 1806; James Moss, bm; M. Duke Johnson, C. C,, wit.

Ware, Joseph H. & Mollie S. Boyd, 5 Nov 1866; Weldon E. Davis, bm; William A. White, C. C. C., wit; m 8 Nov 1866 by J. P. Moore, M. G.

Warthen, James & Nancy Puckett, 26 June 1785; Joseph Lambert, bm; M. D. Johnson, wit.

Warthen, William & Phebey Puckett, 23 Dec 1790; Bennet Hargrove, bm;, bm; M. Duke Johnson, wit.

Washington, John & Rebekah Lanier, 15 July 1805; Jacob Mordecai, bm; Jo Terrell, D. C., wit.

Washington, Nedham H. & Agnes Hickman, 8 Mar 1837; William E. Hinton, bm; E. W. Best, wit.

Watkins, Caleb & Betsey Short, 5 Sept 1818; Jo L. Riggans, bm; W. A. K. Falkener, wit.

Watkins, Demcy & Lucena Stewart, 2 July 1834; Thomas G. Watkins, bm.

Watkins, Edmund W. & Sally Burrows, 12 Jan 1831; Luke H. Paschall, bm; C. Drake, C. C., wit.

Watkins, Elmus W. & Sally Short, 22 Sept 1824; John Andrews, bm; C. Drake, C. C., wit.

Watkins, Henry T. & Sarah E. Watkins, 13 Dec 1852; Charles J. Fleming, bm; Jno W. White, clk, wit; m 22 Dec 1852 by Wm. A. Burwell, J. P.

Watkins, James R. & Martha Talley, 22 June 1853; Mark C. Turner, bm; Jno W. White, clk, wit; m __ June 1853 by J. H. Hawkins, J. P.

Watkins, John & Fanny Lindsay (no date); Caleb Lindsey, bm; M. D. Johnson ,C. C., wit.

Watkins, John & Mary Reaves, 15 Aug 1823; Landy L. Thurmon, bm.

Watkins, John W. & Mary H. P. Nicholson, 11 Jan 1856; George W. Pegram, bm; Jno
W. White, clk, wit; m 11 Jan 1856 by M. M. Drake, J. P.

Watkins, Landy T. & Henrietta L. Paschall, 11 Dec 1843; John Watkins, bm; M. J.
Montgomery, wit.

Watkins, Richard & Nancy Burroughs, 5 Dec 1832; Thomas G. Watkins, bm.

Watkins, Richard S. & Sarah L. Mabry, 22 Jan 1847; Charles E. Watkins, bm; Jno
W. White, wit.

Watkins, Robert & Agnes Flemmin, 30 Nov 1825; Landey L. Thurmon, bm; C. Drake,
C. C., wit.

Watkins, Sanders S. & Mildred Vanlandingham, 31 Jan 1832; Thomas G. Watkins, bm.

Watkins, Thomas G. & Nancy G. Watkins, 12 Mar 1832; Landy L. Thurmon, bm.

Watkins, Timothy (col) & Panthea Hendrick, 25 Sept 1866; Thomas P. Paschall, bm;
William A. White, clk, wit; m 26 Sept 1866 by R. D. Paschall, J. P.

Watkins, William G. & Emily Moss, 20 June 1844; Thomas P. Paschall, bm.

Watkins, William N. & Elizabeth Williams, 24 Apr 1826; James Nicholson, bm; M.
M. Drake, wit.

Watson, Allen (col) (son of Henry Nicholson and Dilcey Rodwell) & Mary Ward (dau
of Jacob Brodie & Amy Brodie), m 27 Dec 1867 in Warrenton, NC, by N. A.
Purefoy, M. G.

Watson, James & Sarah Ezell, 3 Jan 1809; Jones Taylor, bm; J. C. Johnson, D. C.,
wit.

Watson, John & Mary Short, 15 Dec 1797; John Williams bm; M. Duke Johnson, C.
C., wit.

Watson, John & Rowena Rodwell, 17 Feb 1840; Lewis Turner, bm.

Watson, Lewis (col) & Rebecca Green, 21 May 1866; Wm. T. Alston, bm; William A.
White, clk, wit; m 21 May 1866 by T. B. Kingsbury.

Watson, William & Fanny Norsworthy, 4 Sept 1807; Joel Terrell, Jr, bm; M. D.
Johnson, C. C., wit.

Watson, William & Mary Turner, 28 Apr 1829; Gordon Cawthorn, bm; E. D. Drake,
wit.

Watson, William & Louisa V. Wright, 16 Jan 1865; Edward W. Best, bm; William A.
White, wit; m 18 Jan 1865 by W. Hodges, M. G.

Watson, Windsor (col) & Celia Ann Twitty, 5 May 1866; Henry B. Hunter, Sr., bm;
William A. White, clk, wit; m 5 May 1866 by Robert O. Burton, M. G.

Watts, Allison M. & Rebecca J. Preston, 15 Sept 1845; John C. Browne, bm; M. J.
Montgomery, wit.

Watts, Bracket B. & Dicey Clark, 16 Dec 1848; William Pardue, bm; Jno W. White,
wit.

Weatherford, Thomas B. & Tabitha W. Baily, 12 Nov 1837; William Palmer, bm.

Weaver, John & Susan Crowder, 20 Dec 1843; Robert D. Paschall, bm; M. J.
Montgomery, wit.

Webb, George & Sarah Carter, 15 Aug 1806; John Moore, bm; M. Duke Johnson, C.
C., wit.

Webb, Orren & Elizabeth Andrews, 27 ___ 1806; Thomas Jolly, bm; Jo. Terrell, D. C. C., wit.

Webb, William & Parthena Bell, 29 Apr 1835; Thomas Bell, bm; E. D. Drake, clk, wit.

Webb, William & Parthena Bell, 18 Dec 1835; John King, bm; W. H. Foote, wit.

Webb, William E. & Anne Bowen, 18 May 1859; E. W. Best, bm; Jno W. White, C. C., wit; m 6 June 1859 by C. M. Cook, J. P.

Webster, Bartlet & Celia White, 12 Apr 1798; William Robertson, bm; James Moss, wit.

Welch, James A. C. & Susan G. Bobbitt, 24 Sept 1862; Alfred N. Johnston, bm; Wm. A. White, clk, wit; m 24 Sept 1862 by Saml Bobbitt, J. P.

Weldon, Danl & Sarah Falkener, 4 Aug 1798; Benj Falkener, bm; S. Green, wit.

Weldon, Sales & Elizabeth Mathews, 27 Oct 1837; William F. Lampkin, bm; E. W. Best, wit.

Wells, David & Susan Langford, 2 Dec 1825; Samuel H. Riggan, bm.

Wells, John D. & Nancy Harriss, 21 Dec 1846; Benjamin H. Bass, bm; Jno W. White, wit.

West, John J. & Jane Carter, 19 May 1856; John J. West, bm; Jno W. White, clk, wit; m 20 May 1856 by Saml Bobbitt, J. P.

West, John W. & Elizabeth Green, 19 Aug 1835; Oscar Alston, bm; E. D. Drake, clk, wit.

Westray, Samuel & Ann Baskett, 10 Jan 1839; Gideon M. Green, bm; Edmd W. Best, clk, wit.

Wetherinton, John & Nancy Ellis, 31 Dec 1787; Alexander Nicholson, bm; M. D. Johnson, C. C., wit.

Wheeler, Samuel & Salley Laughter, 9 Feb 1781; William Laughter, bm; Thos Machen, wit.

Wheeler, Thomas & Sarah Hill, 15 Sept 1781; John Hills, bm.

Wheless, John & Prudence May, 4 May 1797; Daniel Talley, bm; Thos Malone, wit.

Whitaker, Calvin J. & Elizabeth Campbell, 6 May 1828; George W. Barns, bm; M. M. Drake, wit.

Whitaker, Dudley A. & Sarah Carter, 22 Dec 1824; John Langford, bm; Jos A. Drake, wit.

Whitaker, Eli & Abigal Jones, 24 Feb 1807; Edward J. Jones, bm; M. D. Johnson, C. C., wit.

Whitaker, Spier, Jr., & Fanny DeBarnia Hooper, 30 July 1866; Wm. J. White, bm; William A. White, clk, wit; m 31 July 1866 by William Hodges.

White, Amasa & Eliza A. Johnson, 10 Sept 1830; John V. Cawthorn, bm.

White, Dr. C. & Sallie A. White, 19 Sept 1855; Jno W. Pattillo, bm; Jno W. White, clk, wit; m 17 Oct 1855 by J. P. Moore.

White, Daniel & Lucy Coleman Short, 15 June 1812; William Andrews, bm; Wm. Green, C. C., wit.

White, Edmond & Mary D. Hogwood, 19 Dec 1821; Charles W. Johnston, bm.

White, Edmund & Mary W. Hilliard, 7 Sept 1833; E. D. Drake, bm.

White, Henry P. & Sarah W. Hicks, 13 July 1854; Jno White, bm; Jno W. White, C. C., wit; m 18 July 1854 by T. B. Ricks, M. G.

White, Henry P. & Martha E. Hicks, 18 Nov 1862; Drury Gill, bm; William A. White, clk, wit; m 27 Nov 1862 by Lemmon Shell.

White, James O. & Tabitha Jordan, 26 Oct 1840; Edwd M. Steed, bm.

White, Jesse B. & Mahala Tucker, 9 Sept 1826; John D. Tucker, bm.

White, John & Hannah Langford, 1 Jan 1819; John King, bm.

White, John & Priscilla D. Jones, 28 Nov 1838; H. C. Lucas, bm.

White, John H. & Martha A. Mabry, 10 Oct 1865; Jno W. Pattillo, bm; William A. White, C. C., wit; m 18 Oct 1865 by T. Page Ricaud, M. G.

White, John L. & Mary A. Williams, 8 Feb 1841; Thomas Hamlin, bm; Burl Pitchford, J. P., wit.

White, John W. & Minerva H. Wright, 12 July 1828; Anderson Wright, bm; M. M. Drake, wit.

White, Peter D. & Permelia Andrews, 31 May 1815; Anthony King, bm; W. Green, C. C., wit.

White, Robert & Ann Bush, 9 Oct 1788; Cade White, bm; M. Duke Johnson, C. C., wit.

White, Robert A. & Sarah L. Paschall, 19 Dec 1831; Samuel E. Phillips, bm; Benj E. Cook, wit.

White, Robert A. & Ann Mary Colemon, 7 Apr 1855; M. W. Paschall, bm; Jno W. White, clk, wit; m 12 Apr 1855 by Jas T. Russell, J. P.

White, Robert A. & Lucy Wiggins, 10 Jan 1856; George J. Duke, bm; William A. White, wit; m 15 Jan 1856 by Jas. T. Russell, J. P.

White, Thomas & Elenor Turner, 18 Apr 1808; Sterling Pitchford, bm; M. D. Johnson, C. C., wit.

White, Thomas H. & Martha J. Walker, 3 Nov 1865; Wm. L. Hicks, bm; William A. White, clk, wit; m 8 Nov 1865 by T. Page Ricaud, M. G.

White, Valentine & Elizabeth Ann Pettilloe, 10 July 1793; Avery Connell, bm; Richd Russell, wit.

White, William & Rebecca Bell, 4 Dec 1798; John Langfurd, bm; M. D. Johnson, C. C., wit.

White, William & Polley Wood, 13 Mary 1799; Wiley Wood, bm; Shd Green, wit.

White, William & Rose Henderson, 26 Aug 1866; Valentine Flemming, bm; William A. White, clk, wit; m 27 Aug 1866 by Wm. Wallace White, J. P.

White, William A. & Sallie E. Cole, 27 Sept 1859; W. A. J. Nicholson, bm; Jno W. White, clk, wit; m 28 Sept 1859 by N. A. Purefoy, M. G.

White, Wm Baxter & Jemima Edwards, 8 Mar 1787; Wm Rooker, bm; M. Duke Johnson, C. C., wit.

White, William H. & Silva Bennett, 14 Mar 1840; Isham Bennett, bm.

White, William H. (son of T. L. & F. J. White) & Sallie H. Bobbitt (dau of Samuel & Martha A. Bobbitt), 28 Sept 1867; William A. White, clk, wit; m 2 Oct 1857 by B. F. Long, M. G.

White, William W. & Panthea B. Boyd, 11 Oct 1848; David Parrish, bm; Jno W. White, wit.

White, Willis & Lucy Wilson, 18 June 1792; John Langfurd, bm; M. D. Johnson, C. C., wit.

White, Willis P. & Meriah E. Scoggins, 12 Oct 1846; Thomas M. Wynn, bm; Edmd. White, wit.

Whitehead, Nathan B. & Mary Jones, 21 Sept 1831; George M. Allen, bm; C. Drake, C. C., wit.

Whitehorn, Richard & Mary A. Grizzard, 8 Sept 1852; James A. Grizzard, bm; Jno W. White, wit; m 8 Sept 1852 by Wm. C. Clanton, J. P.

Whitlow, Benjamin & Francis Wright (dau of Nancy), 26 July 1822; Rabun Steegall, bm; Cas Drake, C. C., wit.

Whitten, William E. & Mary E. Wills, 23 Oct 1839; James D. Clanton, bm; Jno W. White, wit.

Wiggins, Gululmus & Polley Royster, 6 June 1801; Reuben Fleming, bm; M. Duke Johnson, C. C., wit.

Wiggins, Harrel & Sarah Royster, 30 Mar 1810; Wiley Smith, bm; Jno C. Johnson, D. C. C., wit.

Wiggins, James T. & Ellen Burroughs, 28 Oct 1859; William M. Wilson, bm; Jno W. White, clk, wit; m 3 Nov 1859 by A. L. Steed, J. P.

Wiggins, John G. & Patsy Adams, 10 June 1857; Jno W. White, clk, wit; m 10 June 1857 by A. L. Steed, J. P.

Wiggins, Robert H. & Louisa Haithcock, 7 Oct 1856; L. W. Roffe, bm; Jno W. White, wit.

Wiggins, William R. & Mary A. L. Hundley, 29 Oct 1853; Nicholas Shearin, bm; Jno W. White, wit.

Wilcox, Julius & Sarah A. Nichols, 16 Oct 1845; H. C. Lucas, bm; M. J. Montgomery, wit.

Wilcox, Julius & Martha J. Holton, 20 Oct 1857; Fran M. Hyman, bm; Jno W. White, wit; m 23 Oct 1857 by N. Z. Graves.

Wilkes, Jesse P. & Hester A. Pitts, 11 Dec 1832; David W. Hunter, bm.

Wilkins, Allen & Susanah Estes (no date); J. Barrow, bm; M. Duke Johnson, C. C.,wit.

Wilkins, Patrick & Mary Green, 16 Jan 1847; Daniel E. Daly, bm; Jno W. White, wit.

Willeford, Brittain & Ursley Pickerill, 22 Jan 1794; James Walker, bm; M. D. Johnson, C. C., wit.

Williams, Alanson & Martha Courtney, 19 Sept 1797; Shd Green, bm; Shd Green, wit.

Williams, Alexander & Cathorine Hodge (no date); Isaac Williams, bm; M. D. Johnson, wit.

Williams, Andrew & Mourning Williams, 24 Dec 1866; William A. White, clk, wit; m 26 Dec 1866 by J. Buxton Williams.

Williams, Armistead (col) & Martha Alston, 26 Dec 1866; William A. White, clk, wit; m 1 Jan 1867 by J. Buxton Williams.

Williams, Arthur (col) & Malinda Cawthorne, 15 Jan 1867; William A. White, clk, wit; m 16 Jan 1867 by William Hodges, M. G.

Williams, Benjamin (col) & Charity Cheek, 8 Feb 1867; William A. White, clk, wit; m 8 Apr 1867 by M. P. Perry, J. P.

Williams, Blake (col) (son of Elijah & Frances) & Winney Collins (step dau of Sye & Hannah), 16 Nov 1867; William A. White, clk, wit; m 16 Nov 1867 by T. B. Ricks, M. G.

Williams, Buckner D. & Elizabeth D. Syme, 2 Nov 1853; John M. Price, bm; Jno W. White, C. C. C., wit; m 3 Nov 1853 by N. A. Purefoy, M. G.

Williams, Butler & Elizabeth Tillery, 2 Jan 1780; John Tillery, bm; Thos Machen, wit.

Williams, Charles & Polley Dawsey, 9 Aug 1799; Charles Megee, bm; Shd Green, wit.

Williams, Doctor G. & Lucindy Clanton, 26 Jan 1822; Anthony Dawtin, Jr., bm; Cas Drake, C. C., wit.

Williams, Edmund (col) (son of Jacob Williams & Silva Hawkins) & Nicey Faulcon (dau of Thomas Faulcon & Betsey Baker), 1 June 1867; William A. White, clk, wit; m 15 June 1867 by John W. Riggan, J. P.

Williams, Francis & Martha Turner, 13 Oct 1819; John Hilliard, bm; Cas Drake, wit.

Williams, George (col) & Viney Wade, 27 Oct 1866; Plummer W. Green, bm; I. H. Bennett, wit; William A. White, clk; m 27 Oct 1866 by N. A. Purefoy, M. G.

Williams, Hardy (col) & Jane Eaton, 9 Apr 1866; Jno C. McCraw, bm; William A. White, clk, wit; m 9 Apr 1866 by N. A. Purefoy.

Williams, Harriss & Arsenath Williams, 22 Apr 1810; Nimrod Williams, bm; M. Duke Johnson, C. C., wit.

Williams, Haywood & Mary Frances Gooden, 21 July 1866; Lewis D. Goodloe, bm; William A. White, clk, wit; m 21 July 1866 by R. D. Paschall, J. P.

Williams, Henderson & Emily A. Darnell, 21 Dec 1852; Drury Gill, bm; Jno W. White, wit.

Williams, Henry & Francis Bowdown, 8 Oct 1798; Nimrod Williams, bm; Shd Green, wit.

Williams, Henry & Polley Wilson, 12 Nov 1799; Wilson Jenkins, bm; Shd Green, wit.

Williams, Henry (col) & Delia Carr, 24 Dec 1866; William A. White, clk, wit; m 26 Dec 1866 by J. Buxton Williams.

Williams, Henry, Jr., & Anna K. Kearney, 28 Apr 1858; Geo R. Clements, bm; Jno W. White, wit; m 5 May 1858 by T. G. Lowe, M. G.

Williams, Henry C. & Elizabeth Smith, 16 July 1824; Thos J. Green, bm; M. M. Drake, wit.

Williams, John & Mary Renn, 2 Sept 1783; William Worrell, bm; M. Duke Johnson, wit.

Williams, John & Frances Watson, 5 Oct 1785; Lewis Williams, bm; M. Duke Johnson, wit.

Williams, John & Polley Rucker, 27 Dec 1792; Bena Kelley, bm; B. Davis, wit.

Williams, John & Polley Pardue, 9 Sept 1805; Isham House, bm; M. D. Johnson, C. C., wit.

Williams, John & Susanna W. Fogg, 23 Oct 1815; Edward Pattillo, bm; Will Green, wit.

Williams, John (col) & Isabella Price, 28 Dec 1866; William A. White, clk, wit; m 3 July 1867 by T. B. Kingsbury.

Williams, Jno A. & Charity D. Alston, 1 Aug 1816; Amos P. Sledge, Wm. D. Freeman, bm; Wm Green, C. C., wit.

Williams, Revd John B. & Ann L. Skinner, 25 Jan 1865; E. E. Parham, bm; William A. White, clk, wit; m 25 Jan 1865 by T. B. Kingsbury, M. G.

Williams, Jno T. & Mary C. Somervell, 4 Aug 1836; Joseph B. Somervell, bm; E. D. Drake, clk, wit.

Williams, John T. & Elizabeth M. Ellington, 8 Oct 1862; Lewis D. Rose, bm; William A. White, clk, wit; m 9 Oct 1862 by Wm. A. Burwell, J. P.

Williams, John W. & Mary Camilla Holt, 17 Nov 1859; Jno C. McCraw, bm; Jno W. White, clk, wit; m 17 Nov 1859 by J. B. Solomon, M. G.

Williams, John W. & Bettie R. Pitchford, 5 Nov 1860; W. A. J. Nicholson, bm; Jno W. White, wit; m 7 Nov 1860 by John S. Cheek.

Williams, John W. & Mrs. Sarah T. McCraw, 25 Oct 1866; Nathan S. Moseley, bm; Williams A. White, C. C. C., wit; m 25 Oct 1866 by T. B. Kingsbury.

Williams, Joseph & Mahalay Howard, 30 Aug 1792; Green Duke, bm.

Williams, Joseph J. & James M. Alston [sic], 11 Nov 1820; Nathl M. Johnson, wit.

Williams, Lewis & Leila Pickrell, 10 Jan 1781; Nimrod Williams, Permenas Williams, bm.

Williams, Lewis (col) (son of Wiley & Charity) & Ellen Pitchford (dau of Arthur & Ellen), 31 Oct 1867; William A. White, clk, wit; m 2 Nov 1867 by John S. Cheek, J. P.

Williams, Littleton (col) & Mollie Skinner, 22 Nov 1866; John Collins, bm; William A. White, clk, wit; m 22 Nov 1866 by Thomas J. Pitchford, J. P.

Williams, Matthew & Elizabeth Myrick, 19 Dec 1826; Hardy Myrick, bm; M. M. Drake, wit.

Williams, Nathaniel & Emily Bowdon, 13 Dec 1841; Daniel Bowdon, bm; M. J. Montgomery, wit.

Williams, Nimrod & Susanah Andrews, 15 Apr 1800; Henry Williams, bm; M. Duke Johnson, C. C., wit.

Williams, Nimrod & Winney Carroll, 27 May 1809; Littlebury Tucker, bm; Jno C. Johnson, D. C., wit.

Williams, Norvel (col) & Louisa Davis, 16 Aug 1866; William A. White, clk, wit; m 16 Aug 1866 by William Hodges, M. G.

Williams, Ossian (formerly slave of J. Buxton Williams) & Evelina Williams (formerly slave of J. Buxton Williams), 26 Dec 1865; John Buxton Williams, bm; C. M. Cook, wit; m 26 Dec 1865 by C. M. Cook, J. P.

Williams, Philip & Polley Worshem, 14 Feb 1799; Robert Alexander, bm; Shd Green, wit.

Williams, Richard M. & Syntha A. Perkinson, 27 Oct 1852; James Malone, bm; Jno W. White, wit.

Williams, Robert & Winney Vanlandingham, 15 Sept 1789; Nimrod Williams, bm; M. Duke Johnson, C. C., wit.

Williams, Robert (col) & Dorothy Williams, 9 May 1867; Benjamin F. Powell, bm; William A. White, clk, wit; m 18 May 1867 by Thos J. Pitchford, J. P.

Williams, Robert E. & U. U. Kearney, 20 Oct 1841; Kemp P. Alston, bm; M. J. Montgomery, wit.

Williams, Samuel & Celia Lancaster, 28 Aug 1781; John Lancaster, bm; thos Machen, wit.

Williams, Saml A. & Sarah M. Hawkins, 20 Dec 1832; Carter Nunnery, bm; C. Drake, C. C., wit.

Williams, Samuel A., Jr., & Anna Baker, 8 Nov 1843; Peter D. Powell, bm; M. J. Montgomery, wit.

Williams, Samuel F. & Jane Coley, 10 Oct 1864; R. M. King, bm; William A. White, wit.

Williams, Seth & Phebe Baskett, 2 Feb 1780; James Basket, bm; Thos Machen, wit.

Williams, Silas (col) & Julia Duke, 14 July 1866; D. Parrish, bm; William A. White, clk, wit; m 14 July 1866 by Thomas A. Montgomery, J. P.

Williams, Silas (col) & Eliza Henry Alston, 21 Feb 1867; William A. White, clk, wit; m 22 Feb 1867 by J. Buxton Williams.

Williams, Solomon & Darcus Simms (no date); Lewis Williams, bm.

Williams, Solomon & Caroline Alston, 22 Feb 1819; Richard Davison, bm.

Williams, Solomon & Maria Kearney, 2 Mar 1835; William H. Williams, bm; E. D. Drake, clk, wit.

Williams, Solomon (formerly slave of S. A. Williams) & Felecia Alston (formerly slave of Miss A. A. Alston), 6 Feb 1866; Saml A. Williams, bm; m 6 Feb 1866 by C. M. Cook, J. P.

Williams, Stephen (col) & Sallie Alston, 1 Jan 1867; William A. White, clk, wit; m 2 Jan 1866 by M. P. Perry, J. P.

Williams, Taverner & Claresa Loyd, 20 Sept 1804; Charles Drury, bm; M. Duke Johnson, C. C., wit.

Williams, Thomas & Virginia Boyd, 17 Oct 1848; Alex B. Hawkins, bm; Jno W. White, wit.

Williams, Thomas Henry & Bettie A. Pegram, 15 Jan 1858; Somervell Saintsing, bm; Jno W. White, clk, wit; m 14 [sic] Jan 1858 by L. C. Perkinson, M. G.

Williams, Thomas W. & Catie V. J. Redd, 18 June 1856; Fayette V. Williams, Wm S. Ransom, bm; Jno W. White, C. C., wit; m 18 June 1856 by Thos S. Campbell, M. G.

Williams, William & Betsey Aslin, 27 May 1793; William Laughter, bm; B. Davis, wit.

Williams, William & Patsey Bowdown, 9 July 1794; James Moss, bm; B. Davis, wit.

Williams, William & Elizabeth Alston, 7 Apr 1810; Henry G. Williams, bm; M. Duke Johnson, C. C., wit.

Williams, William (col) (son of Samuel Burgess & Matilda Williams) & Frances Williams (dau of Frank Sledge & Winney Williams), 26 June 1867; William A. White, clk, wit; m 6 July 1867 by M. P. Perry, J. P.

Williams, William A. & Jane Twitty, 6 Oct 1837; Joseph S. Jones, bm.

Williams, William C. & Rebeckah A. Davis, 26 June 1819; Richard Allen, bm.

Williams, William K. A. & Caroline M. Williams or alston, 22 May 1863; Tippoo Brownlow, bm; William A. White, wit; m 27 May 1863 by A. W. Mangum, M. G.

Williams, Wm. P. & Elizabeth M. Alston, 8 June 1812; Joseph Hawkins, bm; Wm. Green, C. C., wit.

Williams, W. R. & Mollie Thomas, 7 Nov 1864; Jno W. Williams, bm; William A. White, wit; m 7 Nov 1864 by Henry Petty, M. G.

Williams, Wm. W. & Octavia A. Robertson, 23 Oct 1865; Wm. A. J. Nicholson, bm; William A. White, clk, wit; m 25 Oct 1865 by N. A. Purefoy, M. G.

Williamson, John W. & Jane Smith, 5 Feb 1824; Richd Russell, bm; C. Drake, C. C., wit.

Williford, Thoe's & Salley Gwyn, 24 May 1787; William Gwin, bm; M. Duke Johnson, wit.

Willis, Thomas C. & Harriett Hayes, 6 Jan 1836; Austin Plummer, bm; E. D. Drake, clk, wit.

Willson, Jessey & Salley Robertson, 7 July 1792; John White, bm.

Willson, Oliver & Caty Pitchford, 28 June 1823; John Tanner, bm; Edwin D. Drake, wit.

Willson, Richard & Amey Marks, 28 Sept 1780; Thomas Newman, bm; Thos Machen, wit.

Wilson, Bennitt & Mary Kidd (no date); Henry Wilson, bm; M. D. Johnson, wit.

Wilson, David (col) (son of Wesley Pettifoot & Viney Wilson) & Pattie Wilkins (dau of Edgar & Mary), 12 Nov 1867; William A. White, clk, wit; m 12 Nov 1867 by Jas. C. Robinson, J. P.

Wilson, Eaton & Elvy Shearin, 1 Apr 1848; Willis W. Haris, bm; Jno W. White, wit.

Wilson, Edward (col) & Caroline Bobbitt, 19 May 1866; Dr. Thomas E. Wilson, bm; William A. White, clk, wit; m 19 May 1866 by Samuel W. Dowtin, J. P.

Wilson, Elijah & Ann Paschall, 18 Dec 1804; Elisha Paschall, bm; M. D. Johnson, C. C., wit.

Wilson, Hartwell & Lucy Wilson, 21 Dec 1842; George W. Omerry, bm; M. J. Montgomery, wit.

Wilson, Hartwell & Elizabeth Gray, 24 Oct 1837; James Saintsing, bm; E. W. Best, bm.

Wilson, Henry & Judiah Pitchford, 10 Aug 1809; Benja Hawkins, bm; Jno C. Johnson D. C. C., wit.

Wilson, James & Matilda R. Brickell, 6 Oct 1831; Nathaniel Brickell, bm; Benj E. Cook, wit.

Wilson, John M. & Susan G. Bobbitt, 1 Apr 1839; Thos A. Montgomery, wit.

Wilson, Joshua & Molley Williams, 11 Jan 1783; Robert Williams, bm; M. Duke Johnson, wit.

Wilson, Joshua & Melissa Carter, 6 Sept 1842; Robert P. Hamlin, bm; M. J. Montgomery, bm.

Wilson, Joshua & Francis Harris, 2 Jan 1857; G. H. Macon, bm; Jno W. White, clk, wit; m 2 Jan 1857 by M. M. Drake, J. P.

Wilson, Nathaniel & Elizabeth Shearin, 2 Apr 1866; Lewis Little, bm; William A. White, wit; m 4 Apr 1866 by J. H. Northington, M. G.

Wilson, Peter & Patsy Tanner, 6 Apr 1797; Francis Tucker, bm; Shd Green, wit.

Wilson, Pleasant & Mary Howelson, 21 Mar 1798; James Sandefer, bm; James Moss, bm.

Wilson, Presley & Susanah Smith, 4 Feb 1809; John Harwell, bm; J. C. Johnson, D. C., wit.

Wilson, Richard & ____ Newman (dau of Thomas Newman), 29 Sept 1780 (request for license).

Wilson, Richard & Mary W. Harriss, 2 Mary 1825; Pinckney Harris, bm; M. M. Drake, wit.

Wilson, Richard & Martha Wilson, 13 July 1835; Thomas Wilson, bm; E. D. Drake, clk, wit.

Wilson, Sherwood & Peggy Breedlove, 19 Nov 1794; Joab Langford, bm; Richd Russell, wit.

Wilson, Spencer & Delila Keel, 4 Apr 1801; Joab Langford, bm; S. Johnson, wit.

Wilson, Thomas & Nancy Keal, ____ 1795; George Lankford, bm; Th. Plummer, wit.

Wilson, Thomas & Nancy Lanngford, 4 Feb 1823; Mark Clanton, bm; Edwin D. Drake, wit.

Wilson, Thomas, Jr., & Rebakah Wilson, 24 Mar 1839; Little Bury Hix, bm; Burl Pitchford, J. P., wit.

Wilson, Thomas E. & Janet M. Mitchell, 13 July 1847; John V. Cawthorn, bm; Jno W. White, wit.

Wilson, Weldon E. & Henrietta Walker, 9 Dec 1857; Somervell Saintsing, bm; Jno W. White, wit; m 10 Dec 1857 by Jas T. Russell, J. P.

Wilson, William & Nancy Randolph, 19 Sept 1803; Samuel Alston, bm; Gideon Johnson, wit.

Wilson, William & Elizabeth Falkener, 14 Sept 1859; Jno T. Taylor, bm; William A. White, wit; m 16 Sept 1859 by L. Henderson, J. P.

Wilson, William G. & Betsy Marshall, 5 Nov 1814; Thomas Nuchols, bm; W. Green, C. C. C., wit.

Wilson, William G. & Rebecca Vaughan, 26 Sept 1843; Wm. S. Ransom, bm; M. J. Montgomery, wit.

Wilson, William M. & Lucy F. Wiggins, 10 Aug 1852; Wm. G. Wilson, bm; Jno W. White, wit.

Wilson, William M. & Adaline N. Vaughan, 26 Feb 1855; Nathl McLean, bm; Wm. A. White, wit.

Wingate, William & Lurany Maddray, 26 Apr 1796; Benjamin Thurmon, bm; M. Duke Johnson, C. C., wit.

Winn, Andrew J. & Barshaba Ann Lee, 6 May 1851; William P Rose, bm; Jno W. White, clk, wit; m 7 May 1851 by Edmd White, J. P.

Winn, Charles & Elizabeth Wilson, 7 Mar 1827; Robert J. Williams, bm.

Winn, Joel & Elizabeth Hilton, 2 Aug 1819; Philemon Hawkins, bm; Caswell Drake, wit.

Wombell, George & Catharine Dowtin, 29 Nov 1831; David D. W. Dowtin, bm.

Wood, Agrippa & Salley Hawks, 9 Jan 1799; Devena Muston, bm; M. Duke Johnson, C. C., wit.

Wood, Bennet & Nancey Elleton, 12 Aug 1797; Saml Bartlet, bm; M. Duke Johnson, C. C., wit.

Wood, George & Arabella Conn, 6 Jan 1858; Ezra Lee, bm; Jno W. White, wit; m 6 Jan 1858 by Wm. C. Clanton, J. P.

Wood, Henry A & Martha Langford, 31 Aug 1824; Thomas P. Keel, bm; E. D. Drake, wit.

Wood, Isaac & Lewsey Darnald, 10 Apr 1799; John Darnald, bm; Shd Green, wit.

Wood, James B. & Nancy F. Vaughan, 23 Aug 1837; Michael Riggan, bm.

Wood, John & Betty Oakley, 3 Jan 1780; Phillermon Hillard, bm; Thos Machen, wit.

Wood, John & Sarrah Welden, 28 Aug 1846; Thos T. Twitty, bm.

Woodard, William (col) & Lucy Ann Richardson, 13 Apr 1867; Lewis B. Collins, bm; William A. White, clk, wit; m 14 Apr 1867 by M. P. Perry, J. P.

Woodlief, Robert & Lethe Garrett, 4 Apr 1833; Thomas Coghill, bm; Benj. E. Cook, wit.

Woodliff, Irving E. & Ann Eliza Edwards, 11 Aug 1856; C. T. Parrish, bm.

Woodruff, Benjamin W. & Sarah J. Moseley, 15 Nov 1865; J. R. Mason, bm; E. W. Wilkins, J. P., wit; m 15 Nov 1865 by E. W. Wilkins, J. P.

Wooton, John & Susan Wooton, 17 Oct 1855; Tippoo Brownlow, bm; Jno W. White, wit.

Wooton, William & Amey Stokes, 23 Mar 1800; Stephen Marshall, bm; M. D. Johnson, C. C., wit.

World, Drewry & Susannah Thomson, 5 Aug 1819; John H. Mulholland, bm; C. Drake, wit.

Worrel, James & Polly Raiborn, 26 Dec 1810; John Mulholland, bm; Jno C. Johnson, D. C., wit.

Worrell, Alexander W. & Martha D. Wood, 16 Jan 1839; Eli B. Marshall, bm; Edwd W. Best, clk, wit.

Worrell, Ransom & Susannah T. Cleton, 11 Mar 1810; Richard Shearin, bm; Jno C. Johnson, D. C. C., wit.

Worrell, Thomas & Susanna Ellis, 14 Apr 1807; Joseph Wren, bm.

Worrell, William & Sarah James, 16 June 1813; Peter R. Davis, bm; Jno H. Green, wit.

Worsham, Benjamin F. & Rebecca Frances King, 13 Feb 1845; Charles M. Cook, bm; Jno W. White, wit.

Worsham, Green & Polly Fane, 3 June 1804; John King, bm; Gideon Johnson, wit.

Wortham, Augustin W. & Martha Ann Terry, 7 Apr 1829; Gabriel L. Macon, bm; C. Drake, C. C., wit.

Wortham, Benjamin H. & Polley H. Lanier, 15 Oct 1804; James Moss, bm; M. D. Johnson, C. C., wit.

Wortham, Edward & Liticia Power, 31 Aug 1803; Thomas Power, bm; Gideon Johnson, wit.

Wortham, George & Salley Archer, 28 Feb 1809; Dickey Neal, bm; M. D. Johnson, C. C., wit.

Wortham, George & Nancy King, 26 Feb 1836; William J. Archer, bm; E. D. Drake, clk, wit.

Wortham, George H. & Ann E. Taylor, 4 Feb 1860; Frederick King, bm; Jno W. White, clk, wit; m ___ 1860 by John W. Hicks, J. P.

Wortham, Henry (col) & Lizzie Thrower, 19 Dec 1866; William A. White, clk, wit; m 26 Dec 1866 by A. L. Steed, J. P.

Wortham, James & Martha Riggan, 13 Mar 1834; George W. Tunstall, bm; E. D. Drake, clk, wit.

Wortham, James & Martha Taylor, 1 Feb 1861; Elbert Brame, bm; Jno W. White, clk, wit; m 8 Feb 1861 by L. C. Perkinson, M. G.

Wortham, James L. & Charity D. Alston, 25 Sept 1841; Robert H. Wortham, bm; Richd J. Wortham, wit.

Wortham, John & Elizebeth Jordon, 18 Feb 1799; Shd Green, wit.

Wortham, John, Jr., & Patsey H. Langford, 5 Mar 1827; Abner Steed, bm; C. Drake, C. C., wit.

Wortham, Joseph H. & Celia E. Perkinson, 18 Oct 1851; Benjamin Wortham, bm; Jno W. White, clk, wit; m 26 Oct 1851 by Caswell Drake.

Wortham, Robert & Mary Montgomery, 29 Mar 1832; Thomas Wortham, bm; C. Drake, C. C., wit.

Wortham, Thomas & Frances O'Bryan, 20 Oct 1829; Philemon Jenkins, bm; E. D. Drake, wit.

Wortham, William & Francis Laughter, 28 Apr 1834; William H. Foote, bm; E. D. Drake, clk, wit.

Wortham, William & Ann James, 13 Dec 1849; Elbert Brame, bm; Jno W. White, wit.

Wortham, Wm. H. (son of William & Frances Wortham) & Caroline A. Perdue (dau of Thomas & Martha Perdue), 9 Nov 1867; William A. White, clk, wit; m 13 Nov 1867 by Z. M. P. Cole, J. P.

Worwell, William & Sarah Brubank, 15 Mar 1797; John Wrenn, bm; Thos Malone, wit.

Wray, James & Darkey Allan, 4 Aug 1788; William Robins, bm; M. D. Johnson, C. C., wit.

Wray, Thomas J. & Eliza Pearson, 22 Dec 1852; Jno S. Thomas, bm; R. B. Robinson, wit; m 22 Dec 1852 by R. B. Robinson, J. P.

Wren, Green & Jane Worrel, 8 Jan 1821; Harmon Renn, bm; Cas Drake, C. C., wit.

Wren, Green C. & Wenny Robertson, 29 May 1832; Thomas M. Renn, bm; C. Drake, C. C., wit.

Wren, Joel & Chaney Mangrum, 9 July 1803; Charles Allen, Jr., bm; Gideon Johnson, wit.

Wren, Joseph & Nancey Maddry, 2 Jan 1782; William Laughter, bm; Thos Machen, C. C., wit.

Wren, Joseph & Clarasa Breedlove, 16 Jan 1810; William Johnson, bm; Jo Terrell, D. C., wit.

Wren, Samuel & Elizabeth N. Fitts, 29 Sept 1804; Drury Bobbitt, bm; M. Duke Johnson, C. C., wit.

Wren, William & Middy Clark, 6 Nov 1817; William Brown, bm; Will Green, C. C., wit.

Wrenn, Zachariah & Elizabeth Pardue, 28 Dec 1813; Joseph Wrenn, bm; Wm. Green, C. C. C., wit.

Wright, Allen & Nancy Hughs, 6 Nov 1837; Woodson Hughs, bm.

Wright, Allen & Maria Mitchell, 21 June 1860; Stephen Hedgepath, bm; Jno W. White, clk, wit; m 21 June 1860 by N. A. Purefoy.

Wright, Anderson & Elizabeth Shearrin, 6 June 1831; Willoughby Hudgins, bm; C. Drake, C. C., wit.

Wright, Briton J. & Mary Hudson, 5 Mar 1787; Joseph Hudson, bm; M. D. Johnson, C. C., wit.

Wright, Drury S. & Sally Shearin, 19 Sept 1831; Wm. A. Hundeley, bm; C. Drake, C. C., wit.

Wright, Hamilton (col) & Victoria Baskerville or Regan, 25 Dec 1865; Thomas P. Paschall, bm; William A. White, clk, wit; m 28 Dec 1865 by T. Page Ricaud, M. G.

Wright, James L. & Amanda C. Davis, 24 Nov 1852; Wesley W. Warren, bm; Bennett V. Nanny, wit; m 24 Nov 1852 by Richd. B. Robinson, J. P.

Wright, Jeremiah R. (col) & Ann Wright, 26 Dec 1865; H. Palmer, Jr., bm; William A. White, clk, wit; m 28 Dec 1865 by Jas T. Russell, J. P.

Wright, Jesse & Mary Findley, 23 Oct 1796; Alexander Nicholson, bm; Shd Green, wit.

Wright, John & Nanney Tarver, 9 July 1782; Bird Tarver, bm.

Wright, John & Pamelia Brantley, 17 Dec 1812; Henry G. Williams, bm; Jno H. Green, wit.

Wright, Joshua & Mrs. Phoebe Short (no date); Jno Beard, bm; James Moss, wit.

Wright, Lewis & Fanny Dortch, 12 Dec 1806; Wm. Wright, bm; Ro. R. Johnson, wit.

Wright, Robert & Rebecca Turner, 28 Nov 1810; Nathaniel Harrison, bm; M. Duke Johnson, C. C., wit.

Wright, Thomas L. & Martha A. Power, 13 Dec 1832; Bennitt H. Stammire, bm.

Wright, William & Lucretia Lowery, 22 Dec 1859; Haywood Cordle, bm; Jno W. White, clk, wit; m 22 Dec 1839 by N. A. Purefoy.

Wright, William H. & Arrella Loyd, 12 Nov 1859; J. M. Roberson, bm; Jno W. White, clk, wit; m 13 Nov 1859 by A. L. Steed, J. P.

Wright, Zachariah & Catharine Kneel (no date): Neal Brooks, bm; M. Duke Johnson, C. C., wit.

Wright, Zachariah & Margaret Brown, 18 Jan 1828; Turner Allen, bm; M. M. Drake, wit.

Wright, Zachariah & Emaline Harton, 9 Apr 1832; Wm. G. Wilson, bm; C. Drake, C. C., wit.

Writtenbury, Isham H. & Jane Dobbins, 12 July 1831; Hugh L. Griffis, bm; C. Drake, C. C., wit.

Writtenbury, Isham H. & Sally W. Writtenbury, 26 Sept 1832; Baxter M. Rittenberry, bm; C. Drake, C. C., wit.

Wynn, Peter & Julia Wilson, 17 Apr 1856; Somerville Saintsing, bm; Jno W. White, clk, wit; m 23 Apr 1856 by Robt D. Paschall, J. P.

Wynne, Thomas M. & Calista B. Pearson, 8 Dec 1828; Pery Jordan, bm; M. M. Drake, wit.

Wyott, Robert L. & Hattie E. Freman, 9 July 1859; R. H. Ford, bm; Jno W. White, clk, wit; m 11 July 1859 by R. G. Barrett, clergyman.

Yancey, Alexander L. & Elizabeth W. Bragg, 27 July 1836; Henry T. Allen, bm; E. D. Drake, clk, wit.

Yancey, Henry & Sarah T. Green, 10 Apr 1813; Robert R. Johnson, bm; Wm. Green, C. C. C., wit.

Yarborough, James D. & Martha N. White, 10 May 1825; Williamson Harper, bm; M. M. Drake, wit.

Yarborough, Wade L. & Martha J. Turner, 24 Dec 1835; William P. Sledge, bm; E. D. Drake, clk, wit.

Yarbrough, Edward & Polly Mabry, 29 Dec 1802; Buckner Mabry, bm; G. Johnson, wit.

Yarbrough, Henry & Mary P. Duke, 24 Oct 1812; George Anderson, bm; Wm. Green, C. C. C., wit.

Yarbrough, Joel & Salley Sledge, 12 June 1803; Wyatt Williams, bm; M. D. Johnson, C. C., wit.

Young, Joseph & Eliza Wilson, 22 Dec 1837; Bennett H. Stammire, bm.

Young, Joshua & Elizabeth Wilson, 19 June 1822; Thomas Hawk, bm.

Young, Dr. S. D. & A. E. Williams, 16 Aug 1862; Jno H. Young, bm; Jno W. White, clk, wit; m 20 Aug 1862 by Ira T. Wyche, M. G.

Young, Thomas R. & Lucy Ann Minetree, 9 Jan 1838; Gideon Harton, bm.

MARRIAGE REGISTER

List headed "August the 15th 1866"

Edward Williams & Martha Davis m 25 Dec 1855.

Robt Watkins & Nancy Ezely m 4 May 1857.

Samuel Davis & Mary Davis m 1 Oct 1855.

Hardaway Cook & Matilda Reynolds m __ Sept 1854.

George Young & Holly Young m 25 Nov 1863.

Plummer Hall & Caroline White m 1 Sept 1848.

Frank Hagood & Ailsey Davis m __ Nov 1843.

Andrew Williams & Jane Williams m 25 Dec 1863.

Adkin Williams & Chany Shearin m 10 Apr 1840.

Harry Davis & Parthena Alston m 15 Apr 1832.

Demsey(?) Jones & Penny Jones m 20 Mar 1858.

Ellick Coleman & Jenny Somervell m 17 Aug 1865.

Howell Jones & Ann Jones m 5 Mar 1861.

Claiborne Jones & Elvira Jones m __ Nov 1851.

Collin Coleman & Serena Sutton m __ Jan 1865.

Kinchen Alston & Matilda Perry m 28 July 1862

Wm Baptist & Sarah Feild m 16 Oct 1864.

Arthur Feild & Arabella Feild m 15 Mar 1851.

Augusta Falkener & Sarah Green m 20 Aug 1863.

Hilliard Cheek & Anna Williams m 20 Aug 1863.

Peter Green & Martha Williams m 25 Mar 1858.

List headed "August 31st 1866"

_____ Alston & Mourning _____ m __ Sept ____.

____ Jones & Rosetta Somerville(?) m 25 Dec ____.

Maddison Harriss & Polly Nicholson m 25 Dec ____.

Henry Davis & Fanny Shearin m 25 Dec ____.

Ned Mayho, formerly free, & Emily Jones m 28 Aug 1846.

Caesar Johnson & Lydia Turner m __ Oct 182_.

Mark Duke & Angelina Williams m __ Apr 1863.

Trim Skinner & Nancy Skinner m 1 Feb 1862.

Patrick Robinson & Tempy Davis m 12 Mar 1863.

Austin Davis & Eliza Davis m __ June 1862.

Shepard Davis & Lucy Alston m 15 Oct 1863.

Augustina Hawkins & Patience Hawkins m __ Nov 1863.

                    List headed "September 6th 1866"

Dawson Jones & Harriet Pettway m 1 Sept 1847.

Lock Harris & Catharine Powell m __ May 1841.

John W. Riggan & Sarah B. Vaughan m 12 June 1851 by B. Eaton, J. P.

Dr. John Moore & Lucy Burgess, dau of John Burgess, m 11 June 1851 by Robert O. Burton.

Joshua Perry & Elizabeth H. Green m 29 July 1851 by Wm. Arndell, Elder, M. E. C. S.

P. R. Merryman & Mrs. Mary Davis m 9 Sept 1851 by A. C. Harris, M. G.

William T. Alston & Laura Eaton m 15 Oct 1851 by Comr. F. McRae, Pastor of Immanuel Church, Warrenton, NC.

Henry Bolton & Margaret Bishop m 22 Oct 1851 by Jas T. Russell, J. P.

John Vaughan & Caroline Mayo m 28 Nov 1851 by J. H. Bullock, J. P.

Elbert Brame & Indiana King m 10 Dec 1851 by O. D. Fitts, J. P.

Saml Harper & Mary E. White m 14 Dec 1851 by H. J. Macon, J. P.

Asa George & Elizabeth King m 15 Dec 1851 by M. Riggan, J. P.

Thos Richardson & Nelly Mosely m 17 Dec 1851 by Richd B. Robinson, J. P.

Lewis Mustian & Mary C. Whitlow m 15 [Dec] 1851 by O. D. Fitts.

Nathl Harriss & Elizabeth A. Harris m 22 Dec 1851 by M. Riggan, J. P.

Doctor L. Aycock & Lucetta W. Bennett m 23 Dec 1851 by H. J. Macon, J. P.

Joseph H. Wortham & Celia E. Perkinson m 26 Oct 1851 by Caswell Drake.

Thomas R. Tunstall & Elizabeth J. Mabry m 16 Nov 1851 by Caswell Drake.

Nicholas Shearin & Malissa Shearin m 8 Jan 1852 by Wm. C. Clanton, J. P.

William J. Kimball & Elizabeth A. B. Watkins m 31 Jan 1852 by Wm. A. Burwell, J. P.

James A. Kimball & Mary E. Watkins m 20 Jan 1852 by Caswell Drake.

Solomon W. Smith & Martha B. Snow m 26 Jan 1852 by H. J. Macon, J. P.

James Roberson & Martha Brown m [no date] by Abner Steed, J. P.

Mecdoland Seward & Eliza Joiner m 4 Feb 1852 by Jno H. Bullock, J. P.

Hawkins Kenedy & Holly Burrows m 14 Jan 1852 by M. M. Drake, J. P.

John E. Brown & Elizabeth D. Dobbins m 25 Feb 1852 by B. Eaton, J. P.

Benjamin King & Rebecca Conn m 9 Mar 1852 by J. B. Solomon.

Joseph John Harris, Jr., & Linny C. Riggan m 17 Mar 1852 by Wm. C. Clanton, J. P.

Henry Harper & Martha Parrish m 25 Mar 1852 by N. Z. Graves.

Joseph ____ & Eliza Ver___ m 26 Mar 1852 by Saml Bobbitt, J. P.

David Hinton of Wake County, NC, & Mary B. Carr m 31 Mar 1852 by Robt O. Burton, M. G.

James Roberts & Sarah M. Harper m 21 Apr 1852 by Richd B. Robinson, J. P.

Baxter Guy & Elizabeth Volentine m 21 Apr 1852 by R. B. Robinson, J. P.

Robert W. Paschall & Lucy N. Paschall m 21 Apr 1852 by Caswell Drake.

William Kin__ & _____ m 25 __ 1852 by ____ wkins, J. P.

Levi Tally & Mary F. Perkinson m 16 June 1852 by J. H. Hawkins, J. P.

Hilliard Harvey & Delia Ann Vaughan m 16 June 1852 by Edmd White, J. P.

Robert P. Harton & Priscilla J. Clark m 28 June 1852 by A. C. Harris, M. G., of Granville County, NC.

George E. Johnson & Lucy Askew m 7 July 1852 by J. C. Cheek, J. P.

James ____ & Alletha J. Fl___ m by Abner Steed, J. P.

Andrew Harrison & Frances Rotenberry m 11 July 1852 by R. B. Robinson, J. P.

Thomas B. Jones & Martha B. Thomas m 28 July 1852 by R. B. Robinson, J. P.

Joseph Brownaskie & Sarah Drake m 27 Aug 1852 by B. Eaton, J. P.

Richd Whitehorn & Mary A. Grizzard m 8 Sept 1852 by Wm. C. Clanton, J. P.

Wm. H. Raney & Mary T. Cretchfield m 7 Sept 1852 by R. B. Robinson, J. P.

Theophilus Stallings & Martha Brame m __ Sept 1852 by Robt O. Burton, M. G.

Robert Green & Elizabeth Evans m 25 Sept 1852 by John H. Bullock, J. P.

Joseph L. Poythress & Elizabeth J. Crowder m 30 Sept 1852 by R. B. Robinson.

Joseph B. Littlejohn & Sallie Jones Field m 13 Oct 1852 by the Rector of Calvary Church, Tarbro, NC

W. A. Dowtin & Sarah Rodwell m 11 Nov 1852 by Rev. N. Z. Graves.

Charles ____ & Mary T. Pierson, m __ Nov 1852 by Richd B. [Robinson], J. P.

John Kelly & Amanda Wilson m 8 Nov 1852 by B. Eaton, J. P.

Bowlin Evans & Partheny Mushaw m 17 Nov 1852 by Thos P. Paschall, J. P.

James L. Wright & Amanda C. Davis m 24 Nov 1852 by Richd B. Robinson, J. P.

John Adams & Silvey Stokes m 10 Dec 1852 by J. B. Solomon.

John Guearin(?) & ____ Cliborne m 15 Dec 1852 by T. B. Ricks.

George W. Earls & Susan H. Regans m 16 Dec 1852 by Thos P. Paschall, J. P.

John W. Hayes and Miss E. J. Jones m 12 Jan 1853 by N. F. Reid.

Richard Shearin & Rebecca Reid m 28 Dec 1852 by Henry Harris, J. P.

Green Blanton & Elizabeth Lambert m 28 Dec 1852 by J. H. Hawkins, J. P.

Henry T. Watkins & Sarah E. Watkins m 22 Dec 1852 by Wm. A. Burwell, J. P.

John Evans & Margarette Durham m 23 Dec 1852 by John H. Bullock, J. P.

Willis Hervey & Henrietta Seward m 29 Dec 1852 by John H. Bullock, J. P.

Wm. J. Justian & Susannah B. Whitlow m 19 Dec 1852 by O. D. Fitts, J. P.

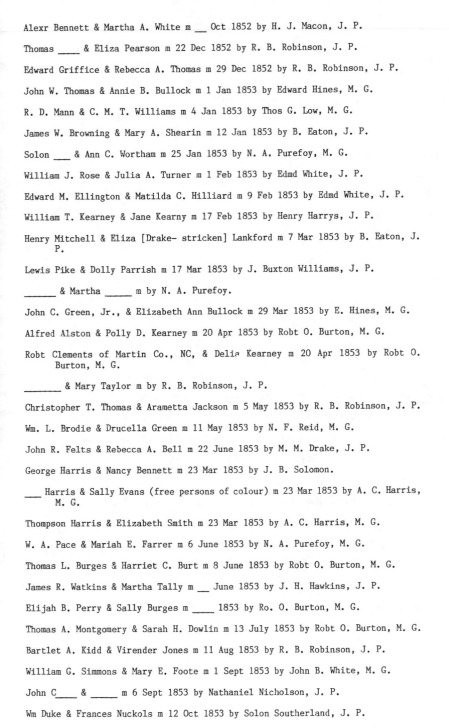

WARREN COUNTY MARRIAGES

Alexr Bennett & Martha A. White m ___ Oct 1852 by H. J. Macon, J. P.

Thomas _____ & Eliza Pearson m 22 Dec 1852 by R. B. Robinson, J. P.

Edward Griffice & Rebecca A. Thomas m 29 Dec 1852 by R. B. Robinson, J. P.

John W. Thomas & Annie B. Bullock m 1 Jan 1853 by Edward Hines, M. G.

R. D. Mann & C. M. T. Williams m 4 Jan 1853 by Thos G. Low, M. G.

James W. Browning & Mary A. Shearin m 12 Jan 1853 by B. Eaton, J. P.

Solon ___ & Ann C. Wortham m 25 Jan 1853 by N. A. Purefoy, M. G.

William J. Rose & Julia A. Turner m 1 Feb 1853 by Edmd White, J. P.

Edward M. Ellington & Matilda C. Hilliard m 9 Feb 1853 by Edmd White, J. P.

William T. Kearney & Jane Kearny m 17 Feb 1853 by Henry Harrys, J. P.

Henry Mitchell & Eliza [Drake- stricken] Lankford m 7 Mar 1853 by B. Eaton, J. P.

Lewis Pike & Dolly Parrish m 17 Mar 1853 by J. Buxton Williams, J. P.

_____ & Martha _____ m by N. A. Purefoy.

John C. Green, Jr., & Elizabeth Ann Bullock m 29 Mar 1853 by E. Hines, M. G.

Alfred Alston & Polly D. Kearney m 20 Apr 1853 by Robt O. Burton, M. G.

Robt Clements of Martin Co., NC, & Delia Kearney m 20 Apr 1853 by Robt O. Burton, M. G.

_____ & Mary Taylor m by R. B. Robinson, J. P.

Christopher T. Thomas & Arametta Jackson m 5 May 1853 by R. B. Robinson, J. P.

Wm. L. Brodie & Drucella Green m 11 May 1853 by N. F. Reid, M. G.

John R. Felts & Rebecca A. Bell m 22 June 1853 by M. M. Drake, J. P.

George Harris & Nancy Bennett m 23 Mar 1853 by J. B. Solomon.

___ Harris & Sally Evans (free persons of colour) m 23 Mar 1853 by A. C. Harris, M. G.

Thompson Harris & Elizabeth Smith m 23 Mar 1853 by A. C. Harris, M. G.

W. A. Pace & Mariah E. Farrer m 6 June 1853 by N. A. Purefoy, M. G.

Thomas L. Burges & Harriet C. Burt m 8 June 1853 by Robt O. Burton, M. G.

James R. Watkins & Martha Tally m ___ June 1853 by J. H. Hawkins, J. P.

Elijah B. Perry & Sally Burges m _____ 1853 by Ro. O. Burton, M. G.

Thomas A. Montgomery & Sarah H. Dowlin m 13 July 1853 by Robt O. Burton, M. G.

Bartlet A. Kidd & Virender Jones m 11 Aug 1853 by R. B. Robinson, J. P.

William G. Simmons & Mary E. Foote m 1 Sept 1853 by John B. White, M. G.

John C____ & _____ m 6 Sept 1853 by Nathaniel Nicholson, J. P.

Wm Duke & Frances Nuckols m 12 Oct 1853 by Solon Southerland, J. P.

Abram Seward & Catharine Durham m __ Oct 1853 by Jno. H. Bullock, J. P.

Buckner D. Williams & Elizabeth B. Syme m 3 Nov 1855 by N. A. Purefoy, M. G.

Thomas M. Egerton & Mary H. Fleming m 7 Nov 1853 by N. A. Purefoy, M. G.

Edward F. Bobbitt & Indiana T. Brame m __ Nov 1853 by Robt. O. Burton, M. G.

Jacob M. Palmer & Bettie F. Rodwell m 17 Aug 1853 by Thos G. Lowe, M. G.

John Hicks & Mary Harton m 17 Aug 1853 by A. C. Harris, M. G.

Robert B. Smith & Emma J. Mitchell m 26 Sept 1853 by R. B. Robinson, J. P.

Beverly B. Vaughan & Esther W. Drumwright m 14 Sept 1853 by N. A. Purefoy, M. G.

Jno. D. Tucker & Eliza M. Parrish m ____ by Caswell Drake.

Richard T. Arrington & Bettie J. Plummer m 2 Nov 1853 by L. L. Smith, Clergyman of the Prof. Epis'l Church.

Frank W. Tatum & Harriet Plummer m 7 Nov 1853 by L. L. Smith, Clergyman of the Prot. Epis'l Church.

Albert Pennell & Henrietta Duke m 30 Nov 1853 by P. H. Smith, M. G.

Miles Evans & Scinnory Mabry m 1 Dec 1853 at Charles M. Cooks house by Henry Harris, J. P.

Wm. H. Smith & Julia A. Spruill m 1 Dec 1853 by Jos Blount, Rector.

_____ & Louisa Taylor m by Richd B. Robinson, J. P.

Benjamin E. Cook, Jr., & Ann Hall m 13 Dec 1853 by T. B. Ricks, M. G.

Charles W. Ogburn & Flury Gill m 13 Dec 1853 by P. W. Archer.

Macon G. Newman & Althier O. Tucker m 14 Dec 1853 by Caswell Drake, M. G.

Samuel Gill & Emily W. Arnold m 13 Dec 1853 by Ph. W. Archer, M. G.

_____ & _____ m by Nathaniel Nicholson, J. P.

William Strum & Mary Harris m 14 Dec 1853 by A. C. Harris, M. G.

James Harris & Elizabeth Brown m 15 Dec 1853 by A. C. Harris, M. G.

Thomas A. Dunn & Lucy Faulkner m 21 Dec 1853 by A. C. Harris, M. G.

James C. Rudd & Emma R. Loyd m 22 Dec 1853 by A. C. Harris, M. G.

Leroy L. Bartlett & Sarah E. Rideout m 18 Dec 1853 by H. J. Macon, J. P.

John L. Neal & Ann P. Rodwell m 17 Dec 1853 by Wm. C. Clanton, J. P.

Richd Conner & Emily Mosely m 29 Dec 1853 by R. B. Robinson, J. P.

____ & _____ m 5 Jan 1854 by H. J. Macon, J. P.

Andrew J. Bowdon & Mrs. Arabella G. ___ m __ Feb 1854 by J. G. ____.

Jefferson Mason & Henrietta Hicks m 7 Feb 1854 by J. G. ____.

_____ & Mary Bartlette m 9 Feb 1854 by J. G. ____.

Wilson W. Ethrage & Rodah McFurson m 12 Jan 1854 by Ph. W. Archer of NC Conference.

Amos Artis & Nancy Green m 17 Jan 1854 by John S. Cheek, J. P.

Giles Bowers & Nancy Felts m 14 Feb 1854 by Henry Harris, J. P.

Jno D. Newell & Emily Brame m 15 Feb 1854 by Thos. J. Pitchford, J. P.

Jerreman Hawks & Parthena Tally m 3 Mar 1854 by J. H. Hawkins, J. P.

Rev. __ H. Jordan & Ann M. Pope m 6 Mar 1854 by J. B. Solomon.

John W. Harris & Eveline Pegram m 11 Mar 1854 by M. M. Drake, J. P.

Frederick C. Vaughan & Martha F. Gholson m 29 Mar 1854 by A. C. Harris, M. G.

William J. Exum & Mary J. Burton m 18 Apr 1854 by Henry Gray, M. G.

William A. Dortch & Elizabeth A. Mise m 9 Mar 1854 by Richd B. Robinson, J. P.

____ Perkinson & Susan ____ m 14 June 1854 by Jno H. Hawkins, J. P.

Granderson F. Glover & Arimente Tridd m 22 June 1854 by R. B. Robinson, J. P.

Thomas M. Crosson & Rebecca Brehon m 10 July 1854 by L. L. Smith of the Prot. Episcopal Church.

Wm H. Polk & Lucy E. Williams m 14 July 1854 by Ph. W. Archer, M. E. Church, South.

Hartwell Roberson & Sarah T. Paschall m 17 Sept 1854 by Jno H. Bullock, J. P.

J. H. Riggan & Adelia A. Seapark m 12 Sept 1854 by N. A. Purefoy, M. G.

Benjamin R. Harris & Nancy T. Womble m 7 Sept 1854 by Thos P. Pitchford.

Jas Haithcock & Susan Lancaster m 20 July 1854 by Saml Bobbitt, J. P.

Henry P. White & Sarah W. Hicks m __ July 1854 by T. B. _____.

_____ & _____ Bartlett m 2 Oct [1854].

Marx Schloss & Mary E. Burrows m 5 Oct 1854 by H. J. Macon, J. P.

W. C. Drake &* Sallie F. Twitty m 18 Oct 1854 by Thos G. Lowe, M. G.

John Cliborn & Sarah Shearin m 18 Oct 1854 by Nathaniel Nicholson, J. P.

George D. Rudd & Martha A. Falkner m 11 Oct 1854 by A. C. Harris, M. G.

Joshua Rivers & E. R. Tally m 15 Oct 1854 by John H. Hawkins, J. P.

_____ Jones & Rebecca ____ m 5 Nov 1854 by B. Eaton, J. P.

Thos P. Levister & Frances S. Robertson m 15 Nov 1854 by Thos J. Pitchford, J. P.

Thos M. Fleming & Sallie A. Johnston m 15 Nov 1854 by H. J. Macon, J. P.

Daniel R. Riggan & Virginia A. Wright m __ Nov 1854 by M. M. Drake, J. P.

Thos Durham & Lucy Harris m 23 Nov 1854 by Thos J. Pitchford, J. P.

Jno H. Myrick & Winifred Stephenson m 28 Nov 1854 by H. A. Foote, J. P.

Wm A. Dowtin & Mary C. Watson m _____ 1854 by N. A. Purefoy, M. G.

Edward C. Jones & Jane B. Thomas m 7 Dec 1854 by R. B. Robinson, J. P.

Jno A. Harris & Elizabeth Lancaster m 8 Dec 1854 by Thos J. Pitchford, J. P.

Weldon E. Bishop & Ann W. Lancaster m 21 Dec 1854 by Thos J. Pitchford, J. P.

Chasteen Dickerson & Mary Hays m 20 Dec 1854 by A. C. Harris, M. G.

John L. Pegram & Jane Robertson m 21 Dec 1854 by Saml Bobbitt, J. P.

William W____ & ___tha L. Bobbitt, m 24 Dec 1854 by Thos J. Pitchford, J. P.

Abbington K. Fleming & Mary C. Smith m 31 Dec 1854 by Will Plummer, J. P.

A. C. McCraw & Sarah Waddill m 22 Nov 1854 by J. B. Solomon.

Wm. E. Edwards & Mary Childs m 1 Feb 1855 by Richd B. Robinson, J. P.

Charles D. Regans & Mary A. Watkins m 5 Mar 1855 by Thomas P. Paschall, J. P.

S. Aycock ___ & Miss M. E. Hicks m ___ 1855 by ____ M. G.

Horace Palmer, Jr., & Sallie E. Milam m 18 Apr 1855 by T. G. Lowe, M. G.

Tony Chavis & Mary A. Vaughan m 26 Apr 1855 by Thomas P. Paschall, J. P.

William Robinson & Lucy A. Hawkins m 1 Feb 1855 by Will Plummer, J. P.

_____ Tunstall to Fra____ m by A. C. Harris, M. G.

Leonidas S. Shearin & Mary A. M. Lewis m 12 Mar 1855 by B. Eaton, J. P.

Fleming Thompson & A. Smith m 27 Feb 1855 by N. A. Purefoy, M. G.

James G. Newton & Lucy J. Newton m 1 Mar 1855 by Jas T. Russell, J. P.

Robt White & Ann M. Coleman m 12 Apr 1855 by Jas T. Russell, J. P.

Solomon W. S____ & Susan D. Harriss m 9 May 1855 by Saml Bobbitt, J. P.

S. M. Cates & Amanda Rooker m 30 June 1853 by William Plummer, J. P.

Dr. C. P. Hyde & Eliza D. Allen m 31 May 1855 by N. Z. Graves.

James H. Harris & Sarah W. Egerton m 16 Mar 1855 by N. Z. Graves, M. G.

John Harris & Elizabeth Moore m 12 June 1855 by John S. Cheek, J. P.

Edward Shroyer & Frances M. Powell m 2 __ 1855 by T. B. Ricks, clergyman.

Thomas T. Fleming & Leticia Regans m 8 Aug 1855 by Thos P. Paschall, J. P.

Green Patterson & Quinney Moore m 18 May 1855 by J. S. Cheek, J. P.

Develly Darnold & Matilda Paschall m 16 Aug 1855 by Robt D. Paschall, J. P.

Octavio Austin & Pattie A. Burgess m 5 Oct 1855 by L. S. Burkhead, M. G.

James A. Cheatham & Lucy A. White m __ Feb 1855 by A. C. Harris, M. G.

Marcellus Ransom & Lucy Sno m 24 Aug 1855 by B. Eaton, J. P.

Littleton Upshur & Frances E. Macon m 15 Oct 1855 by N. Z. Graves.

J. V. Newsom & Nancy Nicholson m 18 Oct 1855 by Buckner Eaton, J. P.

Dr. C. White & Sallie A. White m 17 Oct 1855 by J. P. Moore.

_____ & F. Manor m 24 Oct 1855 by Thos S. Campbell, M. G., M. E. Church, South.

Jacob Parker & Bettie K. Kearney m 21 Nov 1855 by Wm. H. Jordan.

Lewis Mustian & Sarah Bolton m 11 Nov 1855 by Robt D. Paschall, J. P.

Presley Richardson & Rody Richardson m 16 Nov 1855 by Wm. C. Clanton, J. P.

Henry T. Duke & Frances K. Kearney m 15 Nov 1855 by Wm. C. Clanton, J. P.

Ezra Lee & Nancy Hamlet m 15 Nov 1855 by Wm. C. Clanton, J. P.

Henry Hardy & Susan Burrows m 24 __ 1855 by Richard B. Robinson, J. P.

Nelson Brame & Elizabeth Wortham m 11 Dec 1855 by N. C. Harris, M. G.

John Stallings & Eveline Verser m 24 Dec 1855 by H. A. Foote, J. P.

Richard J. Riggan & Margaret F. Lampkin m 17 Dec 1855 by Thos P. Paschall, J. P.

George W. Robinson & Sarah S. Boy m 31 Oct 1855 by Robt O. Burton, M. G.

Robert A. White & Lucy Wiggins m 15 Jan 1855 by Jas T. Russell, J. P.

Harrall Daniel & Louisa Harriss m 18 Dec 1855 by Thos P. Paschall, J. P.

Benjamin Kersey & Elizabeth Epps Kersey m 17 Jan 1856 by Thomas P. Paschall, J. P.

Dr. W. & _____ rk m 21 __ 1855 by L. L. Smith, Presbyter of the Protestant Episcopal Church.

Macon Abbet & Meranda Askew m 20 Mar 1856 by R. H. Smith, M. G.

John A. Delbridge & Martha L. Pierson m 20 Feb 1856 by Richd B. Robinson, J. P.

Andrew J. Mosely & Margaret C. Barner m 2 Apr 1856 by Richd B. Robinson, J. P.

Thos W. Stainback & Martha A. Langford m 12 Mar 1856 by A. L. Steed, J. P.

A. H. Hicks & Betsy R. Burcher(?) m __ Dec 1856 by Thos P. Paschall, J. P.

Marian T. Coghill & Sarah Ann _____ m by A. C. Harris, M. G.

Peter Wynn & Julia Wilson m 23 Apr 1856 by Robt D. Paschall, J. P.

Marian T. Coghill & Sarah Ann Wright m 16 Apr 1856 by A. C. Harris, M. G.

Robert F. Anderson & Renn Anderson m 18 Mar 1856 by Thomas P. Paschall, J. P.

John C. Harriss & Nancy Harriss m 18 Mar 1856 by Henry A. Foote, J. P.

John J. West & Jane Carter m by Saml Bobbitt, J. P.

Thos W. Evans & Permelia A. Renn m 22 Apr 1856 by P. H. Smith, M. G.

L. H. Shuck & M. A. Parrish m 19 June 1856 by N. Z. Graves.

Thomas W. Williams & Catie V. J. Redd m 18 June 1856 by Thos S. Campbell, M. G.

Thomas J. Harris & Martha Hardy m 1 July 1856 by Wm. C. Clanton, J. P.

____ & ____ m 30 July 1856 by N. Z. Graves.

Dr. R. F. Brown & E. H. Mitchell m 5 Aug 1856 by L. L. Smith.

Nat Brickell & Julia Bartlett m 22 Sept 1756 by J. B. Solomon.

Arthur Thompson & Arrena Askew m 9 Oct 1856 by John Watson, J. P.

Wm. H. Thorne & Martha J. Alston m 15 Oct 1856 by Robert O. Burton, M. G.

W. H. Ba____ & Nancy H Robertson m 24 July 1856 by N. A. Purefoy, M. G.

_____ & Ann __eaton m by Samuel Bobbitt, J. P.

John F. Barner & Nancy Mathews m 18 July 1856 by Richd B. Robinson, J. P.

Joseph H. Perdue & Indianna Allen m 31 Oct 1856 by N. A. Purefoy, M .G.

Thomas R. Tunstall & Lucy A Young m 18 Nov 1856 by A. C. Harris, M. G.

John Saintsing & Winnefred Hicks m 29 Oct 1856 by Robt D. Paschall, J. P.

John Perry & Eliz'h E. Sledge m __ Nov 1856 by Samuel Bobbitt, J. P.

Thos R. Hendrick & Catharine W. May___ m 17 July 1856 by Thos G. Low(?), M. G.

____ Bar___ & _____ m __ Nov 1856 by Thos S. Campbell, M. G.

James B. E. Lankin & Maria L. Laughter m 3 Dec 1856 by T. J. Judkins, J. P.

William A. Brame & O. E. Joyner m 17 Dec 1856 by Revd. James Read.

Robt W. E. Tate & Frances E. Renn m 13 Dec 1856 by P. H. Smith, M. G.

Richard Edwards & Jane L. Rudd m 4 Jan 1857 by Abner Steed, J. P.

Presley W. Harris & Louisa N. Riggan m 12 Feb 1857 by Saml Bobbitt, J. P.

John L. Bunchett & Martha A. Tucker m 11 Dec 1856 by Wm. A. Burwell, J. P.

Robert Richard & Jenkins Richardson m 28 Nov 1856 by Wm. C. Clanton, J. P.

A. S. Jenkins & Martha E. Coleman m 3 Mar 1857 by Samuel Bobbitt, J. P.

_____ & _____ m 18 Mar 1857 by N. Z. Graves.

John W. Paschall & Martha E. Paschall m 19 Mar 1857 by Wm. H. Burwell, J. P.

Nathaniel Shearin & Martha E. Marshall m 15 Jan 1857 by J. Buxton Williams, J. P.

Lewis D. Browning & Sephrony Robertson m 2 Feb 1857 by B. Eaton, J. P.

Blake B. Baker & Arilla Johnston m 15 Apr 1857 by O. M. Cook, J. P.

Presley C. Ingram & Eliza E. Bobbitt m 15 Apr 1857 by P. H. Smith, M. G.

J. W. Jordan & Ann M. Steed m 20 Apr 1857 by Thos S. Campbell, M. G.

Jos H. Neal & Caroline T. Harris m 17 May 1857 by Wm. A. Dowtin, J. P.

M. V. Rice & Mrs. Mary L. Brinkley m 17 May 1857 by J. B. Solomon.

Charles Bennett & Mrs. Mary Clark m 22 Apr 1857 by A. Steed, J. P.

Amacy J. Newman & Mary E. Duty m 28 May 1857 by Thomas P. Paschall, J. P.

Dr. Gid H. Macon & Louisa Jenkins m 9 June 1857 by N. Z. Graves.

Benj C. Nicholson & Mary Thomas m 31 July 1857 by Nathaniel Nicholson, J. P.

Wm. B. Foster & Pattie A. Southland m 26 Aug 1857 by Wm. S. Brooks.

Benjamin Davis & Martha A. Fleming m 16 Sept 1857 by Wm. C. Clanton, J. P.

Philip P. Gill & Sarah Paschall m 22 Oct 1857 by N. A. Purefoy, M. G.

John H. Nicholson & Bettie P. Shearin m 15 Oct 1857 by N. A. Purefoy, M. G.

Julius Wilcox & Martha J. Hollon m 23 Oct 1857 by N. Z. Graves.

James Bennett & Lucretia Read m 24 Oct 1857 by William A. Dowtin, J. P.

____ Hawkins, Jr., & Sallie Falkener m 3 Nov 1857 by Robt B. Sutton, clergyman.

Willis A. Hawkins & Leah T. Irwin m 3 Nov 1857 by R. S. Mason, Rector of Christ
     Church.

E. E. Postell of Iredell Co, NC, & A. E. Collins m 3 Nov 1857 by J. Tillet, M.
     G.

John Falkner of Granville Co., NC, & Martha A. Rudd m 18 Nov 1857 by A. C.
     Harris, M. G.

Weldon E. Wilson & Henrietta Walker m 10 Dec 1857 by James T. Russell, J. P.

John H. Chavis & Mary J. Kersey m ___ 1857 by W. N. Bragg, minister.

Isham Mayo & Martha Chavis m 26 Nov 1857 by Thomas P. Paschall, J. P.

William P. Guerrant of Pittsylvania Co., VA, & Jane E. Green, m 17 Dec 1857 by
     John Tillett, M. G.

Robt F. Rose & Bettie P. Duke m 26 Nov 1857 by J. Tillett.

Thaddeus D. Rolland of Granville Co., NC, & Hixy J. Vanlandingham m 23 Dec 1857
     by J. Tillett, M. G.

_____ Robertson, Jr., & Eliza C. Fa____ m by A. C. Harris, M. G.

Jas W. Nuckles & Pink Vaughan m 28 Dec 1857 by R. D. Paschall, J. P.

John W. Watkins & Mary H. P. Nicholson m 11 Jan 1856 [sic] by M. M. Drake, J. P.

Tyra D. King & Mary F. Hicks m by M. M. Drake, J. P.

Joshua Wilson & Frances Hanis m 2 Jan 1857 by M. M. Drake, J. P.

Wm. S. Bell & Martha J. Felts m 24 Dec 1857.

Wm. R. ____ & _____ Omary m 30 Dec 1857[?] by ___ Russell, J. P.

George Wood & Arabella Conn m 6 Jan 1858 by Wm. C. Clanton, J. P.

George R. King & Mary King m 10 Dec 1857 by Wm. C. Clanton, J. P.

John A. Hundley & Eugenia Odam m 14 Jan 1858 by J. Tillett, M. G.

James W. Harris & Tabitha J. Riggan m 15 Jan 1858 by Samuel Bobbitt, J. P.

Thomas H. Williams & Betty A. Pegram m 14 Jan 1858 by L. C. Perkins. n, M. G.

James A. Davis & Mary C. Cheek m 28 Jan 1858 by Mark C. Duke, J. P.

Baker B. Brack & Mary T. Thompson m 30 Jan 1858 by Saml Bobbitt, J. P.

John R. Congleton & Rebecca F. Riggan m 31 Jan 1858 by J. B. Solomon.

John Evans & Priscilla West m 4 Feb 1858 by M. C. Duke, J. P.

Henry Mitchell & Mary E. Ashe m 6 Feb 1858 by A. L. Steed, J. P.

Zeavell Crowder & Surphrone Renn m 31 Dec 1857 by A. L. Steed, J. P.

Robt B. Ridout & Martha F. Wiggins m 20 Jan 1858 by R. D. Paschall, J. P.

Solomon Hunt & ____ Aikin m by Saml Bobbitt, J. P.

Aaron A. Huggins & Caroline J. Williams m 18 Mar 1858 by J. B. Solomon.

Thos James, Jr., & Lucy T. Powell m 30 Jan 1858 by Thos J. Judkins, J. P.

Thomas Painter & Frances Ellington m 14 Sept 1857 [sic] by H. J. Macon, J. P.

John J. Rodwell & Mary P. Rodwell m 5 Apr 1858 by J. B. Solomon.

W. H. Smith & Amarillis Williams m 10 Apr 1858 by J. B. Solomon.

Robert J. Powell & Billie D. Cheek m 4 May 1858 by R. G. Barrett, Pastor of
Warren Circuit, ME Church, South.

Wharton J. Gray & ____ Ellergy m by William Hodges.

Saml P. Arring & Sue Eaton m 6 May 1858 at the residence of Wm. Eaton, Jr., by
William Hodges, Rector of Emanuel Church, Warrenton.

Elijay King & Lucy Tally m 29 Apr 1858 by J. B. Solomon, Pastor Baptist Church,
Warrenton.

W. H. B. Taylor & Mary S. J. Jones m by J. B. Solomon, Pastor Baptist Church,
Warrenton.

____ Williams & Ann K. Kearney m ____ 1858 by T. G. Lowe, M. G.

John R. Burney & Winnie A. Milam m 12 May 1858 by T. G. Lowe, minister.

Makenny Capps & Mary Conn m 27 May 1858 by William A. Dowtin, J. P.

James Green & Bettie Mills m 26 May 1858 by M. T. Hawkins, J. P.

H. H. Hunter & Mary H. Cheek m 16 Feb 1858 by P. H. Joyner.

James P. Terry & Amanda ____ m 24 July 1858 by J. Tillett.

C. H. Bennett & E. B. White m 10 Aug 1858 by Wm. Hodges, Rector of Emanuel
Church.

Dr. J. Chambliss & Miss C. V. Williams m 25 Aug 1858 by William Hodges, Rector
of Emanuel Church.

George W. Harper & Elizabeth Minetree m 22 Aug 1858 by L. E. Perkinson, M. G.

Jno T. Carter & Rebecca F. Thomas m __ Sept 1858 by Saml Bobbitt, J. P.

Augusta A. Cheek & E. J. Newell m 21 Sept 1858 by R. G. Barrett.

William Harris & Elizabeth Evans m 14 Oct 1858 by A. L. Steed, J. P.

Oliver P. Shell & Mary C. Turnbull m 2 Nov 1858 by William Hodges, Rector of
Emanuel Church.

William Morgan Powell & Emily T. Kearney m 4 Nov 1858 by Wm. C. Clanton, J. P.

Samuel A. Paschall & Nancy king m 10 Nov 1858 by L. C. Perkinson, M. G.

Ivy Moss & Rebecca Moss m 24 Nov 1858 by Jas T. Russell, J. P.

Henry Y. Harris & Jane Lancaster m by Saml Bobbitt, J. P.

Robert A. Paschall & Martha D. Roberson m 7 Dec 1858 by Wm. A. Burwell, J. P.

Henry Green & Nancy Hawkins m 21 Dec 1858 by N. A. Purefoy, M. G.

John E. Jones & India E. Royster m 20 Dec 1858 by J. B. Solomon, Pastor of the Baptist Church, Warrenton.

Jno E. _____ & Rebecca W. Tw____ m 24 Nov 1858 by P. H. Joyner.

Durwell B. Kimball & Aggie B. Watkins m 19 Jan 1859 by A. C. Harris, M. G.

John W. Andrews & Susan A. Fleming m 22 Dec 1858 by Thos P. Paschall, J. P.

Thos S. Duke & Parthena Omary m 20 Jan 1859 by L. C. Perkinson, M. G.

Thos Hardy & Matilda Nicholson m 9 Feb 1859 by W. A. Dowtin, J. P.

Isaac Harris & Pattie A. Andrews m 15 Feb 1859 by J. B. Solomon, Pastor Baptist Church.

Nathaniel Kimball & Mary Carroll m 20 Feb 1859 by J. B. Solomon, Pastor Baptist Church.

Robert J. Roberson & Louiza J. Buchanan m 9 Feb 1859 by Thomas P. Paschall, J. P.

_____ & Rebecca Carter m by Nathl Nicholson, J. P.

Edward Pike & Jane Lancaster m 15 Dec 1858 by Nathl Nicholson, J. P.

Thos Shearin & Susan Myrick m 15 Dec 1858 by Nathl Nicholson, J. P.

George W. Loyd & Elizabeth Tunstall m 22 Dec 1858 by A. L. Steed, J. P.

David Roberson & Sallie Clark m 12 Jan 1859 by A. L. Steed, J. P.

Warren H. Capps & Mary L. Regans m __ Dec 1858 by Wm. A. Burwell, J. P.

Nathl Allen & M. E. Powell m 13 Mar 1859 by N. A. Purefoy, M. G.

Gardner Shearin & Lucy J. Pegram m 30 Mar 1859 by Saml Bobbitt, J. P.

___ Coley & Delia _____ m 5 Mar 1859 by Abner Steed, J. P.

Thos Pendergrass & Sallie Nuckles m 1 Apr 1859 by C. J. Jones, J. P.

John C. Powell & Bettie A. Cheek m 6 Apr 1859 by Chas M. Cook, J. P.

Wm. R. Colemon & Lucy A. Hicks m 20 Apr 1857 by J. B. Solomon, Pastor Bap. Ch.

___ Carr & W. Eleanor Kearny m 24 May 1859 by Rev. Thos G. Lowe.

John W. Shearin & Lucy W. Clark m 20 Apr 1859 by A. L. Steed, J. P.

Solomon W. Perry & Sallie D. Stamper m 9 June 1859 by R. G. Barrett.

Wm. E. Webb & Anne Bowen m 6 June 1859 by C. M. Cook, J. P.

Isham W. Dickerson & Celestis Coley m 20 Apr 1859 by C. J. Jones, J. P.

C. E. Hewitt & Lucy Janis m 7 July 1859 by Chas Skinner, J. P.

Robert L. Wyatt & Hettie E. Freman m 11 July 1859 by R. G. Barrett, clergyman.

Lewis Ash & Elizabeth Carter m 4 Mar 1859 by Ridley Brown, J. P.

Charles S. Tucker & Matilda F. Myrick m 22 _____ by R. Brown, J. P.

James A. Pitchford & Sallie E. Davis m 17 Aug 1859 by John S. Cheek, J. P.

J. G. Parrish & Elizabeth J. Harris m 14 Sept 1859 by Saml Bobbitt, J. P.

James G. Thomas & Mary Ann Southall m 18 Sept 1859 by R. G. Barrett, clergyman.

William A. White & Sallie E. Cole m 28 Sept 1859 by N. A. Purefoy, M. G.

Conrad S. Boyd & Alice E. Stewart m 6 July 1859 by J. B. Solomon, Pastor of the
    Baptist Church.

William J. Fulford & Josephine A. Harris m 12 Oct 1859 by Wm. C. Clanton, J. P.

W. E. _____ & Amanda _____ m 19 Oct 1859 by C. H. Harris.

William A. J. Nicholson & Bettie E. Williams m 1 Nov 1859 by J. B. Solomon,
    Pastor Baptist Church.

Jessee Marshall & Rebecca King m 2 Nov 1859 by Wm. C. Clanton, J. P.

Julian V. Perkins[?] & Lucy F. _____ m 8 Nov 1859 by R. G. Barrett, clergyman.

John W. Williams & Mary Camilla S. Holt m 17 Nov 1859 by J. B. Solomon, Pastor
    Baptist Church.

Henry W. Grainger & Martha A. Wilson m 22 Nov 1859 by R. G. Barrett, clergyman.

William Wilson & _____ m __ Sept 1859 by Len Henderson, J. P.

Wm H. Wright & Arrella Loyd m 13 Nov 1859 by A. L. Steed, J. P.

James T. Wiggins & Ellen Burroughs m 3 Nov 1859 by A. L. Steed, J. P.

_____ & Rebecca F. Brown m 1 Dec 1859 by J. B. Solomon, Pastor Baptist Church.

William C. Duke & Obedience Cole m 14 Dec 1859 by Jas. T. Russell, J. P.

John A. Stallings & Sarah A. Robertson m 15 Dec 1859 by Saml Bobbitt.

Nicholas M. Long, Jr., & Sallie Hawkins Williams m 21 Dec 1859 by Jas Blount
    Cheshire.

John W. Rodgers & Mary J. Cole m 7 Dec 1859 by N. A. Purefoy, M. G.

William Wright & Lucretia Lowery m 22 Dec 1859 by N. A. Purefoy.

Micajah Burnet & Martha Ann Mills m 29 Dec 1859 by N. A. Purefoy.

_____ & Mary Davis m 4 Jan 1860 by Thos J. Pitchford, J. P.

Alexander W. Hendrick & Isabella Rowland m 21 Dec 1859 by Charles J. Jones, J.
    P.

Sterling Johnston & M. J. Johnston m 14 Dec 1859 by J. H. Northington, minister
    of the M. E. Church.

_____ us E. Fuller & Lucy R. Ball m 11 Jan 1860 by L. K. Willie, M. G.

Willie Lowry & Winnie Tann m 16 Jan 1860 by N. A. Purefoy, M. G.

Saml W. Eaton & Lucy F. Browne m 17 Jan 1860 by Thos G. Lowe, M. G.

_____ & ___ D. Stallings m ___ Jan 1860 by W. A. Dowtin, J. P.

James Y. Rooker & Sallie A. Thompson m 15 Dec 1859 by Chas M. Cook, J. P.

Thomas R. Hendrick & Mary J. Walker m 8 Feb 1860 by B. F. Long, minister.

____ H. Davis & Mollie _____ m 7 Feb 1860 by John S. Cheek, J. P.

Joseph J. Harris & Mrs. Martha T. Ellington m 18 Jan 1860 by Wm. C. Clanton, J. P.

George H. Wortham & Ann E. Taylor m _____ 1860 by Jno W. Hicks, J. P.

Herman P. Ward & Emma M. Harmond m 26 Mar 1860 by Wm. Hodges.

Robert Ball & Caroline Askew m 13 Apr 1860 by Thos P. Paschall, J. P.

Charles H. Pearson & E. Matilda Burgess m 7 Mar 1860 by Robert O. Burton, M. G.

B. F. Long & Rebecca Brame m 18 Jan 1860 by Ira F. Wyche.

George W. King & Mary N. Carroll m 5 Apr 1860 by N. a. Purefoy, M. G.

Green H. Harris & Margaret N. Carter m 26 Apr 1860 by W. A. Dowtin, J. P.

_____ S. Newsom & Cla___ Rooker m 8 May 1860 by Nathl Nicholson, J. P.

John N. Harris & Ruina A. Harris m 7 Dec 1859 by Nathl Nicholson, J. P.

Nathl W. Shearin & Mrs. Mary C. Sledge m 13 Mar 1860 by Nathl Nicholson, J. P.

_____ & Delia Harris m 29 May 1860 by W. A. Dowtin, J. P.

Levi Walker & Patience C. Paschall m 24 May 1860 by L. C. Perkinson, minister.

Robert C. Twitty & Sallie F. Palmer m 30 May 1860 by Rev. Thos G. Lowe.

Robert B. Pegram & Martha A. Pegram m 6 June 1860 by Samuel Bobbitt, J. P.

R. H. C. M. Paschall & Melissa A. Twisdale m 31 May 1860 by B. F. Long.

W. W. Perkinson & Amanda F. Lambert m 20 May 1860 by L. C. Perkinson, minister.

Allen Wright & Maria Mitchell m 21 June 1860 by N. A. Purefoy.

John W. Cunningham & Martha Helen Somervell m 4 July 1860 by Wm. Hodges, Rector of Emanuel Church, Warrenton.

R. F. Finch & Bettie R. Burney m 3 July 1860 by John D. Southall.

Wm Singleton & _____ Evans m 9 June 1860 by Jno N. Andrews.

Thos Goodmon & Mary Harper m 5 July 1860 by Jno N. Andrews, P. C., Warren Circuit.

Stephen A. Norfleet & M. Louisa Spruill m 23 Aug 1860 by Rev. Wm. Hodges, Rector of Emanuel Church.

_____ & Catharine Sa_____ m 22 Aug 1860 by W. A. Dowtin, J. P.

Thomas J. Green & Jane E. Wortham m 6 Sept 1860 by W. A. Dowtin, J. P.

Robert Tannahill & Sallie Sims m 4 Oct 1860 by Wm. Hodges.

C. W. Champion & M. E. Thompson m 17 Oct 1860 by M. K. Willie, M. G.

James Adkins & Susan Short m 1 Nov 1860 by A. L. Steed, J. P.

R. F. S. Peete & Mary A. Davis m 4 Oct 1860 by Rev. R. G. Lowe.

Samuel Aycock & Sally Ann Conn m 27 Nov 1860 by W. A. Dowtin, J. P.

George King & Martha E. Tutor m 17 Oct 1860 by Jno W. Pattillo, J. P.

Alfred Bishop & Mary Hicks m 21 Nov 1860 by Jno W. Pattillo, J. P.

_____ & Roberta Mi___ m 29 Nov 1860 by R. Brown, J. P.

John W. Williams & Bettie R. Pitchford m 7 Nov 1860 by Jno S. Cheek, J. P.

Robert Cannon & Louisa Victoria Blanton m 5 Dec 1860 by Thos A. Montgomery, J. P.

Samuel P. Arrington & Hannah B. White m 12 Dec 1860 by William Hodges, Rector of Emanuel Church, Warrenton.

Thos C. Reavis & Elizabeth W. Best m 5 Dec 1860 by N. A. Purefoy, M. G.

Armistead King & Lucy Hicks m 2 July 1860 by Thos J. Judkins, J. P.

William Y. King & Mary E. Shearin m 2 Jan 1861 by W. A. Dowtin, J. P.

Theophilus Short & Fanny Loyd m 22 Nov 1860 by A. L. Steed, J. P.

__bert Pendergrass & Elizabeth Perdue m 12 Dec 1860 by A. L. Steed, J. P.

James Saintsing & Lucy Ann Clark m 23 Dec 1860 by A. L. Steed, J. P.

John Daniel Shearin & Fanny A. Watkins m 6 Dec 1860 by C. F. Harris.

Thomas Myrick & Nisha Omary m 23 Jan 1861 by Jno W. Pattillo, J. P.

Miles R. King & Charity W. Paschall m 30 Jan 1861 by N. A. Purefoy, M. P.

Eli W. Ball & Sarah A. Reavis m 28 Dec 1860 by R. D. Paschall, J. P.

Samuel P. Ha__ & Sarah C. Burroughs m 31 Jan 1861 by R. D. Paschall, J. P.

Thomas W. Wade & Permelia P. Golson m 28 Feb 1861 by Rev. L. Shell.

John W. ____ & Mary S. Hicks m 13 Feb 1861 by Rev. L. Shell.

Benjamin W. Darnell & Mary J. Paschall m 10 Apr 1861 by Jno W. Pattillo, J. P.

___ Wortham & Martha Taylor m 8 Feb 1861 by L. C. Perkinson, minister.

Tyra D. King & Susan E. Askew m 24 Apr 1816 by J. H. Wheel, M. M. E. C. S.

N. D. ___ & Mary E. Poythress m 17 May 1861 by Thos A. Montgomery, J. P.

J. M. Bolton & Bettie E. Paschall m 6 June 1861 by Henry A. Foote, J. P.

Wm. T. Pegram & B. M. Hilliard m 14 May 1861 by Wm. Holmes, M. G.

Julius Scott & Frances _____ m 29 June 1861 by Drury Lacy.

S. G. Mabry & Lucy M. Best m 30 June 1861 by A. L. Steed, J. P.

Thos P. Paschall & Elizabeth Andrews m 25 July 1861 by R. D. Paschall, J. P.

John A. ___ris & Frances L. Carter m 24 Aug 1861 by Nathl Nicholson, J. P.

John D. Cole & Ellen J. Newman m 8 May 1861 by Lemmon Shell, minister.

Robert W. Drewry & Annie Hudgins m 28 Nov 1861 by Wm. Hodges, Rector of Emanuel Ch, Warrenton.

Wm. J. Edwards & Mary L. Vaughan m 17 Nov 1861 by Wm. Homes.

___ D. Fleming & Susanna D. Cole m 18 Dec 1861 by J. W. Manning.

William J. Ford & Mary M. Manning m 4 Dec 1861 by James C. Robinson, J. P.

Taylor Tucker & Amanda Burrows m 26 Dec 1861 by John Watson, J. P.

J. H. Robertson & Mary A. Johnson m 8 Jan 1862 by Jno Watson, J. P.

William H. Stark & Mary Jane Moseley m 11 Dec 1861 by Nathl Nicholson, J. P.

Thomas Carter & Jane Brack m ___ Jan 1862 by Nathl Nicholson, J. P.

John S. Mustian & Elizabeth Mustion m 5 Jan 1862 by Jno W. Pattillo, J. P.

Julius S. Brown & Sarah A. Walker m 4 Feb 1862 by Chas Skinner, J. P.

William Robertson & Frances Thompson m 18 Feb 1862 by Chas M. Cook, J. P.

Hugh Ronald & Catharine Baker m 22 May 1862 by William Hodges, Rector of Emanuel Church.

John L. Birchett & Martha A. Vaughan m 30 July 1862 by Thomas P. Paschall, J. P.

Dr. S. D. Young & Miss A. E. Williams m 20 Aug 1862 by Ira T. Wyche, minister.

John Cooper & Martha Cooper m 3 Aug 1862 by Jas C. Robinson, J. P.

James _____ & Susan G. Bobbitt m 24 Sept 1862 by Saml Bobbitt, J. P.

James J. Walker & Lutitia Paschall m 2 Oct 1862 by N. A. Purefoy, M. G.

Joseph B. Jones & Lucy M. Plummer m 15 Oct 1862 by William Hodges, Rector Immanuel Church, Warrenton.

Jno T. Williams & Eliz M. Edington m 9 Oct 1862 by Wm. A. Burwell, J. P.

John Rivers & Elizabeth Collins m ___ Nov 1862 by N. A. Purefoy, M. G.

Samuel Green & Winney Thomas m 26 Nov 1862 by Saml Bobbitt, J. P.

Henry P. White & Martha E. Hicks m 27 Nov 1862 by Lemmon Shell.

Thomas D. Hilliard & Eugenia A. Holloway m 22 Sept 1862 by Lemmon Shell, minister.

Newell Lyne & Mary G. Harris m 17 Dec 1862 by Thos P. Paschall, J. P.

Robert H. Ford & Mary A. E. Johnson m 14 Jan 1863 by Jno B. Williams.

James W. R. Chavis (col) & Sarah C. Kearsey m 15 Oct 1862 by S. V. Hoyle, minister.

John F. Hawkins & Rebecca T. Burrows m 28 Jan 1863 by John B. Williams, M. G.

Crawford Kearney & Charity H. Reavis m 17 Feb 1863 by P. H. Joyner, minister.

James W. Roberts & Mary Eliza Dickerson m 4 Feb 1863 by S. P. J. Harris, M. G.

W. K. A. Williams & Caroline M. Alston m 27 May 1863 by A. W. Mangum, M. G.

J. N. McDowell & Martha P. Washington m 9 June 1863 by Henry Petty, M. G.

Edward H. Plummer & Sallie D. Fitts m 1 July 1863 by William Hodges, Rector of Emanuel Ch.

Wm. T. Hicks & Mary Winn m 5 May 1863 at Ridgeway by J. H. Wheeler.

John G. Hubbard & Sarah E. Brickle m 16 July 1863 by N. A. Purefoy, M. G.

A. E. Thrift & Mrs. Joanna Jamison m 21 July 1863 by John B. Williams, M. G.

Leonard H____ Lizzie M. Green m 10 Sept 1863 by William Hodges, Rector of Emanuel Ch.

Samuel W. Dowtin & Bettie M. Price m 23 Sept 1863 by John Bryan Williams, M. G.

Charles Beddingfield & Elizabeth Williams m 30 Sept 1863 by Henry Petty, M. G.

John J. Smith & John J. Moseley [sic] m 2 Sept 1863 by A. F. Davidson.

_____ & Rhoda G. Whitney m 9 Oct 1863 by John B. Williams, M. G.

Henry Powell & Martha Francis Roberson m 23 July 1863 by S. P. J. Harris, M. G.

L. R. Crocker & Pattie G. Turner m 29 Sept 1863 by W. W. Spain.

John W. Riggan & Elizabeth Fleming m 12 Nov 1863 by Thomas J. Judkins, J. P.

Jacob Brown & Emily B. Mudd m 12 Nov 1863 by Henry Petty, M. G.

James Jonnakin & Anne Weldon m 30 Dec 1863 by Charles J. Jones, J. P.

James S. Foote & Pattie A. Bobbitt m 2 Dec 1863 by Lemon Shell, minister.

Dr. George A. Foote & Sallie J. McDowell m 2 Dec 1863 by Henry Petty, M. G.

Wm. Henry Bobbitt & Winne __ Fleming m 13 Jan 1864 by Henry Petty, M. G.

John E. Twitty & Sally D. Drake m 31 Dec 1863 by Rev. Lemon Shell.

Dr. G. L. Hunter & Lucy Yancey m 23 Dec 1863 by William Hodges, Rector of Emanuel Ch.

William S. Davis & Bettie Jones m 28 Dec 1863 by Lemon Shell, minister.

John Stallings & Lucy A. Womble m 22 Jan 1864 by M. C. Duke, J. P.

Thomas J. Pitchford & Pattie B. Plummer m 23 Dec 1863 by William Hodges, Rector of Emanuel Church.

James Wesley Darnold & Sarah Salmon m 20 Feb 1864 by L. C. Perkinson, minister.

Ellington Scott & Mariah Toney m 2 Dec 1863 by Ridley Browne, J. P.

___es Maclin & _____ m __ Mar 1864 by T. B. Reeks.

Joseph J. Harriss & Mary Ann Hardy m 23 Mar 1864 by C. M. Cook, J. P.

Wiley G. Coleman & J. A. Shearin m 30 Mar 1864 by N. A. Purefoy.

WARREN COUNTY MARRIAGES

D. F. Batson & Sarah W. Weaver m 19 Jan 1864 by Thos W. Rooker, J. P.

Wm Vanlandingham & Sarah Bowden m 31 Mar 1864 by R. D. Paschall, J. P.

Richard Crowder & Miss L. Rivers m 18 Mar 1864 by L. C. Perkinson, minister.

J. M. Robinson & M. A. Harriss m 12 May 1864 by N. A. Purefoy, M. G.

John O. Macon & Indianna Ascue m 12 May 1864 by Solon Southerland, J. P.

Howell Moss & Mrs. Mary A. Duke m 19 May 1864 by James R. Russell, J. P.

Col. William H. Cheek & Alice M. Jones m 9 June 1864 by W. Hodges, Rector of Emanuel Church.

W. J. Carter & Martha J. King m 25 May 1864 by L. C. Perkinson, minister.

Col. Thomas M. Jones & Mary C. London m 29 June 1864 by W. Hodges, Rector of Emanuel Church.

Ridley L. Harris & Lucy A. Pegram m 7 Oct 1864 by B. F. Long.

Col. John D. Barry & Fanny L. Jones m 1 Dec 1864 by William Hodges, Rector of Emanuel Ch.

W. R. Williams & Mollie Thomas m 7 Nov 1864 by Henry Petty, M. G.

___ S. Thrower & _____ m ____ 1864 by J. R. Finley, D. D.

Wm Watson & Louisa V. Wright m 18 Jan 1865 by W. Hodges, Rector of Emanuel Ch.

Jno Drew & Julia Durham m 21 Dec 1864 by John H. Bullock, J. P.

H. M. Blair & Harriet Tally m 8 Apr 1865 by L. C. Perkinson, minister.

Robt H. Read & Pattie A. Patterson m 7 Sept 1864 by John H. Bullock, J. P.

Zachariah T. Shearin & Eliza R. Johnson m 31 Mar 1865 by Henry Harris, J. P.

Wm Hearne & E. J. Cheek m 7 May 1865 by John B. Williams, M. G.

James H. Harris & Mollie E. Shearin m 26 Apr 1865 by Charles M. Cook, J. P.

Charles Fain (col) & ____ Hendrick m 26 Aug 186_ by James R. Russell, J. P.

Ellick Alexander (col) & Clora Somerville m 13 Sept 1865 by W. Hodges, Rector of Emanuel Ch.

J. R. Shearin & Miss C. Thompson m 5 Sept 1865 by Chas M. Cook, J. P.

James Goodson & Mrs. Martha Wiggins m 13 Sept 1865 by W. A. Brame, M. G.

Benjamin Baskerville (col) & Harriet Mayho m 23 Aug 1865 by John W. Pattillo, J. P.

Wm Bell & Lucy Wright m 20 Sept 1865 by B. F. Long, M. G.

F. M. Hyman & Ella S. Jones m 6 Oct 1865 by J. R. Finley, D. D.

Anthony M. Johnston & Octavia D. Shearin m 4 Oct 1865 by Chas M. Cook, J. P.

_____ & Mary A. Wells m 5 Oct 1865 by T. Page Ricaud, M. G.

John F. King & Martha A. Hicks m 23 Aug 1865 by T. Page Ricaud, M. G.

John W. Pattillo & Mary A. Cole m 1 Oct 1865 by T. Page Ricaud, M. G.

Robert Carroll & Sarah Mustian m 1 Oct 1865 by T. Page Ricaud, M. G.

James W. Robertson & Mary E. Kearney m 11 Oct 1865 by Chas M. Cook, J. P.

S. P. Stallings & Sarah A. Stallings m 18 Oct 1865 by T. P. Alston, J. P.

Wm W. Williams & Octavia A. Robertson m 25 Oct 1865 by N. A. Purefoy, M. G.

Simon G. Duke & Eveline Hawkins m 25 Oct 1865 by John W. Pattillo, J. P.

Christopher Walker & Parthenia Paschall m 5 Oct 1865 by John W. Pattillo, J. P.

Solomon Nicholson (col) & Betsy Cole m 15 Oct 1856 by Jno W. Pattillo, J. P.

J. W. Primrose & Mary S. Twitty m 14 Nov 1865 by Jas A. Duncan, M. E. Church, South.

Thomas Lewsey & Mary Goodwin m 18 Nov 1865 by Will H. Wheeler, V. D. M.

_____ & Maggie A. Pegram m 15 Nov 1865 by Will H. Wheeler, V. D. M.

J. H. White & Martha A. Mabry m 18 Oct 1865 by T. Page Ricaud, M. G.

Thomas H. White & Martha J. Walker m 8 Nov 1865 by T. Page Ricaud, M. G.

Emanuel Myrick (col) & Nancy Hunter m 19 Nov 1865 by James C. Robinson, J. P.

_____ (col) & Mariah M____ m __ 1865 by L. C. Perkinson, M. G.

Noah Ashe (col) & Rosa Cheek m 2 Dec 1865 by W. Hodges, Rector of Emanuel Church.

Jacob M. Palmer & Sophie G. Finley m 1 Mar 1865 by J. R. Finley, D. D.

Jacob Johnson & Rebecca Wright m 28 Oct 1865 by James T. Russell, J. P.

Jacob Seward & Ella Russell m 18 Nov 1865 by James T. Russell, J. P.

John Collins & Louisa V. Myrick m 29 Nov 1865 by B. F. Long, M. G.

Chas O. May & Sallie D. Shearin m 6 Dec 1865 by B. F. Long, M. G.

Jeremiah R. Wright & Ann Wright m 28 Dec 1865 by James T. Russell, J. P.

F. _____ & Miss S. A. Perkinson m 21 Dec 1865 by N. A. Purefoy, M. G.

Nicholas Jiggetts & Polly Cole m 26 Dec 1865 by James T. Russell, J. P.

John T. Paschall & Virginia Russell m 26 Dec 1865 by James T. Russell, J. P.

Henry Russell & Winney Johnson m 23 Dec 1865 by Jas T. Russell, J. P.

John E. _____ & _____ Nicholson m 15 Jan 1866 by R. B. Reeks, minister.

Richard Dowtin (col) & Hannah Dowtin m 24 Dec 1865 by F. P. Alston, J. P.

A. A. Hunt & Bettie Wilson m 20 Dec 1865 by J. B. Solomon, M. G.

J. H. Foster & Lucy Ann Duke m 20 Dec 1865 by J. B. Solomon, M. G.

_____ & Martha Colclough m 12 July 1865 by T. B. Kingsbury, M. G.

Henry H. Harrison & Dolly Perdue m 7 Sept 1865 by T. B. Kingsbury, M. G.

John B. Williams & Ann L. Skinner m 25 Jan 1865 by T. B. Kingsbury, M. G.

Archibald H. Davis & Fannie T. Southerland m 2 Nov 1865 by T. B. Kingsbury, M. G.

Henry Smith & Mary Butler m 27 Nov 1865 by T. B. Kingsbury, M. G.

Dr. Benjamin A. Cheek & Laura W. Bobbitt m 30 Apr 1865 by T. B. Kingsbury, M. G.

James A. Marrow & Ellen M. Taylor m 8 Sept 1865 by T. B. Kingsbury, M. G.

Lewis A. Thompson & Sue Alston m 20 Dec 1865 by R. J. Carson, M. G.

_____ T. Rooker & Almeda Newman m 15 Nov 1865 by John W. Pattillo, J. P.

Ellick Davis & Susanna Bullock m 23 Dec 1865 by Wm Wallace White, J. P.

Hilliard Mitchell & Rhoda Birchett m 24 Dec 1865 by Wm Wallace White, J. P.

Willis Green & Ann Mayfield m 24 Jan 1866 by T. Page Ricaud, M. G.

Ralph _____ & _____ Plummer m 27 Dec 1865 by T. Page Ricaud, M. G.

George Vanlandingham & Delia Vanlandingham m 26 Dec 1865 by T. Page Ricaud, M. G.

Amos Jones & Caroline Collins m 25 Dec 1865 by T. Page Ricaud, M. G.

Thomas Plummer & Susan Jerman m 29 Dec 1865 by T. Page Ricaud, M. G.

_____ Wright & Victoria Regan m 28 Dec 1865 by T. Page Ricaud, M. G.

James G. Hicks & Polly Frances Hicks m 25 Jan 1866 by T. Page Ricaud, M. G.

Dr. R. D. Fleming & Miss A. V. Watson m 15 Feb 1866 by T. Page Ricaud, M. G.

John G. Faulkner & Marilla Wright m 16 Feb 1866 by A. L. Steed, J. P.

_____ (col) & Matilda Falkner m 30 Dec 1865 by Jas A. Egerton, J. P.

W. C. Harriss & M. M. Southerland m 14 Feb 1866 b J. B. Solomon.

James W. Alston & Laura C. Terrell m 11 Mar 1866 by N. A. Purefoy, M. G.

Michael W. Paschall & Frances R. Ellington m 19 Dec 1865 by J. W. Wellons, M. G.

Anthony ___ (col) & Diana Russell m 17 Feb 1866 by J. W. Wellons, M. G.

James Hayes & Mary Jane Newman m 15 Feb 1866 by J. W. Wellons, M. G.

Richard Thompson & Emily Thompson m 15 Mar 1866 by Jas T. Russell, J. P.

Henry L. Hopkins of Petersburg, VA, & Betty M. Feild m 3 Apr 1866 by Churchill J. Gibson, Rector of Grace Church, Petersburg, VA.

_____ W. Shearin & __thia Bartlett m 8 Feb 1866 by Jno W. Pattillo, J. P.

Aaron Pitchford (col) & Sarah Alston m 21 Apr 1866 by J. Buxton Williams, J. P.

Wm. H. Paschall & Sarah E. Gill m 25 Apr 1866 by L. C. Perkinson, minister.

J. J. Jones, Jr., & Emma P. Williams m 8 May 1866 by B. F. Long.

_____ & Emma F. Jones m 27 June 186 by J. P. Moore, M. G.

Alex Curry & Jane Carter m 6 June 1866 by S. W. Dowtin, J. P.

Wm. A. Dickerson & Mary J. Parrish m 23 June 1866 by J. B. Solomon.

James G. Thomas & Bettie W. Bobbitt m 12 Sept 1865 by Thomas P. Alston, J. P.

E. K. Harris & Parmelia _____ m 21 Feb 1866 by Wm. H. Meade.

James M. Fitts & Bettie T. Hunter m 7 Mar 1866 by Robt O. Burton, M. G.

Sebastian C. Shearin & Mary C. Marshall m 10 May 1866 by C. M. Cook, J. P.

John R. Turnbull & Bettie M. Eaton m 27 Feb 1866 by C. M. Cook, J. P.

Capt. _____ & Eugenia L. Feild m 5 July 1866 by W. Hodges, Rector Emanl Church.

Anthony Hicks & Nancy Williams m 22 July 1866 by J. P. Moore, M. G.

James M. Hayes & Sallie S. Stanback m 28 July 1866 by J. P. Moore, Elder.

Spier Whitaker, Jr., & Fanny De Bernia Hooper m 31 July 1866 by William Hodges.

William Pool & Mary E. Stewart m 30 May 1866 by W. Hodges, Rector Emanl Church.

Durell A. King & Sarah E. Hawks m 12 June 1866 by John W. Pattillo, J. P.

M. T. Bolton & Elizabeth P. Hawks m 27 July 1866 by Jno W. Pattillo, J. P.

Henry T. Egerton & Mrs. Bettie Powell m 4 Sept 1866 by B. F. Long, minister.

M. S. Pegram & Bettie Duncan m 18 Sept 1866 by J. M. Brame, J. P.

J. R. Shearin & Roxanna Thompson m 5 Sept 1866 by J. M. Brame, J. P.

James K. Plummer & Mary B. Henderson m 3 Oct 1866 by Joseph W. Murphy, Rector of
the Ch. of the Holy Innocents, Henderson, N. C.

John Edwards & Caroline S. Hodges m 9 Oct 1866 by W. Hodges, rector Emmanuel Ch.

Drury Gill & Eliza Felts m 30 Sept 1866 by T. Page Ricaud, M. G.

Frederick A. Hawk & Mrs. Martha E. White m 29 Aug 1866 by T. Page Ricaud, M. G.

Wm A. Newman & Mary E. Newman m 22 July 1866 by T. Page Ricaud, M. G.

Peter F. King & Lucy D. Hicks m 5 Sept 1866 by Z. M. P. Cole, J. P.

James J. Alston & Maria A. Somerville m 18 Oct 1866 by William Hodges, Rector
Eml. Chh.

James Robertson & Susan W. Robertson m 17 Oct 1866 by Saml Bobbitt, J. P.

Burwell P. Davis & Caroline N. Allen m 24 Oct 1866 by N. A. Purefoy, M. G.

Peter W. Arrington & Alice A. Watson m 8 Nov 1866 by W. Hodges, rector Emml Chh.

Willis F. Riddick & Addie B. Currier m 5 Nov 1866 by W. Hodges, rector of
Emmanuel Chh.

Nathaniel Wilson & Elisabeth Shearin m 4 Apr 1866 by J. H. Northington, M. G.

Joseph H. Ware & Mollie S. Boyd m 8 Nov 1866 by J. P. Moore, M. G.

James C. Myrick & Mary E. Shearin m 21 Nov 1866 by J. M. Brame, J. P.

James _ King & Sallie King m 18 Oct 1866 by M. P. Perry, J. P.

M. S. Buchanan & Mrs. E. M. Loyd m 8 Dec 1866 by N. A. Purefoy, M. G.

Geo W. Perkinson & Rosa A. Smelly m 13 Dec 1866 by Thomas A. Montgomery, J. P.

W. G. Haselwood & Virginia V. Perkinson m 13 Dec 1866 by Thomas A. Montgomery, J. P.

Thos M. Egerton & Nancy D. Fleming m 13 Dec 1866 by N. A. Purefoy, M. G.

William D. Newman & Rhoda C. Moss m 19 Dec 1866 by James T. Russell, J. P.

Lewis Coley & Malissa Ann Breedlove m 11 Dec 1866 by A. L. Steed, J. P.

Henry Jones & Mary E. Shearin m 25 Oct 1866 by Ridley Browne, J. P.

James Stallings & Lucy J. Harriss m 11 Oct 1866 by Ridley Browne, J. P.

Henry Kness & Susan D. Stallings m 6 Nov 1866 by Ridley Browne, J. P.

Richard Riggan & Martha Riggan m 18 Dec 1866 by Ridley Browne, J. P.

Dr. V. O. Thompson & S. D. Joyner m 20 Dec 1866 by J. C. Moore, M. G.

Robert Perkinson & Emma M. Perkinson m __ Dec 1866 by N. A. Purefoy, M. G.

Wm. H. Carroll & Pattie Capps m 26 Dec 1866 by J. M. Brame, J. P.

A. W. Smith & Susan A. Coleman m 12 Dec 1866 by Ira T. Wyche, M. G.

A. P. Duke & Hester C. Duke m 20 Dec 1866 by Ira T. Wyche, M. G.

___ B. Lancaster & Angelina Pegram m 17 Jan 1867 by Saml W. Dowlin, J. P.

Paul Palmer & Bettie Twitty m 16 Jan 1867 by Junius P. Moore, M. G.

Wm. H. Shaw & Rebecca H. Shearin m 14 Feb 1867 by N. A. Purefoy, minister.

Solomon Fleming & Maggie J. Watkins m 18 Dec 1866 by J. W. Wellons, M. G.

___ B. Fleming & A. E. Duke m 31 Oct 1866 by J. W. Wellons, M. G.

James Moseley & Mrs. Ann Turner m 18 Feb 1867 by Jno W. Pattillo, J. P.

Henry J. Darnell & Mrs. Mary D. Floyd m 29 Dec 1866 by Jno W. Pattillo, J. P.

James R. Daniel & Winnefred Mustian m 22 Nov 1866 by Jno W. Pattillo, J. P.

James Pearcy & Susan Paschall m 19 Jan 1866 [sic] by Jno W. Pattillo, J. P.

Mark C. Duke & Mrs. Elizabeth W. Powell m 4 May 1865 by Thos J. Pitchford, J. P.

George Conner & Calie Nance m 1 Jan 1867 by Thos B. Reeks, minister.

William Clegg & Mary E. Collins m 9 Mar 1867 by Wm. Hodges, Rector of Emanuel Chh.

Lafayette B. Myrick & Virginia R. Shearin m 14 Mar 1867 by B. F. Long, M. G.

Alfred L. Haithcock & Josephine H. Bobbitt m 4 Apr 1867 by Thos J. Pitchford, J. P.

Thomas Capps & Mildred P. Regans m 22 Sept 1864 by L. Henderson, J. P.

Richard A. Bullock & Isabella B. Bullock m at the residence of John H. Bullock 29 Mar 1867 by F. A. Whaley, M. G.

Robert S. L____ & Sarah E. Riggan m 4 Apr 1867 by Ridley Browne, J. P.

James Felts & Manerve Little m 2 May 1867 by Ridley Browne, J. P.

S. Riggan & Alice F. Pegram m 28 Mar 1867 by Ridley Browne, J. P.

Thomas D. Rodwell & Annie F. Rodwell m 21 Feb 1866 by T. B. Kingsbury, M. G.

Samuel J. Parham & _____ Southerland m 24 Jan 1866 by T. B. Kingsbury, M. G.

J. J. Loughlin & Lucy A. Johnson m 27 Dec 1865 by T. B. Kingsbury, M. G.

M. M. Horton & Lucy A. Terrell m 29 Mar 1866 by T. B. Kingsbury, M. G.

John W. Williams & Mrs. Sarah T. McCraw m 25 Oct 1866 by T. B. Kingsbury, M. G.

Nathan J. Moseley & Mary Jane Woodson m 1 Mar 1866 by T. B. Kingsbury, M. G.

Henry Qualls & Tempy Hamlet m 8 May 1867 by M. P. Perry, J. P.

Norvel Williams (col) & Louisa Davis m 16 Aug 1866 by William Hodges, M. G.

John Christmas (col) & Nelly Green m 1 Aug 1866 by William Hodges, M. G.

Granderson Thornton (col) & Jane Shaw m 30 June 1866 by Z. M. P. Cole, J. P.

Wm White (col) & Rose Henderson m 27 Aug 1866 by Wm Wallace White, J. P.

Frank Alston (col) & Mary A. E. Alston m 25 July 1866 by J. Buxton Williams, J. P.

Haywood Williams (col) & Mary Frances Gordon m 21 July 1866 by R. D. Paschall, J. P.

George _____ (col) & Ellen Darroll m 4 Aug 1866 by R. D. Paschall, J. P.

Faulcon Richard (col) & Rebecca Alston m 2 May 1866 by M. P. Perry, J. P.

Green Basket & Elizabeth Stewart m 8 Sept 1866 by R. D. Paschall, J. P.

Ancil Bullock & Mary Williams m 1 Sept 1866 by R. D. Paschall, J. P.

Horace Jones (col) & Henrietta _____ m 15 Sept 1866 by Thos A. Montgomery, J. P.

Henry Ingraham (col) & Abby Christmas m 26 Aug 1866 by L. C. Perkinson, M. G.

Thomas Mayfield (col) & Rhoda Wright m 16 Sept 1866 by L. C. Perkinson, M. G.

Erasmus Hawks (col) & Lucy Stewart m 1 July 1866 by L. C. Perkinson, M. G.

Waller Henry(?) (col) & Manerva Felts m 1 July 1866 by L. C. Perkinson, M. G.

Stephen Tannahill (col) & Nancy Felts m 1 July 1866 by L. C. Perkinson, M. G.

Rufus Davis (col) & Ella Mayfield m 16 Sept 1866 by L. C. Perkinson, M. G.

Remus Robinson (col) & Elizabeth Boyd m 19 Aug 1866 by L. C. Perkinson, M. G.

Henry Hubbard (col) & Marinda Lester m 9 Aug 1866 by L. C. Perkinson, M. G.

Oscar Clements (col) & Cornelia Alston m 15 Sept 1866 by J. Buxton Williams, J. P.

Haywood Dowtin (col) & Mary Brown m 6 Oct 1866 Saml Bobbitt, J. P.

Timothy Watkins (col) & Panthea Hendrick m 26 Sept 1866 by R. D. Paschall, J. P.

Henry Boyd (col) & Betsy Ann Collins m 7 Oct 1866 by W. W. White, J. P.

Joseph Judkins (col) & Mary Boyd m 21 Oct 1866 by James C. Robinson, J. P.

WARREN COUNTY MARRIAGES

George Williams & Vensey Wade m 27 Oct 1866 by N. A. Purefoy, M. G.

Wesley Hargrove (col) & Martha Plummer m 20 Oct 1866 by W. W. White, J. P.

Solomon W. Kearney (col) & Amy Newsom m 31 Oct 1866 by William Wallace White, J. P.

Harry Browne & Hannah Browne m 10 Nov 1866 by Saml Bobbitt, J. P.

Jerry Browne (col) & Judah Sutton m 20 Nov 1866 by N. A. Purefoy, M. G.

Washington Bobbitt (col) & Nancy Browne m 24 Nov 1866 by Samuel Bobbitt, J. P.

Charles Desborn (col) & Letitia Kearney m 24 Sept 1866 by John S. Cheek, J. P.

Isham Davis (col) & Rebecca Hooper m 14 Oct 1866 by C. M. Cook, J. P.

Littleton Williams (col) & Mollie Skinner m 22 Nov 1866 by Thomas J. Pitchford, J. P.

Norvel Lynes (col) & Sally Birchett m 12 Dec 1866 by Thomas P. Paschall, J. P.

James Bricket (col) & Martha Burnett m 2 Dec 1866 by C. M. Cook, J. P.

Burney Walker (col) & Isabella Bolton m 19 Dec 1866 by James T. Russell, J. P.

John Branch & Harriet Williams m 15 Nov 1866 by Wm. H. Bishop, M. G.

Harry Falkner (col) & Jane Boyd m 16 Dec 1866 by L. C. Perkinson, M. G.

Solomon Talley (col) & Evaline Jefferson m 25 Nov 1866 by L. C. Perkinson, M. G.

Simon Mayfield (col) & Martha Bellemy m 23 Dec 1866 by L. C. Perkinson, M. G.

Abram Ingram (col) & Julia Read m 21 Dec 1866 by Jno Watson, J. P.

William Brame (col) & Chaney Ellis m 25 Dec 1866 by J. M. Brame, J. P.

Lewis Tucker (col) & Amy Pritchard m 27 Dec 1866 by J. M. Brame, J. P.

Jerry Foote (col) & Maria Goode m 26 Dec 1866 by J. M. Brame, J. P.

Washington Christmas (col) & Emily Drake m 29 Dec 1866 by T. Reynolds, J. P.

Jerry Minge (col) & Maria Williams m 29 Dec 1366 by Saml Bobbitt, J. P.

Oscar Henderson & Lizzie Bullock m 31 Dec 1866 by Wm. Wallace White, J. P.

Joshua Henderson (col) & Sarah Sims m 17 Nov 1866 by Wm Wallace White, J. P.

Cyrus Burgess (col) & Nancy Williams m 28 Dec 1866 b M. P. Perry, J. P.

Stephen Williams (col) & Sallie Alston m 2 Jan 1866 by M. P. Perry, J. P.

Stephenson Ransom (col) & George Anna Southerland m 1 Jan 1867 by A. L. Steed, J. P.

Henry Wortham (col) & Lizzie Thrower m 21 Dec 1866 by A. L. Steed, J. P.

Richard Johnston (col) & Ann Johnston m 21 Dec 1866 by Thomas Paschall, J. P.

Samuel Carroll (col) & Mary(?) Paschall m 28 Dec 1866 by Thomas P. Paschall, J. P.

Lewis Love (col) & Fanny Mabry m 26 Dec 1866 by Thos P. Paschall, J. P.

Arthur Williams (col) & Malinda Cawthorne m 16 Jan 1867 by William Hodges, M. G.

Solomon Turner (col) & Catherine Baker m 8 Jan 1867 by Wm. Hodges, M. G.

Armstead Williams (col) & Martha Alston m 1 Jan 1867 by J. Buxton Williams, J. P.

Nelson Alston (col) & Lucinda Alston m 4 Jan 1867 by J. Buxton Williams, J. P.

Henry Williams (col) & Delia Carr m 26 Dec 1866 by J. Buxton Williams, J. P.

Andrew Williams (col) & Manning Williams m 26 Dec 1866 by J. Buxton Williams.

Allen Perry (col) & Manna Williams m 26 Dec 1866 by J. Buxton Williams, J. P.

Adam Alston (col) & Patsey Alston m 18 Jan 1867 by J. Buxton Williams, J. P.

Beckam Paschall (col) & Ann Carroll m 26 Dec 1866 by R. D. Paschall, J. P.

Jas A. T. Carroll (col) & Mariah Jefferson m 19 Jan 1867 by R. D. Paschall, J. P.

Henry Jones (col) & Olivia Edwards m 28 Dec 1866 by James T. Russell, J. P.

Anderson Russell (col) & Silvia Russell m 28 Dec 1866 by James T. Russell, J. P.

Terry Alexander (col) & Jinney Jefferson m 22 Dec 1866 by James T. Russell, J. P.

Matthew Somerville (col) & Dorsey Crosson (col) m 26 Jan 1867 by S. M. Browne, J. P.

Rhoden Alston (col) & Judah Williams m 2 Feb 1867 by J. Buxton Williams, J. P.

James Volentine (col) & Nancy Catherine Overby m 14 Feb 1867 by J. P. Moore, M. G.

Sandy Powell (col) & Mary Jane Williams m 22 Dec 1866 by John S. Cheek, J. P.

John Cheek (col) & Chery Alston m 2 Feb 1867 by John S. Cheek, J. P.

Edward Falkner (col) & Lizzie Hawkins m 17 Feb 1867 by L. C. Perkinson, M. G.

Peter Howard (col) & Peggy L___ m 2 Feb 1867 by L. C. Perkinson, M. G.

Jacob Johnson (col) & Sarah Carroll m 23 Feb 1867 by R. D. Paschall, J. P.

Peter Hayes (col) & Louisanna Alston m 21 Feb 1867 by William Hodges, M. G.

John Dixon (col) & Inez Browne m 25 Dec 1867 by Ridley Browne, J. P.

Israel Patillo (col) & Violet Jones m 31 Dec 1866 by Jno W. Patillo, J. P.

Solomon Somerville (col) & Louisa Cawthorne m 20 Feb 1867 by Wm Hodges, M. G.

Robert Person (col) & Malinda Tillman m 31 Dec 1866 by R. S. F. Peete, J. P.

Lewis Hunt (col) & Rhoda Thornton m 31 Dec 1866 by R. S. F. Peete, J. P.

Howard Browne (Col) & Letitia Thornton m 29 Dec ___ by R. S. F. Peete, J. P.

Robert Palmer (col) & Jinsey Ann Algood m 27 Dec 1866 by R. S. F. Peete, J. P.

Silas Williams (col) & Eliza Henry Alston m 22 Feb 1867 by J. Buxton Williams, J. P.

Brister Alston (col) & Susan Alston m 9 Mar 1867 by Wm. Hodges, M. G.

Allen Davis (col) & Eliza Ann Shearin m 10 Feb 1867 by J. M. Brame, J. P.

Robert Artist (col) & Louisa Williams m 27 Feb 1867 by John W. Riggan, J. P.

Alfred Cawthorne (col) & Mariah Williams m 19 Mar 1867 by Wm. Hodges, M. G.

Dennis Johnston (col) & Mary Cheek m 2 Mar 1867 by A. S. Cheek, J. P.

Micajah Skinner (col) & Ann Shearin m 28 Mar 1867 by Wm. Hodges, M. G.

Gabriel Jones (col) & Fanny Wilson m 9 Mar 1867 by Rev. Wm. A. Brame.

Joseph Alston (col) & Pleasant Williams m 15 Feb 1867 by J. Buxton Williams.

_____ & Maggie Daniel (col) & R. Browne, J. P.

Wm. Kenny Myrick (col) & Lizzie Williams m 26 Jan 1866 by Thos A. Pitchford, J. P.

Parker Bullock (col) & Charlotte Hargrove m 30 Dec 1866 by L. Henderson, J. P.

George Walker (col) & Isabella Hargrove m 1 Feb 1867 by L. Henderson, J. P.

___rge Harvey (col) & Sarah James m 3 Apr 1867 by Wm Wallace White, J. P.

John L. Plummer (col) & Ara Burrell m 18 Nov 1865 by L. Henderson, J. P.

Eaton Alston (col) & Sally Ann Williams m 12 Mar 1867 by J. Buxton Williams, J. P.

Cyrus Milam & Sally James m 21 Apr 1867 by N. A. Purefoy, M. G.

Allen Davis (col) & Eliza Ann _____ m 10 Feb 1867 by J. M. Brame, J. P.

Henry Blanch (col) & Della Milam m 20 Apr 1867 by N. A. Purefoy, J. P.

William Somerville (col) & Indianna Hill m 20 Apr 1867 by William Hodges, M. G.

Hinton Jordan (col) & Martha Steel m 6 Apr 1867 by A. L. Steed, J. P.

Daniel Hawkins (col) & Fanny Steed m 28 Apr 1867 by A. L. Steed, J. P.

Robert Williams (col) & Dorothy Williams m 18 May 1867 by Thos J. Pitchford, J. P.

William Cheek (col) & Sarah Davis m 14 May 1866 by Thos J. Pitchford, J. P.

Anderson Powell (col) & Esther Powell m 14 Apr 1867 by Thos J. Pitchford, J. P.

Nathan Richardson (col) & Martha Birchett at John Birchett's on 21 May 1867 by Thos P. Paschall, J. P.

Peter Perkinson (col) & Rebecca Palmer m 26 Dec 1866 by L. C. Perkinson, M. G.

Abner Duke (col) & Margaret Jackson m 19 May 1867 by L. C. Perkinson, M. G.

Anthony Jiggetts (col) & Frances Hunt m 12 May 1867 by L. C. Perkinson, M. G.

Pompey Robertson (col) & Nancy Richardson m 9 May 1867.

Buckner Alston (col) & Lucy Clements m 18 Oct 1867 by John S. Cheek, J. P.

William Plummer (col) & Catherine Bowser m 14 July 1866 by T. B. Kingsbury, M. G.

_____ (col) & Isabella Price m 3 July 1867 by T. B. Kingsbury, M. G.

Thomas Green (col) & Jacobine Vaughan m 26 Dec 1865 by T. B. Kingsbury, M. G.

James Alston (col) & Louisa Burgess m 7 Apr 1867 by M. P. Perry, J. P.

James Turner (col) & Rachel Hicks m 25 Aug 1867 by R. D. Paschall, J. P.

Benjamin Williams (col) & Charity Cheek m 8 Apr 1867 by M. P. Perry, J. P.

William Woodward (col) & Lucy Ann Richardson m 14 Apr 1867 at Nancy Richardson's
by M. P. Perry, J. P.

June Alston (col) & Julia Burgess m 7 Apr 1867 by M. P. Perry, J. P.

Joseph Kearney (col) & Frances Jones m 28 Aug 1867 by John S. Cheek, J. P.

Duncan _____ (col) & Dolly Kerney m 31 Aug 1867 by John J. Cheek, J. P.

Anderson Kearney (col) & Ellen Williams m 2 Sept 1867 by John S. Cheek, J. P.

John Robertson (col) & Susan Syrus m 28 Feb 1867 by Revd. Dick Alston.

John H. Finch & Miss A. Johnson m 5 Jan 1864 by P. H. Joyner, M. G.

_____ & Rosa Edwards m 16 Aug 1864 by P. H. Joyner, M. G.

George O. Clark & Emaline W. Falkener m 19 Dec 1865 by P. H. Joyner, M. G.

Jordan Pendergrass & Mary Jane Coley m 24 Nov 1865 by P. H. Joyner, M. G.

Wm Pendergrass & Sarah Pendergrass m 10 Dec 1865 by P. H. Joyner, M. G.

___ Brosius & Maggie J. Norfleet m 21 Sept 1865 by P. H. Joyner, M. G.

Wm Filps & Emily Rudd m 28 Nov 1866 by P. H Joyner, M. G.

Richd L. Tapps & Christianna E. Ellington m 27 Dec 1866 by P. H. Joyner, M. G.

Jacob Stamper (Col) & Julia Brame m 2 Mar 1867 by P. H. Joyner, M. G.

_____ Hoyles & Mary K. Wright m __ Dec 1866 by P. H. Joyner, M. G.

J. G. E. Edwards & Darien Alley m 11 Dec 1866 by P. H. Joyner, M. G.

Thomas M. Evans & Martha Hicks m 3 Jan 1867 by P. H. Joyner, M. G.

Charles E. Ivey & Sarah L. Harris m 26 May 1867 by P. H. Joyner, M. G.

Armistead Bram_ (col) & ___ Cheek m 30 Mar 186_ by P. H. Joyner, M. G.

Lewis Allen (col) & Luvenia Champion m 6 June 1867 by P. H. Joyner, M. G.

Christopher Jordan & Tempey Brame m 28 Dec 1866 by P. H. Joyner, M. G.

Harvy Hayes & Lucy Pendergrass m 14 __ 1866 by P. H. Joyner, M. G.

Frank Bridgers & _____ Allen m 2 March 1867 by P. H. Joyner, M. G.

(to brides and bondsmen, p. 3-187)
(to all persons, p. 189-216)

218

Bragg, Catharine 48
Elizabeth W. 186
Jane King 108
Joel P. 43
Sarah 136
Thomas 43, 110, 155
W. N. 36, 199
William 25
Bram--, Armistead 216
Brame, Anderson F. 151
Elbert 184, 191
Elizabeth 138
Emily 117, 195
Indiana T. 194
Indianah F. 22
J. M. 25, 34, 45, 63,
128, 142, 148, 156,
167, 210, 211, 213,
215
James 161
John J. 117
John M. 115
Julia 157, 216
Martha 157, 192
Nancy 75
Nelson 197
Rebecca 103, 203
Sally 76
Tempey 94, 216
W. A. 52, 92, 207
William 213
William A. 198, 215
Branch, Arilla 165
Caroline 165
Charles 165
John 213
Washington 163
Brandom, Thomas 26
Brannum, Peggy 65
Branscomb, Zachariah 95
Brantley, Pamelia 185
Breedlove, Clarasa 185
Francis 93
Malissa Ann 41, 211
N. H. 38
Peggy 182
Breen, Nancy 33
Brehon, George 26
Mariah 26
Rebecca 43, 195
Brewer, Allen 37
Betsey 37
Elizabeth 127
Mary 159
Pattey 32
Reps 3
Sally 25
Brick, William W. 106
Brickell, Mary 35
Matilda R. 182
N. D. 17
Nat 198
Nathaniel 182
Nathaniel D. 50
Bricket, James 213
Brickle, Nathaniel D.
124
Sarah E. 86, 206
Bridgers, Frank 216
J. S. 118
James S. 48, 128
Bridges, Patience 4
William 3
Brinkle, Mary 16
Brinkley, Betsy 4
Mary L. 137, 198

Brinkley, Sally 44
Brintle, Amey 88
Dicey 133
Mary 88
Brodie, Amy 174
Jacob 174
Martha Ann Rebecca 95
Mary R. 12
William L. 193
Brodnax, Thomas 9
Brogdon, Elisabeth 13
Brooks, Elizabeth 30,
158
Mary 32
William S. 199
William T. 63
Brosius, --- 216
Brown, Ann 75
Anne 5
Archabald 53
Archibald 19, 28, 38,
107, 116, 154
Catharine 84
Eliza 118
Elizabeth 4, 74, 194
H. T. 113
Hicksey 18
Jacob 206
James T. 139
Jeremiah 46
John 4, 54, 111
John E. 55, 191
Julius S. 205
Lucy 21, 167
Margaret 186
Martha 140, 191
Nancy 23
Nathaniel 18, 28
Polley 18, 121, 151
R. 14, 202, 204
R. F. 198
Rebecca F. 163, 202
Ridley 37, 202
Solomon 165
Susan 9
William 35, 84, 130,
185
William E. 27
Brownaskie, Joseph 192
Browne, Hannah 27, 213
Harry 213
Henrietta 92
Howard 214
Inez 48, 214
James T. 136
Jerry 213
John C. 174
John E. 149
Lucinda 116
Lucy F. 53, 203
Mary 49
Nancy 213
Phillis 80
R. 166, 215
Ridley 14, 34, 48, 60,
80, 92, 100, 102,
103, 138, 139, 147,
157, 206, 211, 212,
214
Rosa 80
S. M. 214
Sally 80
Sherrod 80
Vesuvia 59
Browning, B. R. 40, 98
Benjamin R. 59

Browning, James W. 193
L. D. 28
Lewis D. 198
R. 28
W. H. 28
Brownlow, Tippee 93
Tippoo 83, 110, 181,
183
Tippoo S. 161
Brubank, Sarah 185
Bryan, Penelope W. 71
Bryant, James 4
Bubhanan, Sarah P. 168
Buchanan, Elizabeth 166
Louiza J. 201
M. S. 210
Buchannon, Nancy A. O.
125
Bugg, Mary A. 60
Bull, Rebecca 72
Bullock, Agness 71
Ancil 212
Ann 82
Ann H. 44
Annie B. 163, 193
Catharine 152
Catharine L. 162
Elizabeth Ann 68, 193
Francis L. 67
Isabella B. 29, 211
J. H. 57, 140, 147,
170, 191
J. J. 142
John H. 50, 95, 136,
147, 191, 192, 194,
195, 207, 211
Len H. 160
Lizzie 82, 213
Parker 215
Richard A. 211
Susanna 46, 209
Bunchett, John L. 198
Burcher, Betsy R. 197
Margaret 52
Burchett, Daniel 21,
29, 32
Edward 70, 124
Elizabeth 70
John L. 142
Minerva 153
Sarah 124
Burchette, Betsey R. 83
Elizabeth 95
John 57
Burchitt, Daniel 16
James 123
Maryann 123
Burckett, Daniel 125
Burford, Mary 71
Mildred 5
Phil. 5
Burges, John 139
Pattie A. 14
Sally 193
Thomas L. 193
Burgess, Albert 47
Cyrus 213
E. Matilda 127, 203
Hagar 47
James 56
Jane 47
John 9, 112, 191
Julia 12, 216
Louisa 12, 216
Lucy 112, 191
Mary B. 152

223

Crutchfield, Amey 75
  Betsey 84
  Charles 116
  Mary T. 135
Cullum, Priscilla 88
Cuningham, Joice 169
  Mary 163
Cunnignham, John W. 203
Cunningham, Anne 126
  Elizabeth 33, 101
  John 43
  Leoa 108
  Parthena H. 53
  Willis 33
Cupples, Charles 3
Currier, Addie B. 138,
  210
Curry, Alex 209
Curtis, Churchwell 117
  Elizabeth 64
  George 52
Cypress, Thursy 106
Cyprous, Mary 87
Cyprus, Ebenezer 58
  Eilza 159
Cyrus, F. W. 92
  Nancy 92

--- D ---

Daiel, Harriet W. 16
Daly, Caroline 111
  Daniel E. 177
  Mary E. 159
Damiel, James M. 95
Dancy, David 62, 90,
  152
Daniel, C. G. 62
  Charlotte 149
  Elisabeth 117, 153
  Emily A. 157
  Frances 154
  Harrall 197
  J. J. 53
  James 26
  James M. 44, 74, 88,
  157
  James R. 66, 211
  John 113
  Joice Ann 95
  Joseph T. 108
  Maggie 102, 215
  Mary 26
  Nancy 113
  Richard 155
  Roxana 74
  Sarah A. C. 88
  Thomas 94, 154
  William W. 84, 144
Darden, Amy 79
  Martha 76
Darker, George M. 70
Darnal, John 112
Darnald, Dwelley 31
  Henrietta 154
  John 183
  Lewsey 183
  Poly 154
Darnall, Ann M. E. 168
  James 125
  Joseph 86
Darnel, Sarah 24
Darnell, B. M. 60
  Benjamin W. 204

Darnell, Emily A. 178
  Harriet 146
  Henry J. 211
  John 67
  Nancy 40
  Priscilla 158
  William 101
Darnol, Jeaney 44
  John 24, 97, 154
Darnold, Develly 196
  Elizabeth 99
  James Wesley 206
  William 45
Darnoll, Fanny 60
Darrell, Martha 97
Darroll, Ellen 212
Daves, Isham H. 91
David, --- H. 203
Davidson, A. F. 155,
  206
Davies, Holly B. 162
Davis, --- 31
  A. H. 30, 46, 82
  Ailsey 189
  Alfred 64, 168
  Allen 215
  Amanda C. 185, 192
  Angeline 161
  Ann E. 121
  Annaca 94
  Anthony 121
  Archibald H. 157, 209
  Arthur 15
  Austin 190
  B. 18, 36, 102, 119,
  141, 179, 181
  Benjamin 172, 199
  Benjamin P. 60
  Betsey 131
  Buckner 60
  Burwell P. 210
  Caroline 70
  Charity 94
  Charles 33, 45
  Cherry 46
  Dempcey Alston 46
  Dioclesian 4
  Dionitia 113
  Edward 96
  Eliza 76, 161, 190
  Elizabeth 96
  Elizabeth C. 37
  Ellick 209
  Frances 45
  George W. 46, 137
  Hanah 97
  Harry 189
  Henreitta 33
  Henry 189
  Isham 213
  Isham H. 45, 75, 108,
  112, 117, 131, 157
  Jacob 70, 109, 159
  James A. 199
  Jane 134
  John 37, 72
  John A. 149
  Joshua 31, 64, 67
  Lisbon 161
  Louisa 179, 212
  Lucy 46, 108
  Lucy Ann 40
  Margaret 133
  Mariah 152
  Martha 23, 85, 133,
  189

Davis, Mary 75, 85,
  109, 189, 191, 202
  Mary A. 127, 204
  Mary H. 106
  Mary J. 53
  Mary S. 84
  Mary T. 145
  Nancey 133
  Nancy 61, 98, 134
  Nancy D. 62
  Nannie 47
  Nelson 133
  Nicholas E. 54
  P. R. 56
  Peter R. 10, 18, 65,
  68, 77, 81, 100, 102,
  105, 109, 155, 184
  Polley 10
  Polly 94
  Quinny 62
  Rebeccah D. 91
  Rebekah A. 181
  Richard 41, 85, 107,
  151
  Richard A. 62
  Rufus 212
  S. 154
  Sabina 33
  Sallie A. 131
  Sallie E. 202
  Sally 21
  Samuel 64, 189
  Sarah 12, 37, 78, 215
  Sarah B. 56
  Shepard 190
  Silvia 70
  Stephen 43, 50, 61,
  101, 120
  Susanna 82
  Tabathy 153
  Temperance 51
  Temperance D. 120
  Tempy 189
  Thamer 157
  Thomas 51
  Thomas H. 122
  Thomas T. 78, 79
  Weldon E. 45, 88, 173
  William 31, 130
  William Macklin 94
  William S. 46, 206
  William W. 24, 98
  Winefred P. 96
Davison, Richard 68,
  84, 180
Dawsey, Polley 178
Dawson, Henry 74
  Polly 141
Dawtin, Anthony 178
  Martha Ann 23
Dawton, John 11
Day, Caty 68
  Rebecca 171
  Robert 95
  Robert J. 25
Deaderick, J. F. 47
  Rebecca L. 47
Dean, Lucy 159
Delbridge, John A. 197
Deloney, Susan J. 122
Denkins, Mary 154
Denson, William 130
Dent, Elisabeth 85
  Susannah 58
Derby, Minerva 106
Derham, Susannah 91

Desborn, Charles 213
Desch, Elizabeth 151
Dickens, Mary 31
  Rebecca 110
Dickerson, Chasteen 196
  Delia 54
  Fereby 14
  Griffin 54
  Isham 48
  Isham W. 202
  J. M. 128
  Mary Eliza 141, 206
  William 25
  William A. 209
Dickins, John 31
  Kelly 48
Dickoson, Charlottee 53
  Young 141
Dignall, Peggy W. 61
Dinckins, Polly 39
Dinkins, Dinatious 19
  Martha 95
  Rebecca 60
Divaney, Jenkins 43
Dixon, Charles 146
  John 214
Dlanton, Susan 27
Dobbin, Sally 23
Dobbins, Eliza 89
  Elizabeth D. 27, 191
  Jane 186
Dodson, Holley 71
Doles, Henry T. 131
Dorden, George 30
Dortch, Fanny 186
  Mariah 170
  Sally 134
  William A. 169, 195
Douglass, Mildred 144
  Richardson 50
Dowden, Anthony 146
  Elizabeth 22
  Lucy 78
Dowell, Suckey 155
Dowland, Darkes 32
  Suasan 125
Dowlen, Elizabeth 9
  Nancy 107
Dowlin, Martha 60
  Mary 162
  Polly 60
  Samuel W. 211
  Sarah H. 193
Dowling, Elizabeth 62
  John 137
Downey, James W. 50
Dowten, Mariah 157
  Winnifred 171
Dowtin, Anthoney 9
  Anthony 77, 78, 87,
    101, 112
  Catharine 183
  David D. W. 76, 183
  David W. 91, 170
  Elizabeth 157
  Francis 165
  Hannah 49, 208
  Haywood 212
  Mary 90, 165
  Nancy 120
  Phillis 171
  Richard 208
  S. W. 209
  Sally 46, 103
  Samuel W. 44, 100,
    103, 181, 206

Dowtin, Sarah H. 111
  W. A. 15, 20, 68, 71,
    73, 99, 103, 116,
    127, 192, 201, 203,
    204
  William A. 20, 32, 91,
    116, 196, 198, 199,
    200
Dowton, Anthony 22
Doyal, Warwick 110
Drake, --- 20
  C. 9, 10, 11, 12, 14,
    16, 18, 20, 23, 24,
    25, 26, 27, 29, 31,
    32, 33, 34, 38, 39,
    40, 41, 45, 46, 47,
    50, 51, 56, 57, 58,
    60, 62, 63, 64, 65,
    67, 69, 71, 72, 73,
    74, 75, 76, 77, 79,
    80, 81, 84, 87, 90,
    92, 93, 94, 96, 97,
    98, 99, 100, 104,
    106, 107, 110, 111,
    112, 113, 114, 116,
    118, 119, 120, 122,
    123, 124, 127, 129,
    130, 131, 132, 134,
    136, 137, 138, 139,
    140, 141, 143, 146,
    147, 148, 152, 153,
    155, 156, 158, 161,
    162, 163, 164, 168,
    170, 171, 172, 173,
    174, 177, 180, 181,
    183, 184, 185, 186
  Cas. 13, 15, 21, 22,
    24, 26, 28, 29, 30,
    31, 45, 54, 58, 60,
    63, 65, 67, 74, 77,
    94, 99, 101, 106,
    107, 111, 115, 118,
    123, 125, 127, 128,
    132, 134, 139, 144,
    145, 151, 154, 156,
    157, 159, 161, 164,
    165, 167, 169, 170,
    177, 178, 185
  Caswell 53, 65, 96,
    117, 118, 125, 167,
    183, 184, 191, 192,
    194
  E. C. 156
  E. D. 10-19, 26-28,
    30, 31, 34, 36, 40,
    42, 44, 45, 46, 50,
    53-56, 59-63, 65, 66,
    67, 71, 72, 73, 75,
    76, 80, 82-85, 88,
    90, 93, 95, 96,
    98-103, 105, 108,
    110-113, 115-119,
    124-127, 129, 132,
    138-145, 147, 149,
    152, 154-159, 161,
    162, 166, 168, 171,
    174, 175, 176, 179,
    180-184, 186
  Edwin D. 13, 24, 30,
    36, 38, 39, 65, 68,
    95, 97, 98, 99, 104,
    105, 107, 118, 123,
    124, 140, 159, 163,
    181, 182
  Elizabeth 3
  Emily 37, 213

Drake, Henry 165
  John O. 49, 109
  Joseph A. 77, 105,
    126, 127, 175
  Joseph E. 50, 137
  M. D. 93
  M. M. 6, 10, 11, 13,
    14, 15, 20, 23, 24,
    25, 28, 30, 31, 34,
    36, 40, 42, 44, 47,
    48, 52, 54, 55, 60,
    63, 64, 65, 68, 69,
    71, 72, 73, 74, 75,
    78, 81, 83, 86, 87,
    89, 90, 91, 95, 96,
    97, 99, 100, 101,
    104, 106, 107, 108,
    111, 112, 113, 116,
    117, 119, 122, 123,
    126, 127, 128, 129,
    131, 135, 137, 138,
    139, 141, 142, 148,
    149, 150, 152, 154,
    155, 157, 159, 162,
    163, 169, 170, 171,
    173, 174, 175, 176,
    178, 179, 182, 186,
    191, 193, 195, 199
  M. W. 145
  Mary A. 143
  Matthew M. 25, 47, 61,
    62, 89, 102, 110,
    158, 160
  Sallie D. 169
  Sally 26
  Sally D. 206
  Sarah 192
  W. C. 195
  William C. 121
Drew, Alexander 95
  Ann 89
  Anna 147
  Casiah 159
  Daisy 76
  Elizabeth 89
  Hardaway 69
  John 89, 95, 207
  Mary 109
  Parthena 26
  Richard 105
  Stanfield 159
Drewery, Charles 48
Drewry, Patsey 156
  Robert W. 205
Drinkwater, John 69
Dromgoole, E. 107
Drue, Hardaway 109
  Sarah 29
Drummons, Rebecca 103
Drumright, E. A. 147
Drumwright, Ester W.
  170
  Esther W. 194
Drury, Charles 38, 39,
    50, 59, 180
Due, Avery 117
Duffey, Polley 153
Dugger, E. H. 163
  Edrick H. 70, 93
  Ezra 50
  John E. 132
Duglas, Catharine 105
Duglass, Frances 105
Duke, A. E. 62, 211
  A. P. 211
  Abigal 164

226

Duke, Abner 215
  Amey 19
  Anne 97
  Anny R. 100
  Arabella G. 24
  Benjamin 51
  Bettie P. 144, 199
  Daniel 88, 122, 164
  Dorathy (Dolly) Ann 92
  Elizabeth 76, 83, 87,
    168
  Elizabeth F. 170
  Emeline M. 26
  Fanny 151
  Frances 99
  George J. 176
  George M. 51, 99, 117
  Green 37, 140, 179
  Green B. 55
  Guilford 131
  H. T. 116
  Henrietta 128, 194
  Henriter 24
  Henry T. 197
  Hester C. 50, 211
  Holley 151
  Indiana L. 66
  James L. 109
  John 4, 50
  Julia 180
  Lewis P. 172
  Lucy Ann 63, 208
  M. C. 57, 157, 200,
    206
  M. W. 139
  Mark 189
  Mark C. 46, 50, 199,
    211
  Mary 31, 90
  Mary A. 113, 207
  Mary C. 81
  Mary P. 186
  Matthew 49, 50, 136
  Melissa D. 84
  Myrick 126
  Nancy 53, 56
  Narcissa 135
  Parmelia 108
  Patsey 101
  Peyton V. 124
  Peyton Vaughan 62
  Ransom 36
  Rebecca 81, 102, 173
  Repps 18
  Richard 16, 51
  Robert W. 51
  Salley 16
  Samuel 15
  Sarah 37, 130
  Sarah J. 108
  Simon G. 51, 97, 115,
    208
  Sylvia 52
  Thomas S. 201
  Thomas V. 42
  William 99, 193
  William C. 202
Duncan, Bettie 128, 210
  Elener 160
  Gordan C. 100
  Henry 79
  Jas A. 208
  Jeane 106
  Milley 156
  Person 100
  Willie 21

Dunkin, Willie 50
Dunn, C. H. 52
  James 61, 160
  Thomas A. 194
Dunnavand, Polley 23
Dunnavant, M. N. 65
Dunnavent, Marble W. 20
Dunston, James 14
Dupriest, Malachi 15
Durham, Ann 109
  Catharine 194
  Chatharine 147
  Eliza 50, 108, 146
  Haywood 18, 80
  Jesibel 139
  Julia 50, 207
  Margarette 57, 192
  Mary 61, 139, 150
  Nancy 52, 95
  Susan 76
  Thomas 195
  William 4, 146
Durom, Benjamin 65
Duty, Elby 122
  Mary E. 117, 198
Dye, Catey 109
  Martin 26, 109, 160
  Polly 88

--- E ---

Eagles, Edward 12, 93
Earles, Nancy 106
  Sally 44
Earls, Elizabeth M. 44
  George W. 192
  Thomas 53
Eaton, Adam 53
  B. 26, 27, 28, 93, 95,
    110, 136, 139, 149,
    191, 192, 193, 195,
    196, 198
  Bettie M. 168, 210
  Buckner 197
  Catherine A. 53
  Elizabeth M. K. 60
  Elizabeth W. 59
  Ella R. 48
  Ezekiel 166
  Harriot B. 60
  Jane 178
  John 123
  Laura 12, 191
  Mary 51
  Mary H. 58
  Matthew 51
  Samuel W. 203
  Sue 14, 200
  Temperance B. 11
  William 53, 200
Edgerton, Nancy 60
Edington, Eliz M. 205
Edmonds, Anne 53
  Hariot 99
  James 53
  Jane 113
  William 20
Edmonson, Cs. R. 120
Edmunds, Sterling H. 99
  Thomas 54, 173
Edmundson, Sarah Jane
    38
Edwards, Ann Eliza 183
  Eliza 71

Edwards, Gideon V. 54
  J. G. E. 216
  James 33, 65, 128
  Jemima 176
  John 26, 76, 141, 210
  Lewis P. 82
  Lucy 4
  Mary 155
  Nancy 41, 78
  Olivia 92, 214
  Rebecca 54
  Rebecca A. 34
  Richard 198
  Rosa 59, 216
  Rose Ann 156
  Sally 50
  Sally Ann 54
  Samuel 21, 82, 132,
    155, 157
  Thomas 58, 164
  Weldon 92
  William 54
  William E. 196
  William J. 65, 114,
    205
  William M. 65
  Zedikiah 135
Edwin, William 166
Egerton, B. J. 47
  Caroline 133
  Elizabeth N. 138
  Gilbert G. 28
  Gilbert Grey 55
  Henry T. 134, 142, 210
  James 55
  James A. 14, 55, 110,
    151, 157, 158, 163
  Jas A. 209
  John 27, 31, 60, 73,
    77, 105, 149
  John J. 74, 75
  Joseph 152
  Martha 28, 110
  Mary D. 143
  Salley 77
  Sarah 74
  Sarah N. W. 78
  Sarah W. 196
  Thomas M. 194, 211
  William H. 148
  Wilmut E. 89
Elam, A. G. 66
Elams, Charles 86
Elenton, Christanner
  Elizabeth 166
Ellenton, Elisabeth 160
Ellergy, --- 200
Ellery, Esther S. 68
Elleton, Nancey 183
  Patsey 44
Ellice, Tabitha 160
Ellington, Amey 97
  Bird 117
  Christianna E. 216
  Edward M. 193
  Elizabeth 58, 116
  Elizabeth M. 179
  Frances 121, 200
  Frances R. 124, 209
  James 21, 55, 58
  John 17, 28
  Lewsey 56
  Martha P. 75
  Martha T. 203
  Parthenia G. 58
  Permealea 28

227

Ellington, Pleasant 166
  Sally 140
  Thomas 56
  William 35
Ellinton, Elijah 55
  James 55, 56
Elliott, William 5
Ellis, A. D. 56
  Abigal 9
  Andrew J. 92
  Angess 153
  Benjamin 166
  Betsey 20, 57
  Betsy 93
  Cealia 149
  Chaney 213
  Chany 25
  Cresey 57
  Ephraim 45
  Francis J. 47
  James 81
  Jane 153
  John 57, 170
  Lewis 148
  Louisa 56
  Lucy 19, 63
  Martha 160
  Milley 90
  Nancy 123, 153, 154,
    175
  Nelly 148
  Obediah 17
  Polley 166
  Priscilla 22
  Rebeca 61
  Richard 57, 85, 166
  Sally 128, 129
  Sarah 43
  Stephen 33, 63
  Susanah 110
  Susanna 184
  Thomas 129
  William 9, 160
  Zachariah 81
Ellms, Winnefret 172
Elloms, Charles 27
Ellums, Charles 106
Ellyson, H. Theodore 62
Elton, Elizabeth 155
Emberson, Sally 142
Emerson, John 4
Emmerson, James 32
Epps, Rebecca 138
Estes, John 69
  Silvey 102
  Susanah 177
Ethrage, Wilson W. 195
Evans, --- 203
  Bowlin 192
  Bowling 147
  Caroline 152
  Celia 165
  Eliza 58, 92
  Elizabeth 68, 77, 192,
    200
  Emily 158
  Fanny 67
  Griffin 108, 130
  Harriett 108
  Isaac 105
  James 57
  Jane 165
  John 192, 200
  John L. 74, 78, 99
  John W. R. 36
  Joseph 69, 76

Evans, Joseph John 58
  Lucy 58, 104
  Lucy W. 87
  Mary 42, 149
  Mary G. 26
  Mary Jane 141
  Miles 194
  Nancy 102, 164
  Noah 75
  Ollive 52
  Patience 107
  Peter 58
  Peter J. 58
  Polley 85
  Richard 108, 144
  Salley 159
  Sally 75, 166, 193
  Susanah 159
  Thomas 58
  Thomas M. 216
  Thomas W. 197
  William 13
Everitt, Simon B. 31
Evins, Mourning 41
Exum, William J. 195
Ezard, Nancy 67
Ezell, J. W. 170
  R. A. 42, 105
  Sarah 174
Ezely, Nancy 189

--- F ---

Fa---, Eliza C. 199
Fain, Charles 207
  Daniel 57, 114
  James 113
  Joel 102
  Mary 102
  Polly 136
  Tyre 153
Falcon, John 172
Falconer, Alexander 89
  Alexander H. 141, 156
Falkener, Augusta 189
  Benjamin 175
  Elizabeth 182
  Emaline W. 216
  Harden 142
  Miranda 14
  Sallie 80, 199
  Sarah 175
  Sarah D. 132
  Sterling 108
  W. A. 115
  W. A. K. 13, 21, 22,
    33, 38, 44, 46, 59,
    60, 83, 111, 112,
    130, 142, 144, 150,
    153, 173
  William 83, 130, 144
  William A. K. 26, 135
Falkner, Edward 214
  Eliza 141
  Ford 54, 145
  Harry 213
  John 199
  Martha A. 145, 195
  Mary 65
  Matilda 209
  Rebecca 126, 140
  Rufus H. 140
  Sarah 161
Falkoner, Martha W. 59

Fane, Polly 184
Fann, Jesse 59
  Molley 118
  Nancy 43
  W. 20
Farrar, Cloye 161
  John H. 74
Farrer, Mariah E. 121,
    193
Farris, C. M. 42, 133
Farrow, John H. 145
Faulcon, Elizabeth 128
  Martha 172
  Mary A. 28
  Nicey 178
  Richard 212
  Thomas 178
Faulkener, Hardy 48
Faulkner, John G. 209
  Lucy 52, 194
  Neverson 38
  Temperance 16
Featherston, John 126
Feild, Arabella 189
  Bettie M. 85
  Betty M. 209
  Eugenia L. 67, 210
Felkener, W. A. K. 132
Felse, Ransom 46
Felts, Alpheus Ann 77
  Barnet L. 127
  Benjamin 141
  Eliza 210
  Eliza B. 66
  Elizabeth 111
  Hardy 60
  Harriet 163
  Henry 61
  Isham 40
  James 102, 103, 211
  John R. 193
  Kinchen 60
  Manerva 212
  Martha 142
  Martha J. 20, 199
  Mary 82
  Nancy 24, 195, 212
  Nathaniel 61
  Randolph 60, 82
  Rebecca 45
  Rowland 71, 73
  Tilmon 45, 108
  William 60, 85
  William H. 45
Fennell, Angelina 93
Ferrell, Littleton 41
  Thomas 64
Field, Sallie Jones
    103, 192
Filps, William 216
Finch, Elizabeth 39,
    172
  George 88
  Ira 167
  John H. 216
  R. F. 203
  Tabby 126
Findley, Mary 185
Finley, J. R. 61, 88,
    121, 207, 208
  Sophie G. 208
  Sophie George 121
Fisher, Harriet 46
  John W. 139
Fitts, Ann E. 146
  C. D. 97

228

229

Gill, Philip P. 199
Samuel 194
Sarah E. 124, 209
Gills, S. B. 57
Given, Rebeccah 18
Glen, James 24
Gloster, Sally 26
Thomas B. 133, 168
Glover, Charles 66
Darnel 105
G. F. 96
Granderson F. 195
Mary 163
Rebecah 146
Rebecca 140
Richard 66
Gober, John 99
Goddin, N. A. H. 80,
131
Godfrey, Elizabeth 122
Sally 122
Golson, Permelia P. 171
Permilia P. 204
Good, Elizabeth 112
Mary 110
Nancy 15
Goode, Eliza C. 151
Maria 213
Mariah 63
Gooden, Mary Frances
178
Goodloe, H. G. 69, 106,
117, 143
Henry G. 93, 148, 153
James K. 86
John 87
Lewis D. 178
Goodman, Jincy 146
Goodmon, Thomas 203
Goodrich, Elisabeth 86
Matthews 70
Goodrum, Emeline 68
Ned 68
Phillis 68
Goodson, James 207
Goodwin, Mary 102, 208
Wiley 135
Goosley, Morgiana M.
135
Gordan, Ann 106
Eliza 152
Randolph 20, 25
Gordin, Martha 158
Gordon, Elizabeth 10
James 65
Mary Frances 212
Tempy 86
Gosee, John 46
Nelley 46
Gossee, John 99
Gotney, Nancey 163
Graces, N. Z. 191
Grain, George 109
Grainger, Henry W. 202
Granger, Anna 43
Grant, John 52
Martha W. 92
Graves, Frances 134
N. Z. 12, 45, 49, 72,
88, 151, 162, 169,
177, 192, 196, 198,
199
Gray, Elizabeth 136,
181
Henry 58, 195
James 93, 145

Gray, Sarah 19
Wharton J. 200
Grayard, Polly 63
Green, --- 36
Allen 136, 165
Ann 47, 86, 156
Austin W. 163
Brind 136
Cornelia 89
Drucella 193
Drucilla 27
Edward 165
Elizabeth 130, 175
Elizabeth H. 191
Fannie C. 152
Frank T. 37
Gideon M. 30, 175
Henry 201
James 67, 200
Jane E. 199
Joanna 59
John C. 44, 51, 85,
102, 106, 114, 169,
193
John H. 9, 10, 11, 23,
25, 32, 38, 44, 45,
51, 54, 73, 76, 87,
90, 93, 97, 100, 103,
118, 121, 123, 126,
143, 148, 155, 160,
166, 172, 184, 185
Laura 52
Lizzie M. 82, 206
Lucretia 57
Martha 57, 93
Mary 4, 68, 106, 115,
177
Mary E. 50
Mary P. 68
Nancy 14, 53, 103, 195
Nathal T. 12
Nathaniel T. 53
Nelly 37, 212
Obed 4, 133
Patience 80
Patsey 30
Peter 3, 189
Plummer W. 178
Polly 42, 120
Priscilla 104
Prissilla 68
Rachel 115
Rebecca 174
Robert 192
S. 9, 41, 47, 49, 55,
56, 57, 59, 66, 69,
82, 100, 108, 112,
127, 156, 175
Salley 89
Sally 4, 123
Samuel 34, 205
Sarah 3, 173, 189
Sarah T. 186
Sd. 162
Sh. 119, 171
Shd. 10, 18, 19, 20,
21, 22, 24, 29, 30,
32, 34, 35, 38, 40,
48, 49, 50, 56, 57,
58, 61, 64, 65, 66,
67, 71, 72, 77, 79,
81, 86, 89, 91, 92,
95, 97, 101, 103,
105, 107, 109, 113,
114, 117, 119, 122,
123, 125, 128, 134,

Green, Shd. (cont)
135, 140, 141, 142,
144, 145, 149, 153,
155, 158, 159, 161,
165, 166, 167, 168,
172, 176, 177, 178,
180, 182, 183, 184,
185
Sher'd. 47
Sherwood 22, 30, 32,
51, 92, 93, 100, 120,
124, 125, 140, 150,
151, 160
Susan 95
Thomas 178, 216
Thomas E. 42
Thomas J. 204
Thomas Jefferson 106
Violet 126
W. 16, 23, 38, 43, 44,
46, 47, 53, 55, 61,
69, 71, 78, 100, 101,
105, 113, 117, 120,
124, 128, 130, 136,
137, 139, 141, 142,
161, 164, 169, 170,
176, 182
Will 33, 39, 46, 52,
79, 88, 101, 125,
133, 179, 185
William 9, 10, 11, 14,
15, 16, 17, 18, 19,
20, 21, 23, 26, 30,
31, 33, 35, 37, 38,
40, 41, 42, 43, 45,
48, 51, 53, 55, 56,
60, 61, 62, 67, 68,
69, 72, 73, 74, 75,
78, 80, 83, 84, 85,
87, 89, 90, 93, 94,
95, 96, 98, 100, 101,
106, 107, 108, 109,
112, 114, 115, 117,
118, 119, 120, 121,
122, 123, 126, 127,
129, 130, 133, 134,
135, 138, 139, 140,
141, 142, 143, 146,
148, 149, 150, 152,
153, 156, 157, 158,
161, 162, 164, 165,
166, 168, 170, 171,
172, 175, 179, 181,
185, 186
Willis 209
Greene, Jane E. 69
Greyard, Betsey 154
Griffice, Edward 193
Rebecca H. 153
Griffin, H. L. 54
Lucy 156
Thomas 25
Griffis, Elizabeth 32
Hugh L. 186
Martha 162
Samuel 162
Grime, Elizabeth 19
Grimes, William 69
Grissom, Oliver 57
Grizzard, James A. 177
Mary A. 177, 192
Guarns, Margarett 109
Guearin, John 192
Guerrant, William P.
199
Gui, Marey 105

231

Hawkins, Nancy 67, 201
  P. 39
  Patience 190
  Pattie 132
  Peter 80
  Phil 18, 123
  Phil B. 81
  Philemon 4, 5, 10, 14,
    37, 43, 80, 115, 151,
    183
  Philemon B. 44
  Philimon 55
  Philip 4, 113
  R. H. 141
  Rebecah 57
  Reuben 140
  Reubin 27
  Sarah M. 180
  Silva 178
  Susanna 80
  Theny 69
  W. J. 68
  William 80
  Willis A. 199
  Wyatt 29, 80
Hawks, Benjamin 90, 95
  Ebeline 51
  Elizabeth P. 23, 210
  Erasmus 212
  Fedrick 100
  Frederick 81
  Henrietta 97
  James 81
  Jane 107
  Jereman 97
  Jerreman 171, 195
  John 101
  Lucy 115
  Nancy 18
  Nathaniel S. 45
  Polly 158
  Rebecca 17
  Salley 183
  Sarah 64, 97
  Sarah E. 97, 210
  Susan 81
  Thomas 17
Hayes, Harriett 181
  Harvy 216
  James 209
  James M. 210
  John W. 192
  Mary 48
  Peter 214
  Sarah E. 31
  Susan S. 36
Haygood, William 90
Hays, Elizabeth 106
  Mary 196
Haythcock, Temperance
  126
Haywood, Joshua 30
Hazard, Betsey 47
  Dianna 135
  John 67
  Lewis 57, 69, 71, 82,
    135
  Lot 47, 82, 102
  Sally 107
Hazelwood, Mary 119
  Sarah 48
  Warwick 60, 61, 78
Hazilwood, Lucy 157
Healvin, John 159
Hearne, William 207
Heathcock, Mary 32

Heavlin, John 158
Heavline, John 80
Hedgepath, Stephen 185
Henderson, Joshua 213
  L. 29, 32, 132, 171,
    182, 211, 215
  Len 202
  Leonard 71, 166
  Mary B. 132, 210
  Oscar 213
  Rose 176, 212
Hendrick, --- 207
  A. G. 83, 159
  Alexander W. 202
  Eley 156
  Elizabeth 117
  George J. 43, 110
  Ginney 58
  H. C. 132
  Mary 43
  Mourning 116
  Nancy 151
  Panthea 174, 212
  R. L. 79
  Stephen 38
  Thomas R. 198, 203
Henry, Waller 212
Herndon, Z. 162
  Zachariah 29, 60, 120
Hervey, Willis 192
Hester, Stephen 83
Hewitt, C. E. 202
Hickman, Agnes 173
  Martha 53
Hicks, A. H. 197
  Anthony 210
  Catharine W. 81
  Charles 83
  Elizabeth 56
  Esther 129
  Harriet R. 43
  Harrison 87
  Henrietta 108, 194
  Isabella 123
  James G. 209
  Jane 94
  John 81, 98, 125, 154,
    194
  John B. 101
  John W. 57, 184, 203
  Lucy 97, 124, 204
  Lucy A. 41, 201
  Lucy B. 132
  Lucy D. 99, 210
  M. E. 129, 196
  Martha 58, 216
  Martha A. 98, 207
  Martha E. 176, 205
  Mary 21, 204
  Mary F. 99, 199
  Mary S. 84, 204
  Nancy 114
  Nancy T. 119, 149
  Polly Frances 151, 209
  Rachel 168, 216
  Rowan 81
  Sally 81
  Sarah F. 46
  Sarah W. 176, 195
  Susan Ann 163
  Tabatha 114
  William 39, 56, 98,
    154
  William L. 176
  William T. 206
  Winifred 146

Hicks, Winnefred 198
  Winnifred 120
Hide, Averriller 92
Highs, James H. 126
Hightower, Betty 126
  Stephen 52
  Tabitha B. 161
Hill, Ann F. 115
  Benjamin 50
  Felicia M. 147
  Hartwell 10
  Indiana 156
  Indianna 215
  Maria 107
  Mathida 81
  Prudence 64
  Richard 4
  Sally 165
  Sarah 175
  Winnifret 39
Hillard, Phillermon 183
Hilliard, Annie E. 84
  B. M. 128, 204
  Dandridge J. 71
  John 84, 178
  Martha B. 19
  Mary 84
  Mary W. 176
  Matilda C. 55, 193
  Micajah 90
  Phileman 104
  Thomas 21
  Thomas D. 205
  William F. 28, 125
Hillman, Saml 64
Hills, John 175
Hilton, Dicey 154
  Elizabeth 183
  Lucy 136
  Susanah 49
Hindsman, Catharine 45
Hines, Benja W. 85
  E. 193
  Edward 163, 193
  Edwin 68
Hinton, David 191
  Thomas 121
  William E. 102, 173
Hix, John 99
  Little Bury 182
Hodge, Cathorine 177
  Frances 102
Hodges, Caroline 54
  Caroline S. 210
  W. 9, 14, 37, 67, 75,
    93, 132, 174, 207,
    208, 210
  William 11, 12, 13,
    14, 17, 20, 35, 36,
    37, 39, 44, 50, 54,
    59, 68, 82, 87, 93,
    102, 119, 131, 132,
    133, 138, 143, 150,
    152, 156, 161, 165,
    166, 168, 173, 175,
    178, 179, 200, 203,
    204, 205, 206, 207,
    210, 211, 212, 214,
    215
Hogwood, Elizabeth 38
  Jane 156
  Mary D. 176
  Nancy 48
  Susanna 50
Holaway, Mary P. 130
Holden, Elizabeth 19

237

239

240

241

242

244

247

Salmon, Ann 27
  Jonathan 94, 146
  Sarah 45, 206
Samford, William 66
Samuel, Elizabeth 102
Sandefer, James 182
Sandifer, Priscilla 72
Sandiford, Mary H. 28
Satterwhite, James P.
  54
Saunders, Martha 92
Savage, Jane 122
Schloss, Marx 95, 150,
  195
Scoggins, Alice F. 122
  Harriet 142
  James 142
  Meriah E. 177
  Sally 142
Scot, Charlotte 57
  Hariot 58
Scott, Catherine 55
  Ellington 206
  John 3, 37, 80, 86,
  166
  Julius 204
  Polley 147
Seapark, Adelia A. 195
Sears, Abner 108
Seaward, Abraham 109
Seawell, Joseph 4
Self, Frances 5
Semmons, Janney 83
Sensing, Charles 147
Senter, Fanny 9
  Freeman 52
Separk, Adelia A. 139
Serug, Lotty 96
Seward, Abram 194
  Henrietta 95, 192
  Jacob 208
  John W. 162
  Mecdoland 191
Sewell, Ann 50
Sexton, John 103
Seymour, M. R. 31
Shackleford, Joel G. 46
Shaw, James 100, 156
  Jane 165, 212
  W. H. 165
  William H. 113, 211
Shearin, --- W. 209
  Albert 131, 148
  Amarellas 119
  Amey 15, 79
  Ann 152, 215
  Bettie P. 199
  Bettie R. 119
  Caroline 89
  Chany 189
  Claiborn 142
  Cynthia 149
  Daniel 16, 171
  David 139
  Dolly 75
  Dorothy 35
  Drewry 74
  Drewy 156
  Drury 97, 127
  E. P. 119
  Edith 111
  Elisabeth 210
  Eliza 163
  Eliza Ann 45, 215
  Elizabeth 90, 153, 182
  Elizh. 96

Shearin, Elizth B. 91
  Elvy 181
  Fanny 78, 189
  Frances 129
  G. E. 78
  Gardener 103
  Gardner 201
  Gardner E. 148
  George W. 89
  Guardner 105
  Henry 81, 131, 149,
  150
  J. A. 41, 206
  J. R. 207, 210
  Jacob J. 150
  James 164
  Jarratt H. 116
  John D. 45, 53
  John Daniel 204
  John P. 23, 73, 150,
  153
  John R. 143
  John W. 201
  Joseph 56, 108, 150
  Judah 20
  Julia Ann 41
  Leonidas S. 196
  Lewis 147
  Loisa 110
  Louisa 110
  Lucy 57, 103
  Malissa 148, 150, 191
  Margaret 19
  Marina A. 75
  Martha 14, 56, 119
  Martha B. 15
  Mary 30, 97, 115, 127,
  131
  Mary A. 22, 71, 193
  Mary Ann 28
  Mary E. 92, 99, 115,
  204, 210, 211
  Mary F. 76, 115
  Mary M. 83
  Mary W. 61
  Mollie E. 75, 207
  Moses 63, 148
  Nancy 30, 123, 143,
  149
  Nathaniel 198
  Nathaniel W. 203
  Nicholas 177, 191
  Octavia D. 59, 91, 207
  Oliver 170
  Pricella 105
  Rebeca 150
  Rebecca 139, 164
  Rebecca H. 148, 211
  Richard 35, 166, 184,
  192
  Robert A. 23, 149
  Rosa 103
  Ruina A. 75
  S. A. 139
  Sallie 108
  Sallie D. 208
  Sally 119, 142, 185
  Sarah 39, 73, 195
  Sebastian C. 210
  Sencord M. 63
  Susan 161
  Susan S. 116
  Syntha 116
  Thomas 201
  Virginia R. 115, 211
  William 148

Shearin, William H. 9,
  60, 93, 97
  Winey 131
  Zachariah 139
  Zachariah T. 207
Shearrin, Elizabeth
  109, 185
  Franky 109
  Jinsey 56
Sheless, John 160
Shell, Annee 144
  Edmond 138
  Jane 57
  L. 204
  Lemmon 40, 47, 63, 84,
  169, 171, 205, 206
  Oliver P. 200
  Patsey 33
  Raney 71
  Richard 71
  Salley 57, 111
  Stephen 57, 150
  William 111
Sherin, Cath 65
  Edward 150
  Gardner 163
  Joseph 65
Sherrin, Nancey 17
  Rosey 105
Sherrod, Thomas 5
Sherwood, --- 145
Short, Betsey 173
  Elizabeth 110
  Lucy Coleman 175
  Mary 174
  Mary Ann 171
  Nancy 137
  Phoebe 186
  Rebeccah 110
  Richard 137
  Sally 173
  Susan 9, 204
  Theophilus 204
  William 35, 139, 167
Shroyer, Edward 196
Shuck, L. H. 197
Simmons, Mary 165
  Samuel 151
  William G. 193
Simms, Darcus 180
  Frances 166
  Francis 71
  Gilley 90
  Zebiah 53
Simon, John 68
  Peggy 68
Sims, Allan 13
  Bathena 168
  Chesley 168
  Elizabeth 168
  Harriet W. B. 152
  Henry 65
  Jane 102
  John 52
  Julius 152
  L. S. 152
  L. Sanders 48, 166
  L. Saunders 151
  L. Swepson 16
  Leonard H. 102
  Lucy 78
  Lusey 166
  Mary 54, 151
  Nancy 13, 65
  Olive A. 155
  Rebecca 65

250

251

252

254

Wright, Virginia A. 195
  Virginia Ann 138
  William 202
  William H. 202
  William R. 16
  Zachariah 11, 56
Writtenbury, John 140
  Sally W. 186
Wuggins, Polley 29
Wyatt, Robert L. 202
Wyche, Ira F. 203
  Ira T. 50, 103, 153,
    186, 205, 211
Wynn, Mary 84
  Peter 197
  Thomas M. 177

Wynn, William 31, 42

--- Y ---

Yancey, Harriet J. 10
  John G. 10, 67
  Lucy 87, 206
Yarborough, Huldy 135
  Martha 104
  Mary 69
Yarbrogh, Elisabeth 130
Yarbrough, James D. 69
  M. 72
  Martha 72
  Mary 149

Yarbrough, Matilda 26
  Rebecca 72
  Sarah Jane 20
  William 72, 130
Young, Abigal 97
  Elizabeth 99
  George 189
  Holly 189
  John H. 186
  Joshua 100
  Lucy A. 167, 198
  Martha E. 129
  Nancy 126
  Precella 40
  R. E. 77
  S. D. 205